Pastor Helvius Thompson, (cuz)
Missionaries are special
a missionary in the black communi
May God bless you.

DeWitt Williams

Precious Memories of Missionaries of Color

Volume 2

DeWitt S. Williams, EdD, MPH, CHES

TEACH Services, Inc.
P U B L I S H I N G
www.TEACHServices.com • (800) 367-1844

Copyright © 2015 TEACH Services, Inc.

ISBN-13: 978-1-4796-0429-6 (Paperback)

ISBN-13: 978-1-4796-0439-5 (Hardback)

ISBN-13: 978-1-4796-0430-2 (ePub)

ISBN-13: 978-1-4796-0431-9 (Mobi)

Library of Congress Control Number: 2015909722

Published by

TEACH Services, Inc.
P U B L I S H I N G
www.TEACHServices.com • (800) 367-1844

PREFACE

The second volume of *Precious Memories of Missionaries of Color* is a treasure trove of inspirational stories and an important declaration—a veritable honor roll—of the tremendous mission service of so many people of color through the years. In search of these accounts, Dr. Williams mined information from personal letters, magazine articles, memories, and even passports! The result of his meticulous work is here to inspire us with the sacrifice, faithfulness, and even heroism of those who went before us.

Sprinkled throughout the book are personal touches that bring the stories to life. Long a fan of Anna Knight, I was delighted to read that in later years she was a well-known figure at Oakwood—a highly respected mother in Israel who brought erring students back on track with a prod of her cane!

I hope, like me, that you will be inspired and encouraged as you read this delightful book.

Gary Krause
Director, Office of Adventist Mission
Associate Secretary, General Conference of Seventh-day Adventists

INTRODUCTION

Adventists have taken seriously the command of Jesus to take the gospel message to the entire world. Just eleven years after the official organization of the Seventh-day Adventist Church in 1863, John Nevins Andrews was commissioned to go to Switzerland. After the Civil War, recently freed slaves also caught sight of the vision of a finished work. In 1892, some eighteen years after Andrews, the first missionary of color left the United States to spread the good news in Jamaica.

Ever since these two pioneers left American shores, hundreds of missionaries have followed them, being sent around the world by the Adventist Church to help in spreading the gospel via our schools, colleges, universities, and medical institutions.

Dr. Carol Hammond felt inspired to write the first volume of *Precious Memories of Missionaries of Color* in 2006. I was present when she invited a group of black missionaries living in the Washington metropolitan area to her home one Sabbath to discuss the idea. We urged her on. Several subsequent meetings followed while we planned how we should proceed.

Elder Maurice T. Battle who had worked in the General Conference Secretariat for many years provided a preliminary list of those who had served. We hunted for addresses and drafted letters and made phone calls, asking for stories and pictures. We were pleased with the response. Forty-nine families responded, and Dr. Hammond portrayed their stories in her book, which was published in 2008.

In the back of *Precious Memories of Missionaries of Color* was a "Black Seventh-day Adventist Mission Service Honor Roll" that contained the names of 125 black Seventh-day Adventist missionaries. I realized that information about more than seventy-five black missionaries was not included in Dr. Hammond's book. I wanted to know more about these people. I wanted to know where these seventy-five people went, when they served, and how long they served. That list became my marching orders for volume two. I *needed* to know more about them. I later discovered that many of them had passed away or retired and moved away. It was a very difficult task to find most of them or even to find information about them.

Thankfully the General Conference archives had some information about many of them. Usually when a missionary was sent overseas, their assignment was recorded on the back cover of the *Adventist Review*. In a few cases this was all I could find. I also did my best to interview those who were still alive or to talk to their relatives, if I could find them.

I spent a great deal of time finding information on the earliest black missionaries: James Patterson, Mabel Branch, Thomas and Henrietta Branch, Dr. James and Marian Hyatt,

Lambert Browne, and Drs. David and Lottie Blake. These had all passed away, but there was information about them in Adventist and non-Adventists sources. I was especially pleased to find a picture of our first black missionary, James Patterson, on his 1917 and 1918 passports.

I discovered that Hannah More was not an African American. She was listed in Carol Hammond's book and cited in Charles Dudley's list of missionaries. I did not write much about Anna Knight since she has been covered thoroughly and had written her autobiography *Mississippi Girl.* My objective was to include only those who were sent out from North America. Sometimes it was difficult to determine precisely whether a missionary was from the North American Division or the Inter-American Division. Some worked in both divisions. Some started out in the Inter-American Division and later moved to the North American Division.

There may be one or two who should not be in this book, and there are a few that I probably did not include but should have. I apologize for this. I discovered about a dozen who were not on the original list but who served as missionaries. I did not include student missionaries, special service, or volunteers who went out for less than a year. I never could find anything for Sherman Aldridge, Leroy Hamilton, Gerald Mouse, or Ron Nelson who were on the original list. Some wanted to write their own stories, and I was glad to receive this information. I let them stand in the first person. I feel that the two and a half years I spent in research were well worth the product that I am able to offer Adventist historians.

I have compiled several lists of missionaries. The first list is chronological and lists the missionaries that were not in the first book by the date they served. This chronological list becomes the table of contents for my book. It includes the ninety-five portraits in this book. The second list in the back of the book includes the ninety-five missionaries of this book combined with those in the first volume but has them listed alphabetically. I feel that this book was worth it just to have a combined list of all the black North American missionaries that served the Adventist Church with the dates and places they served. The third list is also in the back of the book and is the same as the previous list but has the missionaries listed according to the time (chronological) they served. I feel these two lists in the back of the book are very useful and valuable.

I have included one example of the newer form of missionary service, Adventist Frontier Missions (AFM), which sends missionaries to unreached people groups and has them raise their own funds to support them in their mission endeavor. The Polley family worked for AFM, and they recount some of their exciting experiences.

While all Christians love God, missionaries have an intense desire to share that love with others, even if it means sacrificing the comforts of home. Missionaries accept the challenge to go into the entire world to preach the gospel. Black missionaries have served with distinction not only in Africa but in India, Asia, Europe, the islands of the sea, Inter-America, South America, and all around the world. They are still going out. Most of the missionaries I interviewed said the years they spent in service overseas were the highlight of their lives. They still have wonderful memories and strong ties and relationships with the people in the territories they served.

Some assignments were very dangerous. Some missionaries had to be evacuated because of wars and political tensions. Many of the very early missionaries had their lives shortened because of malaria, black water fever, or some kind of plague. There were few pills in those days to protect against these conditions. Phillipa Vanderburg was killed in a car accident in Liberia and her family severely injured.

I thank Carol Hammond for having the vision to begin this project. I thank Dr. Benjamin Baker for the help he gave in the General Conference archives and for digitizing the *North American Informant* and other black journals. I owe a debt of gratitude to Alvin Singleton who had a knack for finding information from passports and census reports and other non-Adventist sources. I want to thank Sarah Gilmor, reference librarian of the Colorado Historical Society for searching and providing me with copies of the 1898–1908 newspapers with information about Mabel Branch. This was invaluable. Oakwood archivist, Heather Rodriguez-James, was very helpful and answered all of my questions and supplied whatever resources she had. I thank my wife, Margaret, and my daughter Darnella for being patient with me and at the same time being an inspiration to me. I thank my oldest daughter, Deitrice, and her son, Neil (my only grandchild), for their constant prayers of encouragement for me and this project.

I feel satisfied and fulfilled now because I know quite a bit more about those on the "Missionary Honor Roll." Having additional information about them helps us to honor and respect them better. We salute the missionaries of color and hope their stories will inspire the next generation of those who will answer God's call to serve wherever God leads.

From Greenland's icy mountains,
from India's coral strand;
Where Afric's sunny fountains roll down
their golden sand:

From many an ancient river,
from many a palmy plain,
They call us to deliver their land
from error's chain.

Shall we, whose souls are lighted
with wisdom from on high,
Shall we to those benighted
the lamp of life deny?
Salvation! O salvation!
The joyful sound proclaim,
Till earth's remotest nation
has learned Messiah's name.

Reginald Heber wrote these words in 1819 at the request of his pastor who wanted to promote his missionary program. It is said that Heber wrote the verses in just twenty minutes. Adventists rarely sing this song today, and it is not included in our new Adventist hymnal, which was published in 1985. However, I remember as a young person singing this hymn, and the words are embedded in my mind even today. Our youth today may not even know this song.

Many of the early missionaries died overseas, but they were determined to bring good news to every corner of the globe. Jesus will not come until the message has gone everywhere. No sacrifice is too great. Wherever there is darkness and sin, there is a need for someone to take the light—a missionary. We don't necessarily have to go to jungles today. Divisions can send workers to their own territories. May this second volume continue to inspire us to spread the gospel message around the world—to our great cities, to dying men and women everywhere. Our desire is for Jesus to come soon. May we all become missionaries. That is my hope and prayer.

Any proceeds from this book will be put into a scholarship fund for students to assist them in getting an education at Oakwood University.

Table of Contents

* – Denotes that this name appeared in volume 1, but it is included here because I have found new information on the missionary.

See the Alphabetical and Chronological Index in the back of the book that combines the names of the missionaries in this book and also those in volume 1.

1.

JAMES E. PATTERSON

1892–1896 / Jamaica, Barbados, Panama, Haiti
1910 / Columbia

Many Adventists believe that Anna Knight was the first black Adventist missionary. She was, indeed, the first black woman missionary of any denomination to be sent to India, going there in 1901. But she was not the first black missionary of the Adventist Church. Nine years earlier, in 1892, James Elijah Patterson left San Francisco to take the gospel to Jamaica.

Anna Knight wrote her well-known autobiography *Mississippi Girl*, and she worked and lived at Oakwood College and in the vicinity of the school for many years, so Adventists are very familiar with her. Yet we know practically nothing about Patterson. He is a blank canvass, an empty book, a clean slate. No picture of him appears in any Adventist publication. No stories or details about him exist in any book. Black historian Louis B. Reynolds readily admitted there was no formal information about him except a record that he went overseas to Jamaica in 1892.[1]

Thanks to modern tools available to trace our roots, we are able to finally capture a glimpse of the first black ambassador from America. Much of what we know about his personal life comes from non-Adventist sources such as passport applications, census records, and naturalization papers.

James Patterson was not an ordained minister like John Nevins Andrews, the church's first missionary sent to Switzerland in 1874. The son of Abraham Patterson, he was a layperson—a sailor, a cook, a porter, a steward, and above all, a colporteur. Information from his applications for passports reveals that he was born on the island of St. Vincent, British West Indies, on November 15, 1857. He came to the United States in 1874 when he was sixteen years old, and at first he lived in New York before he migrated to California.

Somewhere along this journey James Patterson met his wife, Mary, who was born in Jamestown, Virginia, in 1855. After their romance, courtship, and marriage, they had at least four children: Alberta, born in 1883 in Battle Mountain, Nevada; Walter (1890), William (1891), and James (1894) were all born in California. James Patterson was naturalized in California on October 5, 1899. We don't know how or when he became an Adventist. We found two pictures of him on his passport applications.[2]

The story of the Adventist Church in Jamaica is one of stupendous growth. Today there are more than 270,000 Adventist

---

1. Louis B. Reynolds, *We Have Tomorrow* (Washington, D.C.: Review and Herald Publishing Association,1984), p. 323.

2. We found three passport applications for James Patterson dated October 13, 1899; May 24, 1917; and December 21, 1918 (United States of America, State of California). His pictures were on the last two passports.

members scattered across the tiny island in more than 700 churches and companies with more than 220 supervising ministers. Currently about one in ten people in this tropical paradise are Adventists. In 1892 when James Patterson went to Jamaica, there were no Adventist churches, no Adventist ministers, and no Adventists.

The people of Jamaica first learned the Sabbath truth through literature. It was the printed page filled with Bible and Spirit of Prophecy truths that brought Adventism to Jamaica. God-fearing colporteurs like George King, William Arnold, B. B. Newman, and James Patterson risked their lives and made the world their parish to take truth to every man.

In 1890 William Arnold was selling religious books in the tiny Caribbean island of Antigua. He sold *The Coming King* to Henry Palmer in Antigua. Palmer sent the book to his son, James, who lived in Jamaica. Shortly thereafter, the young Palmer reportedly found a religious tract at the Kingston Wharves where he worked, but he paid little attention to it until he realized it came from the same publishing house as the book his father had sent him. He wrote to the publishing house who forwarded his letter to the International Tract and Missionary Society. They sent him additional literature, which he passed out in Kingston.

Palmer reportedly gave a tract to Dr. Ross of the Kingston Public Hospital who, not being a very religious man, passed it on to Margaret Harrison who did charitable work visiting the sick in the hospital. Mrs. Harrison, an English socialite and a devout Christian, was immediately fired up with the message and started sharing it with friends and family. She was convicted of the Sabbath but hesitated to keep the day. She put the Sabbath literature out of her sight.

One Sunday in church her minister read the Ten Commandments, and the members responded after the reading of each commandment with, "Lord, have mercy upon us, and incline our hearts to keep this law." Conviction seized her heart anew. She went home, and alone with God and His Holy Word, promised to obey His law.

Early in 1891 the International Tract and Missionary Society secured several names of people living in Jamaica and sent them reading material. This was followed up by correspondence, and several began meeting at Mrs. Harrison's house to keep the Sabbath.

Elder Lewis C. Chadwick, the president of the International Tract and Missionary Society, nearing the end of a very distinguished career, traveled to many countries to make recommendations as to which countries were ready for the Sabbath truth. Chadwick spent eighteen days in Jamaica, and on Sunday, January 24, 1892, he became the first Adventist minister to preach a sermon in Jamaica. James K. Humphrey, a leading Baptist preacher interested in the Sabbath, invited him to preach at his Baptist Church. Chadwick later met Mrs. Harrison and the few questioning believers.

Chadwick submitted a detailed report to the Mission Board upon his return to the States and recommended the selection of an experienced canvasser to open the work by the sale of subscription books. "The one or ones who go there to work, must expect to meet many difficulties unknown at home, and must go prepared to work hard and perseveringly in order to make their going successful. To the right one there is chance for good work, and I hope and pray that the Lord, whose work it is, may himself direct in the selection of someone to engage in the sale of our books in this island."[3]

In June 1892 Brother Patterson arrived in Jamaica. One of the biggest problems he had to deal with was reaching the white owners of the larger plantations. In the only extant letter we have by him, he mentions some of these problems.

A white brother would do well in this city, while a colored one would do well in the country, the white people in the country not being as prejudiced as their brothers in the city.

I had to work mostly with the second and third classes of people here. In many instances I had to send the book in to be looked at while I stood at the door and waited. A white person would be allowed to enter and give a canvass, and by thus doing could create an interest and doubtless take an order, and then of course would have no difficulty in delivering; while I meet with a good many postponements on account of having to work mostly with the poorer class ... I am very thankful for the small books and tracts which were sent me with my order for books; they have done much good. Five have accepted the truth, and met with us for worship last Sabbath, and were out last evening to prayer meeting. Many of the ministers are warning their congregations against reading the spurious literature which is being spread in the city. Many already see the difference between the false and true; while some accept the truth, others fear the speech of the people around them. For such let us pray.[4]

In spite of the challenges, Patterson met with great success especially in selling *Bible Readings for the Home Circle*. Early in 1893, about nine months after Patterson's arrival, Brother B. B. Newman who had been canvassing in Florida was sent to Jamaica by the Foreign Mission Board to further develop the canvassing work, and they moved Patterson to Haiti, Barbados, and Panama.

Balfour Hurst, for many years the director of publishing in the Inter-American Division, told how his father came into the church by a book which Patterson sold. Patterson's fourth copy of *Bible Readings* was sold to Cecil Shelly of St. Ann. When Shelly found out it was a Seventh-day Adventist book he offered it to Mr. Hurst who exchanged a chair for the book. Hurst forgot about the book for two years and when he opened it his mind was directed to the caption "Who Changed the Sabbath?" That evening he walked eight miles to visit his minister who told him that the Sabbath had been changed. Hurst was still troubled and continued to study and eventually became an Adventist. As a result of that one book over 200 individuals joined the church, among them six colporteurs and four ministers. Four churches were raised up as a result of that one book-one at St. Ann's Bay, one at Ocho Rios, one at Ocho Rios on the hill, and one out by Runaway Bay.[5]

In 1893 Mrs. Harrison went to the Battle Creek Sanitarium for treatment. While there she attended the General Conference session and appealed for a minister to be sent to Jamaica. A year after Patterson first came to the island, in May 1893, the General Conference sent a young minister, Albert James Haysmer, and his wife to follow up on the work of Patterson and Newman and establish a permanent church in Jamaica.

3. "Jamaica," *The Home Missionary*, April 1892, pp. 90, 91.

4. *The Home Missionary,* November 1892, p. 262. From a letter written by Brother J. E. Patterson, dated at Kingston, Jamaica, September 7, 1892.

5. B. E. Hurst, "Stories About Publishing Evangelism In Jamaica", *Inter-American Division Messenger*, October, 1955, p. 9.

Later that year William Arnold arrived in Jamaica to canvass with health books, and still later George A. King arrived. Many of the new members were taught to canvass, and the truth spread rapidly. In less than three years the total value of books sold in Jamaica was $8,240 for health books and about $7,654 for religious books, an incredible amount for that time.[6]

Elder Haysmer tells of the impact of a book that Brother Patterson sold in Jamaica.

I met for the first time a young man who had formerly been a Salvation Army captain … He had come into the truth through reading. Some time ago a young lady from that district had come to Kingston, and some Signs were given her. She took them home, but cared nothing for them; but this young man, calling there and seeing them, picked them up and became interested, and as the Sabbath was mentioned, his attention was called to it.

A few days afterward he called at another place, and found a copy of "Bible Readings" that Brother James Patterson, from California, had sold nearly four years ago, while he was canvassing here. He accidentally turned to the Sabbath question, and as he read, he thought, "What does this mean?" He borrowed the book, and studied it carefully; and being honest, the result was, of course, his acceptance of the truth. He soon became full to overflowing with the message, and was expelled from the [Salvation] Army, but not until he had laid before them the light which God had given him. Several months have passed, and as the result of his faithful labors, twenty are now keeping the Sabbath with him."[7]

The life of a traveling colporteur has always been one of great faith. Usually he carried all of his belongings in a satchel, which would include his hammock, some Sanitarium biscuits, a supply of malted milk, a spirit lamp, his change of clothing, and his Bible. He might carry another suitcase filled with books, and when these were gone he would start taking orders, which would arrive by boat or mail. He rarely knew where he would spend the night. If he could not find a friendly home that would put him up for the night, he would stretch his hammock between two trees. He would carry a small supply of drinking water in a little rubber bag and replenish it with good clean water as opportunity presented itself. The canvasser would work both sides of the streets, not missing a single home or shop, placing the special books in the hands of all who were seeking truth.

After leaving Jamaica, Patterson continued on to Panama. On this trip he demonstrated determination and resourcefulness. He landed in Guatemala and took another ship to El Salvador. He paid part of the way and hoped the captain would allow him to work part of the way to Panama.

Although he remained on board until the vessel left the latter port, and the mate set him to work, the captain forbade his going any further … The passengers collected thirty dollars for him to pay his passage, but the captain refused to sell him a ticket, and started him ashore in a small boat. The passengers gave him the money, however, and instead of going ashore he induced the boat's crew to put him on board the steamer City of Sydney, which was lying at Point Arena with a broken shaft, waiting to be towed to Panama. When another steamer came to tow the Sydney, he paid ten dollars passage to Panama. So the unkindness of the former captain worked a

6. A. J. Haysmer, *The Home Missionary*, July 1895, pp. 20–22.

7. A. J. Haysmer, "Jamaica," *Advent Review and Sabbath Herald*, October 5, 1897, p. 635.

decided advantage to Bro. Paterson ... Arriving in Panama he went to work canvassing ... in about seven days he took two hundred and forty dollars' worth of orders.[8]

In 1896 we find James Patterson as a cook and steward on the fifth voyage of *Pitcairn*. The missionary ship *Pitcairn* was built the summer of 1890 at a cost of $12,035.22. The money was donated from Sabbath School offerings for the Polynesian Field and especially Pitcairn

Island to follow up on growing interests in the Sabbath. *Pitcairn* made its first voyage in 1890, and in all it made six trips to the island of Pitcairn.

After giving a list of ordained ministers, medical personnel, and teachers on board, the registry mentions Patterson among the nine crew members who were required in the vital task of making the ship sail. The *Pitcairn*, with Patterson on board as cook, left the wharf in Oakland, California, on her fifth cruise on Tuesday, May 19, 1896. The ship visited the islands and returned to Oakland in November 1896.[9]

The account mentions that "some of the crew had taken a leading role selling Christian literature."[10] Although hired as a cook, Patterson was probably busy doing what he did best— distributing truth-filled Adventist literature.

In 1897 the General Conference voted to send Patterson back to the West Indies as a self-supporting missionary. They advanced him $200.00, which they expected him to repay.[11]

Patterson's cooking skills must have been outstanding. From 1899 to 1902 he worked as a chef at St. Helena Sanitarium. Four of his tasty recipes were printed in *Signs of the Times*, and two in the *Pacific Health Journal*.[12]

In 1910 after leaving St. Helena Sanitarium, the colporteur spirit stirred in him again. "He is now canvassing in Panama. His first week's work report is as follows: 37 hours, 56 orders for 'Heralds' and 8 orders for 'Coming King,' Spanish. Brother Patterson speaks the Spanish quite well, and we expect to hear continued good reports of his work."[13] A few months later the *Pacific Union Recorder* shared a letter from the field agent in Panama. "Brother Patterson will soon take up the work in Panama City with 'salud y Hogar' ('Home and Health'). Then we are planning to send him to Cartagena, Colombia. This will be pioneer work for him. Recently he took eleven orders in the government building at Colon, including the governor, Secretary of State, and other officials ... His Spanish is serving him well in the Panama country."[14]

From November 15, 1915, until December 1918, we find Patterson at the United States Marine Hospital in San Francisco working as a porter and being treated as a patient. Sailors at the turn of the twentieth century were subject to maladies and injuries as diverse as the lands they sailed to. Deadly contagious diseases spread rapidly on the closed quarters of ships. Respiratory diseases were by far the most common causes of death among sailors. Sailors were also afflicted with heart disease, kidney disease,

8. "From Panama," *The Present Truth*, June 2, 1892, p. 174.

9. Herbert Ford, "Assessing the Advent of the Pitcairn," Pitcairn Islands Study Center, Pacific Union College. http://1ref.us/7j; "75 50 25 Years Ago" *Review and Herald*, May 3, 1946, p. 2.

10. Ibid.

11. "J. E. Paterson, VS. West Indies," Foreign Mission Board Minutes, The Polynesian Committee, Oakland, CA, April 22, 1897, p. 26d.

12. *The Signs of the Times*, June 28, 1899, p. 429; August 8, 1899, p. 509; August 16, 1899, p. 541; November 1, 1899, p. 717; J. E. Patterson, "New Year's Menu," *Pacific Health Journal*, 1899, pp. 14, 15; J. E. Patterson, "Patties and Gems," *Pacific Health Journal*, June 1902, p. 28.

13. "Pacific Press Items," *Pacific Union Recorder*, March 3, 1910, p. 2.

14. Chas. F. Innis, "Pacific Press Notes," *Pacific Union Recorder*, July 21, 1910, pp. 2, 3.

and conditions affecting the brain. Occupational hazards were rampant with great risk of falling from the ship's heights or the development of hernias that would go untreated for months at sea.

Many of the sailors who went to the Marine Hospital died there. Most had no money and no known family to arrange for their funerals. Sometimes a sailor's shipmates or employer would handle these expenses, but often the ship had sailed away from San Francisco before the crew member either recovered or died. When there was no next of kin or friend to contact, the hospital would bury the deceased in the cemetery in back of the hospital.

Attached to Patterson's last application for a passport was a letter from the United States Public Health Service dated December 12, 1918, certifying that he had been under treatment at that hospital for three years for chronic tuberculosis.

"He is anxious to go to St. Vincent in the West Indian islands to benefit his health, and it is believed this trip will be of decided benefit to him," wrote G. Parcher, assistant surgeon in temporary charge, U. S. Marine Hospital, San Francisco, California. Patterson was 61 years old at the time.

The last mention of James Patterson in denominational papers came in 1919. He apparently made it back to St. Vincent, and his health must have improved. He made an appeal to the reading public to send some Adventist literature so he could share the gospel with those around him. "J. E. Patterson, Kingstown, St. Vincent, B. W. I. desires clean copies of the *Signs Magazine*, tracts, *Life Boat*, and other of our papers, to be used in missionary endeavor in that community. Send postage paid."[15]

15. "Wanted for Missionary Work," *The Signs of the Times,*
    August 12, 1919, p. 15.

James Elijah Patterson, the first black Adventist missionary from North America, made a difference for God and man by distributing truth-filled literature wherever he went. Through the long corridors of history, he comes to life. We now have a physical picture as well as a Christian profile of a man who shared his faith around the world.

Picture of J. E. Patterson from his 1918 passport application.

The missionary ship Pitcairn on which J. E. Patterson served as cook, steward, and colporteur on its fifth voyage in 1896.

2

HANNAH MORE

Not an African American

Surprisingly, I discovered that Hannah More was not an African American, although she was a missionary to Liberia and Sierra Leone. When I inquired at the General Conference archives, Dr. Benjamin Baker informed me that I had incorrect information. He said I should talk with Dr. Bill Knott, the editor of *Adventist Review*, who had written his doctoral dissertation on Hannah More. So I contacted Mr. Knot by e-mail. Here is his reply:

Thank you for your inquiry about Hannah More. I do indeed have a clear photo (the only one known to exist) of her, and am attaching it to this message. Please do not reproduce it or transmit it in any form without contacting me in advance.

Ben Baker is quite right: there is no evidence that Hannah More was a person of color, though her story is "remembered" in that way by many Adventists. I discovered a unique phenomenon while I was working on the dissertation: approach any 10 Adventists who acknowledge having heard of Hannah More before, and 8 or 9 of them will say something like, 'Wasn't she that African-American lady who was turned away in Battle Creek?' This experience was so persistent that I began to think carefully about how this linkage of her name to African-American experience might have occurred. You've pointed me to Carol

Hammond's book, but there seems to be something more widespread occurring.

My best guess is that Hannah's story—overlooked, neglected, and "turned away" by the movement she loved—is a functional metaphor for the experience of many African Americans in earlier decades of the church, and so the stories became intertwined. Her years of experience as a missionary in West Africa may have also deepened this perceived association.[16]

Hannah's family was from Union, CT, and the genealogical work I did pointed conclusively to English Puritan ancestors on her mother's side, and probable Irish ancestry on her father's. Having collected, transcribed and carefully read some 95 of her letters, as well as dozens of letters to her from family, fellow missionaries, and Adventists, there is no indication in any of those that she was African American. Her deep passion for groups historically neglected and marginalized—Native Americans on the American frontier, repatriated Amistad survivors in Africa, and West African tribal groups—has also certainly contributed to the "memory" of her life within the broader narrative of Adventism.[17]

16. For those who want to know more about Hannah More, please read "A Winter's Tale" by Bill Knot in the January 22, 1998, issue of *Adventist Review*, pages 8–13.

17 Bill Knot, editor and executive publisher, *Adventist Review* and *Adventist World*, e-mail communication to DeWitt Williams dated June 19, 2013.

3

ANNA KNIGHT

1901–1907 / India

Anna Knight was one of the early pioneers that I (DeWitt Williams) knew personally.

She was at Oakwood College when I attended from 1957–1962. She would usually attend Friday evening vespers and Sabbath services at the college church. Her seat was always up front on the far right. She and Mother Cunningham were treated like "Adventist saints" and were very much respected by the student body. Sister Knight was in her late 70s at the time and would not hesitate to reprimand any student she felt was misbehaving or going a little too far in their social relations. In those days young men were not allowed to hold the hand of any young lady, and the young men sat on one side of the auditorium while the ladies sat on the other side. She usually carried a cane or an umbrella and would tap or poke a student who was out of line.

Some of us had read her autobiography, *Mississippi Girl*, and knew some of the details of her life. Several of the Knights, her relatives, were also enrolled in school with us. She would also publicly correct them if they "acted up."

I will not go into great detail about her since her story is covered considerably in *Precious Memories of Missionaries of Color*, volume 1. But I found the details of her burial marker to be of interest, and I have included that story from *Southern Tidings* here.

On Monday, May 28, 2001, Don Schneider,

North American Division president, journeyed with leaders from the Southern Union Conference, Oakwood College, South Central Conference, and Gulf States Conference to a small burial plot located deep in the pine woods of Southern Mississippi.

"We are gathered here to pay tribute to one of the greatest people the Adventist Church has known," explained Schneider.

When Anna Knight was born in 1874, it would have been difficult to imagine the places she would travel, the things she would accomplish, or the impact she would leave. She was bestowed with a thirst for learning, but as a black child in rural Mississippi, Anna found educational opportunities almost nonexistent. She taught herself to read and write by listening to white neighborhood children read and spell. Having no paper or pencil, she practiced her writing by scratching in the dirt with a stick. By the time she was in her teens she had mastered the subjects taught in the country schools of the time although she had never been inside a schoolhouse.

She was converted to the Seventh-day Adventist faith by reading *The Signs of the Times*. The magazine was sent to her by a member who saw in a New England newspaper a request she had made for reading materials. Through the help of a conference worker in Tennessee, Anna was able to attend Mount

Vernon Academy in 1894. She then went on to attend Battle Creek College, where she trained to be a missionary nurse, graduating in 1898. After finishing her schooling, she returned to her home state to operate a self-supporting school for black children in Jasper County.

In 1901 she was the first woman of any Christian denomination to go to India as a missionary. She served there for six years. After returning home, she served in the Southeastern Union as a nurse, teacher, and Bible worker. When the Southeastern Conference and Southern Conference merged, she served in the education department until retirement.

Anna died in 1972 and was laid to rest in a grave marked with only a small metal tag. In 1999 Florence Blaylock, one of Anna's cousins, shared Anna's story at a ministers' meeting in the Gulf States Conference. Upon discovering there was no marker at her gravesite, Mel Eisele, Gulf States Conference president, and the conference centennial committee began to formulate plans for a marker and a formal memorial service. From the beginning it was decided the service would be a joint effort of the Gulf States and South Central Conferences. Joseph McCoy, South Central Conference president, readily agreed.

Along with the officials, a busload of people from the Gulf States Conference camp meeting and local members from Soso and Laurel, Mississippi, met at the Soso Seventh-day Adventist Church and then traveled to the obscure burial site. At the ceremony Malcolm Gordon, Southern Union president, gave the welcome and prayer. Marshall Kelly sang a musical tribute. Florence Blaylock and Dorothy Knight Marsh, Anna's cousins, shared memories of Anna. Bruce Peifer explained the contributions she had made at Oakwood College. Eisele and McCoy gave tributes.

"I am honored that I knew her," said McCoy. "She was a giant of a woman."

"I feel cheated that I didn't get to know Anna," said Eisele. "Learning of how she lived her life has inspired me to accomplish more for Jesus."

In his closing remarks Schneider said, "Her life calls out to me, to be somebody. When I consider what she was given and what she accomplished in her life, I pray, 'lord, you used her in such a mighty way. If there is anything I can do, please use me. Help me accomplish something for You.'"

Before having the closing prayer, Jim Nix, director of the Ellen White Estate, told of the powerful prayer life that sustained Anna.

As the group left the small clearing, a shaft of sunlight fell on the new tombstone, a tombstone inscribed with the story of what one woman—born in the cotton fields of Mississippi at a time when poverty and racial injustices prevailed—accomplished with her life.[18]

Anna Knight in her later years

18. Becky Grice. "A Giant of a Woman: A Memorial to Anna Knight." *Southern Tidings*. July 2001, p. 3.

Don Schneider, president of the North American Division, speaks at the ceremony that provided a new grave marker for Ms. Knight at her burial site in Soso, Mississippi.

Dr. John Harvey Kellogg who encouraged Anna Knight to go to India.

Anna Knight, 95 years old, shakes hands with R. R. Figuhr, retireing General Conference president.

Anna Knight with star of Morning Star boat at Oakwood College

4

MABEL BRANCH WEBB

1902–1908 / Malawi

Mabel Branch. You may think that her name sounds familiar but you just can't quite place it. There is a reason you may recognize the name. Mabel Branch was the oldest child of Thomas H. Branch who went as a missionary to Nyasaland (Malawi) in 1902 as the first black missionary to Africa. The mission appointment mentioned Thomas H. Branch "and family" and then continued to talk about Elder Branch.

Mabel is hidden in those two words "and family." I have decided to separate her from her family and acquaint you with her because she was an outstanding twenty-four-year-old young lady. Mabel Branch could have chosen to stay home. She had the world before her. She was successfully employed and admired in her world.

Florence Mabel Branch was born in Wyandotte, Kansas, on April 1, 1878. Her parents moved to Denver the same year she was born, and she attended Denver schools. She graduated from West Denver High School in June 1897. *The Rocky Mountain News,*[19] one of Denver's major daily newspapers from the 1860s until its demise in 2009, displayed a bold caption on one of its columns—"First Colored Teacher in Colorado—Graduate of Westside High School Appointed to District 15 School at Pine Ridge."

The article went on to say the following:

---

19. *The Rocky Mountain News,* July 30, 1898, p. 4.

She is the first colored teacher appointed in Colorado, and her friends look upon the appointment as making the beginning of a new era for the colored race in the state. The rapid strides in education made by the rising young Negroes have been gratifying in all sections, indicating that they are hastily embracing their opportunities … She has worked hard for the position with which she is now honored, receiving the support of the directors of the district 15 and the West Denver instructors who taught her.

Miss Branch on both sides of the family descends from slaves. The parents of her father and mother were slaves, but they themselves were born in freedom. Her parents are well-educated, and appreciate the honor given their daughter.

Mabel received an offer to teach in a Presbyterian school in Knoxville, Tennessee, but she declined the offer and instead accepted a position as the first black teacher at Pine Ridge, just outside of Denver. She taught at Pine Ridge for six years before going to Africa.

When her parents received the call, she gladly consented to go as the teacher of her two younger brothers and as a teacher at the Cholo Mission. She wrote several letters to her stateside school friends that were published in the Colorado newspapers. She let the readers know that she had already had several attacks of malaria, was missing her friends, and was trying to learn the language.

> *It is very lonely here for me … Every month she [her friend in Colorado] sends me three or four Statesmen, and I get news that way. How I enjoy those papers, for we receive no newspapers and we do not know what is going on in the world … Two days [after I got here] I began teaching school. I have 112 scholars, divided into three separate schools on this station. Some of the more advanced pupils teach those in lower grades, and I teach the highest classes in English. My hours are from 8 to 12 a.m. and 2 to 4 p.m. Besides this I often make little dresses for the children and women's waists to sell.*

> *All of my pupils are young men and married ones with children. Mamma teaches the women every afternoon. I have charge of all the teaching work, besides cutting up soap once a week and distributing to each pupil to do his washing with. So you see I am quite busy all the time. I do not have time to learn the language—which is Marjahija—as fast as I would like, although I can talk some now.*

> *I shall now tell you about the climate. The altitude is about the same as that of Pine Ridge district. We are located among the mountains, but it seems as if we are about 2,000 miles nearer the sun.*

> *Oh, it is so extremely hot! We dare not go out in the sun without a cork hat and white umbrella, even when the sun is hidden behind a cloud. In a few minutes, without a hat in this country, you will suffer with a severe pain in your head. Malarial fever is the common disease, and I am now having a second attack. I am still trying to perform my duties, but, oh,*

> *it is so hard. Mamma is just getting over an attack of fever. While you are all enjoying the cold we are having the hottest weather in the year. We never have any snow. We are eating green vegetables of all kinds—in fact, we have them the year round.*

> *It does not seem like Christmas to me. December is the hottest month in the year and June the coldest. We have two seasons, rainy and dry, the rainy season being six months and the dry season the same.*

> *It is now the rainy season and while it is raining it is very cold, but immediately after it is hotter than ever.*

> *We are at a large coffee plantation of 2,100 acres, and it is covered with big forests. We are not raising coffee at the present time, but simply running a mission station.*

> *We have plenty of natives all around us. I shall tell you of their customs when I get back.*

> *In all British Central America there are only seven Afro-Americans, we five and two at a station forty miles from here. I was there a month ago to visit the young lady. There are only two ways of traveling here. One is to walk, the other to ride in a machila. A machila is a hammock suspended from a pole and carried by two men, accompanied by twelve, who take the place of the tired ones. It took me all day to get forty miles …* [20]

These details and many other strange customs were related to her friends in Colorado. In another Denver newspaper article, the family recounts some more experiences.

20. "Denver Girl Teaching Her Black Brethren," *Denver Post*, March 22, 1903, p. 18.

If a young woman in British Central Africa finds a young man who takes her fancy the lucky girl does not have to wait until he asks her, but she proceeds to cook him a dinner, which she carries to his home. If he eats the meal she has placed before him they are engaged, then the final arrangements are made by the parents.

The natives of that section live in huts made of grass and their only clothing is a loincloth. Their principal article of food is a sort of porridge made of corn ... [Everybody] here is anxious to learn especially the younger ones ... Until the completion of the railroad last December, freight for the interior was carried by the natives.[21]

Miss Branch wrote a number of letters that were reprinted in Adventist magazines. The one below gives some more details of her life as a young missionary.

Cholo.—Our two school buildings are made of grass and bamboo poles, with grass roofs. The larger one will accommodate about one hundred persons, sitting close together. For school purposes it seats about sixty. This building is used as a church in pleasant weather, and also as a school for English pupils. Both buildings have dirt floors, which are infested with matakenya. The matakenya are small, shiny black insects somewhat resembling the American flea. This insect burrows its way through the shoe and into the foot, where it deposits its eggs. If the insect and its eggs are not removed intact in a short time, the foot becomes infected. Sometimes the natives come to us with the toes and fingers both infected.

Occasionally snakes come out of the grass roof to view the classes in the schoolroom.

Whenever one appears, the school boys drop books and slates, and lessons are suspended until it is killed. There is an opening about three feet wide all around the large schoolroom, through which the wind sweeps from all directions on windy and rainy days. There are no doors, and if we cover the openings with mats, no one is able to see, as there are no windows.

The smaller school building is used for teaching the Manganja scholars, of which we have had two large afternoon classes. Many of the working people attend the afternoon session when their day's work is finished, most of them learning their own language.

The mission house is forty feet long by twenty-six and one half feet broad, with a veranda eight feet wide around three sides of the house. Each end of the back veranda has been enclosed, and is called a room. One is used as a storeroom. It is eight and one half feet long by six feet broad. The other enclosure is used as a kitchen and pantry. It is thirteen by seven and one half feet. A space of eighteen feet is left between the two enclosures for a back veranda. There are five rooms in the house. A dining room, twenty-one feet long and ten feet wide, containing no windows, passes through the center of the house with two rooms on each side of it. This hall is used as a dining room, as a sitting room, as a bedroom when strangers need lodging, and in bad weather as a church; in fact, it is the court for general purposes. The front door of the dining hall is half glass, and on dark, cold days when the door must be shut, this is all the light we receive.

The other four rooms are each twelve by ten feet. The house is covered with corrugated iron, but this has been covered with thick

21. "Good Cook Sure to Win Husband, Says Missionary," *Denver Post*, October 16, 1908, p. 10.

grass, to keep out the sun's intense heat.

There is a great work to be done here. We have a very meager supply of books, slates, and pencils. We are all interested in our work, and trust that the seed sown will fall upon good ground, and bring forth much fruit for the Master.[22]

Her letter to Elder O. O. Fortner, the secretary and treasurer of the South African Union, was shared with the members of the union since Fortner was also editor of the *South African Missionary,* the union's monthly paper.

Dear Brother Fortner,

Your letters have been received, and we are glad to hear from you. We are very glad to hear that Elder Hyatt will visit us soon, for we were quite disappointed when he did not come last year, and I hope he will not disappoint us again. We all enjoy our work here, and realize what a great opportunity we have for doing good.

We have representatives here from several different tribes, many of whom are Christians. The Manganja boys come from the villages every day, to school, and of course they are no expense to us. Those that stay here are of the Angoni and Yao tribes, and come from long distances. And they work in the corn and cotton fields from 6 A.M. to 10 A.M., and for this work they receive a small allowance, which enables them to buy their clothes and soap.

At present we have only thirty-three pupils enrolled, for it is the nature of the native to be always walking from one place to another. As they seldom stop long at one mission, it makes it very bad for all our classes. Just as we are beginning to see some results with an English

class, they will nearly all leave and others take their places, and we must commence at the first again. Thus we never see as much real good accomplished as we would like to see. All missions have the same difficulty, for only a few will stop long enough to be benefited. The branches taught are, reading, translating, spelling, writing, arithmetic, and music. We sing a great deal in school and Sabbath School. This they enjoy very much. I am trying to teach them to sing by note, and although it is very slow work, yet we all enjoy it.

The corn is nearly all dry now, and it is being gathered in and stored away. There is plenty of food everywhere this year, and the natives are making lots of beer. We can hear the drums beating at some near village nearly every night, and great crowds of people are passing, carrying their food and drums, going to these dances and beer-drinkings. In the villages on the station we have stopped their drum-beating and dancing; and every Sabbath some of the Christian boys from here, go to those villages and hold services, while many of the village boys come here to services, and they listen attentively to all that is said.

My father will write to you about the work later.

We are all of good courage in the Lord and enjoy our work, hoping that the Lord will bless our efforts, and that we will be found ready when He comes to gather His own.

With kind regards to all, I am your sister in the work,

Mabel Branch[23]

---

22. Mabel Branch, "British Central Africa," *Adventist Review and Sabbath Herald*, November 12, 1903, pp. 17, 18.

23. Mabel Branch, "Letter from the Nyasaland Mission," *South African Missionary*, June 1904, pp. 5, 6.

Mabel elaborates on the drums, drinking, and her desire to reach more of the Manganja tribe in her letter to the *Adventist Review.*

We have representatives here from several different tribes who are Christians, but of the Manganja tribe, who are living all around us, there are no converts. They seem to be the only tribe in this part who do not accept the Word of God, but continue in their wicked ways, dancing and drinking. They have many fables and proverbs, some of which contain many good lessons. Here is one of their sayings: "If you marry an idiot of a wife, you get shame with her. A gadding woman, who neglects her home duties, brings shame upon her husband, and he loses strength and honor, and has no longer influence."

The drums have been beating every night for a week—and why?—The crops are good this year, and plenty of corn has been raised; now the natives are making large quantities of beer, and the drums are beating to call all, for miles around to participate in the merrymaking. Many families, carrying their food, mats (beds), and drums, have been passing.

All night long we can hear the sound of the drums, for they have many. The rhythm is most perfect. The time is varied, for the smaller drums are made to answer the larger ones. The rapid and slow beats blend in the most perfect time, and the dancers quickly take their places, and all seem to go mad with excitement. Standing the small drums against a long pole, which has been securely fastened to two trees, and holding the large drum, about 4 feet long between his knees, a skilled drummer beats five of them at once. He becomes so enthusiastic in his labors that the beating can be heard for a long distance. The perspiration pours from his half naked body.

With what joy these people will walk for miles, through the hot sun, to attend these dances, and for days labor untiringly in the works of Satan. Yet when we invite them to attend services here, they make excuses, or promises which they never intend to keep. They will not come to hear God's Word, for even a few minutes, nor do they respect Him in whose keeping are their lives.

Every Sabbath some of the Christian boys go to the different villages to preach; and although some will listen, many laugh and make fun of them; but the boys keep on going and preaching.

Many of the village children attend our school, and also Sabbath services, and listen attentively to all that is said. In these children lies our hope of getting this message taught to others. The older people do not like to change their customs, but many of the young ones do not like the village life, so come to the mission to be taught. In school we are teaching the boys to sing, which all enjoy very much; and they are eager to learn our Sabbath-school songs in English.

The work is progressing nicely in all lines. We are all of good courage, and interested in our work for these people who are sitting in darkness and superstition. Our prayer and desire is to know how to best work for them. We know that if we are faithful in sowing the seeds of truth, God will give the increase.[24]

We lose track of Mabel Branch for a while after she returned from Africa. Then she reappears in 1922. We find her marriage license

---

24. Mabel Branch, "Our Nyasaland School," *Adventist Review and Sabbath Herald*, April 6, 1905, p. 18.

and notice that she marries Seymour E. Webb, a contractor living in Watts, California, on November 1, 1922, at forty-three years of age.

Seymour, who is forty-nine years old, had a large family of eight children. His wife Anna had died of an illness, leaving him a widower with eight young children. Seymour had not been a Seventh-day Adventist all of his life. It was about 1906 that Jenny L. Ireland, a young graduate nurse from the Battle Creek Sanitarium, began to do medical missionary work among the colored people in Los Angeles. Not knowing where to start, she was impressed to ask the colored postman whom she saw on the street one day if he knew any colored people who might be interested in studying the Bible. Without any hesitation he told her that he was sure his wife would be interested in studying with her.

Bible classes combined with home nursing and healthful cooking classes were conducted in this postman's home with such good results that Ms. Ireland was able to induce the conference committee at its session in 1907 to erect a building in which to conduct church services.

A new era in Seventh-day Adventist history began on the first Sabbath of August 1908 when the twenty-three believers organized the Furlong Seventh-day Adventist Church, the first colored Seventh-day Adventist Church west of Ohio. Under Sister Ireland's leadership, this church grew to more than 100 members before it ever had a pastor. It later became known as the Wadsworth church with a membership of more than 700 members.

The next church to be organized in California was the Watts church, later to become the Compton Avenue church of Los Angeles and still later the Normandy Avenue Seventh-day Adventist Church of Los Angeles. Sister Ireland, assisted by Sister Amy Temple, a retired Bible instructor, gave Bible studies to this large

family, and Seymour and Anna Webb joined the church. The church grew, and the Webbs were part of the original charter members.

Anna was just forty years of age when she passed away. The union paper carried the story. "After a lingering Illness, Sister Anna Webb fell asleep Feb. 11, 1918, in Los Angeles, Cal., at the age of nearly 41 years. She leaves a husband and eight children to mourn her loss. Her faithfulness to her Lord gives them a good foundation for the cheering hope of meeting her in the first resurrection. Funeral services were conducted in the Watts church, a large audience of her friends and acquaintances attending."[25] Mabel was willing to step in and finish raising Anna's large family. Two of Mabel's stepsons, Adolphus and William Webb, became outstanding ministers in the Adventist Church.

After Henrietta Branch died, Thomas Branch soon retired and moved to California to be near his daughter. Elder Branch died in his daughter's home. Before dying he extracted a promise from his grandson William C. Webb to continue the work the Lord had blessed them to establish in Africa. The younger Webb's intentions were good, but he did not follow up on the promise.[26]

Elder Adolphus Webb died on August 25, 1970. He spent his life serving in many of the larger black churches in various parts of America. Among the churches he served were First Church, Washington, D.C.; City Temple, Detroit; Ephesus, New York City; Beacon Light, Kansas City, Missouri; University Boulevard, Los Angeles; 31st St. Church, San Diego; and many other smaller congregations.

25. G. W. Reaser, *Pacific Union Recorder*, March 28, 1918, p. 7.

26. Charles Dudley, *Thou Who Hast Brought Us Thus Far on Our Way*, book 3, vol. 3 (Nashville, TN: Dudley Publications, 2000), p. 124.

Elder William C. Webb, like his brother, pastored all over the United States, was a dean at Oakwood College, and was well known for his interesting and lively song services that he conducted at camp meetings and even at the General Conference sessions.

Mabel Branch Webb passed away on October 12, 1945, at sixty-seven years of age. Her spirit inspired the young people of Colorado, the young men and women of Africa, her two sons who became outstanding preachers in the Adventist Church, and the rest of the Webb family.

FIRST COLORED TEACHER IN COLORADO

Graduate of West Side High School Appointed to District 15 School at Pine Ridge.

Florence Mabel Branch, a graduate of the West Denver High school, has been appointed a school teacher in district No. 15 at Pine Ridge, near the Arapahoe and Douglas county lines. She is the first colored teacher appointed in Colorado, and her friends look upon the appointment as making the beginning of a new era for the colored race in the state. The rapid strides in education made by the rising young negroes have been gratifying in all sections, indicating that they are hastily embracing their opportunities. The school board making the ap-

FLORENCE MABEL BRANCH, CLASS '97.

pointment is composed of William Bushell, president; J. R. Kinsey, treasurer,

Mabel Branch at twenty-four years of age

Newspaper clippings featuring Mabel Branch in Denver newspapers from 1898–1908.

Mabel with machila team. Strong men would carry a sling on their shoulders with the passenger sitting inside. Usually two (one at the front and one at the back) would walk until tired, and then fresh walkers who had not carried anything would step in to carry the passenger. A team usually consisted of eight men.

DENVER GIRL TEACHING HER BLACK BRETHREN

Bright Young Afro-American's Experience in Far-Off Africa, Where the Sun Shines Hottest at Christmas Time.

Probably the first letter ever received in Colorado from an Afro-American girl teacher in British Central Africa is pub-

few days you see 'twill be nearly five months before I can receive an answer. So please reply to this letter soon after

A Denver newspaper.

Mabel's stepson Elder W. C. Webb was a well-known Adventist pastor. His brother Elder Adolphus Webb was also a well-known Adventist preacher.

Branch family around 1907. Mabel in back, two boys on end and parents seated.

5

THOMAS H. AND HENRIETTA BRANCH

1902–1908 / Malawi

An unusual set of circumstances led the Adventist Church to send its first African American missionary, Thomas H. Branch, to the continent of African in 1902. The idea to send a non-white missionary to Nyasaland (Malawi today) actually came from Joseph Booth, a maverick preacher and denomination hopper (he belonged to seven denominations over his lifetime). Booth promoted the extreme idea of sending 20,000 American Negroes back to their native continent to help Africans reclaim Africa from colonial masters.

Adventists had known Joseph Booth only a few months when he gave an electrifying speech. Returning from Africa in 1901 as a Seventh Day Baptist, Booth went to Brooklyn, New York, in search of Seventh-day Adventists "on the Sabbath day and found them in the hall. Here I met Elder Haskell and his wife."[27] Haskell interviewed Booth and sent his report to the Mission Board, which invited Booth to meet with them in Battle Creek. They then invited him to the Lake Union Conference meeting in Chicago on March 29, 1902.

William A. Spicer, secretary of the Mission Board, was greatly impressed with Booth's proposal to begin mission work in Nyasaland. Spicer recounts that meeting.

When Brother Joseph Booth, who had been carrying on industrial mission work under the First-day Baptists, accepted the Sabbath truth in Plainfield, N. J., about five years ago, a private association of the Plainfield friends sent him out to establish a Sabbath-keeping mission. They bought an estate of two thousand acres, with buildings, and expected to make the mission practically self-supporting by coffee planting. They paid fifteen thousand dollars for the estate, and have expended very nearly ten thousand dollars more in clearing land and in operating expenses …

During these years Brother Booth has felt drawn ever more decidedly to the Adventist position; and when he decided to stand with us, our Seventh-day Baptist brethren were led to consider what they ought to do with their station … Although the friends might, undoubtedly, have secured better terms from first-day societies, they preferred, at a sacrifice, to turn the mission over to us in order that the Sabbath standard which they had unfurled might still remain, and be carried on further yet into the interior … It was arranged that, for the sum of four thousand dollars, the property and mission interests should pass to our board …

When Brother Booth met our brethren … and told his story of Nyasaland, all felt that it was of God that we should enter the field. But

---

27. "The Call for the Message in Central Africa," *Advent Review,* May 13, 1902, p. 14.

the Mission Board had planned work which required all the funds available, and in our mission work we can go only so far as the Lord sends the means. The Lake Union Conference said, "Go ahead," and voted its surplus funds, five hundred dollars, for Nyasaland.[28]

Delegates to that conference circulated the exciting new venture by word of mouth and in union papers. Spicer continues telling how the funds came in.

Altogether, pledges of $7,000 were made to this enterprise ... The board had within sight sufficient to get the workers to the field, and to provide for the work for the first six months, and to make the first cash payment of two thousand dollars for the mission station ... And just as we were waiting to see how deliverance would come, California sent the Mission Board the cheering message by wire: "you can draw two thousand dollars today. Blessings upon Nyasaland!" Thus we take upon ourselves a blessed ministry for the people of Nyasaland,——the land of Livingstone,——with a clear sheet financially. Thanks be to the Lord for this.[29]

Joseph Booth was an independently-minded Englishman who migrated to Australia and became a sheep farmer but later felt a call to preach. In 1891 he sold his business and embarked on his missionary career in Africa. In 1897 Booth published *Africa for the African* in which he outlined a program for abolishing British colonialism. Booth believed in complete racial equality and felt that he was called by God to speak against inequalities. Booth saw the industrial mission as a way to develop financial and educational independence for Africans. By offering to pay higher salaries, he recruited national workers to his mission—eighteen shillings per month when the ordinary rate was three shillings, which greatly irritated other missionary groups.

Booth dedicated *Africa for the African*, firstly to Victoria, Queen of Great Britain; secondly, to British and American Christians; and thirdly, to the Afro American people of the United States. He believed that colonialism deprived 200 million Africans of their birthright and permanently drained the wealth of Africa into European channels. In a separate petition to Queen Victoria in 1899, he specified twenty-one years as the time period to develop African independence after which Britain should hand control back to the indigenous inhabitants of Central Africa.

Booth felt that if he laid this burden on the black people of America a great number of them would return to Africa and help redress the centuries of injustice produced by colonialism. The most innovative and controversial part of Booth's proposal, which the Adventists didn't know at that time, entailed selling most of the Plainfield estate to African Americans in smaller plots.

Booth proposed a new organization, the African Protection and Repatriation Society, to encourage emigration and the establishment of American Negro families on these small land grants. He ran advertisements in many prominent American papers inviting interested parties to join.

Just before visiting the Adventists, Booth traveled to Atlanta and several eastern cities with large African American populations to gain support. He visited Bishop Henry M. Turner and W. E. B. Du Bois. He wrote Booker T. Washington and other prominent African American leaders in Philadelphia and sent them a prospectus about the potential of the

28. W. A. Spicer, "The New Missionary Enterprise Nyasaland," *Advent Review*, May 27, 1902, p. 17.

29. Ibid.

Plainfield Mission estate, which at that time still belonged to the Seventh Day Baptists. It was while waiting to hear from one of these leaders that he succeeded in gaining the backing of the Seventh-day Adventists.[30]

Unaware of Booth's extreme ideas but excited about opening a new mission station so cheaply in Africa, Spicer wrote, "The situation in Central Africa is such that colored workers may render special service, where the white face could not get access. The natives of the interior have besought Brother Booth, if he loved them, to bring out to Africa one of their own brethren, of whom they have vaguely heard. It was therefore decided that we might appropriately send out one of our colored brethren as our first contribution to Brother Booth's party."[31]

The Colorado Conference recommended the "colored" family and graciously volunteered to sponsor the Branches by paying their salary while in Africa if the General Conference would pay their transportation. Thomas H. Branch was born in Jefferson County, Missouri, on December 24, 1856, and Henrietta Paterson was born on March 12, 1858, in Roanoke, Missouri, the youngest in a large family. Somewhere along the line Thomas met Henrietta, and the couple married on December 7, 1876, in Kansas City, Kansas.

We don't know much about their early life. Charles Dudley states that Thomas Branch attended the school that Mrs. H. M. Van Slyke opened to help teach those who had recently been set free from slavery.[32] The *Adventist Review* mentions her school. "I am engaged in teaching a colored school in Ray Co., Mo. My pupils, *ranging in age from six to twenty-four* years, are very anxious to learn, and are apt to remember what is taught, all oral instruction in particular"; and "ten colored persons now read the Bible with so much readiness that we are able to finish a chapter at our morning exercises, and all usually engage in singing."[33]

It is possible that the young newlywed couple, thirsting after additional education, attended the Van Slyke School together in 1877 as some of the older students. The Branch's first child was born in Kansas, a little girl named Mabel, in April 1878. The Van Slyke School might have been their first exposure to Adventist doctrines, for they were baptized in 1892.

The couple moved to Denver, Colorado, in 1878, and three boys were added to the family: Thomas in June 1887; Paul in March 1891; and Robert in January 1896. Henrietta received training as a nurse and would do extra training to be able to act as a missionary doctor. Mabel graduated from Denver West High School and worked five years as a schoolteacher. For the last twenty years, Thomas worked as a porter, cook, steward, and brakeman on the Rio Grande railroad, which later granted him Sabbath privileges.

Brother Branch proved himself to be an able speaker, a diligent Bible student, and an enthusiastic lay worker who made a big impact on the colored population in Pueblo. "Since I returned from Denver the interest has increased very much and to the extent that I am not able to fill all the calls. I am still holding meetings in Bessemer at the hotel, and am

30. Harry Langworthy, *"Africa for the African." The Life of Joseph Booth* (Zomba, Malawi: Kachere Series, 1996), pp. 108, 109.

31. Ibid., pp. 17, 18.

32. Charles Dudley, *Thou Who Hast Brought Us Thus Far on Our Way*, book 3, vol. 3 (Nashville, TN: Dudley Publications, 2000), p. 172.

33. Mrs. H. M. Van Slyke, "Among the Freedmen." *Review and Herald*, February 22, 1877, p. 59.

trying to find a place on the north side to hold meetings."[34]

His energetic and faithful Bible work saw the creation of the first black Adventist company of believers in Pueblo. (The seeds he planted there have grown so that today there are four large African American churches in Pueblo and Denver.)

The Branches were older than most missionaries sent out by the church. Thomas was forty-six; Henrietta, forty-four; and their unmarried daughter, Mabel, had just turned twenty-four. The three boys were fifteen (we find no evidence that the oldest son, Thomas, went with them), eleven, and six, but they were eager for the new adventure.

No other black person from the Adventist Church had been sent to Africa. They had no role models to copy. It took courage, bravery, and a great faith in the providence of God to accept this Macedonian cry. But they gladly accepted the call to serve overseas.

The Colorado Conference ordained Thomas Branch on May 22, and the account of their departure is recorded.

Immediately taking leave of brethren and fellow laborers, and of those for whom we labored, we went to Denver, our former home, to make ready for the journey ... we packed a few necessary articles, and bidding our friends good-by, we left for Chicago. Elder Spicer met us there, and gave us all needed instructions for our journey.

... Wednesday morning, June 4, [1902] we set sail for London, England, arriving there June 12. We spent our first Sabbath in ... the Duncombe Hall church. We were given a hearty welcome by all the brethren.[35]

We left London Friday, June 27th, and have seven weeks before us yet. As we left the harbor at Southampton and were well out at sea it seemed that we had left the world behind us, but we know there is a great harvest field to which the dear Lord is taking us and we are glad for a place in his vineyard.[36]

The first sign of trouble comes in their next correspondence.

In company with our co-laborers, Brother Joseph Booth, his wife and little daughter, we sailed from Southampton on the 'R. M. S. Saxon,' June 28, 1902, for our future field of labor ... .

At Chinde, East Africa, situated at the mouth of the Zambezi River, we were detained nine days by the British consul, because we were educated Afro-American missionaries ... After the expiration of nine days, we were permitted to proceed up the river. We left Chinde on the 14th of August, and arrived in Cholo on the 29th.[37]

It was probably while being detained that the Branches found out who Joseph Booth really was and the possible political problems their ethnicity might produce. Many officials believed that the teachings of colored Americans induced a spirit of independence and insubordination among Africans. This movement of African nationalism, termed "Ethiopianism," began in South Africa around 1890 when independent African churches

---

34. "Pueblo," *Echoes from the Field*, February 5, 1902, p. 3.

35. Mr. and Mrs. T. H. Branch, "Called to Africa," *Advent Review*, July 15, 1902, p. 20.

36. Thomas Branch and Family, "On the Ocean," *Echoes from the Field*, September 3, 1902, p. 2.

37. Mrs. Thomas Branch, "British Central Africa," *Advent Review*, November 18, 1902, p. 17.

started forming. These churches claimed what had been promised Ethiopia in the Old Testament—"Ethiopia shall soon stretch out her hands unto God" (Ps. 68:31, KJV). The colonialists equated Ethiopianism with the educated American Negro. But it was Joseph Booth, not Thomas Branch who presented a danger to the country.

Adventists had no idea that Booth had written *Africa for the African* or that by sending Thomas Branch would raise the political implications of Ethiopianism. Booth neglected to tell Spicer anything about this.

Booth left the Branches in Chinde after staying with them for three days trying to convince the authorities that the Branches were not involved in Ethiopianism and proceeded to Plainfield. Here he met with Jacob Bakker who had been his assistant while Plainfield belonged to the Seventh Day Baptists. He informed Bakker of the sale to the Adventists and Bakker left in late August.

By now the Adventists were beginning to see Booth's true nature. Spicer wrote "It was against our best judgment that a colored worker be sent, but he [Booth] made so strong a plea, based on the sentiment of blacks, so we yielded."[38] If Spicer had consulted missionaries with experience in South Africa, he probably would have been reluctant to meet Booth's call for a colored missionary. Booth later wrote that there was prejudice among the South African Adventists who refused to host the Branch family, forcing Booth to spend his limited money in Durban for hotel accommodations for the newly arrived missionary family.[39]

A letter from E. R. Palmer to General Conference President A. G. Daniells mentions more concerns about Booth.

It would not be a great surprise to me if there should be unpleasant developments in the future, in view of the fact that Brother Booth knows only the ABC of our message, and is not at all acquainted with our methods of working. I have spent quite a little time with Brother Booth ... and I believe that he is a man of great energy and capacity, and that he is very inventive, and will always have great plans far in advance of the common people. He is like Dr. Kellogg in that particular.

He has already a plan in mind, and in fact tells me that he has entertained it for some time, of forming an organization in England and America, the object of which shall be to secure hundreds and thousands of coloured people from the South and locate them on self-supporting stations ... He says there are hundreds of thousands of dollars available in the United States for any organization, which will in an intelligent way attempt to locate the black man in the country from which he was taken.

He thinks that he thus sees the salvation of Africa and the relief of the oppressed coloured man in the South, in such an effort. His plan is a magnificent one, but to what extent it is proper for us as a denomination to enter into such a religio-political undertaking, may be a question. However I have seen enough of Brother Booth, and have heard enough of Central Africa to convince me that it would be nothing short of a criminal caution for us not to enter into this opening of Providence, and do all that we can for that field ... I still believe that a strong white man ought to be selected for the mission as soon as possible.[40]

---

38. Letters, Spicer-Booth, September 25, 1903; Spicer-William S. Hyatt, July 9, 1903.

39. Harry Langworthy, *"Africa for the African." The Life of Joseph Booth* (Zomba, Malawi: Kachere Series, 1996), pp. 164–166.

40. Letter dated June 13, 1902, from London.

There were great problems at Plainfield Mission between Branch and Booth. The Branches were interested in teaching and preaching the gospel and were not interested in Booth's proposals. Booth was always involved in some project and never had enough money to pay the mission bills or pay the Branches their salary. After just six months Booth was recalled by the Mission Board and asked to become a colporteur in England. With Booth gone, Branch labored alone as the director of Plainfield Mission until a white man was sent by the Mission Board.

Joseph H. Watson with his wife and son arrived, but in less than a year the climate had ravaged Watson, and he passed away at age thirty-three. His wife and son returned to their home. Young Watson was buried on the grounds of the mission station. Branch continued as director, and on July 14, 1906, he organized the very first Adventist Church in Malawi.

Branch continued to direct the mission until another white missionary, Joel C. Rogers, came who renamed the mission Malamulo, which means commandments, and the Branches moved to South Africa in 1907 in search of a better climate and to put their boys in school. It was a great disappointment to them when they found out that their boys could not attend the white Adventist schools. In 1908 they returned to the States because of Henrietta's inability to cope with the fevers, and Elder Branch was placed once again in charge of the colored work in Denver. He traveled to various churches in the conference, telling of his experiences in Africa. He became a member of many church committees. In 1910 he was called to the East to develop an interest in the city with the largest black population in America. We have a very detailed account in the union papers as to his work in the East.

We are told that in the eastern cities, including Philadelphia, the Lord desires us to proclaim the third angel's message with power. As a result of this admonition the work has been advanced to meet the needs of all nationalities. Philadelphia having a negro population of 107,000, more than any other city in the United States, efforts have been put forth in behalf of this city.

Elder T. H. Branch and family from Denver, Colorado, were procured last September, arriving in Philadelphia Thursday, September 29, 1910. He entered the work with zeal and earnestness and the Lord has blessed his efforts from the beginning. The colored members of the North Philadelphia church have heartily affiliated with him, and as a result of this cooperation, the First African S. D. A. church of Philadelphia was organized Sabbath, February 11, 1911.

Elder W. H. Heckman conducted the service, his subject being "The Church, Its Organization and Purpose, and, the Relation of Individuals to the Church." The spirit of God came in with power, uniting the hearts of all, so there was not one dissenting voice. After a brief, but earnest discourse, the organization was effected with sixteen charter members.

The church officers having been elected, Elder Branch as pastor, a church fund with which to purchase a suitable house of worship was started, and in a very short time over $300.00 was raised. All were encouraged, and we firmly believe that with the blessing of God resting upon the beginning of this great work, much will be accomplished, and many will be brought to the knowledge of this last warning *message to a dying world.*

The ministers who were present and participated in the service were Elder W. H. Heckman, president of the East Pennsylvania Conference, Elder H. Myers, pastor of the First German S. D. A. church, Elder S. D. Hartwell, secretary and treasurer of the East Pennsylvania Conference, and the writer. Inasmuch as it is God's purpose that the truth for this time shall be made known to every kindred, nation, tongue, and people, let God's people remember in prayer this beginning, that the special blessing of the Lord be over the colored work thus started in Philadelphia.[41]

A year later another report told of the progress of the work in Philadelphia.

Sabbath, February 10, the members of the First African Seventh-day Adventist Church celebrated the first anniversary of its organization by rendering an appropriate program. Elder T. H. Branch gave a history of the organization and growth of the church, showing that thirteen new members had been added to the church in the twelve months past … The work of the church is in good condition. The outlook is only encouraging.

The report of the treasurer, given by the state treasurer, Elder S. D. Hartwell, showed a tithe paying church, and that the ten cents a week for missions was by the church paid in full to date. These two reports certainly were a source of great encouragement, and each member felt inspired to strive to do more in this year for the spread of the message to the world, and for the upbuilding of the church.

Scripture recitations, and other quotations

followed, with some excellent papers by members of the Sabbath-school, and hymns and solos befitting the occasion. Much credit is due to those who took part in these exercises, all having been done to the glory of the Lord, who "has done great things for us."[42]

Two years later another report indicated that the Philadelphia church was still growing.

It has now been two years since our little company was organized into a church. We spent the first eighteen months in educating the people. They had not been thoroughly taught. While teaching them we were also engaged in giving Bible readings and doing missionary and colporter work. For the last six months great interest has been shown, and all are actively engaged in giving the message.

Soon after my arrival here, I was fortunate to enter the old folks home at Forty-fourth and Girard Ave., to hold services on Sabbath afternoon. Our membership has increased from sixteen to thirty members, with $263.83 for tithes. Sabbath school has increased from six to thirty-two members. We are now building a new church.[43]

Later the church was renamed Ebenezer, and it became the mother of nearly a dozen African American churches that exist in the Philadelphia area today.

Henrietta Branch died in Philadelphia on April 4, 1913. Her death delivered a devastating blow to Thomas. He had not been able to get a good education for his boys, and they both joined the army. His health was

41. B. M. Heald, "East Pennsylvania." *The Columbia Union Visitor*, February 22, 1911, p. 5.

42. Henrietta Branch, "East Pennsylvania," *The Columbia Union Visitor*, February 28, 1912, p. 5.

43. T. H. Branch, "Philadelphia," *The Gospel Herald*, June 1913, p. 3.

also failing from having had malaria so many times in Africa. He married a much younger woman, Lucy Baylor, with a five-and-half-year-old daughter. Lucy became a follower of A. T. Jones. When Thomas wouldn't compromise his beliefs and adopt her peculiar beliefs, Lucy's parents urged her to leave Elder Branch and return to their home.

Alone and without any family in Philadelphia, he moved to California in 1918. He served in Watts for a short time but then took sustentation, which the new leaders from East Pennsylvania Conference were reluctant to recommend for him. He moved in with his daughter, Mabel Webb, and spent the last few years of his life with her and her family in Los Angeles. He passed away on November 6, 1924. Elder P. Gustavus Rogers gave the eulogy.

The Branches were pioneers in Colorado, Malawi, and Philadelphia. They steered clear of politics, overlooked prejudice, left an amazing legacy to the Adventist Church, and became an inspiration to other black missionaries to venture overseas.

Joseph Booth is still regarded as the maverick missionary who advocated several unusual political, social, and religious causes and was instrumental in the founding of seven major denominations in Malawi. He was prohibited from entering Malawi in 1907 but continued working in Africa and inspired several Africans to form indigenous denominations. Europeans regarded Booth as a hopeless visionary, a religious hitchhiker, a threat to race relations and the colonial order, and even an inciter of sedition and treason. But it was his vision that opened the Adventist Church in Malawi.

The new Seventh-day Adventists missionaries in 1902. The Branches and the Booths in London just before leaving for Nyasaland, Africa. Seated in the back row (from far left): Henrietta and Thomas Branch, Mabel Branch, Joseph and Annie Booth. The children in the front (from far left): Emily Booth and Paul and Robert Branch.

Fred Mead and Thomas Branch at the gravesite of young J. Watson who died in Nyasaland not long after arriving.

DARKEST AFRICA

Thomas H. Branch, Railroad Employe, Becomes Preacher and Chooses Distant Field.

His Wife and Daughter, Latter a High School Graduate, Will Accompany Him.

After eight years of preparation for the missionary field Thomas H. Branch, a colored employe of the Denver and Rio Grande for over twenty years, leaves to-morrow with his family for Central Africa, to preach the gospel to his own race. He was ordained only last Thursday. Mr. Branch will have the co-operation of his wife and daughter in his new work, both having special interest in the new opening that has come to them, and for which they are unusually well fitted.

Miss Branch is 24 years old, and a graduate of the West Denver High school.

REV. THOMAS BRANCH,
Ordained Thursday for Missionary Work in Africa.

She has been teaching school for several years near Parker, in district No. 15 of Arapahoe county. She will take charge of the school work, and will also have the education of her two brothers, one 12 and the other 7, who accompany them to Af-

Story in the Denver Daily News on May 24, 1902, about Thomas Branch leaving for Africa.

Pastor and Mrs. Malinki and their two daughters. Pastor Malinki was one of the first national leaders in Malawi.

An assembly at the Nyasaland mission house.

Indigenous teachers at Malamulo.

6

JAMES AND MARIAN HYATT

1903–1907 / Ghana, Sierra Leone, Nigeria

On April 24, 1901, after voting to pay $2,000 cash at that time and another $2,000 a year from then for the transfer of the Nyasaland (Malawi) Mission to the Adventist Church, the Mission Board next voted "to correspond with J. M. Hyatt, of Denver, Colo., concerning work in Nyasaland, and that we petition the Colorado Conference to support him in the field and pay his expenses thereto, in case he is sent."[43]

For some reason, the Mission Board took no further action on Hyatt and voted later to send Thomas H. Branch to Nyasaland, and the Colorado Conference happily supported Elder Branch.[44] Two years later "it was agreed that Minnesota should be asked to support Brother J.M. Hyatt on the Gold Coast, and that arrangements be made for his departure, if possible, with Brother Hale and family, the present month."[45] Thus, Dr. James Hyatt and his wife became the first black missionaries to enter the Gold Coast (Ghana), arriving there in 1903.

James M. Hyatt was born in 1869 in Kentucky to Milton and Maggie Hyatt. He later met and married Marian E. Williams (her parents were Charles and Eliza Williams) who was born in 1867 in Michigan. James and Marian were married on December 21, 1892, in Battle Creek, Michigan. We don't know why and when they moved to Colorado, but there is a high probability that they were acquainted with the Branch family. Brother Hyatt was a dentist, but we don't know where he studied. Earlier records say he was a tinner. Marian was a seamstress and dress maker. It does not appear that they had any children.

James Hyatt wrote more than a dozen letters from Africa that were published in the *Advent Review and Sabbath Herald* and *The Signs of the Times*. In one of the earliest letters he wrote, he stated:

After a slight delay in perfecting arrangements for our journey, we left Minnesota for New York [probably February 1903]. We stopped in Cleveland for a week's visit with friends and relatives. While there, we visited among the colored people, and had some interesting experiences, especially on Sunday at the largest Baptist church, where we were offered financial aid. Surely, a consecrated colored laborer could do much good among the thousands of intelligent negroes of Cleveland.

After riding a night and a day, we were in New York, where we were met by Brother Calvert, of the Bible Training School, who took us to that institution, where we spent the night. It truly

43. Mission Board Minutes, April 24, 1901, p. 65.

44. Mission Board Minutes, May 15, 1902, p. 67. The minutes incorrectly say Brother F. A. Branch.

45. Mission Board Minutes, January 5, 1903 p. 107.

is a haven of rest. The spiritual atmosphere is invigorating. Here we met Elder Luther Warren, whom we had not seen for years. We were glad to hear of the good interest that was manifested among the colored people, under his labors, and would have been glad, as was suggested, to spend some time in the school, and at the same time assist with interests that had been awakened.

After a trip of eight days we disembarked at Liverpool, where we found Elder Hale and his family ready to sail that day. In England we met some good friends, one a wholesale grocer, not of our people.

After ten or twelve days more of sailing, we sighted the coast of Africa for the first time— Freetown, Sierra Leone. We had the privilege of going ashore here, and were much surprised to find that all the natives are not illiterate, as has been said, but some are well educated. All government offices are filled by natives, except that of the governor-general. Some of our American colored brethren could do much good by settling here and living the truth, especially such as have trades. Among the trades that may be mentioned are dentistry, carpentry, blacksmithing, and farming. To such there are inducements offered in the matter of passage.

After dinner with the harbor master, we were soon on our way to our final stopping place. We reached Cape Coast Castle in four days. We were warmly greeted by the natives generally. There are less than five on the Gold Coast who make any pretense of keeping the Sabbath. We are very glad, indeed, to get here, and like it very much. We hope that it will not be long before we will have more of our American brethren on the Coast at different points; for it is true, as stated by others, that there is an

affinity between the natives and other negroes that is not known by some at least.

While talking with the passengers as I came down from Freetown, I made the acquaintance of a man from the West Indies. He was going to one of the towns on the coast below us. In conversation with him, I learned that his sole mission was to carry the Sabbath to his people. He is a native. We were glad to see the direct working of the Lord in this matter. We are sure that he will use many agencies that are unknown to us to reach the millions of natives here. We are of good courage and hope to see the work make fast progress.[46]

He arrived in Ghana on March 10, 1903, a week after Elder Hale. A few months later Hyatt wrote another letter that was printed in the *Advent Review* about the progress of the work in the Gold Coast (Ghana). He mentioned that the work was moving along quite well there and they were being greatly blessed. They were holding street meetings on Sundays, and their congregation blocked the street off entirely.

He discovered how easy it was to find things that you wouldn't expect in Africa. He needed a portable organ, and to his surprise, he discovered that his neighbor had one. Apparently Hyatt was a good musician, and he discovered that the people of the Gold Coast really enjoyed music, which helped to attract them to the street meetings. The meetings were also very well attended on Tuesday and Thursday evenings.

Hyatt also mentioned the great need for at least two more teachers. They had six classes, the sessions lasting from ten to twelve o'clock in the morning, and from two to four in the

46. J. M. Hyatt, "West Coast, Africa," *Advent Review and Sabbath Herald,* June 2, 1903, p. 17.

afternoon. The work was graded from elementary to classes in algebra.

Hyatt rejoiced over an unexpected blessing. A well-to-do native merchant called on him and presented him with a new expensive chapel organ. They had just lost the use of the other organ the Sabbath morning before. Hyatt did dental work when time permitted and was able to help many this way. At one point he had two boys living in his home—one about twenty years of age and the other a small boy. The older boy was hoping to go into the work sometime and had become a member of the church.[47]

The work in the Gold Coast had started in 1888. The captain of a ship that was anchored in the harbor of Apam agreed to distribute tracts and literature in the Gold Coast and a roll of tracts fell into the hands of honest seekers. F. I. U. Dolphijn, a native Ghanaian, read the literature and began to observe the Sabbath. Some missionaries had been sent there in 1893, but the climate was very difficult for the white missionaries. They started calling the Gold Coast the "white man's grave." All of the missionaries had to leave after a short while because of malaria and black water fever. When they left, F. I. U. Dolphijn and G. P. Grant, a neighbor whom Dolphijn had converted, took charge of the work. There were no missionaries in Ghana for several years.

Then Dr. Hyatt and Brother D. U. Hale (who had been there once before but had to leave because of sickness) arrived in 1903. But in less than a year, Elder Hale and his family had to return to the States because Elder Hale came down with his third attack of black water fever. For two weeks he was not expected to live, but by the most careful nursing, he finally rallied. Before he was able to sit up, three of his children were in the hospital with him. The doctor informed them that to remain would be nothing less than suicide, and so the family reluctantly left their missionary post. Thus, the Hyatts were left in the Gold Coast all alone. Thankfully, they remained healthy and continued to oversee the work in the Gold Coast.

Dr. Hyatt was able to convert several Ghanaians who helped to establish the Adventist Church in Ghana. Among the most prominent was Christian A. Ackah who organized churches at Kikam and Axim in 1909. In subsequent letters Dr. Hyatt tells how the nationals loved anything American and were anxious to read the literature he distributed. As a result of their work, many people were convicted of the Sabbath truth; however, few were taking a stand for it.

The Hyatts later spent some time in Sierra Leone (1905). It was cooler than the Gold Coast, and they used the time away to revive their health. Dr. Hyatt wrote from Freetown, "I am holding a very interesting Bible reading on Thursday evening, at one of the houses, and prayer-meeting on Wednesday evening at my home."[48] They also distributed tracts. They were soon joined there by Elder and Mrs. D. C. Babcock, and the work in Sierra Leone began to blossom. Together they opened a day school. Hyatt was the first known black missionary to work in Sierra Leone. Lambert W. Browne would come a little later in 1906. C. E. F. Thompson, a Jamaican, would be baptized in Sierra Leone in 1907 and begin working there. I am not sure Thompson would be considered a missionary to Sierra Leone since he was already there when he was baptized. However, he would be sent later as a missionary to Ghana.

47. J. M. Hyatt, "West Africa," *Advent Review and Sabbath Herald*, August 11, 1903, p. 19.

48. J. M. Hyatt, "West Africa," *Advent Review and Sabbath Herald*, August 31, 1905, p. 13.

Dr. Hyatt later worked in Nigeria (1906–1907) and was the first black Adventist American to work there. Hyatt returned to the States in 1907. We find him speaking and selling literature in Philadelphia with his friends Elder Thomas and Henrietta Branch in 1912, and then we lose track of him. Marian Hyatt seems to have remained in Monrovia, Liberia.

Another expatriate black worker would soon come and pick up the work in Ghana. Brother C. E. F. Thompson, a Jamaican who had received his literary training at Kingston College in Jamaica, had come to Sierra Leone independently and became acquainted with the Adventist message while living in the country. Thompson was baptized in Sierra Leone in 1907 by D. C. Babcock and served as a faithful worker for the church there. Brother Thompson had visited Ghana for a short time in 1909 to conduct a series of meetings among the Nsimbia people in Kickam and Axim but had returned to Sierra Leone after the meeting.

When Mrs. T. M. French, who had been a teacher in Ghana, passed away because of a fever, her husband was advised to leave Ghana and go home to regain his health. With no expatriate workers in Ghana, Brother Thompson was advised to drop his work in Sierra Leone and go to the Gold Coast (Ghana) full time to continue the work that had been done by the French family. C. E. F. Thompson arrived in Ghana again in February 1910. He could be considered a black missionary from Sierra Leone to Ghana. Unfortunately, after working honorably in Ghana for about two years, Thompson died from Bright's disease on March 25, 1912. He was just thirty-six years old.[49]

We have no pictures of the Hyatts. This picture is of C. E. F. Thompson, a Jamaican who worked in Ghana and Sierra Leone with L. W. Browne and the Hyatts from 1907 when he was baptized to 1912 when he died of Bright's disease.

Early workers in Ghana. Standing in the back row is Mrs. Kerr, F. I. U. Dolphijn (the first baptized Adventist in Ghana), and G. P. Grant, Dolphijn's neighbor. Seated are Isaac Dolphijn, Mr. George T. Kerr, D. U. Hale, and Fred Dolphijn.

49. The *Advent Review and Sabbath Herald* carried articles about Thompson's work and his death: D. C. Babcock, "West Africa," *Advent Review and Sabbath Herald*, December 21, 1911, p. 13; "Thompson" Obituary, *Advent Review and Sabbath Herald*, May 23, 1912, p. 23.

7

LAMBERT WELLINGTON BROWNE

1907–1908 / Sierra Leone

Lambert Wellington Browne was born on May 22, 1883, in Barbados, West Indies, to Samuel and Rosalie Browne. As a young man of twenty years of age, Browne is listed as a worker in the 1904 Seventh-day Adventist Yearbook serving in the East Caribbean Conference in British Guiana, South America, and in the 1906 Yearbook he is listed as serving in Trinidad.

He is first mentioned in our church papers when he describes his experience of speaking at an evangelistic meeting on the night of February 15, 1905, in the village of Conneltown, Barbados, in the St. Lucy parish. Although still a schoolmaster, he enjoyed preaching, and he described another meeting where he spoke the next night in a different place two miles away. Six people were ready to join the church and others were desirous of learning more.[50]

About four month later, on Friday, June 9, 1905, Pastor George F. Enoch baptized five precious souls in the sea, the first fruits of Browne's labor in the parish of St. Lucy, Barbados. Less than a month later on Sabbath, July 1 in Bridgetown, Barbados, eleven more precious souls were buried with their Lord in baptism and twenty-four added to the church through Browne's efforts.[51]

It must have been his intense desire for more education plus the talents the church leaders saw in this young man that led him to make plans to attend school in America. The passenger arrival list of the *SS Trinidad* shows L. W. Browne arriving at Ellis Island on July 30, 1906, after having left Barbados on July 26. He went straight to Emmanuel Missionary College (EMC) in Berrien Springs, Michigan, for more theological studies.

After just a few months at EMC, in April 1907, he sailed from New York to Sierra Leone to join Elder D. C. Babcock. He wrote from Sierra Leone:

It is now a month and a half since I came to Sierra Leone, and my observation has taught me that a great and effectual work has already been done here; but there yet remains a greater work to be accomplished, which is a herculean task, looking at it from a human standpoint, and can be performed only by the influence of the Spirit on us as workers, and on the people … Truly may it be said that the city is stirred from center to circumference … Our school now has an enrollment of sixty, and there is an increase occurring weekly. It may be observed that we have made no effort to obtain students, but there is a tendency on the part of the people to send their children to the school,

50. L. W. Browne, "Barbados," *Advent Review and Sabbath Herald,* July 20, 1905, pp. 14, 15.

51. "Our Work and Workers," *The Caribbean Watchman,* August 1905, pp. 10, 11.

even taking them from other schools, because they believe that the training received by the children is of a substantial nature.

A gentleman in the city told me a few days ago that if we had a boarding school, he would gladly send one of his sons to live with us. This remark was made by him spontaneously, without any request on my part for his child to attend school. We are endeavoring to fit the students to become workers for Jesus; for we know that soon-and very soon-children must witness where persons of mature age cannot go.[52]

In 1905 the General Conference voted to send Elder D. C. Babcock to the West Coast of Africa to revive the work. He visited the Gold Coast (Ghana) and Sierra Leone and decided that the headquarters for the work should be in Sierra Leone since it was much cooler. Early in 1906 a mission house was built on the side of a hill outside of Freetown. The weather there was good for their health.

Mrs. Babcock opened a school, and the enrollment climbed to 125. A new 40 x 60 foot tent was set up in Freetown and the first meeting was held on January 10, 1907. Each evening the crowd increased until there were about 1,500 people attending. Thirty-one people were baptized as a result of the meetings, and a church was organized.

The work grew rapidly:

The necessity of organizing a church in Sierra Leone was discussed for several weeks, and Sabbath, July 20 [1907], was appointed as the day on which it should take place. It was a bright sunny morning (although this is the rainy season), and quite a favorable day for those who lived at some distance from the place of worship. There was a good attendance, including those who had given their names for organization, as well as other interested persons.

Elder Babcock spoke impressively of the benefits of organization, and of the duties that devolved upon the related members of an organized body … As points of interests were touched, 'Amen' was heard from different ones, thus signifying the desire to comply with the principles presented … twenty persons entered into the bond of Christian fellowship and concord. Seven of these were accepted subject to baptism, which was arranged to be administered on the following day … Six of the seven baptized are young men who have expressed a desire to work for the Master … Officers were elected, their duties pointed out, and thus closed the experience of a never-to-be-forgotten occasion.[53]

C. E. F. Thompson, a Jamaican who was already living in Sierra Leone, and R. P. Dauphin were baptized in this tent effort. Both of these men turned out to be good workers. These two men went with L. W. Browne to Waterloo, a town about twenty miles from Freetown, to open the work there. A company of believers grew out of their efforts.

Elder Babcock describes the progress of the work in Waterloo.

On the morning of October 16 [1907], Brother Browne and the writer [D. C. Babcock] boarded the train for Waterloo. A limited amount of our literature had been sold among the people of this town; but aside from that, nothing had ever been done to advance the message in this town of more than 3000 souls … The following week Brother Browne returned, and through the

---

52. L. W. Browne, "West Africa," *Advent Review and Sabbath Herald*, September 19, 1907, pp. 18, 19.

53. L. W. Browne, "The First Church Organized in Sierra Leone, West Africa," *Advent Review and Sabbath Herald*, October 3, 1907, p. 16.

kindness of Mr. Faulkner, the district Commis-
sioner, he secured the town market, a spacious
room not now used, in which to hold a series
of meetings. The first of November, Brother
and Sister R. P. Dauphin and Brother C.E.F.
Thompson accompanied Elder Browne to
Waterloo, and in a short time an excellent inter-
est was manifest … A bitter opposition soon
arose, and the minister of the leading church
disfellowshipped several of his members for
attending the meetings at the market.

On Sunday, March 14, our first baptism took
place … twelve earnest souls were buried with
their Lord in baptism … a meeting was called
to consider the building of a church … Long
before the hour appointed for the doors to be
opened, the people began to come; and by the
time the services began, every inch of seating
room was occupied … On the platform were
prominent lawyers and city councilmen.

The dedication of this new, neat building,
the first Seventh-day Adventist Church in all
West Africa, marks an advanced step. While
we have no haughty pride in the edifice, we do
praise the Lord that we have a place of wor-
ship to which we can invite the public.[54]

In May 1908 Browne returned to the
United States because of ill health and spoke
to his fellow students and teachers at Emmanuel Missionary College about the work in
Sierra Leone. He also enrolled in school to
continue his studies. The General Conference
voted that "the treasurer be authorized to loan
him $25 to help him in finishing his course at
Berrien Springs."[55]

54. D. C. Babcock, "West Africa," *Advent Review and Sabbath Herald,* June 4, 1908, pp. 14, 15.

55. General Conference Committee Minutes, April 20,
1909, p. 618.

The enrollment form gives us a bit more
information about him. His father was a wheel-
wright, and his name was S. R. Browne, but
he was not an Adventist. His mother was an
Adventist and named R. A. Browne. He would
be twenty-six at his next birthday and wanted to
continue in foreign missionary work.

Having finished his course of studies at
Emmanuel Missionary College, Browne was
assigned to pastor a colored church in Springfield, Illinois. The church building there was
small and unattractive. He encouraged the
members to paint it, and he helped make
other necessary repairs to transform it into a
beautiful edifice. Next the new pastor pitched
a tent and conducted a series of meetings for
six weeks. The church was revived and people
were baptized.

On January 2, 1910, Pastor Browne was
ordained to the gospel ministry in Springfield.
A year later on the night of February 24, 1911,
around midnight, young Pastor Browne was
awakened with the sad news that his church
was burning. When he arrived at the scene
of the conflagration, the firemen were bus-
ily fighting the flames to protect the building
to the north where the fire had originated.
Thanks to the neighbors, most of the furniture
in the church was saved except some of the
school desks, which had been fastened to the
floor. Undaunted Browne began to raise funds
for a new building.

About a year later Browne was sent to Indianapolis to pastor a colored church there.

Here he was met with great illness, and the
tent meetings that he was holding had to be
canceled. After recovering his health, he began
his second tent effort. The first Seventh-day
Adventist Church for colored people in the
state of Indiana was organized in the city of
Indianapolis on July 25, 1914. Elder Browne

reported that eighteen persons were a part of this new church organization and that others would be added in a future baptism.[56]

On Thanksgiving evening, November 25, 1915, Elder Lambert Wellington Browne was united in holy matrimony to Lalla Vivian Poole in Indiana. Lalla, a nurse, was the daughter of Albert and Bettie Poole of Louisville, Kentucky, and was born on June 16, 1892.

In 1918 the Brownes were called to the Kansas Conference to grow the colored work. The Kansas City Church had about sixty members, and he went to work immediately erecting a nice church. The last reference to him was in the 1921 yearbook, stating that he worked in the Kansas Conference.

In 1926 Lambert Wellington Browne became a naturalized citizen of the United States while he was living in Chicago, Illinois. The 1930 and 1940 census showed Lambert Browne and his family still residing in Chicago, Illinois. They had a daughter, Rosalie Browne, and a son, Leon Browne, both born in Chicago.

The man who is credited with starting the work in Waterloo, Sierra Leone, and who assisted with starting the very first church in Sierra Leone passed away on December 2, 1966, in Chicago. He is also credited with starting the first black congregation in Indiana and advancing and increasing the progress of the black work in Illinois and Kansas. His wife, Lalla Browne, died in Illinois in April 1984 at the age of 92.

We have no pictures of L. W. Browne or his wife, Lalla. We were able to find pictures of his children who attended schools in Chicago. Pictured is Leon Browne when he attended Chicago State University in 1942.

Daughter Rosalie Browne at Englewood High School, Chicago, Illinois, in 1940.

The very first Seventh-day Adventist Church building in all of West Africa was dedicated in Waterloo, Sierra Leone, on March 29, 1908, just before L. W. Browne returned to America.

___

56. L.W. Browne, "A Church Organized," *Lake Union Herald*, August 26, 1914, p. 4.

8

DAVID AND LOTTIE BLAKE

1913–1917 / Panama, Haiti

Lottie Cornelia Isbell was born on June 10, 1876, in Appomattox Courthouse, Virginia, next door to the house where General Lee surrendered to General Grant. When she was three her family moved to Columbus, Ohio, where she was educated in the public schools.

The Isbells were staunch Baptists until they met Sister Swift, a white Seventh-day Adventist who confronted Thomas and Fanny Isbell, Lottie's parents, with the Adventist message. In 1896 Thomas, Fanny, Lottie, Mamie, her sister, and their aunt Grace Kimborough (who also became a medical doctor) were baptized and joined the Adventist Church.

At the time of her baptism, Lottie was twenty years of age and had just completed a teacher's training course. She was looking forward to working as a teacher, but her Bible instructor encouraged Lottie to attend Battle Creek Sanitarium and Hospital Training for Nurses. That year Lottie enrolled and studied nursing at the sanitarium. She lived in the home of Dr. John Harvey Kellogg who acted as a surrogate father and mentor for her. Kellogg, who reared several black children in his own home, wanted her to go beyond nursing and chose her to attend the American Medical Missionary College, which was also located in Battle Creek. Dr. Kellogg encouraged and assisted his protégé to take the medical course, from which she graduated in 1902 as the first black physician in the Adventist Church.

After graduating from medical school in 1902, Lottie had her heart set on serving in Africa, but Dr. Kellogg advised her to go down south and establish a sanitarium and nurses training program as her first missionary assignment. She accepted with youthful fervor, but the sophisticated black community where Meharry Medical College, Fisk University, and Walden University were just getting a foothold looked with disdain on her "rag treatment" or hydrotherapy. They seriously questioned her practice of medicine without drugs, and she was never able to establish a nursing school in the South.

Dr. Isbell served as director of a health facility, the Rock City Sanitarium, which became the forerunner of Riverside Sanitarium and Hospital in Nashville, Tennessee. Then she served as a practicing physician in Birmingham, Alabama. In 1903 Lottie went to Oakwood College to organize a nurses training program. That year an epidemic broke out in the Oakwood orphanage and many of the children seemed on the verge of death. Dr. Isbell rolled up her sleeves and worked untiringly to arrest the epidemic.

Lottie passed the Alabama state medical board examination in 1904, scoring a perfect paper. For three years Dr. Isbell practiced in Birmingham, and during this time she met a strikingly handsome young minister, Pastor David Emanuel Blake, who had migrated to the United States from Jamaica to attend school, which later became Atlantic Union College, in South Lancaster, Massachusetts. (His parents were George and Eliza Blackwood Blake). Lottie and David began to correspond.

After Pastor Blake graduated from South Lancaster Academy, he was sent south to pastor a church in Nashville, Tennessee. While pastoring there, he completed the medical course at Meharry Medical College. He was now both a pastor and a medical doctor.

The two doctors were married in 1907. Before the couple embarked on their lifelong ambition of becoming foreign missionaries, David Blake visited Columbus and organized the few believers there into a church. Leaving the young flock in the care of the Ohio Conference, the couple then sailed for Central America and Panama where they did self-supporting medical missionary work.

Dr. David Blake left in early 1913[57] to go to Panama to secure lodging and make arrangements for his family. A few weeks later Dr. Lottie Isbell Blake left the United States for Panama with their three little girls: Frances, the eldest, then Sarah, and Marcia. Alice Evelyn Blake (Brantley) made her appearance after they reached Panama. Alice was born on November 22, 1913, in the Canal Zone and was followed by the final child of the family, a boy, Thomas.

It was just before the outbreak of World War I that the Blakes found themselves in Panama as self-supporting missionaries. The greatest engineering feat that Uncle Sam had ever ventured upon was on the drawing board, the Panama Canal. With so much going on, the services of a physician were greatly appreciated. The Blakes found that there was much need for their medical skills. Yellow fever and malaria were rampant. Along with caring for the sick, there was active missionary labor for those who were unchurched.

The Canal Zone was teaming with black men and women from all over the Caribbean who came to build the Canal. Dr. David Blake, fluent in French and Spanish, was a welcome sight as he traversed the Canal Zone taking care of the people. As a medical evangelist he was busy on two fronts, saving lives and saving souls. Dr. Blake shared some of his experiences after being in Panama for a year.

A year ago I landed in Colon, having separated from the Sanitarium work in Nashville, Tenn., to engage in self-supporting medical missionary work in this field. We were welcomed by the brethren here, this being a very needy field with but few workers.

The town of Empire, an important section about twelve miles from Panama City, was chosen for beginning our medical work, and as there was a small, struggling company at this place, we felt that our assistance would be needed in strengthening the believers, also in making additions to the church.

The Lord has blessed us in our medical work far beyond our highest expectation, and our efforts in evangelical work have also been very gratifying.

The need of a small sanitarium was one of our early observations, but as the government of the Canal Zone forbids the acquisition of land and the putting up of buildings, we were perplexed to know how to meet this pressing need.

57. J. F. Crichlow, "Nashville, Tenn," *The Gospel Herald,* February 13, 1913, p. 8.

We were thus compelled to work with what facilities we had at hand, and await developments of certain plans we had in view.

Two weeks ago we were favored with the lease of twelve rooms in a large building in Cristobal, the American settlement adjoining Colon, at a very reasonable price, the owner giving twenty-five dollars for the special electrical installation in our section of the building.

The Isthmian Canal Commission maintained a hospital in Colon, but owing to the early completion of the canal, it was decided to discontinue it. This action removed the only hospital from Colon, thus leaving the field clear for our work.

We were also privileged to secure the equipment we needed from Commission's Colon Hospital, in the way of surgical instruments, beds, bedding, etc., some of these new, and at an exceedingly low price. Thus within a few weeks our institution will be ready for business.

We feel very thankful for these evidences of divine leading. They encourage and strengthen us. We are also thankful for the hearty support of the conference brethren.

Our only purpose is to assist in the furtherance of the third angel's message. Our success is not measured by the money made, but by reaching souls with this glorious message. To the above end we solicit your prayers for the success of our work in this needy field.[58]

Dr. Lottie Blake devoted most of her strength and energy to training her five children and establishing a school to educate

them. Other wealthy parents wanted their children to attend her little school. For about three years the Blakes remained in Panama, but the missionary venture took a toll on the family—every member was, at some time, afflicted with malaria.

Dr. Blake wrote about his work in the *Review* again.

The Missionary Volunteer Society of the Mount Hope church has been doing commendable work. The society is divided into bands, and these hold meetings in various parts of the neighborhood, some going in boats across the sound to small villages peopled with Spanish, French, and a few English-speaking people. A lively interest is being aroused among the Spanish people. They are eager to hear our message. It was my privilege to attend a Spanish Bible reading conducted by two of our native brethren. It was a pleasure to note the interest manifested by those present, in finding and reading the Scriptures and in listening to the exposition. At the conclusion, a Spanish lady asked her friend what she thought of the things she heard. She said she liked our teachings and desired to know more. The brethren will follow up the interest, and we hope that by the Lord's help the pathway of many of these unfortunate people will be lightened with the third angel's message ...

Medical missionary work is meeting with gratifying success, financially and otherwise. Through its influence we are able to reach many of the influential men of the republic. Recently I had the privilege of an introduction to, and a short interview with, the governor of the province in which I live. He manifested great friendliness, and promised to render any aid he could when called upon to do so. I have also had a call from a prominent attorney. He

---

58. D. E. Blake, M. D., "A Year on the Canal Zone," *Advent Review and Sabbath Herald*, January 15, 1914, p. 12.

has decided to take a course of treatments in our treatment rooms.[59]

After Panama Dr. David Blake worked as a medical missionary in Haiti and helped establish a church in Port au Prince, the capital. Their coming was greeted with great joy. "Dr. and Mrs. D. E. Blake, who are both physicians, are now located in Port au Prince and we are very grateful to the Lord for their presence to give prestige to our work and to help in a material way to build up the cause of God in this Republic."[60]

With five children to care for, while in Haiti their savings were almost depleted. The General Conference tried to encourage them in their work in Haiti. "Voted, That the treasurer be authorized to appropriated $200 for church and school building enterprises in Haiti. Voted, That $150 be granted to Dr. D. E. Blake, recently landed in Haiti from Panama to take up self-supporting medical missionary work, this amount being a grant in aid, to encourage him in establishing work at Cape Haitien."[61] After two years of revolution, destruction, and devastation, the Haitian people were agitated because U.S. Marines occupied the country. Once again malaria left its shattering mark on the family. It was too much. After three months they decided to leave Haiti.

Dr. Blake took his family to Jamaica, where they remained for about eighteen months with his relatives. He then moved to Charlestown, West Virginia, to establish a medical practice. Once settled, he sent for the family. The Blake's future seemed bright and full of promise, but on a cold day in October Dr. David Blake went out in the rain, developed a chill, and returned home wheezing and coughing. Within a week, on October 31, 1917, Dr. David Blake, just forty years old, was pronounced dead from pneumonia.

Dr. Lottie Blake took her children to live with relatives in Columbus, Ohio, while she returned to Charleston to practice medicine for the next five years. She then moved to Columbus and practiced medicine there for fifteen years, from 1920 to 1935.

She added the Pennsylvania State Board to the five others she had passed (Ohio, Tennessee, Alabama, Panama, West Virginia), and from 1935 to 1957 she practiced medicine in Pittsburgh, Pennsylvania, specializing in the treatment of women and children. But it was her discovery of a cure for "Smokey city" pneumonia, which was caused by the smog in Pittsburgh, for which Dr. Blake is best remembered by the medical world.

In 1957 Dr. Lottie Blake retired at the age of eighty-one with more than fifty years of service. She was honored by the American Medical Association. She passed on her love for the church and academic achievement to her children and grandchildren, who have made great contributions in education and medicine. Frances Blake served as a dean and educator; the late Dr. Sarah Catherine Blake Fraser was an anesthesiologist in New York City and a graduate of Meharry Medical College; Marcia Louise Blake Neil is the mother of a physician, Dr. Richard Neal of Loma Linda University; Alice Blake Brantley served as a teacher, missionary, and principal for many years, and her son, Dr. Paul Brantley, served the church for many years and is currently at its world headquarters; a younger aunt, Dr. Grace Kimbrough, a

---

59. D. E. Blake, "Isthmus of Panama-Canal Zone," *Advent Review and Sabbath Herald,* July 2, 1914, p. 13.

60. Mrs. Margaret E. Prieger, "Hayti-The Island of Revolutions," *The Life Boat,* August 1916, p. 235.

61. "Haiti," Minutes of the General Conference, May 11, 1916, p. 423/155.

niece, Dr. Muriel Robinson, a grandson-in-law, Dr. James Holmes, and a great-grandson. Dr. Keith Wood, all became medical doctors, also.

Dr. Lottie Blake spent her time in retirement giving Bible studies and distributing literature as a hobby. Born a centennial baby (1876), she died in the bicentennial year on November 16, 1976, in Huntsville, Alabama, at the ripe age of 100. Her daughter, Alice Blake Brantley, also lived to be 100 years of age.

Dr. Lottie Blake was the first black female doctor in Alabama and the first physician of color in the Seventh-day Adventist Church. She was also the first black faculty member at Oakwood School and the first with a degree. Never affluent, she donated much of her services to the poor. She knew her reward would come in heaven.[62]

LOTTIE C. ISBELL.

Dr. Blake attended the American Medical Missionary College in Battle Creek, from which she graduated in 1902 as the first black physician in the Adventist Church.

Lottie Blake as a young medical student with the other members of her class.

Dr. David E. Blake in his doctoral cap and gown at his graduation from Meharry Medical College. The two doctors were married in 1907.

62. I am grateful to background information that I obtained from Stephanie D. Johnson, "Dr. Lottie Isbell Blake: Dean of Black SDA Physicians," *North American Regional Voice*, March 1987, pp. 1–3, and Dr. Blake's grandchildren Paul Brantley and Charlotte Brantley Holmes.

Drs. Lottie C. and David E. Blake (seated) who worked with the initial sanitarium venture in Nashville, shown with their nurses and assistants.

Dr. Lottie Blake in her later years.

The Blake family in Panama.

9

HENRY T. SAULTER

1928–1929 / Bahamas

Henry T. Saulter was born on October 30, 1906, in Lexington, Kentucky, and graduated from Oakwood College in 1926. He began denominational service immediately by teaching in Jackson, Mississippi, and Louisville, Kentucky. He was contacted by Frank L. Peterson, then assistant educational department secretary of the Southern Union, and asked to go to Nassau, Bahamas, as a teacher. When he accepted, he was told to go to Oakwood College for further arrangements.

At Oakwood, Joseph A. Tucker, Oakwood president, gave him train and boat fare to Nassau, and he was on his way. Saulter taught the Shirley Street church school in Nassau for the 1928–1929 terms and then returned to the United States. The Bahamas Mission was at that time a part of the Antillean Union, with Alfred R. Ogden as president. The Shirley Street congregation was the only church in Nassau, but there were other companies on surrounding islands. Saulter was not married when he served as a missionary.

Elder Ogden, the president, was quite pleased with Sautler's work and wrote the following: "Brother Saulter is much more than a teacher; he is a real missionary, and a great help in the work of the church, assisting generally in every way possible for its advancement."[63]

Returning to the United States, he married Leona Saulter from Indianapolis, Indiana, and taught school until 1942. After a two-year break from military service, he served at the Allegheny Conference Book and Bible House from 1945 to 1951. He was ordained to the gospel ministry in Baltimore, Maryland, in 1951. A year later in 1952 a new conference in the Kansas area was created, and Sauter was selected as the first secretary-treasurer, serving with the president, Frank L. Bland. Then for the next eleven years he was secretary-treasurer of the Central States Conference.

Later he returned to Oakwood College where he served as assistant business manager and director of student finances until 1962. Elder Saulter was then called to the Southeastern California Conference and worked with the regional churches as an interim pastor until he became pastor of the Encanto Company in San Diego. He later accepted the invitation to become auditor of the conference.

In 1981 members of the Kansas Avenue Church in Riverside, California, opened their new multipurpose building and named it the H. T. Saulter Hall. As a retired minister, Elder Saulter had volunteered his time in the development of this third phase of the church complex. Charles E. Bradford, General Conference vice president for North America at the time, preached on the opening day.

---

63. A. R. Ogden, "In the Bahamas," *Advent Review and Sabbath Herald*, January 24, 1929, p. 15.

Elder Saulter passed away in Riverside, California, in 1995 at the age of eighty-nine, and Leona passed away in Clinton, Maryland, at ninety-two years of age. Sister Saulter had moved to live with her daughter Joyce Saulter Daniels and her husband Lucius Daniels in Maryland.

Elder Henry T. Saulter served as a teacher in the Bahamas in 1928.

10
DONALD AND DOROTHY SIMONS

1947–1950 / Sierra Leone

Donald Simons came from an outstanding black Adventist family. His mother, Naomi Simons, was the daughter of Franklin G. Warnick, the first colored teacher to work with James Edson White on the missionary steamer, the *Morning Star*, which carried the gospel to black people in Mississippi. She and her husband, English Glenn Simons, were former students of Oakwood College, graduating in 1914. All seven of their children attended Oakwood College, and five worked for the Adventist Church. Three would serve as missionaries: Donald, Richard, and Lois Benson.

Elder and Mrs. Donald B. Simons and their little four-year-old daughter, Carmelita, and eight-month-old baby, Geneva, left New York City on July 21, 1947, by plane under appointment of the General Conference. They were traveling to Freetown, Sierra Leone, to engage in evangelistic work in the great but needy African city.

Elder Simons had been ordained to the gospel ministry the last Sabbath of the South Central Conference camp meeting at Oakwood College in 1946.

Upon getting settled in Sierra Leone, Elder Simons wrote a long letter to Elder Peters letting him know of their progress in Africa. The letter was published in *The North American Informant*.

Many things have happened since last we saw you … It would take many words to describe in detail our most enjoyable trip by air. Leaving LaGuardia Field in New York, July 21, 1947, we soared up into the airy heights-up, up to 17,000 feet. In a few hours we were in Gander, Newfoundland.

We had several hours' layover here, so we ate breakfast, and early morning found us once more en route to Lisbon, Portugal. We were to have stopped in the Azores Islands, but the weather was excellent, with good tailwinds, and there were no passengers for the Azores; so literally flying "in the midst of heaven," we crossed the entire Atlantic Ocean in one hop of nine hours, and slid gracefully out of the air in view of the rugged coast of Lisbon. Red-tiled roofs and light-colored buildings present a beautiful picture from the sky, and doubtless from the ground also.

Tuesday night found us sailing high above the clouds and weather en route to Dakar, Senegal, while stars gazed down in silent benediction. We stopped in Dakar a short while; the weather on ground, as we stepped from the plane, was hot and humid. That we were in Africa was no mistake, but it was to us almost as unbelievable as a dream or nightmare-so brief was the time en route.

Early Wednesday we continued this delightful flight via Pan American World Airways, four-motored constellation clipper, straight to Accra, Gold Coast, arriving about Wednesday at noon. We were cordially met by pastor William McClements, the West African Union Mission superintendent, who carried us in the mission Dodge pickup to our headquarters, … We stopped here and enjoyed the kind hospitality of Sister Duplouy until aroused early Sabbath morning and notified that our plane would be ready about 9:00 A.M.

Pastor McClements saw us to the airport, where we took a two-motored British aircraft, which carried us more than seven hundred miles back up to Sierra Leone to Waterloo Airport, about twenty-five miles from Freetown. A few minutes by taxi over a bumpy black-tar-paved road found us in the quaint, historic, caste-ridden city of Freetown.

We were impressed with the extreme poverty of natives—no exaggeration to say that many—emphatically hundreds—meet the eye clad in tatters. This is no misstatement—ragged, frayed semblance of clothing! Any clothing, in whatever condition it is, would be welcomed by these people …

Our first month here was one of constant adjustment and makeshift in that our household goods had not arrived. We have only praise and thanks to our heavenly Father for His hand of Providence in our personal affairs, and with the advent of a new year, we earnestly desire to be used of Him in the salvation of souls.

At the request of the local mission committee we delayed our evangelistic meetings until after the Christmas and New Year's festivity, which

we can describe now as riotous, drunken fetish dancing, with drumbeating, parading all night and all day, devil dancers, medicine man, and an array of activities to keep one constantly aware of the mighty challenge of the Dark Continent. We hope to begin evangelism sometime this month.

We are very happy to report that our entire family is in excellent health … Two weeks before Christmas we made a visit into the interior, spending a fortnight. I took my family back as far as Bo (160 miles inland), where the Sierra Leone headquarters are, and left them there at the mission compound, then trekked on about eighty miles further inland, beginning mission work in a new chiefdom. It was a new experience for us to be greeted by a welcome procession of the chief and his villagers, one blowing a horn made from elephant tusk. About twenty miles from this village of Sandaru is elephant country. Leopards are also seen frequently by the natives here, and they trap and kill them. Hiking nine miles over rough, hilly terrain, by native bush path, we were able to see monkeys swinging in the trees, hear parrots chatter, also the guttural voice of a large baboon. He was seen by one of our group.

Returning to Freetown the day before Christmas, we found a note tucked under our doorway which, to our astonishment, had been penned by Philip Giddings, who had looked us up when his boat stopped at Freetown for a few hours. We were keenly disappointed that we had missed him. I conclude that he was headed home on furlough.

This is Saturday night, and I shall trace our activities of the day, the first Sabbath of the New Year. It will give you some idea of our work here. Early in the morning my wife and

I were up getting the children ready. We drove to Freetown, picked up Teacher J. B. Terry and headed out twenty-five miles to serve ordinances to colony churches. En route we stopped at Kissytown, where we have a small company. Here we dedicated four small children to God, then to Samuel-town to administer the ordinances. Here I spoke through an interpreter.

The members met in a mud building with thatched roof, about 25 or 30 in number. To hear the members singing familiar songs in their native (Mendi) language is quite a pleasure. From Samueltown we went to Waterloo, where for years back our mission headquarters were located until it was occupied by the British militia, and later sold to the government. We have a church here with about thirty members, and a school. The building is of concrete and fairly nice. After preaching here (in English) and celebrating the church ordinances, we returned to Freetown, where my wife has introduced our M.V. Society. We have perhaps a dozen members here. The building where we met is also of concrete construction and fairly representative, except that like the others, it stands in need of renovation. Lest I forget, old Sabbath school picture rolls are welcome in quantity here.

We renew our consecration to God, and we ask the continued interest and prayers of our people in the homeland; we urge them to greater liberality for the West African mission field, and we address ourselves to the grand privilege of a part in the proclamation of the gospel of the kingdom and the consummation of God's work in the earth.[64]

---

64. *The North American Informant*, February 1948, pp. 1–3.

Another lengthy report came from Freetown two years later in March 1950.

After our arrival in Sierra Leone on July 27, 1947, our early weeks were devoted to getting settled and acquainted with our members, itinerating among our mission stations in the protectorate, attending workers' meetings and committee meetings, and engaging in the Ingathering campaign.

On Sunday night, January 25, 1948, our first public lectures were launched in the Wilberforce Memorial Hall after a four-week preparatory distribution of literature. The hall, with an estimated seating capacity of seven hundred, was filled to overflow with a very interested and appreciative audience. The subject featured Daniel 2 under the caption "Next World Ruler—Who Is He?" A huge life-sized cutout symbol of the great image and appropriate pictures on the screen helped to emphasize the subject effectively.

The hall was used for cinema shows, dances, city council meetings, traffic court, and other public gatherings. As a result, our weekly meetings were confined to three lectures a week. Nevertheless we rejoiced to see most of the meetings well attended.

At the presentation of the Sabbath truth we had occasion to witness a demonstration of God's intervention in behalf of the proclamation of this vital subject. Thinking we had booked the hall for this particular night, we had advertised our subject and arrived at the hall at almost meeting time to find it in total darkness. Fortunately we took our car, located the custodian, and brought him to open the doors of the hall. Hundreds of people had assembled at the hall to attend the meeting. Other hundreds collected in the street, curiously concerned about the crowd outside the dark hall. Thus, when the doors swung open there was a literal stampede into the hall to hear the message. Many could not obtain entrance. Others who were unable to find seats in the hall shared the platform, standing on either side of the speaker as they drank in this testing truth. As a sequel to this narrative, we discovered later that other people had booked the hall for this same night, but for some unexplained reason had not come to occupy it. Thus God interposed for the propagation of the gospel.

During this first campaign our working force consisted of Pastor J. Terry, Charles Karmo, Mrs. D. B. Simons, and T. E. Harding. Pastor Terry, district leader in the colony area, rendered indispensable support in playing the piano, directing the ushers, and leading out in our Bible class conducted in the community center each Thursday in connection with the public lectures. The home Bible course was used for this instruction. Brethren Harding and Karmo and Mrs. Simons gave needed support in the personal visitations, and assisted the speaker at each meeting. The offerings for forty public meetings during our first lecture series averaged more than one pound ($4 U.S.) a night. Our highest offering for one night was four pounds, five shillings and sixpence ($17.40 U.S.); thus, our offerings were more than sufficient to pay for the hall rental.

The list of names in our hearers' class soon grew to more than five hundred. The enrolled membership of our Bible class numbered more than fifty persons.

After this campaign the Freetown church membership and workers became a Minute Man church for the first time in the church's Ingathering history (perhaps among the first in the West African Union).

Sunday night, April 3, 1949, marked the beginning of a second series of meetings in the same hall. However, we were confined to Sunday nights only. Although these meetings were not attended as well as the former ones, the attendance was encouraging, and consisted largely of people who had followed the previous lecture series. Pastor Terry and the writer persisted in these meetings in spite of limited supplies and workers because of circumstances beyond control.

On May 28 we were made happy at the arrival of Pastor D. Agboka, of Gold Coast, and evangelist J. Adeoye, of Nigeria, who had come to join in the campaign. We appealed for enrollments in the home Bible course during this series also; in one night we received applications for the enrollment of eighty persons.

Sunday night, July 3, the lectures were transferred to our church, and the responsibility of preaching was divided among the workers. Persistent torrential rainfall forced us to conclude our lectures prematurely.

The city has been undergoing a profuse sowing of the gospel seed. It is not ours to predict the harvest. It is our conviction that we have a mighty open door in West Africa through the program of city evangelism.

We thank our heavenly Father for the measure of success that has attended our work here. It has been gratifying to see one of our converts, a carpenter, doing the work of renovation on the Freetown church, another carrying the responsibility of the secretarial work in the mission office, another teaching in our headquarters school at Bo, another now pursuing studies at Oakwood College in America, and still others making their contributions in some way to the work of the church.

In our contemplation of plans for future evangelistic campaigns we strongly visualize the pertinent need of an attractive tabernacle in which to conduct our meetings to greater soul-winning advantage. Likewise, we keenly feel the need of at least one more couple from the States who could do Bible work and be responsible for the music.

We thank Pastor William McClements and the West African Union Mission committee for their loyal support of city evangelism in West Africa. We also thank the West Nigerian, the Gold Coast, the Liberian, and the Sierra Leone missions for sending men to assist in the work here.

The members of the Freetown church rendered appreciable help in passing out literature, ushering, and singing. We dare not overlook the self-sacrificing, missionary-minded wives of our workers, particularly Mrs. Agboka and Mrs. Adeoye, who kept the home fires burning during the extended absences of their husbands for the benefit of the Lord's work.

In closing this report we share with you the contents of the following unsolicited letter received from a student of the Bible class conducted in connection with our meetings:

"In forwarding my last two lessons I wish to express my appreciation and thanks for the benefits I have derived from your Bible lectures and lessons, and I can safely say that never before has the Bible been as lucidly explained. I am sure many like myself bear this testimony, and look forward to more of these lessons and lectures which are the prerequisites of a regenerated Freetown. To you and Mrs. Simons, Mr. Terry, and other workers I send very best wishes for good health and abundant success in His vineyard.

‘Rise up, O men of God!
   The church for you doth wait,
Her strength unequal to her task;
   Rise up and make her great."

We are impressed with the wonderful yet solemn privilege and responsibility of being co-workers with Christ. These words present anew a mighty challenge to us as laborers in this field, and constitute a call to sober, godly living and for a ministry fired with greater zeal to win souls for Jesus. To this end we rededicate ourselves and solicit the prayers of our brethren and sisters in the homeland."[65]

In 1950 the Simons returned home. Elder George E. Peters reported the event in *The North American Informant.*

Elder Donald B. Simons, union evangelist of the West African Union, formerly located in Sierra Leone, arrived in New York with his wife [Dorothy Rice Simons] and two children aboard the S.S. Queen Mary, March 24. They spent a week in Washington reporting at headquarters and visiting our two congregations, the First church and Ephesus.

Elder Simons' report of his work in Sierra Leone, where he spent a three-year term, proved both interesting and enlightening. His lectures were made very realistic by his use of some 120 films.

Mrs. Simons, who is a registered nurse, proved

65. *The North American Informant,* March 1950, pp. 8–10.

very helpful in the mission fields as she lent her assistance in visiting and in health work. Elder Simons stated that on many occasions Sister Simons arrived to give needed medical aid to some native in the 'nick of time.'

The Simonses will take some needed rest, will visit parents and friends in Wisconsin and Chicago, and then will fill appointments in our churches and camp meetings in many of our cities from Florida to California.[66]

After returning from Sierra Leone, Elder Simons served as departmental secretary in the Lake Region Conference and then went to the Allegheny Conference in 1956 where he served as a departmental secretary. They later had a third girl, Carol. On January 1, 1967, a new conference was formed, and he went to serve as a departmental director in the newly formed Allegheny West Conference. He later became the second president of the Allegheny West Conference. After working for the Allegheny West Conference, he served as the public relations director of Christian Record Braille Foundation.

Elder Donald Simons and wife, Dorothy Simons.

Elder Simons as president of the Allegheny West Conference.

Pastor S. C. Nicol-Komara, delegate to the General Conference session from Sierra Leone, visits with Elder Simons after sixteen years of separation.

66. *The North American Informant.* April-May 1950, pp. 5, 6.

11

RICHARD AND RUTH SIMONS

1952–1960 / Liberia, Nigeria

Richard W. Simons, his wife, Ruth (born Marion Ruth Williams), and their two children, Shirley and Richard Jr., left New York City on January 17, 1952, for Monrovia, Liberia, in West Africa. At the time of his call, Brother Simons was serving as manager of the school store at Oakwood College. He would serve as secretary-treasurer and acting superintendent of the Liberia Mission.

One of their responsibilities was to supervise the boarding academy at Konola. While under their leadership, the enrollment increased from 77 to 145 during the first year. Konola students were from some of the best families in Liberia, and most of them were from Monrovia. Since 95 percent of the students were non-Adventists, there was a great opportunity for evangelism within the school.

On Sabbaths more than two hundred people crowded into the school building and others clustered under nearby trees to hear the sermons that were preached in English and translated into three of the native dialects. There was a great need for an auditorium or chapel at the school, and one of the ways that they raised funds for the building project was to have the choir perform at various functions. One time the students from the Konola Training Center were asked to give a concert in the Executive Pavilion in Monrovia, the capital of Liberia. They were promised more than a thousand dollars for the performance.

Professor and Mrs. Philip Giddings and Mrs. Ruth Simons carried two truckloads of students into the city in order to publicize the work being done at the mission. The venture was called the Singing Crusade, and the citizens were impressed by the performance.

Some Monrovians, according to the local paper, commented that while other schools in the country were famous for football, the Konola Training Center might very easily lead the entire country in singing. However, regret was expressed that the students only received $64 for the trip. The public asked Elder Henry and other mission leaders to have the group sing again in a more promising area.

After their furlough the Simons family (now increased to three children after the birth of Beverly) moved to Aba, Eastern Nigeria, where he accepted the position of secretary-treasurer of the East Nigerian Mission.

After they returned to America, Mr. Simons served as principal of Los Angeles Academy, and then the Southern California Conference committee appointed him as the new auditor for the conference and later the assistant treasurer. He would later join the Northern California Conference and serve as the secretary and briefly as the president.

*Richard W. Simons, missionary,
auditor-treasurer, administrator.*

12

THEODORE AND FRANKIE CANTRELL

1955–1968 / Liberia, Ghana, Nigeria

As a young man, Ted Cantrell was quite a Bible student as this little story in our denominational paper points out.

> *Recently six of the young people of the Ephesus church received prizes that were given by the New York Bible Society for essays written on portions of the Bible. There were two thousand Harlem contestants for the six prizes, and in the face of this large number of contestants, two of the six prizes were won by Seventh-day Adventist young people …*

> *"In addition to the six prizes, thirty others of the two thousand received honorable mention and a Bible each, and among these again our young people came to the front. Four of the thirty receiving this award were also Ephesus young people. Their names are Ruth Robinson, Theodore Cantrell, Helen Horton, and Gladys Miller.*[67]

Ted attended Adventist schools and was in the class of 1939 at Greater New York Academy. He was the sergeant at arms of his graduating class. He then went on to attend and graduate from the University of Pittsburgh before moving to Oakwood College to teach.

Frankie Lee Mitchell attended Oakwood

for four years and worked for Ted, who was also her instructor at Oakwood. She took a class from him her senior year and got to know him better. Two months after graduating from Oakwood with her bachelor of arts degree, Frankie and Ted married on August 8, 1950.

Two weeks later the newlywed couple relocated to Loma Linda University (College of Medical Evangelists), and Frankie began studying to become a nurse. Three years later Frankie Cantrell graduated from the school of nursing at the College of Medical Evangelists, having spent the first eighteen months at the Loma Linda campus and the last eighteen months on the Los Angeles campus. This program allowed the students to complete a program of college study with a major in nursing and a minor in public health and social studies and receive a bachelor of science degree.

Two years later the Berean Seventh-day Adventist Church of Uniontown, Pennsylvania, hosted a farewell reception for the Cantrells, because they had just been appointed as missionaries to Liberia, Africa. Theodore Cantrell was the son of Mr. and Mrs. Ralph Cantrell of Edenborn, Pennsylvania, and had been a member of that church. The couple left for the new post on Sunday, March 20, 1955. The two would serve in four distinct lines of activity—administration, nursing, teaching, and dentistry.

Frankie said that she did everything—she

67. Blanche Markham, "Achievement of the Youth," *Atlantic Union Gleaner*, April 17, 1935, p. 5.

taught anatomy and physiology at Konola Academy, pulled teeth, sutured wounds, gave tetanus and other shots, and administered medicine to counteract snake bites. She sent her degrees to the certifying boards of the country, and they sent her certificates that she could hang on the wall so that people would know she was not a bush doctor but well-qualified to help.

Shortly after she arrived in Liberia, she secured some antivenom serum from Durban, South Africa, just in case she ever encountered someone suffering from a snakebite. She kept it in a kerosene refrigerator. Sure enough, she had to use it on a young man who was bitten by a large snake. Thankfully, she administered the needed remedy to save his life.

Ted started off teaching biology and anatomy and physiology at Konola Academy. Richard Simons was the principal of the school. When he left, the union leaders selected Ted to be the principal. After serving as principal for a time, the union leaders noted how carefully Ted kept records and asked if he would serve as the treasurer of the mission.

A little less than four years after arriving in Liberia, in December 1959, they became the parents of a beautiful baby girl, Linda. Their second baby, Frank, followed soon after.

The Cantrells kept the folk back in America aware of what they were doing. In one letter from the Cantrells, which was read by Elder Fordham at Oakwood College, the members were informed of the need for money to purchase a tractor to cultivate the ground with more ease. The baskets were passed, and an offering of $63.78 was collected to help with this worthy project. Additionally, a message was sent out in the *North American Informant* labeled "Tractor for Africa" so that others might contribute.[68]

68. "Conference Regional Meeting a Success," *The North American Informant*, July-August 1958, p. 13.

Later when they were stationed in Nigeria, they had to be airlifted out because of the political situation. They took a plane from Port Harcourt to Lagos. The American Embassy staff met all the Americans there and tried to determine whether each group was going to be evacuated to America or reassigned someplace in Africa. They were asked, "Are you a missionary, businessman, or just a vacationer?" The Cantrells let them know they were missionaries, and there were other Adventist missions nearby in Ile Ife and even in Lagos.

The political upheaval occurred when the Eastern Region of Nigeria seceded from the federal government and formed the new Republic of Biafra. War between the two factions made life difficult for all expatriates.

For many years the Ibos of the Eastern Region (Biafra) had been among the country's elite. They had played a major role in its economic and administrative structure. The Ibo region of the country was the first to be entered by the British, and hence the first to receive the advantages of European civilization. Later, when the British explorers pushed northward, it was the Ibos who befriended and assisted them.

Still later, when missionaries established schools, the Ibos were among the most apt pupils. When the British finally took political control of Nigeria, the natives who were best prepared to fill important positions in government and business were Ibos. In fact, they soon held most of the important posts reserved for nationals, particularly in the North where Muslim influence resulted in poor reception of missionary schools.

In addition, because they were gifted in commercial lines, the Ibos established their own trading businesses. They developed large fleets of trucks that carried produce over Nigeria's expanding road system. They painstakingly saved their money, investing and reinvesting it, so that eventually many of them were able to send their children to the best universities in Britain. Being a very ambitious people by nature, they wanted their children to have the best civilization could offer. Thus many of their number filled key positions in the government when Nigeria became independent in 1960. However, Ibo tribesmen were not elected to political leadership of all Nigeria at this time. This was probably due to the fact that the tribe was a comparatively small one.

When the northern tribes belatedly raised educational horizons, and their graduates began to look for employment, they discovered that most jobs were already held by Ibos who were not at all willing to relinquish them. Moreover, the Ibos in the North had many relatives in the East, and as new positions became available, they persuaded their employers to hire their relatives.

Thus more Ibos were constantly coming to the North looking for jobs, since the East was a relatively small territory where overcrowding and unemployment were constant problems. As more and more graduates of schools in the North were unable to find jobs, tribal jealousy and mistrust developed. In many cases, jealousy finally grew into hatred that periodically exploded into aggression against the Ibos living in the North.

In January 1966 Nigeria's civilian government was overthrown by the army. Major Gen. Johnson Aguiyi-Ironsi, an Ibo, emerged as leader of the new military regime. During the coup, Ahmadu Bello, political head of Nigeria, and spiritual leader of all Nigerian Muslims, was killed. Many other political leaders were slain, but strangely, few Ibo leaders lost their lives. This led the people of the North, who constituted most of the foot soldiers in the Nigerian army, to conclude that the sudden take over had been masterminded by the Ibos. Consequently, in July of that year a second coup was carried out. This time it was led by northern soldiers, and Ironsi was assassinated.

The control of the federal government then passed into the hands of Lt. Col. (now Major Gen.) Yakubu Gowon, a handsome, British-trained member of a small northern tribe. After the northern takeover, a systematic assassination of all Ibo military officers was undertaken. At that time most of the officers in the army were Ibos.

Following the action against the Ibo officers, uprisings began against Ibo civilians living in the North. Eventually these led to wholesale slaughter of Ibos all over the North. The Ibos could not even depend on the northern police and soldiers for protection. It is estimated that by October 1966 approximately 30,000 Ibos had lost their lives in the North, and more than one million refugees fled to their native territory, Eastern Nigeria. Similar, less violent uprisings took place in the Western Region.

It was the massacre that led Ibos to feel that if they could no longer be safe anywhere in Nigeria, they no longer had any common ties with the rest of Nigeria. Therefore, in May 1967 they seceded from the federal government, and the newly independent Republic of Biafra was born. Lt. Col. Odumegwu Ojukwu, former military governor of the Eastern Region, was asked to be its first leader. The federal government at Legos immediately cut off all mail and telegraph services, closed major highways and bridges, and stopped all passenger service by air and sea. It also sent warships to blockade Port Harcourt, the new republic's only major outlet to the sea.

Preparations for military action against the secessionists were soon underway.

With the mail service disrupted, and all travel between Biafra and the rest of Nigeria greatly restricted, missionaries began to wonder how long it would be before they saw their family and friends again.[69] For a period of time Brother Cantrell was released from his mission responsibilities for part-time services with the Relief Department of the National Council of Churches. Brother Cantrell was responsible for the distribution of tons of foodstuffs sent to Liberia by this organization for hospitals, schools, and the needy. This is the first time that the Seventh-Day Adventist Church has been requested to assist Church World Service.

In 1970 after the Cantrells returned to the States, the Northeastern Conference asked Ted Cantrell to be the director of a new nursing home, Victory Lake Nursing Home, in Hyde Park, New York. Shortly after overseeing its construction, they received a call from the Southern Union Conference for Cantrell to serve as secretary-treasurer of the South Atlantic Conference headquartered in Atlanta, Georgia.

Theodore Cantrell passed away in 2011 in Knoxville, Tennessee. Frankie Cantrell lives near her children in Tennessee.

The whole family in West Africa (from right to left): Frank, Ted, Frankie, Linda.

Ted talks with a local Masai tribesman during some time in Kenya.

69. Ronald E. and Nathaniel Krum, "Directed by God's Providence," *The Youth's Instructor*, April 2 and 9, 1968, pp. 4–13.

Elder Ted Cantrell while working for the Southern Union Conference.

At the 2009 General Conference session, Ted and Frankie meet with some old friends from the mission field.

13

DOUGLAS AND HELENA TATE

1955–1957 / Liberia

Douglas Tyrone Tate was born in Memphis, Tennessee. His wife, the former Helena Brantley, was born in Tampa, Florida, and was a fifth generation Adventist who always wanted to be a missionary.

They met at Oakwood College. Douglas graduated in 1953 at the top of his class. Helena studied math and music but did not graduate from Oakwood. After completing the seminary in Washington, D.C., Pastor Tate was appointed to go to Liberia as a missionary.

On Sabbath, December 3, Tate was the guest speaker at a church in Ephesus, New York, speaking on the subject of "The Pearl of Great Price." The next sermon he would preach would be in Africa. Pastor Tate, his wife, and a baby boy, Cedric Douglas Tate, left Brooklyn on Friday, December 9, 1955, aboard the Norwegian freighter *Grandville* of the Barber line. Their ship briefly stopped in Portland, Maine, before setting sail for Africa on December 13.

On arrival in Liberia, after being on the boat for ten days, Pastor and Mrs. Dunbar Henri met them at the port and took them to their home. They were surprised to be accommodated in a brand new two-bedroom block house painted in soft pastel colors, the best on the block.

They quickly made friends with the other expatriates, among them Ted and Frankie Cantrell. Douglas was put in charge of five churches and was tasked with beginning and evangelistic work in the area. One church was on the border of Sierra Leone and another was at the Konola Academy where he also served as principal. The country was peaceful, but the members were somewhat afraid of the government, which made it was very difficult to do evangelism. During his short stay, he baptized almost seventy individuals. Pastor Tate frequently traveled to the rural areas looking for opportunities for evangelism. The people had strange ways to show their hospitality, but Pastor Tate was always mindful of its effect on the future of the work.

Their second child, Karen Marie, was born in Liberia and was given the name Doma, which means born on the road, by the natives since they did not reach the hospital in time for the birth because of the road conditions. In addition to caring for her children, Helena directed the choir at Konola Academy. It is impressive to note that one student and choir member was the son of the Liberian president.

The Tates enjoyed their new surroundings and the local food. They especially liked eating the green vegetables. The collard greens were so large they resembled the elephant ear plant.

They were enjoying their work and wanted to stay for life, but Pastor Tate had repeated bouts of malaria and the U.S. Public Health Service recommended that he return to the

States for treatment. The family was sorely disappointed. Douglas went home alone, and Helena traveled later with the two children. On returning Pastor Tate joined the Psychology Department of Oakwood College as a faculty member. He worked at Oakwood full time and part time at Alabama A& M University. Later he accepted a full-time position at A&M, retiring from there in 1995.

Douglas and Helena are both retired and live in Huntsville, Alabama, near their daughter Saundra. They testify that their years as missionaries greatly enriched their Christian experience.

Douglas Tate in 2014

14

LUCIUS AND NAOMI DANIELS

1957–1964 / Liberia

Lucius Edward Daniels Sr. was born in St. Augustine, Florida, on May 7, 1926. He was the third of seven children from the union of Alex and Bertha Daniels. At an early age, Lucius expressed an interest in becoming a minister.

He attended Oakwood Academy and then enrolled in Oakwood College from which he graduated in 1947 with a bachelor's degree in theology. Lucius married his college sweetheart, Naomi Hamlin, on November 2, 1947. Naomi was a native of Ohio, having grown up in the small, colorful village of Oberlin, which is thirty miles from Cleveland. They had two sons: Lucius Jr. (deceased) and Arthur.

Before going to Africa, they served for twelve years in several congregations in North and South Carolina and Georgia. Mrs. Daniels was a nature enthusiast. As a teacher in Georgia, she introduced her students to the study of plants, rocks, insects, birds, fish, and stars. Their last church before leaving the country was in Winston-Salem, North Carolina.

The Daniels' family sailed from New York on July 24, 1957, on the "S. S. Waterman" to Southampton, England, en route to Monrovia, Liberia. Elder Daniels had been assigned the post of secretary-treasurer of the Liberia Mission; however, he was soon elected president of the Liberia Mission. Part of the Daniels' ministry was performing together. Naomi would play the piano while Lucius sang uplifting songs about God's love.

Lucius lived a hearty, energetic life that integrated a variety of responsibilities and activities after returning from the mission field. Among those was serving as a food stamp supervisor in Jacksonville, Florida, and owner-manager of Alex Texaco Service Station and Taxicab Company in St. Augustine, Florida. Elder Daniels was extremely interested in health and authored several books, among them the book titled *Healing Balm in Quality Foods.*

Elder Daniels passed away on January 18, 2013, in Michigan at age eighty-six.

Mrs. Naomi and Elder Lucius Daniels and sons, Arthur (left) and Lucius Jr. pose for an informal picture before leaving for Liberia in the early summer of 1957.

15

GRETEL GRAHAM ASHLEY

1957–1958 / Uganda

Gretel Graham was determined to be a nurse. The daughter of Frank and Esther Graham of Andrews Memorial Hospital in Jamaica, she attended West Indian Training College from 1945 to 1949. She earned her full way from the sixth standard until graduation as a nurse.

In 1950 she moved to Alabama to complete her pre-nursing work at Oakwood College. After one year of school, she realized that she would not be able to receive additional funds from her family to finish her dream of becoming a nurse, so she enrolled in *The Message Magazine* scholarship plan during the summer. Five young ladies were chosen to work in Pittsburgh, and she was one of them. She stayed in the home of Nancy Harris, the magazine leader, in Pittsburgh, Pennsylvania. Even though this was her first attempt at canvassing, the Holy Spirit guided her, and she earned her scholarship in twelve weeks. She was also able to work at one of the Pittsburgh hospitals after completing her scholarship. Her goal was to continue her education at Loma Linda and become a nurse.

Upon graduating in 1955 with a bachelor's degree in nursing from the College of Medical Evangelists (Loma Linda University), she spent one year at White Memorial Hospital and then about nine months at a hospital in New York City. She had finally fulfilled her personal dream of becoming a trained nurse.

Her call from the mission field was to Malamulo Mission in Nyasaland (Malawi), Africa. The General Conference was not able to fulfill this request because immigration laws would not permit her to enter Malawi, so her call was transferred to Ankole Hospital in Uganda. Upon arriving and working there, she endeared herself to both the medical staff and the patients at Ankole Hospital. But when she heard Cupid calling her, she returned to the United States to marry Edward B Ashley, an X-ray and lab technician. In 1974 they returned to Kingston, Jamaica, to work at Andrews Memorial Hospital where her parents had worked.

She later moved to Florida to work at Walker Memorial Hospital and received her master's degree in public health from the off-campus program of Loma Linda University.

Gretel Ashley was an active member of the Adventist Church in Avon Park, Florida, and helped open a community center there.

Gretel Graham in 1957.

16

WILLIAM AND HORTENSE ROBINSON

1957–1959 / Uganda

Elder W. R. Robinson and his family sailed from New York on the S. S. Queen Elizabeth on February 15, 1957, en route to England and the mission fields in East Africa. He had accepted the position of president of the Uganda Mission.

A forty-one-year-old veteran worker, Elder Robinson had already faithfully served the Adventist Church. He had been a departmental leader, evangelist, and pastor of the largest churches in the Allegheny Conference. From the Allegheny Conference he was called to the Home Missionary Department of the Northeastern Conference with offices in New York City. It was while in the Northeastern Conference that Elder Robinson received and accepted the call to Uganda.

The Robinsons had four children, three boys and a girl. The two older boys, Sonny (William R. Robinson Jr.) and David, were both attending Pine Forge Academy but accompanied their parents on the trip to the mission field. Eugene was not old enough to attend school and his sister, Marjorie, was even younger.

Hortense had been a church school teacher in Baltimore at the time she married. Both husband and wife served as teachers at some time in their careers, and they carried to their new field of labor both experience and technical "know-how" that was fortified with Christian zeal.

The family stopped in London, England, leaving the Cunard Line there, and embarked directly for Africa. Because of the Suez Canal difficulty, the Robinsons sailed around the Cape of Good Hope and came up the east coast of the continent. When they arrived Elder Robinson penned the following letter, dated April 7, 1957, to Elder F. L. Peterson.

We arrived safely and soundly in Kampala Friday, April 5, after traveling 12,900 miles in seven weeks. We have been received warmly and royally. We preached Sabbath to a packed church in Kampala. The Prince of Buganda, members of congress, physicians, lawyers were in attendance. Newspapers in Kampala and Nairobi, Kenya, carried the story. The radio announced it in the newscast.

This is a wonderful country with many wonderful people. The truth is held in high esteem. Hundreds still speak favorably of Elder Cleveland and his work. We have had a busy schedule. We had committee meetings Monday and Tuesday. Four meetings are scheduled for Wednesday. Union committee in Nairobi will be held within two weeks. Sixteen camp meetings are scheduled in our mission field, and I will attend twelve of them. The other four have already convened. A large effort is planned for Kabale in the Ankole district. I will spend two weeks there.

The people are of good courage. Continue to pray for us.

Arrangements are being made for me to see the king of the country in the near future. I would like to present him with a copy of that wonderful book, The Hope of the Race. . . .

All join me in sending kindest personal greetings.[70]

Those seven weeks of travel, much of it on water, led Elder Robinson to pen an article titled "No More Sea."

This verse in Revelation 21:1 took on a new significance while I was on my voyage to the far-flung mission fields. We spent thirty-three days on two expansive oceans. For days we could see nothing but water. The first thing that could be seen as one looked out of the stateroom window was water and sky; the last thing at night that could be seen was sky and water.

We could walk to the bow of the ship, and as far as the eye could see, there was nothing but water. We would go to the stern of the ship and gaze out over vast horizons, and as far as the eye could see there was water. We would go to the port side and peer into the distance, and all that could be seen was water. Then we would go to the starboard side and train our sights on water! There was not a park nor palace, nothing but water. There was not a tree nor train, nothing but water! Water to the north! Water to the south! Water to the east! Water to the west!

Nothing but endless stretches of water before us and behind us. We were surely in the midst of a measureless ocean! But that is not all. We went upstairs to read the ship's log and learned that we were plowing through water that was 18,075 feet deep! There were three miles of water beneath us. And we were 138 miles from the nearest land! Today the water of the seas covers three fourths of the world's surface. The four great oceans—the Pacific, Atlantic, Indian, and Arctic—occupy 129,428,859 square miles of territory, and the seas claim an additional 10,144,840 square miles. (World Almanac [1957] p. 565.) But the day is coming when there will be "no more sea."

What is meant by the phrase, "no more sea"? The sea was a symbol of terror to the ancients. The Jews throughout their long history never became skilled sailors. There was no compass at that time, and the sailing vessels rarely ventured beyond the sight of land. The dangerous shoals were yet uncharted, and lighthouses were unknown. Only the most daring mariners would risk their lives on the treacherous waves. The Bible speaks of the "raging waves of the sea" and its "voice roareth," and "the wicked are like the troubled sea." (Jude 13; Jeremiah 6:23; Isaiah 57:20.) No wonder, then, that the sea became a symbol of terror and fear . . .[71]

The two oldest boys returned to the States to enroll at Pine Forge in the fall of 1957, rejoining their graduating class of 1958.[72] The return trip to Pine Forge was the trip of a lifetime. Sonny and David, just in their early teens, boarded a plane at Entebbe, flying the Airworks British line. They stopped at Khartoum,

70. F. L. Peterson, "Robinson Family in Kampala," *The North American Informant*, April-May 1957, pp. 1, 2.

71. W. M. Robinson, *The Message Magazine*, February 1958.

72. A. V. Pinkney, "Robinsons Return to Pine Forge," *The North American Informant*, Oct.-Nov. 1957, p. 15.

then at Wadi Haifa where they spent the night at the Nile River Hotel. Breakfast there was homelike—eggs, toast, and hot chocolate. Their flight then took them to Libya, and from there to the island of Malta. Their next stops were Nice, France, and London, England. The entire flight was more than 4,000 miles.

They spent four days in England. These days were packed with exciting visits to Buckingham Palace, Westminster Abbey, the House of Parliament, 10 Downing Street, Piccadilly Circus, Trafalgar Square, and Scotland Yard.

Next they booked passage on the S.S. Flandre, a French ship leaving from Southampton for New York. The crossing took longer because of continued storms and fog; however, Sonny and David successfully returned to school and joined their classmates. They returned with a wealth of experience and were in good health, just a little thinner. They said they had missed the good meals served at school.

Elder and Mrs. W. R. Robinson celebrated their 50th wedding anniversary on Sunday, June 25, 1989, in Nashville, Tennessee, in the new F. H. Jenkins School. Friends and well-wishers came from as far away as California, New York, Maryland, Washington, D.C., and from as close as Huntsville, Alabama, Louisville, Kentucky, and other cities in the South Central area. Their children and grandchildren were also present. It was a glorious occasion. Elder Robinson talked about the day he married Hortense. He said it was truly "a date to remember."

It was a bright, balmy Sabbath day, June 24, 1939, when they began their life's journey together. Hundreds had come to camp meeting on the campus of Nannie Burroughs School in Washington, D.C. In the afternoon, three young people stood before Elder F. L. Peterson, the highest-ranking ethnic minister in the

General Conference. A beautiful beaming bride, Hortense Robinson became the wife of William Raymond Robinson. Longtime friend W. Albert Thompson stood by the groom. It was a unique ceremony in that the bride never changed her name; she merely changed her status from single to married as the wedding vows were exchanged.

It was pointed out that for more than fifty-three years, Pastor and Mrs. Robinson had served the church with distinction in many capacities and in many places, from coast to coast and overseas. Avenues of service included the positions of colporteur; church school teacher; pastor; conference evangelist; and director of a half-dozen departments, including Sabbath School, personal ministries, publishing, and communication. He served as editor of *The Message Magazine*, circulation manager, and missionary to Africa and Trinidad. The list of labors necessitated moving their complete household twenty-six times. They no doubt set a record for frequency of moves.

In February 1956, after burning the mortgage at the Baltimore Berea church, they were transferred to Cleveland, Ohio, to pastor the church in Glenville and complete the building of Ramah Academy with Elder Harry Dobbins. Just a few months later in October they were invited to New York to become the Sabbath School and personal ministries director of the Northeastern Conference. A house was purchased in Mount Vernon, New York, two weeks later.

Little did they know that a short time later Elder Ralph Watts, president of the Trans Africa Division, and Elder W. Duncan Eva, secretary, would fly from Africa to see them personally and urge them to come to Africa as president of the Uganda field. It took them until February 1957 to complete health tests, etc., in preparation for work in a foreign country. So, from February 1956 to February 1957, the mission appointees moved from Baltimore, Maryland, to Cleveland, Ohio, to Mount Vernon, New York, to Kampala, Uganda, covering 14,000 miles.

As I look back over my files, I see a letter that I (DeWitt Williams) sent Elder Robinson on his eighty-fifth birthday. It expressed my sentiments and the sentiments of other young admirers.

Dear Elder Robinson, Congratulations! And happy birthday!

God has blessed you to see your 85th birthday. Psalms tells us that 70 years is the normal. And if by reason of strength we make it to 80 then we are most fortunate. But God has seen fit to keep on adding years to your life. Praise the Lord!

I can remember you when I was a little boy. At that time, I was a member of the Philadelphia Ebenezer church. From time to time you used to preach there. I always looked forward to your enthusiastic preaching. Your messages were always exciting, inspirational, and powerful. I always wondered where you got so much energy. And whenever I had the opportunity to go to the Allegheny camp meeting I always looked forward to hearing you speak.

I remember when you went to Africa. The thrilling stories you told when you returned inspired me to want to go to Africa. And in 1967 I followed in your footsteps and spent five years in Zaire. Later on my family and I returned to Africa and spent an additional three years in Burundi. You were a part of my inspiration for going.

Thank you also for the books that you published which focused on the black man and the great possibilities that the Bible promised him. These books, added to the articles that you published while you were editor of The Message Magazine, gave African Americans renewed hope for the future.

Edward B. Butler said "one man has enthusiasm for 30 minutes, another for 30 days, but it is the man who has it for 30 years who makes a success of his life." For nearly 65 years you have been an enthusiastic spiritual leader. I thank God for you and the example you have set.

Thank you for your vision, your leadership, and your dedication to the cause of the Seventh-day Adventist church. May God bless you and your family and may you have many more birthdays.

William and Hortense Robinson

Sonny and his brother David wearing the Kanzoo garment dress for the Bugunda tribe that lives in Kampala. The boys are holding a camel caravan carved from ivory.

The Robinson family on the deck of the Ivernia. This liner carried them to Halifax where they boarded the Queen Elizabeth, which could not dock in New York because of the tugboat strike.

Elder and Mrs. Robinson entering the F. H. Jenkins School for their fiftieth wedding anniversary.

17

Claudienne Gordon-McKenzie

1958–1960 / Nigeria

Born in Lincoln, Nebraska, Ms. Gordon moved to Boston at an early age. She made a vow when she was only five years old in Sabbath School that she would one day become a foreign missionary. On Wednesday, April 16, 1958, that dream came true. Then a member of the Berea Adventist Church in Boston, she left on the "Queen Elizabeth" for Ile Ife Mission Hospital in Nigeria.

At the boat to wish her Godspeed were her parents, Mr. and Mrs. Gordon; Ms. Frankie Lawton, teacher at the Berea Elementary School; Mrs. E. A. Lockett; Ms. Ruby Jones; Elder F. L. Jones; and Pastor O. A. Troy Jr.

Ms. Gordon had taken the pre-nursing course at Oakwood College and was a graduate of the New England Sanitarium and Hospital. The School of Nursing of the New England Sanitarium had its annual capping ceremony on January 7, 1951. Eighteen young women received the cap of the school, and three young men had badge insignia attached to their left uniform sleeve. Ms. Joyce Saulter, the daughter of Elder and Mrs. H. T. Saulter, and Ms. Claudienne Gordon were two of the first nursing students (if not the first) from Oakwood College to attend and graduate from the New England Sanitarium.

After graduating she worked as a nurse at Boston Lying-in Hospital, Boston City Hospital, Beth-Israel, and the University of Kansas in Kansas City, Kansas. Seven years after finishing her degree she headed for the mission field.

When Ms. Gordon arrived in Nigeria, two overseas doctors, four overseas nurses, and a large group of consecrated Nigerian nurses made up the staff of the 125-bed Ile Ife Hospital.

Each morning some 600 African patients with their accompanying relatives would be waiting at the side of the building to gain admission. Hundreds of well-dressed mothers clothed in native garb waited for medical attention. Most of the women wore a turban-like headpiece draped about in a flourishing sweep and tied in such a way as to add a beautiful contour to the fine features of the Yoruba tribe that lived in that part of the country.

The babies were carried on their mother's backs, supported by a scarflike cloth that encircled the mother and the baby and passed underneath the mother's arms. These mothers would unwrap their babies and show them to Claudienne Gordon who cared for an average of 200 little people every day.

Even when she deserved a break, most times she did not take it. The *Messenger* told how Ms. Gordon spent her local leave in Accra, Ghana, serving as pianist for an evangelists effort by E. E. Cleveland.

She returned home on January 14, 1960, because of sickness in the family.

Miss Claudienne Gordon headed up the baby clinic at Ile Ife Hospital.

Eighteen young women received the cap and three young men had badge insignia attached to their left uniform sleeve on January 7, 1951, at the New England Sanitarium nursing graduation. Miss Joyce Saulter is seated on the left front row and Miss Claudienne Gordon is standing in the second row in the middle.

Just as we were going to press I found Claudienne and discovered that she had married Harold McKenzie, a colporteur/evangelist from Jamaica who had migrated to the United States. Elder A. R. Haig, pastor of the Hanson Place and Garden Heights churches in New York, would ask Brother McKenzie to preach at one of his churches while he visited and preached at the other one. While preaching at the Garden Heights church, Brother McKenzie met Claudienne Gordon who had recently returned from Nigeria and they were married December 27, 1964 at the Ephesus NY church.

Brother McKenzie worked in finance for more than twenty years but his heart was always in church work. They moved to the Jamaica SDA church in 1965 where he has served as the first elder for thirty-eight years and also served as interim pastor. Claudienne, being a registered nurse, worked at a number of different hospitals in the area including Mt. Sanai and Jamaica Hospital.

More than twenty-five years ago, they began to keep foster children and over the years have had scores of children in their home. They arranged for several church members to adopt some of these children and a pastor even adopted one. They offered love and a home to the homeless children and on four occasions they adopted a boy. One of the boys they adopted had Downs Syndrome and was only given three years to live when they adopted him but he is thirty-one years old now. They have one daughter of their own.

18

GLORIA MACKSON HEMPHILL

1958–1961 / Tanzania

Miss Mackson is a native of Baton Rouge, Louisiana. Gloria graduated from Oakwood Academy and obtained her bachelor's degree in home economics from Union College in 1953.

While engaged in civil service work in Seattle, Washington, she completed graduate work at the University of Washington and Washington State College in pursuit of a master's degree.

As a credentialed teacher in home economics from the State of California, she spent two years teaching homemaking at Los Angeles Academy before joining the Southern California Conference office staff where she served as the secretary to the director of the Southern California Conference health and welfare department for two years.

When the call came to serve overseas, Ms. Mackson thought she would be going to Bombo, Uganda. Later, she was told she would be going to Katikamu, East Africa. However, it was finally decided to send her to the Ikizu Training School in Tanganyika, which is today Tanzania. She set sail on December 16, 1957, from New York, going to Southampton, England, and from there to her mission appointment in Tanganyika (Tanzania).

The August 1961 issue of *The Message Magazine* printed a letter from her after she arrived. "Here at Ikizu I do enjoy my work very much. I am the girls' worker; teach domestic science, history, and geography. It keeps me very busy—28 periods a week, besides a work program of 15 hours a week … Thank you again for sending *The Message Magazine* to Ikizu."

The picture included with the article showed her with the students in the library, and close observers noticed that *The Message Magazine* occupied a prominent place on the reading racks in the library of Ikizu Training School.

At the Ikizu Teacher Training College in Tanzania, they didn't have a formal graduation ceremony with invitations, programs, caps and gowns, etc. If they had a celebration, everything was much simpler, even though it was just as thrilling to the participants and spectators. Ms. Mackson helped to develop a formal graduation program at the school. An earlier letter printed in the November-December 1959 issue of *The North American Informant* tells about graduation.

Hello Folks,

It is all over but the shouting, and I am certainly doing that today. This week I have worked harder than any other time since I've been here at Ikizu. It reminded me of home and how I worked from early morning until late at night and went to school also. It was wonderful to just sit down this morning and do nothing.

It all started on Sunday, October 4, with the senior dinner, the first to be held at Ikizu. We had American food, so it all had to be bought, and prepared and cooked, including three cakes. The girls helped me prepare the food in the domestic science kitchen. We were still working when the lights blinked, but the principal let them stay on for a while longer. The next day we came back to finish the cooking and decorate the dining room. We used reeds from the dam; painted some of them and hung them on a wire. They made the most unusual partition, with the false crepe-paper ceiling.

Each table had a white tablecloth. It was a real pleasure, for many of the students had never eaten on a white tablecloth. The grade nine students served, and with their white uniforms on they looked lovely and served quite well. The principal brought his recorder, and we had soft dinner music during the meal. With all the large potted plants the place really looked inviting.

During the week, a trip had to be made to Musoma to do more shopping for shoes, shirts, and ties, all for the seniors. This, of course, took a whole day. Three dresses then had to be made in one week, including the belt, which I have asked the tailor to make, but on Friday one hour before sundown he sent them to me saying that he didn't have time to make the belts, so I sat right down and made them.

Among the preparations that became my responsibility were the following: the church had to be decorated, the students had to practice their marching, the program had to be rehearsed for Thursday night, the music to be selected for the singing, the printed program made out and sent to the press, signs to be made, my regular classes to be taught, and final examinations to be made and given. I had company at my house on Sabbath, twelve people, and I have no regular help. At one time I was sure I would never make it through the week. On top of all the responsibilities I had a severe cold.

The principal and his family will be leaving Ikizu soon, so we gave him a farewell party in the dining room on Thursday evening before the class night program; all of that had to be planned and decorations provided. The students are not like those at home, where one says "do this or that," and it is done the way you say. Here when the students eat only with a spoon, it is hard to set a proper table. We are working on this. One must stand by to see that everything is done right.

I cooked the food at my house for the staff members, and the dining room cooked for the students. We had a wonderful program. I have much to be thankful for, and the Lord really did bless the program. Everything went along so very smoothly. One could see how thankful I was when all the ninth graders and the graduates left for home. I really did SHOUT. Now I can get some curtains made, and clean my house.

In November we will leave here, Mrs. Beavon and myself, to go to Kenya. She will stop there, and I will go on to Uganda for a short visit and on to Teachers' Institute. Do pray for us here, that the Lord will be with us and this next year will be a good one. We're getting a new principal and one new overseas teacher. Give my regards to all who may ask about me.

Yours in Christian service, Gloria Mackson.

Graduation services would get better and better. Yvonne Davy wrote about the last graduation service that Gloria participated in before she returned to the States.

Sunday was a big day for some of us, since all the board members and their wives had been invited to dine with the Ikizu graduates ... One of the members of the graduating class had made the place cards for the tables. But when those in charge looked over the room just before the doors were opened, they discovered that somehow the young man had forgotten to make cards for two of the guests, Elder Duncan Eva, the Division Secretary, and Brother Marx, who would take Elder Cuthbert's place when he went on furlough. Eda Medford, however, came to the rescue, and within the twinkling of an eye she had two cards ready for her husband to wave dry as the first guests sauntered into the room ... Miss Gloria Mackson, the young lady in charge of the girls' school, had trained her students well, for those who served at the tables did an excellent job. Even though the girls had not waited on tables before and so were very bashful and nervous, there was never a hitch as they passed between the tables handing out food to hungry guests.

After dinner the class president delivered an excellent speech, thanking those who made it possible for us to meet in this manner. The DC and Elder Eva both gave after dinner speeches that were witty and instructive. Bob McGhee introduced the graduating class to us by projecting slides of them onto the screen.[73]

Pastor Eva, secretary of the Southern Africa Division, gave a stirring appeal to the class to consecrate their all to Jesus. And Gloria Mackson responded for the class by singing "I'll never walk alone, Christ walks beside me." The graduates felt rich and fortunate to have participated in such a special celebration, complete with a special marching tune thanks to a teacher who brought his Hammond organ from his house for the event.

Miss Mackson requested permanent return effective December 1961 because of her concern for her aged parents.

A news notes appeared in the *Pacific Union Recorder* on December 25, 1961. "Two ladies, formerly from Los Angeles, will be arriving from Africa on December 31. They are Miss Gloria Mackson from Ikizu, Tanganyika, East Africa and Miss Celeste Lewis from the West African Training School in Nigeria. Anyone wishing to welcome them back to southern California might be interested in meeting their plane. They're coming in on American Airlines from New York. The flight number is 621."

Miss Mackson said that she wondered what diplomat was arriving on the plane because so many people were there at the gate waving. And then she discovered that she and her friend were the object of their attention. About 100 people had seen the note in the *Recorder* and had come to the airport to welcome them home.

Later on someone sent in her name to the Queen for a Day show. She was invited to appear on the nationally televised ABC broadcast on February 21, 1962. Emcee Jack Bailey, assisted by model Maxine Reeves, placed the crown on her head and congratulated her for her life of service. She also won some prizes and some money on the show as appreciation for her work overseas.

Gloria Mackson Hemphill currently resides in California close to Loma Linda University.

---

73. Yvonne Davy, "Routines of Mission Life," *The Youth's Instructor,* November 6, 1962, pp. 3, 4, 15.

Gloria Mackson

After returning from Africa, Gloria Mackson was crowned Queen for a Day on the nationally televised ABC broadcast.

Miss Mackson with students in the library at Ikizu Mission.

The 1961 graduating class at the Ikizu School in Tanganyika.

19

CELESTE LEWIS

1960–1964 / Nigeria. Liberia

We don't have much information about Celeste Lewis. The minutes of the General Conference meeting on August 4, 1949, state, "Voted, to pass on to Oakwood College the call from the Pacific Union for Miss Celeste Lewis to connect with the Los Angeles Academy as librarian and English teacher."

We then have record of her at the Nigerian Training College, for the *Pacific Union Recorder* ran an announcement about her return with Miss Gloria Mackson.[74]

"Two ladies, formerly from Los Angeles. will be arriving from Africa on December 31. They are Miss Gloria Mackson from Ikisu. Tanganyika. East Africa, and Miss Celeste Lewis from the West African Training School in Nigeria. Anyone wishing to welcome them back to southern California might be interested in meeting their plane. They are coming in on American Airlines from New York. Their flight number is 621."

More than 100 people met these two young ladies at the airport.

In the General Conference minutes dated March 21, 1963, we find another action related to this young woman: "Voted, to pass on to Miss Celeste Lewis, of Los Angeles, California, a call to connect with the Northern European Division as a teacher at Konola Academy, in Liberia. Miss Lewis formerly served a term in the Nigerian Training College."

---

74. "News Notes," *Pacific Union Recorder*. December 25, 1961, p. 12.

20
CADDIE JACKSON HOWELL

1961–1963 / Nigeria

Caddie Howell was born in Whitestone, Virginia, to Charles and Ruth Jackson. Her mother and father were both graduates of Oakwood College. Pastor George Earle, her uncle, was the former president of the Northeastern Conference.

The family moved to New York in 1942, and at eleven years of age Caddie began playing the piano at the White Plains Adventist Church for both the children and senior Sabbath School departments for a period of five years.

At age sixteen she became the official organist for the First White Plains Seventh-day Adventist Church. Caddie graduated from Northeastern Academy and then from Atlantic Union College in 1961 with a degree in nursing. Shortly after graduating she received a call to go to Nigeria to work at the Ile Ife Hospital where she taught nursing.

The cornerstone for the 125-bed hospital was laid in 1940. At that time Ife was one of the ten largest cities in Nigeria and also the holy city of the Yoruba people. According to traditional beliefs Olo-dumare, the supreme deity, created the world in four days. When Ile Ife Hospital was founded, it had one American physician and one British nurse.

When Caddie worked at the hospital, there were thirty nurses on staff, most of whom had been trained in the hospital's own school of nursing and midwifery, and four

doctors. Annually the hospital treated more than 100,000 patients for a multitude of maladies. The first patients usually arrived before dawn and formed a line to register and get their clinic records and a number card, which determined when they would see the doctor.

There were many, many children who were sick and many of them arrived at the hospital too late to save their lives. Too late! Too late because of fear, uncertainty, and ignorance! Those were the real foes of the medical worker, not the germs and parasites that modern science could overwhelm with its potent weapons. Nearly 50 percent of all the children born in Nigeria at that time would die before the age of five. The hospital's main medical task was to teach the gospel of preventive medicine and health education to persuade the masses to accept the protective powers of cleanliness, immunizations, and proper diet.

Caddie recalled her time in Nigeria with fond memories:

Let me tell you in more detail about my work there. It was most interesting and rewarding. It was a college education in itself. I worked at Ile Ife Hospital for two and a half years. My mornings began with worship time in the chapel, then out to the wards. Under the leadership of Dr. Sherman Nagel and matron Beryl Turtill, I was the supervisor of wards five and six, which were the children's wards and the orphanage. The orphans were well fed, but they also seemed to gain on "love" alone. We fed them Quaker Oats, and they fattened right up.

We got a midmorning break, and I always went back home for breakfast and last-minute chores. Taking care of the orphans and pediatric wards paid off great rewards. How I wished I could've adopted one of those precious little ones—especially one eventually adopted by a family. Being frail, after about a year he was admitted to ward four of the hospital and soon passed away.

A family celebration brought Brother Enoch Dale to Atlanta, Georgia, a few years ago. I saw him then and also this year. He was the choir director of the Ile SDA Church senior choir, and I was the pianist. I also enjoyed working with quartets and groups as well as teaching piano lessons and doing recitals.

One evening while counseling a student in my living room, I heard a loud knocking noise on my front porch. I quickly went to the door and there were several workmen who saw a five-foot spitting cobra on my porch. They yelled, "Snake, Madame, snake!" They proceeded to kill the snake, and I was greatly relieved. I'm so thankful God took care of me while being around those snakes.

One thing I really enjoyed was being served a cold drink at break time. The drink was given to us to help us get over the sun-heat, which we were not accustomed to. The turns to serve were rotated through the homes of missionaries.

While on an all-day shopping spree to Ibadan or Lagos, which we did once a month, I became acquainted with the "siesta" after lunch. That was something I had only read about in Spanish countries. We enjoyed our lunch, which we had packed, and then went for a short swim in the pool. Yes, wonderful times.

I remember one time when a bug flew right down into my ear and would not come out. I had to get Dr. Larry Longo from his dinner table. I'm so grateful to him. He took me to the emergency room at the Ile Hospital where I worked and removed the crazy bug.

A few years ago I saw Dr. and Mrs. Nagel at a Nigerian Ibo wedding. It was so nice to see them again. It will be so great when all God's children can be together in one place and not scattered all over. That place is called heaven, and He is coming real soon. I look forward to that.

In 1964 Caddie married Francis Howell, a builder from St. Lucia, and became the mother of three children—Joseph, Nancy, and Lily. She continued to work as a nurse until she retired, but she was always available to play the piano and organ for her church. Caddie served the First White Plains Seventh-day Adventist Church for more than fifty-seven years as head of the music department, choir directress, organist, pianist, nurse on duty, and secretary in the Personal Ministries Department. She performed in concerts and on television all over the East Coast and produced records on her own label as a recording artist on the organ.

A national nurse, two Finnish nurses, and Caddie give love to some of their babies.

Caddie Howell, center, her husband, Francis, of forty plus years, and their children, Lilli Howell, left, Nancy Howard, and Joseph Howell, attended the testimonial and retirement dinner given by the First White Plains Church. They are holding the first record made by Caddie on her own label as a recording organist.

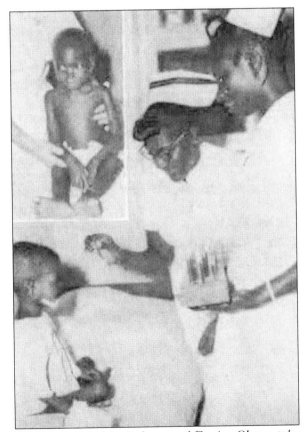

Two nurses, Caddie Jackson and Eunice Olowe, take a native child's temperature.

21
LORETTA DANIELS

1962–1966 / Ethiopia

Loretta Daniels graduated as a nurse from Glendale Sanitarium and Hospital in Glendale, California, and also received a certificate from the Barnes Hospital, School of Anesthesia, in St. Louis, Missouri. She departed from New York on October 23, 1962, for Addis Ababa, Ethiopia, to work as a nurse anesthetist in the Empress Zauditu Memorial Hospital.

While working in Ethiopia, she met and married Mr. L. Wassie who was employed by the government of Ethiopia. She returned to the United States for a short time in 1966 but left again to live in Ethiopia as Mrs. Loretta Wassie.

22

MILTON AND IVY NEBBLETT

1963–1966 / Guyana

Mission service, by its very definition, is often viewed in its stereotypical context. A person has a desire to serve, is called to serve, and ultimately spends time preaching or providing education or badly needed medical services to impoverished communities outside of their country of origin. However, nothing about Milton E. Nebblett's approach to "mission service" ever fit the traditional mold.

Born the son of a master tailor in Le Ciba, Honduras, his love for service to others was nurtured as a young child through his parent's love for helping people regardless of personal stature or economic status. As a teen working in his father's tailor shop, he learned a strong work ethic and a practical skill that brought him pleasure throughout his life. Like a good tailor, he developed the ability to know when something in the garment, or in ministry, "wasn't quite working right," and how to make necessary adjustments for the "right fit."

Spanish was his mother tongue. As a result, he was forced to start his formal college education by first attending Oakwood Academy to master English and grammar. He subsequently graduated in 1950 with honors from both Oakwood Academy. Four years later he once again graduated with honors, this time from Oakwood College. While attending the academy, he created a Pathfinder Master Guide Club, which was so successful that it was recognized

by the college president and used by the college to train many aspiring ministers as Pathfinder leaders, many of which became youth directors across the country.

After finishing his degree at Oakwood, he married the former Ivy Tynes of Nassau, Bahamas, who also grew up in a home that emphasized mission service. Ivy became his partner and collaborator throughout his lifelong ministry of service. He went on to earn a master's degree in divinity from the Seventh-day Adventist Theological Seminary, then located in Washington, D.C., in 1952.

Soon after completing his studies at the seminary, he was called to serve in the East Caribbean Conference by the Inter-America Division leadership. His love of service within the local church of his youth in Honduras was recognized and rewarded by Elder Norman W. Dunn, field secretary of the General Conference for Inter-America, and Elder Arthur Roth, president of the Inter-American Division, who occasionally visited Honduras and became acquainted with Milton as a young man and saw the mission work of the Nebblett family. He was posted as a district pastor in Trinidad and Tobago and was ordained to the gospel ministry in 1958 in Bridgetown, Barbados, before moving to South America where he served as home missionary, Sabbath School, and missionary volunteer secretary in

Georgetown, British Guiana (now Guyana).

Nebblett later pastored in various locations within the Caribbean—at one point pastoring twelve churches simultaneously. From 1963 to 1966 he served as president of the Guiana Mission. During that period at the Guiana Mission, Nebblett's interest in, and attention to, meeting the needs of not only parishioners but the larger community as well led him to spearhead the groundbreaking and construction of the Goshen Youth Camp and the Davis Memorial Hospital, then the largest hospital in the country.

Later, during civil unrest within Guyana, many were left without food for months.

Because of his American citizenship and his community service leadership, he was personally entrusted with the coordination and distribution of the U.S. Government's Food-for-Peace supplies within the country. He became responsible for distributing more than 1.5 million pounds of food each year to thousands of needy families throughout the country. This was accomplished through his establishment of Adventist Welfare Centers within sixty-five churches throughout the country. People from surrounding communities could only receive food aid by coming to a Seventh-day Adventist Church. The visibility and good will toward the church was greatly enhanced throughout Guyana, and the program was so well run that the United States used his program as a model for other distribution programs in other countries around the world.

At the conclusion of his term in Guyana, he returned to the United States, serving as an assistant pastor as well as a senior pastor in several churches within southern California. In 1968 the U.S. federal government, remembering his service in Guyana, asked him to use his talents in the organization and distribution of humanitarian aid in Vietnam. He was granted a leave of absence from his pastoral responsibilities by the Southeastern California Conference, and he accepted the challenge to serve mankind, this time on behalf of the United States of America, as an advisor to the South Vietnamese government during the peak of the war.

He began his work in Saigon in 1969 by coordinating and building refugee camps and designing rehabilitation activities for millions of displaced persons in South Vietnam who were fleeing from the bombings in their villages. Carrying out humanitarian mission work under the powerful authority and financial strength of the U.S. federal government, Nebblett was always mindful of his responsibility to first represent Christ, through love, to his fellow man—even in the middle of war. He was able to make a difference on a much grander scale than he could have ever imagined helping the people of Vietnam, both believers and non-believers alike.

In 1974, close to the end of the war, Nebblett returned to the United States to pastor several churches in Maryland and Pennsylvania before accepting another call to "mission service" in 1980. This time he accepted a position at the Adventist Church's world headquarters as deputy director of the Seventh-day Adventist World Service (SAWS). Because of his experience and knowledge of the inner workings of the United States Agency for International Development (USAID), the former refugee advisor for the South Vietnamese government and the U.S. Department of State within Vietnam brought a new energy and a broader vision of international development and relief to the church.

At that time, his vision and exposure to global possibilities was much greater than church leadership could imagine. He pointed toward trails that the church was not yet aware of or prepared to blaze. His vast knowledge and contacts within USAID enabled him to secure the first grant of $10 million dollars for the church to use for international humanitarian relief through SAWS.

With Nebblett's grant proposal writing and project development expertise, and his insistence on changing the church's humanitarian scope from a locally focused to a global emphasis, he pushed the agency to expand its vision and operations, which transformed Seventh-day Adventist humanitarian mission outreach in the early 1980s. As a direct result of the initial grant, SAWS' name was changed to Adventist Development and Relief Agency (ADRA) to better reflect its new, larger mission. During his tenure as a deputy director for SAWS/ADRA, the organization employed twelve people in its home office and 300 people worldwide and was by and large a global "community service" based organization. In just five years, Nebblett was successful in securing more than $100 million dollars in federal and private grants.

ADRA now employs eighty-five people in its international headquarters and 6,000 people worldwide. The Adventist Church is now a major player on the international development scene, developing, coordinating, and implementing humanitarian projects and essential health and educational outreach throughout Africa, Latin America, Asia, and the South Pacific. Because of those early efforts and successful funding grants, the church had access to most of these countries and governments that were previously closed to it. Nebblett worked nonstop and traveled extensively, working on multiple projects throughout Africa, Asia, and Latin America to assess humanitarian needs and work closely with high level government leaders. In his combined mission service, he visited 150 countries and lived in forty-two different houses during his ministry. His projects included large-scale countrywide food distribution, farming, education, health and disease prevention, clean water, and the expansion of several hospitals and clinics around the world under the Seventh-day Adventist Church's name.

Ivy Nebblett had a passion for nutrition and was a well-recognized health consultant. She visited more than 200 countries, teaching the value of a plant-based diet. As director of the Sta-Well Center in Pennsylvania, she hosted a weekly radio program titled "It's Your World of Good Health." She conducted seminars and cooking schools, and her preaching and teaching were in great demand. She was also a nutrition consultant for the Department of Aging in the city of Philadelphia and was the administrator for the District of Columbia public schools' food services. Since she worked in food services for several city governments, Ivy was in a position to influence the quality of meals served to those segments within the population who were at the greatest risk—the young and the elderly. Ivy is thankful for the part the Lord allowed her to play in sharing the Adventist health message with the world.

Milton left ADRA in 1985 and returned to pastor in the Washington, D.C., metropolitan area. However, his focus on missions and helping those in need did not stop there. After retirement, he was asked by Elder Danny Davis of the Allegheny East Conference to help secure major funding from the Department of Housing and Urban Development (HUD) for the creation of the first church managed senior citizen housing facility in the conference called Chillum Oaks. As a result of that first project, others have used Nebblett's model and proposal templates to obtain funding for other facilities in our conferences around the country. He and his family also formed an independent humanitarian organization (LIFT, International) and operated it for a few years before Alzheimer's disease set in, which he lived with for the final decade of his life. Nebblett died on September 13, 2012, at age eighty-eight.

Although he did not fit the traditional definition of "missionary," he contributed to the church's mission through the demonstration of love in action by feeding countless thousands of hungry people. Clothing the poor and healing the sick was evident through his vision of serving mankind on a global basis as an expression of his love for Christ and his responsibility to his fellow man. This was his vision of mission service—whether local or global.

Most sermons preached throughout his ministry were about God's enormous love for us and how we have a responsibility to love and care for others. From a simple hug to clothing and feeding millions, he believed that LOVE for people in need was the driving force behind Jesus' ministry and, therefore, should be his life's ministry as well. Depending on who you are, or where you were when you encountered him, there is no doubt that you were left with the indisputable fact that he was a man who set out to change the world by simply uplifting people wherever he could.

"Oh Love That Will Not Let Me Go" was his favorite hymn, simply because its lyrics so eloquently illustrated God's love for him and his love for God. There was never a doubt that he cared and that he would do whatever he could to help those in need, whether it was the shirt on his back; the very food on his table; digging fresh water wells; or building hospitals.

Many missionaries who are currently called to serve in faraway places are harvesting in vineyards that were first planted though the efforts of Milton Nebblett. The reputation and trust of the Seventh-day Adventist Church with governments and peoples throughout the world were enhanced through his dedication to demonstrate love in action and through his vision of a global mission brought about through his service to the Lord.

While not one to self-promote or tout his numerous successes, among his greatest stated achievements that he is most proud of during his lifelong ministry was that of his love and commitment to his wife and family. His four children and ten grandchildren continue his legacy of service and ministry to mankind.[75]

Milton with his wife, Ivy, in British Guiana while serving as president of the Guiana Mission.

Elder Nebblett in his office while serving as president of the Guiana Mission in British Guiana.

75. Contributed by Milton Nebblett Jr.

The Nebblett family in 2011: (left to right, standing) Jude Boyer-Patrick, M.D., M.P.H., Milton E. Nebblett Jr., Edwin E. Nebblett, M.D., M.P.H., Marina E. Coleman; (left to right, seated) Ivy S. Nebblett, M.P.H. and Elder Milton E. Nebblett.

Milton Nebblett posing with Buddhist monks in South Vietnam after helping to rebuild their monastery in 1973.

Ivy and Milton during their retirement years.

Making plans with some young people.

23

LINDSAY AND EVELYAN THOMAS

1964–1966 / Ivory Coast

Lindsay Thomas Jr. was born in 1929 in Waynesborough, Georgia, and grew up in Savannah where he completed his early education. He was the eleventh of twelve children. Neither his father nor his mother could read or write.

Lindsay attended Oakwood College and La Sierra College before graduating with his bachelor's degree in French and theology from Le Seminaire Adventiste in Collognes, France. He later received another bachelor's degree from Boston University and his doctor of philosophy degree in French from the University of California at Los Angeles.

Evelyan Patterson grew up in Los Angeles and received her high school diploma from Los Angeles Academy. While in elementary school, she decided to become a physician. Then, in her teen years she read an article about apartheid, and decided to pursue international service.

She attended La Sierra University and the University of California before graduating from Loma Linda University with a medical degree. Upon graduating she completed residencies for general surgery, obstetrics and gynecology, and anesthesiology.

Dr. Evelyan Thomas first realized her dream of international service in the country of Ivory Coast in 1964 when she and her husband were sent to Africa as missionaries. Although that initial stint was only for two years, both of them have returned to Africa numerous times since then. In 1971 Professor Thomas and Dr. Thomas returned to North Nigeria where Lindsay taught French at Ahmadu Bello University and Evelyan offered medical services to the people.

In 1999 Evelyan founded PAPS Team International, an organization that establishes cervical and breast cancer screening clinics in impoverished areas. So far, the clinics have screened more than 18,000 women. Teaming up with Loma Linda University's School of Medicine, she has served as a medical missionary in five countries in Africa. She established the James Alfred Smith Scholarship Fund at Loma Linda University's School of Medicine. The fund is named after her late stepfather who nurtured her dream of becoming a physician. The fund assists female students aspiring to make a difference in the world.

Lindsay and Evelyan have continued to keep Africa in their hearts and have engaged in many activities to develop pastors, evangelists, and teachers in Africa. In 1980 the second Seventh-day Adventist Church was built in Togo, West Africa, thanks to Lindsay's efforts. One Sabbath afternoon Lindsay was visiting homes in Fontana, California, when he met Mami Spencer. They struck up a conversation and somehow got on the subject of mission work. As she became more and more interested in his description of the Adventist Church's mission activities, she asked what she could do. Thomas suggested donating funds for a church, which she did.

Not even an Adventist, Mami Spencer donated enough money to build a church in Togo, once she was assured that the church could be named in honor of her deceased husband, Arthur Spencer. Lindsay was the agent who oversaw the project. Two years later the church was built on land purchased with funds donated by several Adventists from Southern California. Spencer Memorial Church seats 150, and many people have been baptized in the church since its dedication.

Guy Valleray, secretary of the Africa-Indian Ocean Division, launched a five-week soul-winning series titled Happy Life Seminar in Abidjan, Ivory Coast. More than 500 Ivoirians attended the first meeting. The audience included the mayor, other officials, professionals, university students, and many from the general population of the capital city. Each person had preregistered at a fee of approximately $3.50, about the average daily wage for an unskilled laborer. This was done to determine initial public interest and also to help cover the cost of materials that were used by participants during the five weeks. The Happy Life Seminar constituted a training program with some sixteen ministers from six French-speaking countries. A handsome tent, donated through the initiative of Lindsay Thomas, was erected next to the evangelistic center and was served by closed-circuit television to take care of the overflow crowd.

Dr. Lindsay Thomas had a heart for evangelism in Africa and worked with the Concerned Layman for Evangelism in Africa to set up a crusade in Monrovia; however, the group was unsuccessful in finding a noted black evangelist to speak for the meetings. When Dr. Thomas contacted Dr. E. E. Cleveland and asked him to recommend a student to conduct the crusade, Dr. Cleveland immediately recommended Joseph Rodriquez, a junior ministerial student at Oakwood College who had conducted a six-week crusade in Liberia that resulted in the baptism of 629 persons.

The Layman Committee consisted of members from California and Arkansas, and it paid for the entire crusade. They bought the tent, paid all of Joseph's expenses, and provided hundreds of small books to be given away during the series.

On January 5, 1983, Joseph and his friend Jonathan Ward, also a ministerial student at Oakwood, boarded the flight to Monrovia. All night during the flight Joseph prayed, "Lord, you can trust me with more than 100 souls." He didn't have a figure in mind, and by not limiting the power of God, he was rewarded beyond his greatest dream. Several times during the meetings Joseph was threatened with death.

Attendance the first night totaled 1,500 with 700 enrolling in the Real Truth Bible Course, which was held each evening before the main meeting. By the fourth week average nightly attendance had swollen to 2,300. When he preached on Sabbath, the sermon was televised nationally. The Lord blessed young Joseph, who was only twenty-two years old and had only been an Adventist for five years.

When Joseph became a Seventh-day Adventist at the age of eighteen, after being a Catholic all his life, he encountered fierce opposition from his father. One reason his father opposed Adventism was because this was during the time of the Jonestown mass suicide and most people from Trinidad and the surrounding Caribbean islands were suspicious of other religions. His father threatened to put him out and refused to feed him because he continued to adhere to this strange religion. Joseph refused to bow under his father's wrath; he determined to remain true to his principles. He became accustomed to standing up for what he believed, even if it meant standing alone.

On the day of Joseph's baptism, April 14, 1978, after having attended the Adventist Church for only two weeks, he began to preach. He set out on his divinely appointed mission by taking a battery-powered loudspeaker into the bus terminal and the highways and byways.

Finally he opened up his father's garage and conducted services while his father was at work. Little did he know that this was one of several dress rehearsals ordained by God to prepare him for his life's work.

During this time, God loosened his tongue that he might speak. All of his life he had suffered from a severe speech impediment. His mother had taken him from doctor to doctor and tried all kinds of folk remedies. One remedy consisted of Joseph gargling with fresh seawater and sea shells, but to no avail—he continued to stutter. When he became a Seventh-day Adventist and accepted his life's work, God loosened his tongue. One day he heard himself speaking and remarked in amazement, "Hey, I'm talking correctly!"

In 1983 Lindsay Thomas and the same group (a nonprofit organization called ABOKIN, Inc.) sent John E. Collins, associate director of Sabbath School and personal ministries for the Pacific Union Conference, to Sierra Leone to teach laypeople the art of one-to-one soul winning. However, training members was not easy because some could not read. There were also tribal language barriers and absolutely no tools with which to work. In addition to training in how to prepare a Bible study, instruction included home visitation,

how to find people interested in a Bible study, and gaining decisions. Children and families were urged to participate and become a soul winning team.

In 1984 Dr. Lindsay Thomas returned to Africa to participate in a training course.

Recognizing active laypeople as a possible solution to Ghana's pastoral shortage, Lindsay and Hubert Goodlett conducted a three-week Bible Study Institute for laypeople. Six hours each day, six days per week, they taught 150 laypeople how to give Bible studies using the Encounter Bible lessons. Each person received a new Bible and other evangelistic materials thanks to donations by laypeople in Arkansas and California. At the conclusion of the Institute, forty-four laypeople were employed to do evangelistic work—their salaries would be paid for by the same American group.

In 1984 Lindsay Thomas returned to serve as a leader for a training institute in Nigeria. The major ethnic group in this area adhered to Islam. Because it is nearly impossible to conduct public evangelistic campaigns, door-to-door work is the best method of outreach. Lindsay and his group paid the salaries of twenty-four full-time laypersons and sponsored several training institutes.

In 1985 Hubert Goodlett and Lindsay Thomas organized a twelve-day Bible Institute in Kinshasa, Zaire, and 250 people, representing several tribal groups, attended. During the institute a non-Adventist who had been attending the meetings daily responded to an appeal for laypeople to give Bible studies in their neighborhoods. The man, Mpaye Kimbole, told how his mother, a devout Christian, but not an Adventist, had set a good example in his home. At an early age, however, he had become addicted to various harmful drugs.

One day one of Kimbole's cousins visited

a village witch doctor in search of money. The witch doctor agreed to give the man money if he delivered nine individuals to be killed by the witch doctor as part of his fiendish ritual. The cousin delivered to the witch doctor three children who were massacred. When Kimbole, the fourth person, was escorted to the witch doctor, the man did not take his life at that time. But when he returned home, he became deathly ill. Twice relatives gave him money to buy medicine; twice he bought marijuana instead.

While feverishly attempting to smoke the second lot of marijuana, he heard a voice calling him. He looked everywhere but saw no one. Then he passed out. During the night he was terror-stricken by nightmares—devils eating his frail body, wild animals attacking him, arrows piercing his skin. Yet in the dreams an invisible figure kept defending him. A voice repeatedly said to him, "Go get someone to pray for you or you will certainly die."

When Kimbole woke up, he asked his mother to pray for him. Christian groups prayed for him. Kimbole himself began to pray. And as he prayed, he began to regain peace of mind. His frail body became stronger. He stopped smoking cigarettes and marijuana. He ceased drinking alcoholic beverages and using other addictive drugs. While attending the training session, he made plans to join the Adventist Church and witness for his newfound faith.

Over the years Dr. Lindsay Thomas and his group sponsored Elders Ivan Warden, Stephen E. Patterson, Walter Pierson, Henry J. Fordham, Robert Lister, Calvin Watkins, Robert L. Tolson, Leslie Pollard and his wife, Arthur S. Bushnell, James Melancon, and others to conduct evangelistic meetings and to organize evangelistic training in Africa.

On July 16, 1987, the General Conference voted a special thank you: "to express appreciation to Lindsay Thomas for his interest in overseas missionary work. Following a regular mission service (1964 to 1966) he has worked, on a self-supporting basis, as an evangelist, a leader in layman's institutes, Bible seminars and spirit of prophecy meetings."[76]

Lindsay and Evelyan Thomas have been perpetual missionaries on the continent of Africa. Dr. Lindsay has visited and worked in Senegal, Ivory Coast, Ghana, Rwanda, Burundi, Nigeria, Liberia, Sierra Leone, Zaire, Kenya, Cameroon, Tanzania, Malawi, Uganda, Egypt, Togo, Benin, Ivory Coast, South Africa Republic, Lesotho, Swaziland, Cape Town, Mozambique, Madagascar, Zambia, Zimbabwe, Uganda, and Botswana. They have seen to it that instruction has been given by organizing and teaching in Bible Institutes for Laymen, Spirit of Prophecy Seminars, and seminars for local church elders.

The couple has raised funds to hire lay preachers on a full-time basis; distribute food to widows and children and clothing and shoes to needy; erect churches and chapels; dig wells; sponsor young people in school; provide tapes, CDs, DVDs, religious and Spirit of Prophecy books; provide tents for evangelistic meetings, bicycles for lay preachers, and wheelchairs; financial assist pastors and their wives; build parsonages; and host medical and dental fairs.

In 2006 Dr. Lindsay Thomas was awarded an honorary degree, the doctor of divinity, at the University of Eastern Africa in Baraton, Kenya, for his work in twenty-six different African countries, which has resulted in the conversion of 50,000 people. Since that time an additional 60,000 have accepted Christ, making a total of 110,000 new members to the Adventist

---

76. "Thomas, Lindsay---Appreciation," General Conference Minutes, July 16, 1987, pp. 87–253.

Church as a result of his efforts. Lindsay and Evelyan expected great things from God, and then attempted great things for God! Praise be to His holy name!

Dr. Thomas feeding the people in the community in Kenya in 2013.

Dr. Lindsay Thomas Jr. and his wife, Evelyan, enjoying a meal with friends.

Dr. Thomas in Kenya with a group of friends following one of his seminars.

Dr. Roger Hadley, dean of Loma Linda University's School of Medicine, and Dr. Evelyan Thomas enjoy a moment of celebration with the international service award Thomas received in recognition of her years of selfless dedication to the health needs of impoverished women in Africa and Jamaica. The award was presented during the Women in Medicine luncheon in 2012.

24

DOLLY ALEXANDER-JOHNSON

1965–1967 / Zambia; 1970–1972 / Rwanda; 1975–1979 / Ethiopia

Teaching for nine years in three African countries convinced Dolly Alexander that generally speaking Adventist missionaries were woefully lacking in language skills, and she sought to do something to help change the situation.

A native of British Columbia, a Canadian province not known for its interest in the French language, Leola Dolly Alexander became enthralled with French as she heard it on the radio and read it on cereal boxes at breakfast. (By law, nearly every public communication had to be presented in both French and English in Canada.) Her parents, Thomas Foster and Leola Alexander, moved to Langley, British Columbia, in 1934, and Thomas donated the wood for Langley's first Adventist Church. Dolly had two sisters and four brothers.

Dolly attended Canadian Union College where she used her talents of singing by joining a ladies quartet at the school. She later transferred to Andrews University where she graduated in 1962 with a bachelor's degree in home economics. After obtaining her degree, she taught school in British Columbia. One of the courses she had to teach was French. She soon decided she wanted to learn French better, so she went to France. While studying French in Paris, Alexander supported herself by teaching English at the Berlitz language school. Then

she received a call to teach home economics and French at the newly established Rusangu Secondary School in Zambia.

In Africa at that time (1965–1967) many more boys went to school than girls, so she ended up teaching a lot more French than home economics. This was a factor in her decision to earn a master's degree in French at the University of Illinois when her term of service ended.

Her experience in Zambia also made her realize that she needed not only to learn more French but also to speak the local language of her students if she really wanted to get close to them and understand them.

Dolly determined to learn the local language at her next overseas mission assignment. From 1970 to 1972 she served at Gitwe Secondary School in Rwanda. She soon discovered that Gitwe was isolated, and there was no possibility of her attending a regular language school, so Dolly recruited one of the students to teach her. Learning a language without even having a dictionary is a formidable challenge, but she finally learned enough basic Kinyarwanda to talk with the people at the marketplace.

Dolly didn't fare so well in Ethiopia, where once again she found herself teaching home economics at an isolated Adventist secondary school, Ethiopian Adventist College. The language schools were located in the capital city of Addis Ababa, a four-hour drive south of the school, and she could go into the city only once a month. Although she and several other missionaries stationed at the school persuaded the church translator who spoke fluent Amharic and English to teach them during one summer vacation, none of them mastered the language.

Dolly's determination to do something about language learning for missionaries led her to the Ivory Coast where she spent several months doing research for her doctoral dissertation in linguistics from Georgetown University. Washington, D.C. Although her dissertation was a comparison of African and Western oral discourse styles, her real interest was in helping Adventist missionaries become more effective in the field.

During her second year of study at Georgetown University, she attended a linguistics conference where she met Dick Davidian, the former principal at Gitwe. They compared notes and discovered that they were pursuing doctorates in linguistics for the same reason—Adventist missionaries needed an effective language program.

Dolly felt that women especially needed to learn the local languages in Africa because the majority of African women did not speak the official language of their respective countries. She believed that women in Africa were limited to communicating with other women. A foreign woman who comes to Africa is seen in the wrong light if she speaks only with men, and yet she is often limited to that because men are the ones who speak the official language.

She used her linguistic skills to help the church. She prepared several surveys for Adventist missionaries to determine their attitudes and experiences in language learning. She was very much concerned about making language learning a bridge instead of a barrier in the worldwide mission program of the Seventh-day Adventist Church.

Besides being a great teacher, Dolly Alexander's great desire was to see the church establish an effective language program for Adventist missionaries so they would quickly fit in with the nationals. More important, she felt that if missionaries could speak the language of the people, they could form closer relationships and have greater opportunities to impact them spiritually. It was probably through her efforts that the church later set up required mission institutes and language programs to help new missionaries better prepare themselves for usefulness when they arrived in their mission field.

The last record we have of Dolly Alexander shows her teaching language at Pacific Union College from 1990 to 1993 with the hyphenated named L. Dolly Alexander-Johnson.[77]

The Canadian Union College ladies' quartet— Rose Dubyna, Dolly Alexander, Kathy Gustavsen, and Juanita Melashenko—presenting a musical program at the Peoria MV rally.

---

77. Much of this article was taken from "To Every Nation, Kindred, Tongue, and People" by James L. Fly, *Adventist Review*, January 2, 1986, p. 29.

25

GEORGE AND LOIS BENSON

1967–1970 / Libya and Ethiopia

George Nathaniel Benson grew up on a farm that his great-great-grandfather received as a government grant in Indiana. The Benson family was the only black family in that county and the only Adventist family. The inspiration to become a doctor came to him through his mother's encouragement. He applied for and was accepted as one of the first black medical students at Loma Linda. After graduating from Loma Linda University's School of Medicine in 1953, he became board certified in radiology and nuclear medicine.

Although he planned to stay for only a year or two, he worked for a number of years at Riverside Sanitarium and Hospital in Nashville, Tennessee, where he was director of nuclear medicine and at Meharry Medical College where he was clinical associate professor of radiology and nuclear medicine. While in Nashville he served as a local elder and as temperance secretary for the Riverside Chapel Church. As part of his missionary effort, he subscribed to ten copies of *The Message Magazine* for his office waiting rooms.

Each year Dr. Benson left his busy practice to spend a few days at one or more of the camp meetings to give health lectures, to perform medical examinations, and to counsel with those in attendance regarding personal medical problems.

George Benson married Lois Simons, a registered nurse. Lois' brother Richard Simons was a missionary to West Africa and another brother, Donald B. Simons, was a missionary in Sierra Leone. The Bensons had two sons, Paul and Stephen.

With such a missionary tradition in Lois' family, when the Bensons were called to the Benghazi Adventist Hospital, they accepted and left with their two sons for Libya in 1967. On November 23, 1969, the local government nationalized the hospital, which was under Dr. Benson's direction as acting medical director. The new government of Libya took over the operation of the sixty-five-bed hospital but with an all national staff. Relations between the government and the church-owned hospital continued to be friendly, and the move was interpreted by the hospital officials as a step toward nationalization of the country rather than an anti-church action. Other hospitals in Libya were nationalized at the same time. The Benghazi Adventist Hospital had first opened in a downtown hotel in 1956, and in January 1968 it had moved to a brand new building.

After the government takeover, it soon became evident that the Adventist staff, which was made up of forty-eight families with a large number of Far East missionaries (Filipinos, Koreans, and Indonesians, could not remain in Libya and work under the new government arrangements, so the General Conference

made efforts to reassign the Adventist personnel to other responsibilities. Some had to be
sent home on permanent return. Dr. Benson
was reassigned to Gimbie Hospital in Ethiopia
to finish out his term of service.

In 1976 Dr. Benson accepted the position
of director in chief of the Radiology Department of Martin Luther King Jr. Memorial Hospital in Kansas City, Missouri, and Lois became
the obstetrics charge nurse for Shawnee Mission Medical Center. They joined the Beacon
Light Church and used their skills to conduct
several Five-Day Plans to Stop Smoking. Dr.
Benson served as head church elder and Sabbath School teacher. In 1980 they returned to
Nashville where he headed up the Radiology
Department at Meharry Medical College.

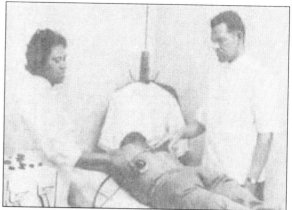
Mrs. Joyce Watson assists Dr. Benson in treatment of a patient using the ultrasound muscle stimulator combination.

Drs. George Benson and Carl Dent operate new artificial dialyzer at Riverside Sanitarium.

Dr. Benson speaks at the Lake Region Conference camp meeting.

Riverside Sanitarium staff physicians: (left to right) Drs. D. Warren Harrison, George N. Benson, William Coopwood, and Carl Dent.

Dr. and Mrs. Benson with their sons, Paul and Stephen, as they prepare to leave for mission service in Libya.

The medical team at Riverside: (left to right) Drs. Carl A. Dent, William A. Coopwood, Gardner L. Dixon, Samuel DeShay, Green Shurney, and George N. Benson.

Dr. and Mrs. Benson after retirement.

26
NAOMI BULLARD

1967–1982 / Rwanda; 1996–2002 / Kenya

Naomi Bullard was the youngest daughter in Robert and Susan Bullard's large family. Her teachers were good role models in the schools she attended. Naomi attended the Phyllis Wheatley Elementary School in Miami, Florida, and then Booker T. Washington High School. Attending these fine institutions, Naomi thought a lot about the influential black heroes that they were named after.

Graduating at the top of her class in Miami, she went on to attend Oakwood College where she studied pre-nursing. In 1961 she received a bachelor's degree in nursing from Loma Linda University. There were only two black students in her class, and she maintained the highest scholastic average in the program. Two years later she earned her master's degree. She remained at Loma Linda after graduating and taught on the nursing faculty for three years.

Then she received three simultaneous calls to work as a missionary in Ethiopia, Zambia, or Rwanda. Naomi accepted the most difficult call to the French-speaking country of Rwanda in Central Africa to establish a new nursing program at Mugonero Hospital.

This was a very challenging task. First, she had to learn French well enough to teach in it, and secondly she had to develop the course of study for this new program—in French! On January 20, 1967, she sailed on the *SS United States* to begin studying French in Neuchatel,

Switzerland, for six months before heading to Rwanda. There would be very little money for starting this new program, but Naomi was determined that with God's help her mission would be accomplished. One year later the program began with twenty students who were instructed in French.

Three years after the program began, on July 2, 1972, a graduation ceremony was held, and eleven male nurses received their diplomas. Mugonero is built on a small plateau with a beautiful and commanding view of Lake Kivu. It was a gorgeous day, and the graduation exercises were held out of doors. All government requirements had been met and approved. The minister of public health for Rwanda, Dr. Theodore Sundkiunuko, and his sister were in attendance to give the graduating address and present the diplomas to the graduates. Some nurses graduated with honors and received special acknowledgment.

Missionaries from nearby Catholic and Protestant missions and hospitals attended, and the visiting minister of public health emphasized the value of Christian education. He stated that the world did not need men of great intellect as much as men of noble character. Character building, he said, was the most important work ever entrusted to human beings. The Mugonero Hospital staff presented the minister with one of Mrs. White's books.

In this first nurses training course there were no girls graduating since none had sufficient prior education to begin the course. The course started every two years, and there were seven girls in the new class. Naomi Bullard was very pleased to see the fruits of her labor in the very first graduating class. She looked forward to her well-earned furlough after more than five years of arduous mission service.

After fourteen years of service in Rwanda, Miss Naomi Bullard returned to America to work in health services and serve as a professor of nursing at Oakwood College in Huntsville, Alabama. She later received a call to Kenya to set up the nursing department at the University of Eastern Africa at Baraton, Kenya. She took on this new challenge and worked in Kenya for six years before moving to Florida.

Naomi received numerous awards for academic excellence during her career; among them is the President's Award for the School of Nursing at Loma Linda University, 1961, and Alumnus of the Year, School of Nursing, Loma Linda University, 1972.

Naomi Bullard and Dr. Lydia Andrews stand around a graduating student at the University of Eastern Africa, Kenya.

Naomi Bullard pins a graduation pin on a student.

Naomi Bullard in her Loma Linda University graduating cap and gown.

Naomi Bullard stands with fellow teachers.

27

JOHN AND DORA RODGERS

1967–1979 / Puerto Rico; 1980–1991 / Costa Rica

Dora Mae Echols was born in Detroit, Michigan, to Magnolia and Wellington Echols. She was the eldest of eight children.

John Edward Rodgers was born in Alabama but as a little baby his family moved to Coshocton, Ohio, a little town in the eastern mountains. He always thought he was born in Ohio like his sixteen other brothers and sisters. The entire family belonged to the Methodist church.

John's aunt who lived in Detroit invited him to come there, and he moved to Detroit to live with her. John took a great interest in the Adventist Church there and joined. He especially appreciated the way the Adventist young people treated him. It was the Adventist young people of Detroit who convinced him to go to Oakwood College. His parents also joined the Adventist Church, but his other siblings did not.

An excellent student, Dora loved reading, poetry, writing, music, and languages. In 1942 she graduated from Northern High School with honors. She received scholarships that financed her education through Wayne State University in Detroit, where she majored in French and received her master's degree from Wayne State in 1946. She became a teacher in the Detroit Public School System.

In 1947 while on an outing with her French club at Belle Isle, a park in Detroit, Dora met John Rodgers who was at the park for a church picnic. Since John would be attending Oakwood College that fall, they kept in touch with him by mail. Dora was baptized into the Seventh-day Adventist Church around 1949 while John was away at Oakwood. In the meantime John, a gifted tenor soloist and recent music graduate of Emmanuel Missionary College, teamed up with Dora, and they presented an inspirational joint recital of drama and voice in the lecture hall of the Detroit Institute of Arts. They made a nice musical couple, and on June 14, 1953, John and Dora decided to tie the knot and get married. Out of their union came two children: Sharlita Michelle and Edward Jai.

The couple moved to Southern California in 1960, and then in 1967 they moved to Mayagüez, Puerto Rico, where Dora taught at Antillean Adventist University and John took some additional graduate classes and studied Spanish. He says the Lord helped him learn Spanish because he doesn't understand how he learned it so fast. John says he was surprised that he made all As in his classes because they were taught in Spanish, and he was still learning the language. Dora was already very proficient in French, Spanish, elocution, and recitation.

Later the General Conference voted that John should serve as a professor of psychology and education at Antillean Adventist University. Dora became chair of the English Department and headed up the committee for the college's independent study for accreditation.

John said that at one time he thought about becoming a minister. But soon that thought left him and he thought about becoming a medical doctor. Then as he studied he became more and more convinced that he should become a teacher. He prayed about it, but he also asked his two children what they thought. They both shouted loudly together, "Be a teacher, Dad, be a teacher!" So with that affirmation, he dropped the medical aspirations and concentrated on education and teaching. He taught biology and many other subjects before he decided that he really liked psychology.

Some of the outstanding leaders of the Spanish Adventist work sat in their classes while they taught at Antillean Adventist University. Juan Prestol who later became a treasurer of several conferences and a division and is now a treasurer in the General Conference was Dr. Dora's student. Angel Rodriguez who is director of the General Conference Biblical Research was another one of her students. Time will only tell the great influence the Rodgers exerted on the development of Spanish leaders during their many years at these leading Spanish institutions.

The 1973 college yearbook, the Flamboyan, was dedicated to the Rodgers. The dedication page was sprinkled with art and pictures and said, "KIND ... , AMIABLE ... , MUSICIANS ... , THE MOUNTAIN NIGHTINGALE ... , FOND INTERPRETERS OF HUMAN BEHAVIOR ... , COURTESY PERSONIFIED ... , AN INSPIRATION TO YOUR STUDENTS ... ,YOU LIVE AND TEACH ... , BECAUSE OF LOVE ...

"And it is by the influence of your beneficial ways of doing things among us and for us that we commend you. And therefore, we dedicate these pages to you."

In 1975 they took a sabbatical and with the children moved to Berrien Springs, Michigan. There they enrolled at Andrews University and completed their doctorates in education and counseling/psychology in 1978. The two doctors returned to Puerto Rico but came back to Andrews in 1980 to march in the same graduation with their daughter, Sharlita who received her undergraduate degree. The family says that Dora was the first woman to receive the doctoral degree in education from Andrews University.

In 1989 Dora and John received a mission call to go to Costa Rica to teach at the Universidad Adventista de Centroamerica (UNADECA). Upon completion of this service in Costa Rica, they received the Merit of Honor for distinguished service at that institution. In 1991 they returned to the United States and settled in Dayton, Ohio. Dora worked from 1997 to 2007 with the Kettering Medical Center's counseling department and with its Ministry Care Line.

On May 28, 2013, Dora fell asleep in Jesus. Her husband of sixty years still lives in Dayton, Ohio.

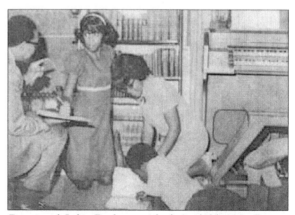

Dora and John Rodgers with their children in Puerto Rico.

John and Dora Rodgers and their car.

Dora and John Rodgers with their children in Puerto Rico.

Dr. Dora Rodgers with her English and elocution students in Puerto Rico.

Drs. John and Dora Rodgers

28

HERMON AND PHILIPPA VANDERBERG

1967–1969 / Liberia

Sometimes mission service means paying the ultimate sacrifice, which turned out to be the case for Phillipa Vanderberg.

Hermon and Phillipa had looked forward to overseas mission service ever since they were young. Hermon was a native of Detroit, Michigan. He received his degree from Oakwood College in 1955 and then completed his seminary training at Andrews University. He began his ministry in 1963 as associate to Elder H. M. Barker in Jacksonville, Florida. Later he became pastor of the Charleston district. He made many improvements to all the churches in his district, including a new church home at Bonneau, South Carolina. Elder Vanderberg was ordained to the gospel ministry Sabbath, May 20, 1967, at the Atlanta Berean Church.

Philippa Latney was born in Richmond, Virginia, but grew up in Camden. She could read and write at the age of two and made her first public appearance when just two and a half years old at her church. She was the church pianist at the age of five. She was a skilled performer on piano, trumpet, and organ. She was the first African American to become a member of the Esperanto Society of Philadelphia, Pennsylvania, and to teach at the all-white Ashburton Elementary School in Maryland. Her desire to become a missionary had its inception when she was three years of age.

Philippa attended the public schools of Camden, New Jersey, and graduated from Camden High School. She attended Oakwood College for part of her undergraduate work, but received a bachelor's degree in elementary education from Washington Missionary College in 1959. Two years before, in 1957, she married Herman.

The Vanderbergs with their two children left New York City on July 17, 1967, for Monrovia, Liberia. Pastor Vanderberg worked in Liberia as a district leader and evangelist for the Bassa district and also the pastor for the Buchanan Church. Mrs. Vanderberg was a teacher at the school. In July 1968 Pastor Herman Bauman from the Adventist College of West Africa teamed up with Pastor Vanderberg to conduct a field school of evangelism. The field school had a double purpose: to preach the gospel to those who didn't know it and to train the workers of Liberia in more effective methods of proclaiming the Adventist message. It was held in Lower Buchanan, in Grand Bassa County, in Eastern Liberia. Pastor Hermon Vanderberg was in charge.

Liberian pastors and evangelists came from every part of the country. A total of twelve (virtually all the pastors and evangelists of the Liberia Mission) very energetic and zealous men attended the field school. One came from the far north in elephant country. Another walked for nine hours to get from his station to the road where he could get transportation to come. Within the heart of each one was a burning desire to do something greater for the Lord.

Classes were taught each morning by Pastors Bauman and Vanderberg in church leadership, evangelism, Bible doctrine, and Spirit of Prophecy. The students studied hard and even took quizzes and examinations. At the conclusion of the field school there was a graduation service in which each student received a certificate and a record of the grade they had earned.

The main feature of the field school was the evangelistic campaign itself. Meetings were conducted six nights a week in the community center building. Pastor Bauman directed the meetings and did the preaching. Pastor Vanderberg served as coordinator, and the students assisted with music, ushering, and visitation, as well as other phases of the program. An average of about 300 people attended each meeting, and eighty-five people, including a pastor and an assistant pastor of another church, made decisions to prepare for baptism.

A young man named David Mason who was serving as an assistant pastor in an African Methodist Church decided to become a Seventh-day Adventist. With the kind and dedicated guidance and instruction of Pastor Vanderberg, Mr. Mason received the encouragement he needed and was baptized into the Seventh-day Adventist Church on December 21, 1968.

In September 1969 David Mason was sent to the Adventist College of West Africa to become a student to prepare himself for a place of service in the Adventist Church. Pastor Vanderberg also was responsible for building the mission church in Grand Bassa County.

Once at a temperance program in his district where the young people talked about the dangers of alcohol and cigarettes, Elder Vanderberg called for an offering at the close of the program. He asked, not for a monetary offering, but an offering of cigarettes to indicate a decision to quit smoking. Several stood, and one man, Mr. Greenfield, stepped up and gave his entire pack of cigarettes. He was later given the magazine *Smoke Signals* to help him maintain his decision.

Darkness and death, however, would soon settle over the Vanderberg family and the church in Liberia. In February 1969 Hermon was conducting a week of prayer at Konola Academy and Phillipa was assisting with the choir and music for the program when they met with a tragic accident while going home one evening.

On Thursday night, February 6, 1969, as Pastor Vanderberg and his wife and children were driving home, they slammed into the back of a parked petrol truck that was sitting unlit on the road. Phillipa Vanderburg, just thirty-two years of age, died from her injuries shortly after the collision, and Pastor Vanderberg and his five-year-old daughter Robin were hospitalized due to fractures and shock. At the request of the relatives, Mrs. Vanderberg's body was sent home to America for burial. She was buried in Camden, New Jersey, on March 13.

Phillipa Vanderburg was a young lady of deep piety, exceptional musical ability, and great compassion. This young missionary's life was short, but eventful. She was a kind and thoughtful daughter, wife, and mother. Her last letter home to her mother read in part, "The months are going by quickly and bringing us closer and closer to our reunion date." The Liberia Mission, the West African Union, and the Northern European Division, and many others paid tribute to the sweet natured woman whose missionary service had so suddenly and unexpectedly ended.

Pastor Vanderberg hung between life and death, but with skilled care from the Firestone Hospital in Monrovia and much prayer, he began to make a slow recovery. Robin, although quicker to respond to treatment, had fractures that were extremely difficult to set. Despite the attention of the best doctors in Liberia, the bones refused to line up properly even after several attempts. After about a month Pastor Vanderberg returned to the United States to continue to recuperate at the New York University Hospital in New York and to finally reset Robin's fractures. Dwayne, their eight-year-old son, also traveled with them. Under such lugubrious circumstances the union recommended permanent return for Pastor Vanderberg and his children.

As his health improved, Elder Vanderberg was assigned to the Southern California Conference, pastoring several churches throughout the area. He shared his mission experiences at numerous camp meetings and church gatherings for a while.

Hermon later married Cynthia Cathcart and had an additional child, Peter. He continued pastoring in the Los Angeles area and retired from the Southeastern California Conference in 1988 after suffering several strokes that had a devastating effect on his memory.

Pastor and Mrs. Vanderberg with their two children in front of one of the churches he pastored in America.

Pastor Vanderberg in his Liberian garb.

Wreckage of the Vanderberg automobile, which hit a parked petrol truck without lights and in which Mrs. Vanderberg was fatally injured, on a road in Liberia.

29
ROBERT AND CORDELIA ANDREWS

1969–1978 / Jamaica

"It is always a pleasure for the West Indies Union to welcome new workers to our shores.

West Indies College has been favored in having three new couples join its staff. The first to arrive were Brother and Sister E. D. Brantley ... (then) Dr. and Mrs. Robert Andrews ... Dr. Andrews will head the department of history and will be an instructor of Biblical languages in the theology department. They came to Jamaica from Michigan, and already they have endeared themselves to both the faculty and students. We trust that they may have a long and fruitful period of service here." Thus the *Inter-American Messenger* announced the arrival of a wonderful couple that would bring spiritual and intellectual strength to the college.

Robert Thompson Andrews Jr. was born in Detroit, Michigan, September 18, 1932. His father was a tool and die craftsman for Ford Motor Company; his mother, a former student of Oakwood College, was a third-generation Adventist. Although his father did not share his mother's religious beliefs, he did not object to her taking Robert and his two brothers to church on Saturday. Robert enjoyed church, and at a very early age, he gave his heart to the Lord. He attended Adelphian Academy in Holly, Michigan, and was baptized on his sixteenth birthday. It was then that he decided to become a minister. He colporteured during the summer to help pay his tuition while he attended the Adventist college closest to his home, Emmanuel Missionary College, majoring in religion. When he was eighteen years old, he was injured in an automobile accident, but God spared his life.

One summer Robert met an Oakwood student selling books in Detroit. The student, Cordelia Wethington, invited him to go to Oakwood College. He changed colleges and graduated from Oakwood in 1956 as president of the class. Robert and Cordelia married that summer and moved to Washington, D.C., where Robert attended the Adventist seminary, graduating with a master's degree in New Testament Greek and systematic theology.

In 1959 Robert and Cordelia were blessed with the birth of their first child, a daughter whom they named Esther, followed by the birth of a son, Michael, in October 1960. After pastoring in Southern California, he was called to the Lake Region Conference in 1962. In April 1963 Deborah was born.

Pastor Andrews was ordained to the gospel ministry at the 1963 Lake Region Conference camp meeting. An overflow audience of nearly 2,000 persons gathered to witness the ceremony, which took place on Sabbath afternoon. Elder J. H. Laurence, retired veteran minister who was instrumental in baptizing Robert Andrew's grandparents, gave the prayer of ordination.

Their last child, Karen, was born in 1965.

In 1967 Robert felt impressed to take a study leave from the ministry and pursue a doctoral degree in speech communications at Michigan State University. After graduating from this program in 1969, Robert and Cordelia received a call to mission service at West Indies College in Jamaica (now known as Northern Caribbean University). At West Indies College he was chair of the history and humanities departments. He taught biblical Greek, Bible, and history. He revised the college bulletin, developed a proposal for external accreditation, and helped to develop and expand the graduate extension program for ministers and teachers.

While there, Dr. Robert Andrews assisted the college in developing an extension graduate-studies program with Andrews University. This program enabled Adventist ministers and teachers who worked in the Caribbean Union and wished to upgrade their education to the master's degree level to do so at West Indies College during the summers. The Andrews served the college in various capacities for two four-year terms. Cordelia taught shorthand, typing, and secretarial science and shared her musical abilities.

In the midst of the two terms they returned to the States for a one-year furlough. They spent that year at Andrews University where Cordelia upgraded her education, and Robert was encouraged to pursue a second doctorate in higher education administration.

In 1978 the Andrews received a call to Oakwood College. Dr. Andrews worked at Oakwood both as an administrator and teacher until his retirement in 1997.

Shortly after celebrating their 50th anniversary, Cordelia's health declined. After she passed away, Dr. Andrews married Mandy Martin on November 13, 2010. Mandy has received many awards working for the less fortunate in many capacities and is a strong supporter of Christian education and Adventist missions.

Dr. Andrews' great missionary spirit was expressed by several letters he received at the time of his retirement in 1997. One came from as far away as Uganda and another from a place fifty miles from his home.

One aspect of true missionary work is the "planting of churches." This special gift is evident in Dr. Robert Andrews' life. Not only has he served the church's missionary capacity at "exciting" places like Jamaica, but continues today "planting churches" in communities across North Alabama.

Dr. Andrews and his family came to Guntersville Seventh-day Adventist Church about ten years ago. We were a handful of struggling Adventists, many of us new in the faith, and desperately needing to be spiritually fed.

Dr. Andrews saw our need and used his many, varied gifts. He filled roles such as teacher, pastor, advisor, exhorter, and friend. His wife, Cordelia, helped in the Sabbath School program as superintendent and teacher, as well as, pianist when necessary. And the children have continued in the missionary spirit of their parents. Esther shares her beautiful voice with us when she visits. And Steve and Debbie have recently agreed to come teach the adult class once a month (which has been a true answer to prayer).

On many occasions, Dr. Andrews shared these words with us: "Lord, lay some soul upon my heart, And love that soul through me; And may I do my humble part, To win that soul for thee!"

These words aptly convey the life and times of Dr. Robert Andrews. He has lived by these words every day, as he set an example for others … We know he will never "retire from the Lord's work," and God will richly bless him and his family for the efforts!

Robert and Cordelia Andrews

C. E. Bradford, Lake Region Conference president, extending official welcome to newly ordained Elder and Mrs. Robert Andrews.

Cordelia Andrews and her brothers

Robert Andrews at his ordination to the gospel ministry at the 1963 Lake Region Conference camp meeting with Cordelia and family.

Dr. Robert and Cordelia Andrews and son, Michael

Dr. Robert and Mandy Andrews, June 2013, Huntsville, Alabama

Cordelia Andrews and her daughters: Esther, Deborah, and Karen.

Dr. Robert Andrews and Cordelia Andrews

30

ELYSEE AND ALICE BRANTLEY

1969–1972 / Jamaica

Alice Evelyn Blake was born in Panama on November 22, 1913, the fourth daughter of self-supporting missionary parents, Drs. David and Lottie Blake. A fifth child, a boy, Thomas David Emmanuel Blake, would be born after her. Alice's parents left the United States to serve in Panama and the surrounding area on a self-supporting basis from 1912 to 1916. When they returned to America, her parents started a medical practice in Charleston, West Virginia.

Shortly after arriving in America, her father caught the Spanish flu. With the loving care of his wife, Dr. Lottie Blake, he began to recover. Feeling good, and overestimating his strength, Dr. David Blake returned to his normal work. Malaria had weakened his system in his missionary travels, and shortly he was back in bed. Shockingly, within a few days he was dead.

At the age of three and fatherless, Alice was raised for the next few years by her aunt, Alice Bowman, in Pittsburgh while her mother tried to save the medical practice in Charleston. In the fourth grade she was reunited with her mother and the rest of her family in Columbus, Ohio. She attended East High School in Columbus and graduated at the tender age of sixteen. Alice went to Oakwood College but because of lack of funds she lived off campus and had to walk several miles to school each day—at times hitching a ride with some gracious person seeing her predicament.

She graduated in 1934 and went on to enroll in an elementary education program at Akron University.

Elysee Dillard Brantley was born in Talladega, Alabama, and the family became Adventists when a colporteur sold them a few books. His three older siblings went to Tuskegee and took trades there. Booker T. Washington had advocated the trades. His two brothers became jewelers, and his sister became a nurse. The family moved to Pittsburgh, Pennsylvania, when Alice was living there. Alice was about six years older than Elysee, but she remembered the Brantley family living in Pittsburgh.

Elysee graduated from high school in Detroit and took violin at the Detroit Conservatory of Music. In 1936 Alice and Elysee were married in Fort Bend, Indiana. They connected with one another while Alice was attending Emmanuel Missionary College in the summer.

Elysee learned the principles of electricity at a school in Detroit and began working for Ford Motor Company, which, in those days, was considered an excellent job for a black man. For some time while living in Michigan the family resided on a farm where Elysee had more than forty goats, and the family drank goat's milk regularly, all except Alice.

One day life changed for the family when, while attending a camp meeting, Elysee became convinced that the Lord was calling him to become a literature evangelist. Thus, he quit his job and went into the colporteur ministry. He was very successful in his new literature evangelism program and was called to the Kentucky-Tennessee Conference to be in charge of the publishing work among the colored membership. This was before regional conferences. The family moved to Nashville, Tennessee. Later the family moved to the northeast.

The Brantleys were working in the Northeastern Conference when they got the call to go to West Indies College in Jamaica (Alice's father's birthplace). Elysee was an outstanding literature evangelist and publishing leader. They left from Miami, Florida, on September 15, 1969, for Mandeville, Jamaica. Alice was following in the steps of her parents and going overseas to help where she was needed. At their new post, Brother Brantley was in charge of instrumental music, and Sister Brantley taught in the department of education.

The two Brantleys were quite musical. Alice played the piano and Elysee the violin. They gave performances often, and Alice was always willing to accompany anyone who wanted to sing or play. She was a wonderful Bible worker and agreed to lend her talents by playing for the many evangelists who held tent efforts. She also directed and made recordings of a male chorus. The Brantleys returned to America in 1972.

Alice accepted a call to connect with Oakwood College as principal and instructor at the Anna Knight Elementary School (1972–1979). Much later in her career, during the 1992–1993 school year, she served as assistant principal of the elementary division of Oakwood Academy. For her many years of service as a Christian educator, the school board approved naming the administrative suite of the new elementary building in her honor.

Elysee and Alice volunteered to go back to West Indies College as SOS workers to serve as teachers of music and education at the school they had worked at earlier in their lives.

They left Huntsville on January 4, 1980. They would later accept another SOS call to serve as teachers at Bethel College in South Africa in 1984.

They were parents of five children: three girls, Marion, Marjorie (by his first marriage), and Charlotte; and two boys, Kenneth and Paul. (Alice Brantley had five children and her mother, Dr. Blake, had five children.)

Brother Brantley, born on April 3, 1907, passed away at Oakwood College on October 31, 1993, at eighty-six years of age. Alice was thankful to have her mother's longevity. (Her mother lived to be 100.) But she found out that living a long life demanded lots of courage. She had several falls, one of which left her with a broken hip and some fractures. Less hearty persons would have given up, but her plucky spirit and sense of humor kept her going. Alice celebrated her 100th birthday on November 22, 2013, with a host of family and friends. A few months later, on January 1, 2014, New Year's Day, she passed away at the home of her daughter and son-in-law, Charlotte and James Holmes, M.D., of Stockton, California. I include here a poem written by her daughter Charlotte, which tells her life story quite succinctly and beautifully.

My Mother

by Charlotte Brantley Holmes, 2007

My mother is in size petite,
She's always been quite small,
But viewed through her accomplishments,
I'd say she's rather tall.

When just a little girl of three,
Her loving father died,
Her family had to separate,
And many nights she cried.

When very young she learned to cope,
With things beyond her years,
Determined that she'd live her life
By conquering her fears.

She gave her heart and life to God,
While in her early youth,
She faithfully obeyed her Lord,
And stood up for the truth!

A student very diligent,
With intellect most keen,
From high school she did graduate
When only age sixteen.

A short delay from following
Her goals for education,
She worked two years to give her mother
Needed transportation.

Then on the Oakwood College
To pursue her teaching aims,
Though often lacking food and funds,
Her diploma she did gain.

A dedicated teacher
In classrooms, large and small,
Fashioning young characters
In answer to God's call.

She found her life's companion
When she was twenty-two,
And fifty-seven years remained
A faithful wife and true.

The mother of five children,
Though not all hers by birth,
She tried to love them equally,
And build a sense of worth.

In later life she traveled
To missionary lands,
Continuing to heed God's call
And lend a helping hand.

And so her life continues
To be both rich and full,
Each day lived in the thought that she
Should heed the golden rule.

She counsels all her children,
Her "grands" and "greats" and friends,
Aware that we are living
So very near the end.

How fortunate to have her,
A mother so endowed,
With many, many qualities,
Of which I am most proud!

See selection #8 on Dr. David and Lottie
Blake. Dr. Lottie Blake is the mother of Alice
Brantley.

Elysee and Alice Brantley

Alice Brantley in her nineties

Mrs. Brantley receiving an award for outstanding service at Oakwood Adademy

Alice Brantley in her twenties

31
WILLIAM AND CYNTHIA BURNS

1971–1974; 1985–1988 / Rwanda, Ivory Coast, Ethiopia

Both Cynthia Ruth Giddings and William Lee Burns III had grown up in the mission field. When Dr. and Mrs. Johnny D. Johnson sailed for the mission field on September 4, 1957, on the *SS Queen Mary*, going to Monrovia, Liberia, West Africa, they took Dr. Johnson's nephew, William, with them. They were happy to take the twelve-year-old young man with them because they had no children of their own.

Dr. Johnson was a graduate of Emmanuel Missionary College and the University of Illinois, and he had accepted a call to teach at the Konola Academy in Liberia. After seven years in Liberia, they returned to Africa again following their furlough in 1964 but this time to Ghana.

Ghana holds a special place in the hearts of the Johnsons because after twenty-three years of a childless marriage God blessed them with a daughter, Afriyie. The timing was perfect because in 1965 William returned to the United States from Bekwai, Ghana, for educational reasons.

Elder Philip E. Giddings Jr. and his wife, Violet Blevins Giddings, were pioneer missionaries to Liberia. Elder Giddings spoke fluent French and was the director of education, and Mrs. Giddings was a music teacher and director of the school choir. The choir was one of the best known in all of Liberia. They also served in other French-speaking countries. Elder Giddings parents, Louise Peters and Philip Giddings, were also missionaries. Elder

Giddings died of a heart attack in 1979 and is buried in Nairobi, Kenya. The Giddings had three children: Cynthia and Philip III were born in Liberia, and Don in California. Cynthia Giddings would marry William Burns III, and they would return to Africa as missionaries.

Both William and Cynthia attended Seminaire Adventiste in Collonges, France, although they both graduated from Atlantic Union College (AUC), William in 1971 and Cynthia in 1975.

William never forgot his experiences in Africa as a young man, and he later accepted a call to Africa, saying,

I accepted a call because it has been my personal desire to be a missionary since I first came to Africa at the age of 12 with my uncle and aunt, Dr. and Mrs. J. D. Johnson. When I returned to North America I promised myself that I would return to Africa someday—and I did in 1971. We have since then had the privilege of serving a little more than six years in the Ivory Coast, Rwanda, and Ethiopia.

My degree in modern languages with emphases in French proved to be my ticket to French-speaking Africa. There my eyes were open to the real need for practical education. My students responded enthusiastically to this branch of education.

Would we go again? We are eager to fill the need of African young people for practical skills by returning to mission service to teach industrial arts.[78]

In 1971 William Burns, now grown, married, and with a little daughter, accepted an appointment to work at Kivoga secondary school in Burundi. The call was later changed, and they went to Gitwe College in Rwanda. Brother Burns was a teacher and maintenance supervisor, and Sister Burns taught grades one through eight. When they returned to the States in 1974, they attended Andrews University to get additional training.

Cynthia Burns was happy to speak to the grade school students at the Ruth Murdoch Elementary School close to Andrews University for a special kick-off assembly program. Her color slides of the Gitwe students and campus made her efforts to raise funds for Africa more meaningful. About $900 was raised as a 1975 Christmas gift for Gitwe College.

On September 17, 1985, William and Cynthia and two of their children left San Francisco en route to Africa again—this time to the Ethiopian Adventist College in Ethiopia. As with one of their present posts, William served as maintenance engineer and industrial education teacher, and Cynthia taught in the elementary school, grades one through eight.

Mr. and Mrs. John Johnson and twelve-year-old William Burns waving farewell from the ship that took them to Liberia.

The Burns family was featured in the Sabbath School program of the Idlewild SDA Church in Michigan after they returned from Ethiopia: (left to right) Bill Burns, Vileeta, Cynthia Burns, Billy, and Mark.

78. "Special People," *Adventist Review*, August 10, 1989, p. 23.

32

JOSEPH AND ELMYRE CHERENFANT

1972–1978 / Ivory Coast; 1979–1982 / Togo; 1983–1986 / Cameroon

The Cherenfants are originally from Haiti. From an early age they were taught to love God, love family, and love others. Joseph Michelet Cherenfant, son of a pastor, completed his studies at the seminary in 1948 and then served as district leader in Plaisance, Haiti, until he was called to head the work of the departments in the South Haiti Mission in 1961.

January 31, 1961, was a big day for the district of Plaisance, Haiti. A great baptismal service took place on that date under the leadership of Pastor C. L. Powers, Franco Haitian Union president. Spectators gathered on both sides of the river. Sixty-six precious souls were baptized in the name of the Father, the Son, and the Holy Ghost. It was the zealous spirit of young Joseph Michelet Cherenfant who, during 1960 (not yet ordained), brought more than 150 souls in baptism.

On January 9, 1963, in the South Haiti Mission, Joseph, already departmental secretary, was ordained to the gospel ministry. Pastor Monier prayed that the Holy Spirit would completely possess this new minister and there was hardly a dry eye in the audience when veteran worker Pastor Maxi Cherenfant had the honor of giving the pastoral charge to his son.

If you were to ask Pastor Maxi Cherenfant, a centurion evangelist who regularly baptized more than 200 souls each year, "What is the secret of your success? Tell me about your evangelistic campaigns," he would answer simply, "I prefer to talk about my lay preachers and the work of the 1,200 baptized members in my district. It is because of their work that I baptized 208 souls last year. For ten years I have baptized an average of more than 200 souls each year, and I have never found a better method than that of using the enormous potential of the laymen."

In 1972, armed with his father's philosophy of soul winning and a great faith in God, Joseph accepted a call to serve as an evangelist in the Ivory Coast in the city of Daloa. Although the French work in Africa was difficult, God blessed Pastor Cherenfant with many souls. The family was also increasing. Before their term of service was over, their family totaled six members: four sons, Andre, Elihu, Emec, and Michelet Jr., and two daughters, Urnia and Myrna. Each member of the family loved to sing, and they would often draw a crowd with their beautiful harmonies.

The People's Republic of Benin experienced a special and thrilling occasion when Pastor Cherenfant, his wife, and two of his children and the Togolese Voice of Prophecy Quartet and some local visitors came to the house of worship in Cotonou on Sabbath, June 23, 1979.

Members started arriving at 7:00 a.m. and stayed right through to 2:30 p.m. Pastor Cherenfant preached about the significance of baptism by immersion and then the congregation made their way to the ocean.

Beach lovers and a small crowd from a nearby village looked on as one by one, the new persons in Christ, sealed their commitment to their Lord and Savior. Following the baptismal ceremony, a communion service united the new members with their brothers and sisters and a warm bond of Christian fellowship. In the early afternoon Cotonou's twenty-three baptized members were ready to proceed with a much appreciated church business session that was to organize themselves into a company and later into a full church organization.

One person who was happy to be baptized was Avognon Firmin, a former school teacher, and father of a family of seven children. He had left the classroom for the office because his health was beginning to deteriorate. While undergoing medical treatment for physical and mental exhaustion, Avognon began his quest for inner peace and serenity. Somehow he became convinced that in order to regain his overall equilibrium he needed Christ in his life.

The first church to which he belonged with the rest of his relatives could not satisfy a genuine spiritual hunger. For a while some people who claimed to know God's truth studied with him in his home. Soon he and his family discovered the inconsistencies in their teachings. Next, he tried one of the popular Christian groups in the area that emphasized the gifts of the Spirit. However, the noise during the church services and the impossibility engaging a reasoned discussion with the leadership on biblical topics gradually drove him away from that congregation where he had become a leader himself.

Avognon felt the only option left was to stay at home and worship God alone with his family, although he was seriously considering the advice of his friends to join a church. But which one? None had appealed to his mind and heart.

In this reflecting mood, Avognon was at the beach one day when he heard someone calling, "Pastor, pastor!" He looked around and saw a young man greeting another rather small young man who had come to the beach with his wife for a moment of relaxation. That couple was none other than Pastor Cherenfant and his wife. Avognon's curiosity was aroused. He

approached them and shortly afterwards, a most gratifying relationship developed between him and the missionaries.

From then on, you could be sure to see Avognon attending every church meeting. He quickly completed the French Bible correspondence course with top grades. Being an avid reader, he read every book and magazine given to him. Home Bible studies reinforced and complemented his religious instruction.

Each time he was introduced to a new fundamental Bible truth, he responded positively. He gladly returned an honest tithe to the Lord, which amounted to about ten times as much as most baptized members. He thus frequently testified to God's marvelous blessings.

Six months later, after overcoming, by God's grace, many an obstacle, Avognon was immersed in the warm waters of the ocean. Today Avognon is actively participating in witnessing to other about the difference that God and the Adventist Church have made in his life. He is a leader in the church and intends to follow Christ all the way.

In September of 1982 Joseph and his family returned to Africa after a short furlough, but this time he came back to the continent to serve as president of the East Cameroon Conference. In 1987, after a long missionary career, he moved back to Haiti and accepted the position of president of the North Haiti Mission.

Elmyre Laurent Cherenfant has passed away, but her husband lives in the States and continues to raise funds for Haitian and African students and for other projects in these countries.

Joseph Michelet and Elmyre Cherenfant

Pastor Cherenfant in his later years

Thirteen new members were added to the church in a baptism ceremony in Ivory Coast. Pastor Michelet Cherenfant is wearing a dark suit.

The four sons in the Cherenfant family

Elder Cherenfant with his daughter

33

ROLAND AND SOLANGE JOACHIM

1973–1996 / Ivory Coast, Burkina Faso, Senegal, Cameroon, Ghana

Roland L. Joachim and his wife, Solange, are both originally from Haiti, and their native language is French. The French work in Africa was suffering because of a lack of good French-speaking pastors, teachers, and French materials.

In 1973 at the end of their studies in France at Collonges-sous-Salève, they received a call to go to Collège Adventiste de Bouaké. This high school is located about 250 miles north of Abidjan, the capital city of Côte d'Ivoire. In 1974 the high school had an enrollment of 475 and a staff of fifteen (mostly missionaries from France, Belgium, the United States, and Haiti). The students were 3 percent Adventists, 30 percent Catholics, 10 percent Protestants, 57 percent Muslims, and others.

One of the objectives of the Bouaké School was to prepare ministers for the Adventist Church in Côte d'Ivoire and for the French-speaking countries of West Africa. This was not an easy task, especially when French educated teachers were rare, and when the constituency didn't have one thousand members yet. Unfortunately, the seminary students had no place to stay unless in the dormitory with the high school students.

As principal, Mr. Joachim and his dedicated staff began an extensive expansion program.

During this period, and administration unit, additional classrooms, a new elementary school building, and the boys' dormitory were erected.

In 1976 Mr. Joachim presented Mana Yao Lambert of Côte d'Ivoire and Agbodza Félix of Togo, the first two graduates of the Adventist Seminary in Bouaké, Côte d'Ivoire, with their diplomas after three years of theological studies. The two graduates were put to work in their respective countries as evangelists. The seminary, the only French-speaking one of its kind in the West African Union, opened in 1973/1974 as a necessary branch of the secondary school that had existed since 1958. It was a modest beginning but soon more graduated and began spreading the gospel in French-speaking West Africa.

Elder Joachim was ordained to the gospel ministry at a camp meeting in 1977. From 1978 to 1981 he served as the president of the Adventist mission in Burkina Faso. This "country of honest people," as its name implies, remains a poverty-stricken Sahel country.

In 1981 they returned to the states where Roland attended Andrews University and completed the requirements for his doctoral degree in 1984 and received his degree in 1985. The rest of the family had already returned to Sénégal in November 1984. In November 1985 Dr. Joachim became president of the Central African Union with its headquarters in Cameroon. Five years later, after that term, he became special assistant to the president and field secretary for the Africa-Indian Ocean Division located in Abidjan, Côte d'Ivoire.

Once while Roland Joachim, then division field secretary, was traveling with Leo Ranzolin, the General Conference youth director, and J. J. Nortey, the division president, in Togo, an uprising forced them and several church workers to be confined to their hotel rooms in the country's capital, Lomé. By November 28, borders, airports, and inner-city transportation were shut down and overseas communication was cut off.

By listening to the news via the BBC and Voice of America, they were able to follow what was happening. These men spent much of Thanksgiving Day praying and reading their Bible and *Steps to Christ* in their rooms.

On Sunday morning after eight o'clock, Ranzolin and Joachim went to the airport and found it open with a plane about to arrive. They notified other workers and five of them managed to board the only plane to leave Togo that week. They later learned that the airport was closed again half an hour after their departure. They had asked for God's blessings and protection, and God was faithful to His promises.

The Joachims remained in Abidjan until 1992. From then until 1996, they served in Ghana where Roland was Valley View College (now University) president, and later dean and translator of materials for the newborn Adventist University Cosendai, now a fully-fledged university in Cameroon.

The Joachims have six children and are now living in Loma Linda, California.

Roland Joachim, principal of the seminary in the Ivory Coast, at his ordination service. He stands with his wife, Solange, and Pastor Jean-Jacques Bouit, president of the Ivory Coast Mission.

The Adventist College and Seminary, Bouake, Ivory Coast, in 1973.

In 1976 Mr. Joachim (right) presented Mana Yao Lambert of Côte d'Ivoire and Agbodza Félix of Togo, the first two graduates of the Adventist Seminary in Bouaké, Côte d'Ivoire, with their diplomas after three years of theological studies.

34

EARL AND ANN RICHARDS

1973–1985 / Kenya

Edward Earl Richards' parents were natives of Jamaica, West Indies, but they moved to New York City before Earl was born. Earl grew up in New York, and in 1950 he graduated from Greater New York Academy. From there he went to Atlantic Union College where he completed four years of pre-dental college work. While there he served as president of the Science Forum and of the Phi Delta Chi fraternity. He graduated in the spring of 1954 and received his acceptance to Loma Linda University where he graduated in the second class of the newly created dental college.

Dr. Richards is married to the former Ann C. Smart, a registered nurse from Augusta, Georgia. They have three children: Earl, Andre, and Joi.

Upon completing his degree, Dr. Richards moved to Atlanta and practiced dentistry for eight years. Besides his private practice, he worked with the Fulton County Health Department providing dental examinations and medications for underprivileged individuals. In 1966 he received a grant from the United States Public Health Service and attended the University of Michigan where he received a master's degree in public health.

He did a residency in dental public health service in Frankfurt, Kentucky, and finished a residency with the Georgia Department of Public Health in the spring of 1968. At that time he was chosen to serve as director of the dental service for the Equal Opportunity Office of Atlanta.

In the midst of all these career changes, he did not forget the church. He served as dental secretary of the South Atlantic Conference, local elder of the Atlanta-Berean church, and Sabbath school chorister. From 1962 to 1964 he served as pastor of the Mount Olives Athens, Georgia, church, and from 1964 to 1966 as pastor of the Bethany Rome, Georgia, church.

Dr. Richards shared his story with the readers of *Southern Tidings*:

It all started when I was a young boy. My father was a preacher and my uncle a doctor. I admired both of them and wanted to be like both of them. In the adolescent years of my life, I was seized with an overwhelming impression that I ought to dedicate myself and my life to the gospel ministry. Pride, ambition, and rebellion gained the ascendancy, and I decided to study dentistry. I wanted to be "somebody"—and to be independent. I pacified my conscience with the self-assurance that I would use my success as a dentist to the glory of God.

My acceptance into the second class of Loma Linda University School of Dentistry was a glorious experience. I was awarded the Doctor of Dental Surgery Degree in 1958.

After an intense internal struggle, I accepted an invitation to the South Atlantic Conference to practice dentistry in Atlanta, Georgia.

Fourteen rewarding years, one lovely wife and three children later my impression has crystallized into the realization that my decision was in harmony with the will and purpose of the Omniscient One.

In 1966, after eight years of private practice to a predominantly affluent clientele, I became disillusioned. My disillusionment arose out of a failure to achieve spiritual fulfillment in my professional activities. Taking advantage of what I saw as an opportunity to enhance my witness, I pursue and obtained a Master's degree in public health from the University of Michigan in 1967.

For five additional years in the area of community health, I ministered to the needs of the poor and disadvantaged. I did achieve a modicum of conscience easement, but the Holy Spirit would not allow complete relief from the sense of the lack of complete spiritual fulfillment. At last I could fight no longer.

One Wednesday in late June, 1972, after a series of vexing episodes, I fell to my knees behind the closed doors of my office, begged the Lord to reveal Himself to me, and to show me what He would have me do. As I rose from my knees an overpowering impression led me to seek immediate counsel from Elder R. L. Woodfork, president of the South Atlantic Conference. After a reassuring 40-minute audience, we had prayer. Then he said, "Doctor, let's ask the Lord for a definite sign."

I shared my impression with my wife and we decided to attend prayer meeting that night. The meeting included the usual request-for-prayer season. Without revealing the nature of the matter, I asked the church to pray for me as I faced a crisis in my life. The meeting ended; my wife and I made our way forward to greet the pastor, Elder Taylor.

I was stunned almost into fright when, instead of taking my outstretched hand, he shook his finger and with penetrating eyes and voice said to me, "the Lord has something else for you to do. I do not know what it is, but I have been impressed to tell you so!"

The following week found us on a long-awaited Jamaican family vacation. While there I shared with my dad, a retired minister, our unusual experience, and together we prayed about it. He expressed the hope that perhaps the Lord wanted us on that Island. Because of my love for Jamaica, I too shared his hope. However, I seemed to receive the impression that the Lord had something else in mind.

We returned to Atlanta on July 17 and there, to our utter amazement, was a week-old cable from Elder C. D. Henri, president of the East African Union, inviting us to consider a mission appointment in Nairobi, Kenya.

No one can convince Ann and me but that this entire experience is a modern-day miracle, an unquestionable revelation from God, a direct and divine call. We dared not refuse, lest we grieve the Holy Spirit.[79]

79. Ernestine Mann, "Appointment to Nairobi, Kenya." Southern Tidings, March 1972, pp. 6, 7.

The family left New York City on March 25, 1973. Once in Nairobi, Kenya, Dr. Richards developed a practice that was so successful that the leaders felt they needed to call a second dentist. His practice was made up of ambassadors from many nations, government officials, and businessman, both black and white, located in that bustling metropolitan area.

There were a large number of Adventist young people attending the University of Nairobi, and Dr. Richards served as their chaplain. He held a series of evangelistic meetings at the university, and many of the young people took their stand for Christ. He conducted a large baptismal class at the main church on Sabbath that met at the close of the 11 o'clock hour. In his first two years in Nairobi, fourteen people were baptized as a direct result of his labors.

A Better Living Center was procured in Nairobi, and it quickly became well known for its efforts to help people stop smoking. Drs. Richards and Kenneth Bushnell joined forces to conduct the Five-Day Plans to Stop Smoking.

V. Rajani, a Hindu, smoked heavily. He came across a small advertisement in the *Daily Nation* newspaper advertising the first Five-Day Plan to Stop Smoking to be held in the new Better Living Center. He attended, lost his forty-a-day cigarette habit and gained a whole new set of insights. He wanted to help advertise the next session.

Instead of the usual few lines in the *Daily Nation* that the Temperance Department had been able to afford, Mr. Rajani financed a succession of large display ads in strategic places, such as the back page of the sports section. The Better Living Center and Five-Day Plan to Stop Smoking began to be well known in downtown Nairobi. The result was a quadrupling of the routine attendance at the monthly meetings.

Besides, Mr. Rajani escorted several Hindu business friends into the opening session.

At the next session he strategically placed display ads, but he also interspersed primetime television programs with commercials recommending the group therapy sessions at the Better Living Center.

The outcome of this lavish and most effective promotion was one of the brightest, best, and largest Five-Day Plans to Stop Smoking campaign ever held in the Kenyan capital. Among the seventy or so people attending were Kenyans, Asians, and European business executives and diplomatic corps members of varying religious backgrounds from Buddhists to Muslims to Hindus. (Mr. Rajani brought six of his Hindu friends.) The assembly was a fair representation of the upper echelons of Nairobi's civic, professional, and business community.[80]

At the time of their appointment to Kenya: Ann Richards, Joi (seated), Earl Jr. (left), Andre (far right), and Dr. E. Earl Richards.

---

80. Jack Mahon, "Better Living Center Lights Up," *Adventist Review*, August 9, 1979, p. 20.

35

ALFONZO AND ESTELLA GREENE

1974–1977 / Jamaica

Alfonzo Greene and his twin sister Alean were born in Candor, North Carolina, on August 20, 1926, and were raised by their grandparents, Columbus (the son of slaves) and Emma Greene.

Alfonzo had a natural gift for business, a skill he developed while growing up with his grandfather who owned and operated the Community General Store, a cotton gin, and a family farm. In his early years he tried his hand at constructing a chicken coop for his grandfather. By the age of nine he was managing the family farm himself. Later, while in high school he received certification as a welder through the National Youth Administration and obtained a job welding on Navy ships.

Alfonzo's family was quite active in the Congregational Church (United Church of Christ). His grandparents believed that all Christians should abstain from alcohol and tobacco. He was taught to work hard, respect others, and to conduct his affairs with integrity and honesty. Every Sunday afternoon at the Dry Creek Community Church vespers, the family would sing the Temperance Song: "Away with whiskey, tobacco no more. It robs me of money and I was poor enough before. I despise the filthy weed, I will chew and smoke no more … As long as I call myself a Christian."

After graduating from high school, he pursued a career in the insurance industry where he worked for the National Accident and Health Insurance Company. He was so successful in the insurance business that it was not long before he started Greene Insurance Agency in Charlotte, North Carolina. His business flourished.

After reading a number of pamphlets and books on the Sabbath, Alfonzo joined the Seventh-day Adventist Church in Fayetteville, North Carolina. Soon after joining the Seventh-day Adventist Church he met and began to date Estella Gully, a 1949 Oakwood College graduate and conference Bible instructor.

On October 14, 1951, Estella Gully and Alfonzo Greene were married. Soon afterwards they moved to Berrien Springs, Michigan, where Alfonzo Greene completed his bachelor's degree in business administration at Andrews University.

After graduating Mr. Greene accepted a call to manage the Oakwood College Market and Bookstore where he worked from 1962 to 1965.

Desiring to further his quest of knowledge, he moved back to Michigan, where he completed his master's degree in business administration. At this time Estella also went back to school, attending Western Michigan University, where she completed her master's degree in reading. Upon completion of his degree, Greene returned to Oakwood to teach in the Business Department where he taught until 1970.

After leaving Oakwood, Professor Green returned to Michigan and taught in the Benton Harbor Area School Systems and at Lake Michigan College until receiving a call from the General Conference to teach at West Indies College (Northern Caribbean University) in Mandeville, Jamaica.

They were not so certain that they should accept the call. Elder Fletcher, the president, came to their house in January for dinner and spoke to them about the college and its needs. They first thought about their four children. Fred was in the eighth grade and Crystal was in the eleventh grade. Alfonzo Jr. was at Oakwood, and Anthony at Andrews University. The two oldest children were doing well in college, and they didn't want to disrupt their schooling, so they decided that if they went they would only take the two youngest children.

They were still somewhat reluctant about going, but decided to make the issue a matter of prayer. Mrs. Greene especially was not sure they should go. She asked God to do something that she says she will never do again. I prayed, "Please let something happen today that will let me know that the Holy Spirit has intervened to keep me alive."

On that very day while going to work in her car, she noticed a man following her in a semi-truck, and he was drinking. She decided to pull off the road and let him pass. But when she pulled off the road, he pulled off the road right behind her and crashed into her vehicle, causing her back wheels to roll off. Her car was completely demolished. Fortunately, there were police close by, and they quickly pulled her out for they were afraid the car might explode at any minute and rushed her to the hospital. The doctors put her on two weeks total rest, and her body recovered. There is a big knot on her head and foot even today from the incident.

She knew that the Holy Spirit had intervened to save her life, and she was ready to go. In spite of that, they asked to make a special trip to look at the living conditions in Jamaica the summer before they left. While visiting she discovered that her next door neighbor would be her good friend Cordelia Andrews, whom she had known since childhood. She also knew the Jackson family and was glad to find out they were there at the college. She considered this to also be signs of God's leading.

With his wife and two youngest children (Fred and Crystal), they left Miami, Florida, on September 12, 1974. Getting out of the Jamaican airport was a difficult job for them. The customs officials told them they must have round trip tickets before they would let them in the county. But they only had a one-way ticket. Mrs. Greene sent Fred to tell Brother Samuel Jackson, who was supposed to meet then, that they couldn't get through customs since they did not have round trip tickets.

Little Fred waved a homemade sign at the window, but Brother Jackson didn't see it. She then told Fred to stand with another couple that had passed customs who had several children and act as if he belonged with them and he got through. He went to Brother Jackson and told them their plight. Brother Jackson knew the officials and told them they were connected with the school. They were required to give the number of their American Express credit card and let them know that a round trip ticket was pending to be purchased. The officials then let them through customs. Estella had to go back to the States on Monday and get her visa and purchase the tickets.

Estella Greene says that the principal wanted her to teach first and second grades, each having about fifty-six students. She thought the classes were far too large and she let it be known that she didn't want to teach these large classes, especially since she was new in Jamaica. The word got around that she didn't want to teach the classes. Brother Samuel Jackson was also on the staff as a teacher of music. Sister Greene and Sister Sarah Jackson would go up into the mountains each morning and pray. She asked God to help her with this situation. School was to start that Monday, and since she was traveling, the principal gave the job to someone else. The problem was solved.

As they got settled, Estella visited the laundry one day and saw the kids washing sheets with a washboard. Joan Thomas was in charge of the laundry, and she talked to Estella about the situation. Mrs. Greene wrote back to her friends in Michigan and got them to donate six washing machines. When the washing machines arrived, all of them did not go to the laundry. They wanted to put two in the kitchen and two in the girls' dorm, and the laundry ended up with only two.

Mrs. Greene held a degree in religion, and when the religion teacher left, she was asked to teach Bible and Christian beliefs. The class had 150 students. She was the first female to teach religion at West Indies College. At first the students were very unkind to her because they had never had a woman teacher in religion. Sister Greene and Sister Jackson continued to go up to the mountains every day to pray.

When the seniors went on their annual retreat six weeks after school started, Elder Campbell and Elder Boyd asked her to be in charge of the students and get the students to clean up the cabins and the campus since the person who normally had this responsibility was sick and unable to be there.

She gave the students numbers and those who had "one" worked in the kitchen, "two" on the grounds, and "three" cleaning the cabinets.

The students didn't like these assignments and started to complain. She showed them how to put a nail on a stick to pick up the paper. The boys didn't want to peel the potatoes, but she showed them how to do the job quickly. Pretty soon the work was finished, and they were getting along fine.

Estella then had to make nut patties from scratch with no recipe, which she had never made in her life. Not knowing where to start, she went into the bathroom and prayed. "Teach me how to make them today." God gave her wisdom, and when she was finished, the cashew patties looked like chicken and tasted like chicken. The Lord helped her out.

The sun was getting ready to set, and the Sabbath was about to begin, and dinner and breakfast were all ready. When Elder Campbell came in and saw that all of the cleaning was done and the meals were all ready, he picked her up and shouted, "Thank God for American women!" Her husband and the rest of the students came up for Sabbath. From then on the students were her friends.

The Wednesday before Thanksgiving, Alfonzo came in and the following dialogue took place between the two of them:

"I need to talk to you."

"What?" Estella asked.

"I think we are going to take our savings and pay the General Conference back for moving us down here. I don't think I can take any more of this." His office overlooked a vacant lot and there was no greenery or shrubbery. "This is not working for me at all."

Estella started laughing.

"Please don't laugh," he said.

"You have been telling everybody that you men have adjusted and us ladies are having trouble adjusting. And now you're telling me that you want to go." She continued laughing.

Then he started laughing.

They talked and prayed and waited a little longer and the problems went away. Estella fixed a nice Thanksgiving dinner, and they had a houseful of their friends and fellow professors over. Alfonzo taught business and did workshops all over the island.

While living in Jamaica, Alfonzo became sick and was diagnosed with diabetes. He changed his diet, but later he still had to take insulin.

Professor Greene served his three and a half year commitment there as professor in business administration, and then the family returned to Michigan in 1977 where he again taught business administration at Lake Michigan College until accepting the position of business manager at Lynwood Academy in Los Angeles, California.

Longing to be in the classroom where he could stimulate, challenge, and motivate the minds of his students, Professor Greene left Lynwood Academy to accept a professorship at Kentucky State University where he served from 1978 to 1992 with two brief interruptions in service. From 1980 to 1981 Greene was a visiting professor at Livingston College in Salisbury, North Carolina, where he helped to stabilize the fledgling Business Department. From 1985 to 1986 he was chair of the Business Department at Columbia Union College.

In 1985 Greene completed his doctorate degree in in management at the International Business School. In 1992 Dr. Greene returned to Oakwood College where he taught business until his retirement at the end of 1994.

Dr. Greene was a licensed builder in Michigan for more than fifty years and built homes for many of his colleagues and professional associates in Kentucky, Michigan, and Alabama.

The Greenes loved Oakwood University and moved there in their retirement. Alfonzo and his wife worked tirelessly to raise thousands of dollars of scholarship funds for worthy students. He served as president of Oakwood University's J. L. Moran Alumni Association and regional vice president for the Oakwood University National Alumni Association. All four of their children spent their entire grade school, high school, and early college years in Adventist schools.

In September 2011 just before their sixtieth wedding anniversary in October, Alfonzo got very sick, and the doctor said he would be dead in three days. When the doctors found out that they were that close to their anniversary, they began to research and found one thing they could try, and it worked for about six months. About 1,000 people attended their special anniversary celebration at the Oakwood College Church. Alfonzo was sick for seven months after the anniversary. Dr. Alfonzo Greene passed away on May 18, 2012, in Huntsville, Alabama, where his wife still lives.

Dr. Alfonzo and Estella Greene

36

MORRIS AND SHIRLEY IHEANACHO

1975–79 / Nigeria

The following account was written by Shirley Iheanacho:

My name is Shirley C. Iheanacho, wife of Morris A. Iheanacho. I was born on the beautiful island of Barbados. At the completion of high school, I attended Caribbean Union College (now The University of Southern Caribbean, Trinidad) where I received my diploma in secretarial science. I began my professional career at my alma mater and later at the Port-of- Spain Adventist Community Hospital, for a total of four years before I could save the $1,000 deposit required of international students before entrance in a school in the United States. In 1965 I enrolled at Andrews University and received my bachelor of science degree in 1968. After graduation I accepted a position as secretary to the chair of the Department of Pediatrics at Howard University in Washington, D.C.

It was during my matriculation at Andrews University that I met Morris, the love of my life. In 1969 we were married in Washington, D.C., at First SDA Church, where Luther Palmer served as the pastor. After our honeymoon, I moved to Kalamazoo, Michigan, because Morris was pursuing his master's degree in library science at Western Michigan University. I was blessed to be hired as secretary to the

administrator for the Kalamazoo County Board of Supervisors until the summer of 1970 when Morris was awarded a master's degree in librarianship. He accepted the position of librarian with the state of Michigan, and we moved to Ionia a week after our first child was born. Several months later I accepted the position as secretary at the Ionia Community Hospital and remained in that position until our departure for Nigeria.

In the fall of 1975 Morris accepted a call to return to Nigeria, and I was invited to teach secretarial science courses. In addition to teaching, I taught children's Sabbath School, and sang in the choir and for weddings and special events.

Morris A. Iheanacho was born in east Nigeria. He attended the Adventist College of West Africa and graduated with a diploma in theology. Later he attended Newbold College in England where he received his diploma in theology and history and was awarded a bachelor's degree from Columbia Union College because of Newbold's affiliation with CUC. Morris served as a pastor for a number of years and was privileged to be the translator for the late Pastor C. D. Henri when he conducted evangelistic meetings in east Nigeria. He also assisted with evangelistic meetings conducted by the late Elder E. E. Cleveland in Accra, Ghana.

In 1967 he attended Andrews University, and later Western Michigan University where he earned a master's degree in librarianship in August 1970. He began his professional career as a librarian a few months later at the Michigan Training Unit in Ionia, Michigan.

It was a beautiful fall day in 1975 when he received a call from Dr. Richard Hammill, president of Andrews University at the time, inviting him to head the library at the Adventist Seminary of West Africa in Nigeria (now Babcock University). The college was seeking affiliation with Andrews University and desperately needed a professional librarian. Morris was reluctant to accept the call and presented many reasons why he couldn't— the main one was the sale of our house. He proceeded to list it for sale but didn't expect it to sell because other houses in the neighborhood, which had been on the market for several months, were unsold.

Several weeks passed without a buyer. He contacted Dr. Hammill and informed him of his dilemma. Dr. Hammill assigned Dr. Joseph Smoot, the vice president for academic affairs at Andrews University, to work with Morris in the transition. Dr. Smoot was informed of the house situation, and he arranged for Dr. Wilson Trickett, a business professor at Andrews University and a realtor, to travel to Ionia to market our house. He came, looked it over, expressed that it was a lovely house and that we shouldn't have difficulty finding a buyer, and proceeded to list it in the newspaper. Before returning to Berrien Springs, he prayed that God would bless our family and our house. By

mid-week we received an offer and our house was sold. God removed the obstacles, leaving Morris without valid reasons not to go.

With the sale of our house completed and household goods shipped, our family (including our two daughters, Ngozi, age five, and Chioma, age three) said goodbye to our church family and friends in Ionia and traveled to Washington, D.C., to visit with family and friends before departing for Nigeria. Late in December 1975, we arrived safely on the campus of the Adventist Seminary of West Africa. The house to which we were assigned was not ready so we stayed in a one-bedroom duplex until it was completed and our goods arrived from the United States.

In a short time our family settled in and adjusted to our new environment. Ngozi attended a private school several miles away; however, Chioma remained at home. In the fall of 1976 Ngozi was permitted to attend the school on campus for the children of missionaries, which was located within walking distance from our house. Chioma attended the same school when she reached the age of five.

Daily, Morris worked untiringly to upgrade the library. In addition to his library responsibilities, he taught history courses and served as church treasurer.

In December 1977 God answered my mother-in-law's prayer for more grandchildren and a beautiful baby girl was born. Morris named her Akunna (father's treasure). His mother was overjoyed and gave her the special name of Akunne meaning mother's treasure. After the delivery I experienced a life-threatening ordeal—the placenta refused to come out although the nurse tried to remove it manually. Earlier when we arrived at the hospital my husband mentioned to the nurse that the doctor wanted her to call him as soon as we arrived; however, she refused. By this time I was in excruciating pain and could feel my delivery gown soaked with blood all the way up my back.

Morris was present during the delivery and couldn't tolerate what was happening. He shouted to the nurse to call the doctor that his wife was bleeding to death. She did and the doctor came hurriedly. He ordered her to check my pressure, pulse, and a host of other things. Finally, he was able to remove the placenta. Afterwards the nurse told me to return to my room; however, when I tried to stand up I was dizzy and very weak. The doctor instructed her to get a wheel chair and she wheeled me back to my room. Later I overheard her tell a nurse that I had lost a lot of blood and was very weak. This was my most traumatic experience living in Nigeria. I am eternally grateful to God for saving me from the jaws of death.

I cherish fond memories of four wonderful years on the campus of the Adventist Seminary of West Africa, as well as visiting and spending time with my mother-in-law and other family members in east Nigeria. Our children enjoyed the time spent in Nigeria and often refer to it as their best childhood days.

At the time we arrived in Nigeria, the political situation was pretty stable; however, a few months later Murtala Muhammed, head of the Federal Military Government of Nigeria, was shot. This sent shock waves throughout the country, including our campus. Although

his assassination created deep sadness and much concern as to what would happen next, at no time were we in jeopardy. We thank God for His loving care and protection.

In the summer of 1979 Dr. Calvin Rock, president of Oakwood College, and his wife, Clara, visited several West African countries, including Nigeria. It was during this visit that Morris first met the Rocks. He had the honor of escorting them on their tour of the campus. Nearing the end of the tour, Morris casually mentioned that he was planning to return to the United States in December to work for the state of Michigan. Dr. Rock extended the invitation for him to work at Oakwood instead. He told him: "If you want to work for Caesar, you can go to work for the state of Michigan; but if you want to work for the Lord, you should come to Oakwood." Working at Oakwood College was not in Morris' plan so he did not accept Dr. Rock's offer at the time.

In December of 1979 plans were in place to return to the States; however, we were faced with an enormous hurdle—our American car was still not sold, causing us many anxious moments. Morris decided to leave it for a friend to sell. Here again God intervened on our behalf. A few hours before our departure from the campus, He provided a buyer with cash. We were ecstatic and thanked Him profusely for His wonderful miracle.

The following evening we arrived at the airport and again came face to face with another obstacle. My Nigerian visa had expired in November, and since we were planning to return to the United States in December, we didn't think it was necessary to renew it. Standing at the check-in counter, the officer informed me that I could not leave the country because my visa had expired and that I was in the country illegally. We were shocked and pleaded with him to let me leave. He refused and insisted that I had to obtain a new visa, which would probably take several weeks if not months. Silently, we prayed for God to provide a way for us to leave together as we waited with bated breath. Quietly, Philemon Onwere, Morris' relative and colleague, went to the side of the counter and secretly handed him some cash. Immediately, he stamped my passport, and we were able to leave together. We thank God for answering one more prayer on our behalf.

Sometimes we may make the best of plans for ourselves, but God, the All-knowing One, can turn us around and send us in another direction before we realize it. And that's what happened. When we returned to the States, we stayed with family in Washington, D.C., awaiting the official letter of employment from the State of Michigan, which took longer than Morris anticipated. In the meantime he decided to accept Dr. Rock's invitation to come to Oakwood for an interview. He was offered the position of catalog librarian, which he accepted. The following day after returning to Washington to get us, he received the official letter of employment from the State of Michigan. It came a day too late. God had overruled, and Morris was blessed to serve at Oakwood University for twenty-eight years until his retirement in 2007.

Since his retirement he has continued his dream of global outreach ministries and has assisted Maranatha volunteers in building two churches in Mucatine and Celula 5, Mozambique. I led out with VBS in these two

villages. In October 2013 we again teamed up with twenty-five Maranatha volunteers to build a twelve-classroom elementary school in Tamale, Ghana. I assisted with VBS in three villages as well as sang and preached at the Kaphonin Estates SDA Church.

In a conversation with a local pastor, we learned that he had recently conducted an evangelistic meeting and baptized seventy-five new members, an increase from twenty-five. His challenge was lack of seating to accommodate the new members and their families. Together we were impressed to assist in this worthy cause and contributed money to purchase thirty benches.

Both of these global outreach experiences have not only been life-changing, enriching, spiritually fulfilling, and rewarding, but we have experienced God's miracle-working power in spectacular ways.

After our return to the United States, I got a job at Alabama A&M University. I worked there for two years before I received a call from Dr. Calvin Rock on a rainy evening in January 1982 offering me the position of secretary in the office of the president at Oakwood College. I was delighted and surprised. I have had the unique experience of not only working for Dr. Rock but for three additional presidents over a span of twenty years—the longest period in the history of the president's office for a secretary/ administrative assistant. During my last six years I served as administrative assistant to Dr. Mervyn A. Warren, provost and senior vice president. In 2007 I retired, bringing to a close twenty-six incredible years of employment at Oakwood University.

I'm still amazed at the way God has so lavishly blessed my husband to complete a total of forty-three years of denominational service and myself thirty-four years. He blessed our daughters as well. Ngozi is a pediatric anesthetist at a children's hospital in Georgia; Chioma is a project manager at one of the world's largest computer companies; and our Nigerian-born Akunna has completed the requirements for the doctor of philosophy degree in cellular and molecular physiology at The Johns Hopkins University School of Medicine in Baltimore, Maryland. My God is an awesome God, and we give Him all glory, honor, and praise. Great and marvelous things He has done!

As I reflect upon my life, one of my favorite Bible verses comes to mind of which I have been the beneficiary. It's found in Jeremiah 29:11: "For I know the plans I have for you; plans to prosper you and not to harm you, plans to give you hope and a future."

Growing up as a youngster in Barbados, never in my wildest imagination did I think that God had such beautiful and magnificent plans for me. Today He still continues to bless me to touch lives around the world through my writing ministry and devotional articles published in numerous General Conference women's devotional books and other church-related journals. Words are inadequate to express my joy and gratitude for all His many incredible blessings and miracles and the opportunities He continues to provide for us to serve Him and to encourage fellow travelers on our journey to the kingdom. The lyrics to a song written by Alma Bazel Androzzo back in 1945 come to mind: "If I can help somebody as I pass along then my living shall not be in vain."

God has blessed Morris to be able to provide scholarships and other financial assistance to family members and young people in Nigeria and other countries to help them improve themselves academically and to live more productive and fulfilling lives.

Morris and Shirley continue their weekly ministry of visiting the sick and shut-in at nursing homes, inviting students to their home for Sabbath lunch, providing scholarship assistance to worthy students at Oakwood University and abroad, and serving as elders at the Oakwood University Church. They are thankful to God for the opportunity to serve in their local community and in distant lands, and they give Him the glory for the marvelous things He has done.

Morris and Shirley Iheanacho

Nigerian-born daughter, Akunna, completed the requirements for the doctor of philosophy degree in cellular and molecular physiology and graduated from The Johns Hopkins University School of Medicine in Baltimore, Maryland, in 2014.

Morris and Shirley Iheanacho

Shirley and girls with Voice of Prophecy quartette

Shirley with students in typing class

Iheanacho family with Nnena Onwere during our first visit to East Nigeria

Family's first Christmas in Nigeria

Ngozi celebrating sixth birthday with children from the church school

Morris and family

Morris and Shirley carry metal sheets to construction site in Tamale, Ghana.

Shirley telling children's story in Maputo, Mozambique

Shirley and girls standing in the driveway of their home

37

CRAIG AND JANIS NEWBORN

1975–1989 / Kenya, Iran, Lebanon

Craig Harris Newborn was born in Seven Springs, North Carolina. He completed his college education at Pacific Union College in Angwin, California, earning a bachelor's degree in history and religion and in 1970 a master's degree in history with a secondary education emphasis.

Janis Stephens, whom Craig later married, also completed her studies at Pacific Union College, graduating magna cum laude. Thereafter, Pastor Newborn spent four and a half years as a Bible teacher at San Diego Academy, and Janis taught grade three in the elementary school for two years and kindergarten for two years. They had two children (Sheree and Craig Jr.), both born during their stay in San Diego.

Just before accepting a call to overseas missionary work, Elder Newborn was ordained to the gospel ministry on January 8, 1975, at the Pine Springs Ranch Ministerial Retreat. Special guests at the ordination service were fifty San Diego Academy students who were bused to Pine Springs for the event.

A farewell chapel service for the Newborns was held in the academy gym, featuring Adventist missions in general and the Kamagambo Secondary and Teachers Training College in Kenya in particular. This is where the Newborns would go at the close of the first semester, taking with them the hearts and prayers of both students and faculty. Pastor Newborn

would later serve as chair of the Department of Religion and pastor/chaplain of the Adventist University of Eastern Africa.

In 1978 it was voted that they should go to the Iran Field where Pastor Newborn would become pastor-evangelist and president. In 1981 Pastor Newborn took on a new role, serving as youth, Sabbath School, and lay activities director of the Middle East Union, and Mrs. Newborn began work as director of the School of Intensive English at Middle East College in Beirut, Lebanon.

In April, after a period of relative calm, war broke out again in Beirut. At first the sound of rockets came from the direction of the harbor. Black smoke and ships appeared to be moving out to sea. Suddenly rockets began to whir over the heads of the missionaries, students, and workers at the college and the press. The apartment of one of the press workers was hit by two rockets and almost destroyed. The bombs, rockets, and bullets continued for more than a week. Everyone was thankful that calm came by the time Easter arrived, and they were able to enjoy the Easter cantata.

In 1983 they moved to Kenya again. In 1984 it was Pastor Newborn's privilege to be the commencement speaker for the thirty-one students who graduated in a historic ceremony as Kamagambo's first class of ministerial students. When the ministerial training school was established at Kamagambo in January of 1982, five students were accepted from each field/conference in the East African Union. During their two years at the college, students took classes in languages (including Greek), history, health, music, biblical theology, and vocational arts.

In all the Newborns served more than fourteen years in Kenya, Iran, and Lebanon in varying capacities, including church pastor, Bible teacher, evangelist, field president, departmental director, and university chaplain.

After returning to the United States in 1990, he accepted a teaching position at Loma Linda Academy in Loma Linda, California. While teaching at Loma Linda Academy, he also earned an master's degree in theology and a doctorate in theology and personality from Claremont School of Theology. In 1997 Dr. Newborn moved to Huntsville, Alabama, where he became the vice president for Student Services at Oakwood University. From January 1999 through August 2006, he was the founding director of the Oakwood Branch Office of the Ellen G. White Estate and was also a professor in Oakwood University's Department of Religion and Theology.

On August 26, 2006, he was installed as the senior pastor of the Oakwood University Church and Mrs. Newborn, director of institutional effectiveness at Oakwood University.

He is now the director of Sabbath School and Spirit of Prophecy ministries at the South Central Conference. He and his wife are avid birdwatchers.

Craig Newborn, wife, Janis, children, Sheree and Craig Jr., leaving San Diego Academy bound for East Africa.

The apartment of one of the workers at the Middle East Press was almost destroyed when two rockets fell on the hill where many Adventists lived.

Sandbags protected shop fronts in the battle-scarred, far from peaceful, city of Beirut.

Craig and Janis resting after a long hike.

Elder Craig Newborn as pastor of Oakwood University church.

38
HELENE HARRIS

1976–1981 / Zambia

Helene M. Harris was born in Jamaica and was a product of Christian education. She received her formal education there, graduating from West Indies College with an associate degree in elementary education. She came to the United States in 1966 and attended Atlantic Union College for two and half years and received her bachelor's degree in home economics and education.

Helene taught for ten years at Bethel Elementary School in Brooklyn, New York. During this time she attended classes at Hunter College in New York City, earning a master's degree in guidance and counseling. While at Bethel she received a call from Elder Maurice Battle at the General Conference to serve overseas.

This was a difficult assignment for Ms. Harris to accept at that time. Her childhood dream would be realized if she accepted. She had been inspired to become a missionary while listening to mission stories in Sabbath School as a child. She was dedicated and determined to put God first in my life. However, her mother was very sick with cancer and her father, who still lived in Jamaica, felt that Helene should not accept the appointment. For a long time Helene pondered her future. Should she go? Should she remain? Then she decided to follow the text in the Bible that says that if any person loves God more than his father or his mother he or she is not worthy of God (Matt. 10:37). She decided to answer the call because she believed this was God's desire for her life and also that He was better able to care for her mother than she could. This decision proved to be very challenging to her Christian experience because her mother died while she was overseas. It, however, cemented her relationship with God.

When she had finally decided to go, she became the guest of honor at a farewell party as the members of the church and the teachers from Bethel and other church schools in New York City bade Ms. Harris farewell and wished her Godspeed as she left for Zambia. She flew out of New York City on January 15, 1976.

Zambia (formerly Northern Rhodesia) had been a British colony. The capital city, Lusaka, had a population of fewer than 300,000 when Ms. Harris arrived. Besides speaking English, three large language groups existed: Bemba, Tonga, and Lozi. In addition to these three, there were a number of smaller language groups. Chief Monze had granted the Adventists a 5,436-acre plot of ground on which the Rusanga Station had been built.

I will let Ms. Harris tell the rest of the story in her own words.

My time in Africa lasted from January 15, 1976, to August 3, 1981. During that time I was privileged to head the Home Economics Department.

Working in Africa was very rewarding, and I was greatly enriched. I enjoy traveling and making new friends, and this gave me that opportunity. Africa was a beautiful place to travel, and I saw many scenic sights such as Victoria Falls. I also saw how Africa cares for those who are sick when I visited the lepers at Malamulo Hospital. It was extremely rewarding and fulfilling preparing students from poor backgrounds to pass the same exams that children from England were given in order to attend college. It was a joy for my students to earn 100 percent on the home economic portion of the exam. The students didn't have any textbooks. They only studied the notes written on the blackboard. The school principal commended me for the success the students had achieved through the preparation that I provided for them.

I had many opportunities to share Christ with students and adults in the community. I taught cooking to students and their wives at the ministerial school. Working with the men was very interesting, since culturally men are not involved in the kitchen. However, the men seemed elated over their cooking experience and enjoyed eating food they themselves had cooked.

While serving as senior class sponsor, I met Cornelius Matandiko, a young man of the Catholic faith. He requested Bible studies from me and later became a baptized Seventh-day Adventist. I became his mentor and financed his college education at Solusi College in Zimbabwe. He later became a pastor and evangelist, serving the Zambia Union Conference. Zambia Union Conference sponsored his education at Andrews University where he received a doctorate in ministry.

He was a dynamic evangelist and the first national to become president of the Zambia Union Conference. Hundreds were baptized under his leadership. He died, leaving a wife and two daughters who recently graduated as nurses from Southern Adventist University.

Being a missionary in Africa gave me an opportunity to enhance my public speaking. There were many expectations for me to make public presentations, often on short notice. Though frustrating at times, it was a learning experience. On one Sabbath I took some students to a village church. They led out in Sabbath School, and to my surprise, I was not only their transportation, but after Sabbath School I was asked to preach. I picked up my Bible as I prayed and quickly prepared. Additionally, I preached for a week of prayer on campus.

Often, I visited homes in the village. On one occasion I met a family with a sick child and developed a relationship with them. I helped them with varying needs such as food, transportation to the hospital, and other needs. When he eventually died, I was asked to bath and dress him. Of course, this was a challenge to me, but I responded to their request. I also preached at his funeral.

Another interesting activity I participated in was the training of students to lead out in Vacation Bible School on Sabbath afternoons. One Sabbath we arrived at the appointed location, but no one was there. Our students went to search the area and found them at a ballgame. The students invited the children to come to VBS, and to our surprise one hundred of the children came.

I found that the people of Zambia, even the children, were very interested in learning new things. They were very teachable. They had a positive response to learning more about God and many were baptized.

There were political upheavals in neighboring countries such as Botswana and Zimbabwe, but there was no threat to our lives. There was often no food in the stores, but again we were not affected because we brought food and supplies from the United States, and we also shopped in Malawi, Botswana, Zimbabwe, and South Africa.

I had a rich, rewarding experience as a missionary, but my dad wanted me to be nearer to him since losing my mom; therefore, I did not accept another term. I keep in touch with several nationals who are former students and coworkers. I also communicate with several missionaries with whom I served.

Since returning home, I taught at Orchard Park Elementary Adventist School in Chattanooga, Tennessee, and recently retired after working at Greater Atlanta Adventist Academy in Atlanta, Georgia, from 1983 to 2013 as the home economics teacher, registrar, and counselor. In 1990 I adopted two baby girls, Shederrian and Brittany. I am now a grandmother to Amiyah, six years, and Alaysia, fifteen months, and I am enjoying retirement.

My life is fulfilling and rewarding, and the rest of the journey is dedicated to helping others and having a closer relationship with God.

Miss Harris (second from left) receives a farewell gift from Benito Hodge, principal of Bethel Elementary School, as Pastor W. C. Jones and Home and School leader, Mrs. A. Kent, look on.

Helene Harris at the time she left for Africa

Rusangu Secondary School Administration building

Baptism of students following week of prayer by Pastor Eagan, the Bible teacher and campus chaplain.

National teachers with Helene Harris in the center

A national teacher and family with staff in the background standing in front of the campus church.

39

Irwin and Laura Dulan

1977–1985 / Ethiopia

Irwin Reed Dulan is a native of California and a graduate of Oakwood College in 1967. He received his master's degree from Andrews University. In 1971 Brother Irwin Dulan became the associate in the Missionary Volunteer Department of the Northern California Conference.

He worked in the Sacramento area after he returned from the seminary. In 1973 approximately 3,000 people crowded into the main auditorium on Sabbath, August 18, at Vallejo Camp Meeting to witness the highlight of the week-long series of meetings bringing inspiration and encouragement to the constituency of Northern California. The ordination of Dulan and others to the ministry was a solemn and inspiring occasion.

Later in 1973 Elder Dulan became the Bible teacher at Golden Gate Academy. While he was there a program was continued that offered an opportunity for students to get involved in community service activities. This program was begun so that Christian young people could have an opportunity to share Christ with the surrounding community. Elder Dulan's philosophy was that "the only way a student will keep what religion he has is by sharing it. Love born of God reaches out to one's fellowmen. It is unselfish in character. The feeling of satisfaction that comes from doing things for others is what the youth are looking for when they experiment

with drugs. One can get a real 'high' from community service. If you don't believe it, just try it."

In 1977 Elder Dulan, his wife, Laura, and their three children left the states to begin work in Ethiopia. Elder Dulan started out as a Bible teacher at Ethiopian Adventist College. He later became principal of the college and then the education and youth director of the Ethiopian Union Mission.

Sixty-six students graduated from Ethiopian Adventist College in May 1979, and the new school year began with an enrollment of 445 students. More than half of these resided in the dormitories. Irwin Dulan was serving as principal at that time. The college operated an exemplary agricultural and animal husbandry program, and its mechanical engineering training courses and repair shops were well known and appreciated over a wide area.

The great famine hit Ethiopia while the Dulans were there, and the *Gleaner* magazine documented the challenges that faced the Dulans as they continued their work in Ethiopia:

Gleaner: Is there starvation in Ethiopia?

Dulan: There is starvation. This is no myth; it is a fact. I visited one of the camps, where in one month's time 90,000 people were processed. These people have come from the drought area in Wollo Province, where there has been no rain for several years. The people are being evacuated and relocated in provinces where there is more of a chance of survival.

However, many of the people die on the way to the camps. Only the strongest make it to the stations.

Gleaner: Are conditions as bad as they are depicted in our news?

Dulan: Yes, but they are not the same in every area. There are differing degrees of famine. You see only the worst cases. The camps are pitiful sights. People are herded together like animals.

I walked into one room, the size of your office, and asked, how many people are staying in this room? They said about 45. Can you imagine 45 people in a room 15 x 15 feet? They have to live body to body, like mat. Consequently disease goes quickly through the whole group. This is why they have to have medical assistance at the camps to treat the diseases.

Gleaner: Is the Ethiopian government attempting to help these refugees?

Dulan: The government is doing all they can with their limited resources. One third of their national budget goes for war purposes because there is so much warfare with surrounding countries.

Gleaner: Are American relief efforts helping? Are materials getting through?

Dulan: Materials are getting through, though not as fast as we would like them. Sometimes not everything gets through because there are anti-government rebels who waylay the shipments. The Ethiopian government is being very careful that they guard the commodities as they are going to the needy areas.

Gleaner: What can we do as Adventists in America to aid the Ethiopians?

Dulan: The biggest thing we can do as a church is to support our efforts through ADRA (Adventist Development and Relief Agency). They see that the money goes to the places designated. Often when money comes into a country, it is reallocated to other lines. There is a fear by many that this is being done with relief funds. But we know ADRA is putting the money in the proper places.

Gleaner: What has caused the problems in Ethiopia?

Dulan: Drought is the major factor. But it is also drought coupled with the lack of education in agricultural lines. There are great variations in elevation in Ethiopia. There are areas that look like the Grand Canyon in Arizona, with tremendous gorges and sheer cliffs. To grow food crops on the slopes is an impossibility.

Where the land is more or less level, it has been denuded of greenery and wood because the people use wood to cooe with. When the rains did come, they washed away the topsoil. Vast areas are now covered with boulders and rocks. It seems when there are no trees, rain doesn't come to those areas.

Gleaner: Is agriculture quite primitive?

Dulan: Yes, many are still plowing with oxen. In some places they dig with a sharp stick and turn the soil. In other sections they dig with a hoe. They plant grain crops such as corn, sorghum, wheat and barley.

Gleaner: Is this a temperate climate?

Dulan: most of the country is a high plateau. The government is working in the low-lying areas that are hot. They are experimenting with cotton and citrus and are quite successful.

Gleaner: Is there a future for the refugees?

Dulan: There are many problems with the relocation efforts. The government agencies are putting them in areas where they are mixing tribal groups, and this is a great problem. Tribal groups are closed societies. It is difficult for rural tribal groups to accept members of another tribe into this society. This is causing friction.

The best technique would be to move a tribe into an area where they could be by themselves, but there are no empty spaces. There are people everywhere.

Gleaner: Does Ethiopia have natural resources?

Dulan: Yes, it has many natural resources, especially waterpower, but it is relatively untapped.

Gleaner: How can you have waterpower and drought?

Dulan: This is always a big question. If we had the same waterpower here that they have, it would be highly developed. There is an education toward technology, and so you have people living next to a large body of water, on the brink of starvation, because they don't irrigate with that water. They don't know how to irrigate. It has never been done in their area before. The famine is bringing new dimensions in development. The government is sending out individuals to train rural people.

Gleaner: What is the status of the Adventist Church in Ethiopia?

Dulan? The church is accepted by the government, but it is being curtailed in many ways.

Gleaner: How?

Dulan: In one conference-we call it a field there-we had 235 churches before the 1974 revolution. Since then only three are open and operating.

Gleaner: Is this typical?

Dulan: No, this is probably the hardest hit of any of the fields.

Gleaner: What is the membership?

Dulan: About 33,000.

Gleaner: Does the government inhibit evangelism?

Dulan: Evangelism has to take on a totally different approach to be successful. Instead of running long public meetings, everything has to be in a church or a school, and it can be only for a week or two.

Gleaner: Is the college still in operation?

Dulan: Yes, but not on a college level. It operates only up to the high school level. All secondary and higher education is under the government Higher Education Commission, and they have stringent guidelines as to how we can run the school. The main disagreement is that the curriculum, budgeting and acceptance of mission policies are under their supervision, if we go into the higher education level. This we have not been willing to do.

Gleaner: What about the ministry?

Dulan: One of the great needs is for a trained ministry. Most of our workers aren't trained. We have hundreds of workers, but only about 5% have a grade 12 education.

Gleaner: Can they go to other countries for the education?

Dulan: This is difficult because no money can be exported from the country. Unless they are fully sponsored by the denomination or individuals outside of Ethiopia, it is virtually impossible for them to go outside. They all want higher education. They feel that's the solution, and I think it is.

I have been encouraged as I have seen developments through the years in spite of the fact that individual rights aren't always respected as we know them here. Still the people are trying to do their best. I think there is hope for Ethiopia.

Gleaner: Are Adventists affected by the famine?

Dulan: No knowledge has come to us of Adventists starving to death. Most of the drought is in the North, where our membership is small. This is a Muslim section, and we have had few convert there. At the present time we have fewer than 500 members in the whole northern conference, the area primarily affected by the drought.[81]

When the Dulans returned from Ethiopia, they were featured speakers at the Northwest black members annual convocation. They inspired many audiences with their mission experiences.

Irwin R. Dulan

Just returned from Ethiopia, Laura and Irwin Dulan present a mission appeal.

81. "Former Worker Provides Impressions of Conditions in Ethiopia," *Gleaner,* March 18, 1985, pp. 4, 5.

40

LUCILLE PAULETTE HUBERT

1977–1978 / Guyana

We don't know much about Dr. Hubert. The only information that we were able to find is that she graduated from Loma Linda University in 1975 and went to serve as a dentist at Davis Memorial Hospital in Georgetown, Guyana.

At the time that she left, she lived in Atlanta, Georgia, and she left Miami, Florida, on March 22, 1977. She served as a dentist in Guyana for about a year and a half.

41
MONICA MCKENZIE

1977–1981 / Zaire

The following account was penned by Ms. McKenzie:

My name is Monica McKenzie. I was born in Jamaica and spent most of my formative years in England where I completed my primary and secondary education in addition to my professional education—registered nurse and midwifery training.

While still a very young child between the age of six and seven years old, I remember listening to mission stories and being impressed by them. One story in particular that had the greatest impact was one titled Mighty Mary. Although I cannot recall all the details of the story, I do remember thinking at the time that I wanted to go and serve overseas like she had.

Nursing had not been my first career choice. I wanted to learn languages and travel, and I thought at the time that being a flight attendant would enable me to meet these goals, but that did not work out. I had also been asked to consider joining the police force. In the racially charged climate of the time, I did not think that was such a good idea, so I declined the recruiter's offer.

One of my teachers, however, thought I would make a good nurse. This teacher contacted one of her colleagues on the board of one of the hospitals in the surrounding community. He in turn arranged for me to take the entrance exam and interview with the matron of the hospital. During this time the idea of my going into mission service surfaced once again, and I set off not just to complete my nurses training but to obtain other skills that might prove useful in the mission field, hence the additional training as a midwife.

While completing midwifery training, I came across an ad for a French language summer program at Seminaire Adventiste in Collongès, France. I was very interested in the program but the timing of the program conflicted with my midwifery studies. I contacted the college and asked if they had other dates or similar programs during the year. Although they only offered the condensed language program during the summer, they invited me to attend the regular full-time program. This was something to think about. I concluded that if I truly wanted to serve as a missionary speaking another language would be useful to facilitate communication.

Upon completion of my midwifery program and working a suitable time to gain experience, I enrolled in the French language program at Collongès. During the year I spent in

Collongès, I met several missionary families who were assigned to various French-speaking countries and were attending Collongès to learn French. The children of these families were soon speaking French fluently and often translating for their parents.

It was during my stay at Collongès that one of my friends, upon learning about my intention to engage in mission service, encouraged me to contact the Inter-American Division where her parents were serving to inform them of my wish to be of service. It would be more than one year later before I received a reply to my letter.

Having completed my French program at Collongès and not having received any response from the Inter-American Division, I decided to solidify my newly gained French skills by working as a midwife in Lausanne, Switzerland. Shortly after commencing my employment in Lausanne, I received a call from the Inter-American Division. Unfortunately, I had just commenced my one-year contract with the Clinique Montchoisi and had to decline the call, but I indicated that I would still be interested in serving as soon as my contract was completed.

Mission outreach on Sabbath afternoons with nursing students and staff from the hospital were memorable times also. We would present a public health lecture followed by singing and Bible stories for the children using felts.

At the end of my contract, there was no call from the Inter-American Division. My sister who had immigrated to Canada from England invited me to join her in Toronto. She initiated the immigration paperwork, and after a short stint back in England, I was cleared to join her

in Canada. After several months in Canada, I was finally getting established. I passed my Canadian RN board exams and was about to be offered a full-time position at one of the downtown hospitals when I received a letter from the General Conference asking me if I was still interested in mission service. This letter had been sent to my home address in England and was forwarded by my family.

The answer to their question was yes, although I was torn with the idea of just settling down in Canada with the offer of a full-time position after months of working per diem and my wish to serve. Soon after responding in the affirmative to this letter, I received a phone call from someone at the General Conference. I was again asked if I was still interested in mission service and would I consider going to Songa. My answer of course was yes.

Upon concluding the conversation and reflecting on the invitation, which I shared with my sister, my question was "Where on earth is Songa?" My sister and I poured over the globe and map of the world to no avail. There was no country named Songa.

As communication continued between the General Conference, we soon found out where Songa was located in the former country of Zaire (Congo). Songa Hospital is one of the oldest mission stations in Africa. Mission work among the Baluba people was established in 1921 on a 500-acre plot, and medical work began in 1927. The station is about 400 miles northwest of Lubumbashi, the second largest city in the Congo.

The first nurses to work at Songa were Sybil de Gourville and Lydia Delhove. In 1933 hospital wards and a dispensary were opened, and a maternity unit was opened in 1940. In 1948 Dr. O. Rouhe began a one-year training course for African nurses' aides, which was increased to a two-year course in 1960. This revelation was not reassuring to my family and friends once they heard the news. At that time there was a lot of fighting in Zaire, and every day my sister or someone else would ask if I was sure I wanted to go because of the atrocities that were going on over there, especially when they heard about missionaries being killed. I had already committed my decision to the Lord, and I asked Him to work everything out, and so my response to these concerns was always "if it was the Lord's will everything would be fine."

In 1977 I left Canada for the first two years of my four-year mission service as nursing director and interim director of the nursing school. Due to the ongoing fighting in Zaire and concern for the missionaries' safety, the missionary team from Songa had been evacuated to Lusaka, Zambia. I arrived in Lusaka and met some of the team members who were about to relocate to Songa. I joined them a few weeks later.

Prior to my arrival at Songa, I had driven across the Zambia/Zaire border to Lumbumbashi. I spent several days at the mission headquarters in Lubumbashi awaiting a flight in our mission plane to Songa. Here I was encouraged to purchase simple staples such as sugar, salt, flour, soap, etc. Not recognizing the importance of this advice, I shopped as I would in most other places, not realizing how difficult it would be to obtain these items once at Songa.

Finally the day arrived when I took the two-hour flight to Songa in our mission plane piloted by Dick Davidian. Due to the hasty evacuation and return of some of the missionary team previously, there was no designated accommodation for me, so I spent the next few months cleaning and moving from one house to the next based on whose house was still vacant and their return. I guess I can say that I lived in most homes on the mission compound.

The work at Songa was truly rewarding. I came to bless but was blessed in so many ways. It was not a question of being on the clock and working to a schedule. The variety of duties enabled me to put into practice all I had learned professionally and more. My duties included running the hospital, working in surgery, delivering babies, implementing and working in a mother and child clinic, teaching nutrition, teaching nursing students, working in the shop (basic food products), and conducting health and religious outreach in the surrounding villages.

The time spent at Songa was the most rewarding time of my professional life. The people we served dealt with life and death situations with great resilience, and although we the missionaries were always being commended for our sacrifice in leaving our families/homeland to minister to the needs of the less fortunate, I personally feel that it was the other way round. The people we served were the ones making the greatest sacrifice.

The sick individuals were brought to the hospital by whichever mode of transport they could find—by rail, then walking the 12 kms to the hospital, by bicycle being pushed by a family member/friend, or by truck. The mission truck would take patients who had been treated into the nearest town (90 kms) once a week and pick up supplies (if available) and patients in need of care. This 90-kms trip was fraught with the unknown, and instead of making the round-trip journey in one day, there were many occasions when the journey took several days due to bad road conditions or some mishap with the vehicle.

Some of the more memorable stories included being called out of church one Sabbath with the news that a passenger had been thrown off the train more than 12 hours previously and had spent the night by the tracks where he had been found by some railroad workers. They had taken the man to the station 12 kms away from the hospital but needed transportation to get him to the hospital. His condition did not sound promising.

The driver and several of the nursing staff left in the only vehicle that was operational to transport the patient while the rest of us prepared for his arrival. There had apparently been some kind of altercation between the patient and some of his companions during which he was pushed off the moving train. The wheels of the train ran over one arm, and both of his legs. He was in danger of losing both legs and one foot. Fortunately, we were able to save both legs, but he lost his foot.

Another memorable moment was being called in the middle of the night to attend to a young lady in labor in one of the surrounding villages. It was her first child, and according to her husband she had been in labor for several days, and the baby's head had been visible for more than 12 hours with no progress. As a midwife, this patient information did not sound good for the patient or the unborn child. To further

complicate matters, the only available mode of transportation to and from the patient was a tractor. We had to rig up some form of cart behind the tractor to transport the patient while the doctor and I sat on the hubs over the wheels.

Fortunately for the patient her husband had greatly exaggerated her condition. We were able to transport her back with us to the hospital where she eventually went into full labor several days later and delivered a healthy infant.

Having completed the first two years of my mission service, I went on a three-month furlough and returned to complete an additional two years of service until 1981. During my time in Zaire, the political situation was not good, but God had His hand over us. The governor (grand chef) of the territory in which Songa was located was a friend of the mission, in addition to one of the chiefs in the air force, both of whom would visit from time to time. There was a blackout on news within the country, so we were blissfully unaware of the gravity of situations in the country, but I would be questioned about them by my family. Overall, apart from the snakes, I felt safe even among machete carrying men. People were friendly, and everyone knew where I was and what I was doing! Although I have lost touch with national friends, I remember their warmth, patience, and their gift of music.

Did my mission experience enrich my overall quality of life and Christian experience? My mission experience gave me an appreciation for the things we take for granted, i.e. running water, electricity, transportation, food. I felt the divide between us and them, which reminded me of the imperfections in our world.

All in all I remain a missionary at heart, and I look forward to being able to return to mission service for some short-term stints, maybe to replace individuals on furlough, etc. Since my return home I have worked in various healthcare institutions, pursued my education to the doctoral level, and have embraced more fully the principles of our health message, the knowledge of which I wish I had had while serving overseas. I am currently employed at Loma Linda Healthcare and enjoy volunteering for medical missionary work locally, nationally, and internationally.

Monica McKenzie in her nurse's uniform

Monica McKenzie

Louise, a student nurse, (right), her sister Rose, a nurse, (left), and Monica (middle)

42

DONALD AND CARRIE CROWDER

1978–1982 / Jamaica

Donald Leroy Crowder was a native of Pittsburgh, Pennsylvania. After graduating from Oakwood College, on April 4, 1948, Donald married Carrie Patterson, a teacher, of Asheville, North Carolina, while he was pastoring the Asheville-Greenville district.

Crowder proved to be a skilled speaker and evangelist. He often said, "There is a statement in *Testimonies*, volume 7, page 52, which has proved an inspiration to me in my work of evangelism. I quote: 'The conversion of souls to God is the greatest, the noblest work in which human beings can have a part … Every true conversion glorifies Him, and causes the angels to break forth into singing.'"

God blessed his efforts in the West Palm Beach Florida district and in the Fort Lauderdale area in the 1950s. Crowder tells the story of his fight to evangelize the city.

We encountered a great deal of opposition from the city commissioners as we planned for this campaign (at West Palm Beach Florida). The city manager wrote us a letter in which he refused a request for permission to erect the evangelistic tent. There was a city ordinance, he said, that forbade the erection of tents within the city limits.

Such a turn of events certainly called for real consecration and prayer. The church

members join with the workers in special prayer. I contacted some of the leading men of the community and they gave me wholehearted support. I then went to see the commissioners individually, praying before I entered each office.

I told these men that they permitted circuses and carnivals to put up many tents. We were only asking for the privilege of erecting one tent in which to preach Christ and to help make the city a better place in which to live. Then we were given an opportunity to meet the city commissioners. When they had heard our case they gave us permission to put up the tent provided we could get the backing, in the form of a letter, from the Ministerial Alliance. I was a member of the Alliance so permission was granted. Truly this was a wonderful victory for the Lord because we knew other organizations had been refused permission to put up tents for religious services.

We held meetings for seven weeks in the tent and then moved to the church. There were thirty baptized at the close of this effort. Truly we can say, "If God be for us, who can be against us?"[82]

---

82. V. G. Anderson, "Evangelism in the West Palm Beach District," *Southern Tidings*, August 8, 1951, p. 12.

Later he was called from the Miami church to a district in Birmingham, Alabama. He later pastored the Louisville, Kentucky, church and was called from there to pastor the Spruce Street and Tacoma churches in Washington, D.C. He was then assigned the Omaha-Lincoln district in Nebraska. While serving as pastor of the Park Hill Church in Denver, Colorado, on June 27, 1971, he was elected the fifth president of the Central States Conference.

In June of 1974 he left the presidency and returned to pastoral and evangelistic activities.

In 1978 he went to the West Indies Union to serve as stewardship director and evangelist.

By the grace of God he was responsible for baptizing more than 240 people in 1978, and in a 1979 effort in Port Antonio, East Jamaica, he baptized 436 souls. The *Inter-American News Flashes* reported that he ended this ten-week crusade with a candlelight service, encouraging both new and old members to share the light of the gospel with their friends and neighbors.

During the last months of 1981, the Seventh-day Adventist Church conducted its most extensive and successful evangelistic revival in the hundred year history of the church in Barbados. The main speaker for the "Barbados Crusade" was Donald Crowder. He was supported by a team of ten other Adventist clergy and three Bible instructors. Some of the largest numbers ever assembled in Barbados to listen to an Adventist speaker came to the campus of the Barbados SDA Secondary School at Dalkeith, St. Michael, to listen to his nightly presentations.

R. L. Hoyte wrote about this outstanding evangelistic series, which concluded on December 5, 1981, with an impressive and spectacular candlelight service. The service highlighted the new experience of the three hundred and thirty converts to Adventism.

The Crusade started with a tremendous impact even though the printers failed to print and deliver the handbills and letters of invitation to the public. Two tents with the joint capacity of 1500 were pitched on the playing field …

On the opening night … There was standing room only as more than 2,000 were in attendance. The second Sunday night, the crowd, which kept growing, was in excess of 3,500, and by the fourth week, over 5,000 crowded the tents and grounds. By the end of the sixth week, two more tents had to be pitched, but yet the crowds could not be housed.

Don Crowder … preached the gospel in the manner of the early advent preachers, with Biblical proof for every concept presented. The Holy Spirit's presence and power was so manifest that each night one had the feeling of being in the presence of God. Don's style of preaching is unique, having mastered the techniques of relaxing his audience and commanding 99.9% attention and interest span. He is able to present the naked truth with clarity, urgency, awe, amazement, and compelling impact. He preached a Bible-based message charged with the Holy Spirit that demanded from his hearers introspection and radical reformation with a happy delightful joyous dynamism that caused me to think he would be cheating himself if he did not attend the meeting. So the people came from all parts of this land for nine weeks when the Adventist message held centre [sic] stage in Barbados.[83]

83. Glenn O. Phillips, *Seventh-day Adventists in Barbados-Over a Century of Adventism 1884–1991* (St. Michael, Barbados: Caribbean Graphics & Letchworth Ltd., 1991), pp. 91, 92.

Donald L. Crowder

43

BRUCE AND PAULINE FLYNN

1978–1984 / Great Britain

Bruce E. Flynn is a native of Kingston, Jamaica, and was educated at West Indies College and Oakwood College, graduating from the latter in June 1964. He then canvassed in Lawton, Oklahoma, and Texas for a short time. In 1966 he served as principal as well as teacher of history and Bible at Southwest Region Academy in Dallas, Texas. He had met a talented young lady at Oakwood College, and in 1968 he married Pauline C. Turner. (The wedding was performed by William C. Jones in Dallas.)

In 1969 Flynn went to Andrews University and graduated with his master of divinity three years later. From 1971 to 1974 he was a Bible and history teacher at Pine Forge Academy before returning to Jamaica for ministerial service. Pastor Flynn returned to pastor the Mandeville, Jamaica, church for three years and then back to the States as pastor of the Metropolitan Church in Maryland. While at Metropolitan he was instrumental in building a new church and starting and designing the new G. E. Peters School.

In October of 1978 Elders G. Ralph Thompson and B. B. Beach shared with him the conditions in England, and Pastor Flynn responded to a call to serve in the North British Conference. He was appointed to Camp Hill, Birmingham, where he was senior minister at the largest church in Birmingham. He would serve there for three years until his appointment as secretary of the North British Conference.

You might wonder why Great Britain, a highly industrialized country, would be a place that would require missionaries. If you were to have visited the Adventist Church in England during the 1970s, you would have found that blacks comprised more than 70 percent of the church membership whereas in the general population blacks comprised only a few percent of the British population.

During the 1950s West Indians began migrating to Britain. Several acts initiated by the United States Congress brought a halt to the previously unrestricted movement of Caribbean peoples to the United States. This led the West Indians to turn to Britain as an alternative. Britain needed additional labor and encouraged West Indian immigrants to its shores. And most

Caribbean people saw Britain as the motherland, since in the 1950s most of the English-speaking West Indian islands were under British rule and West Indians regarded themselves as British.

In the major cities of England, Adventist congregations that in the early 1950s were wholly white had become almost entirely black.

By the late 1970s blacks were either approaching a majority of the church in Britain or were already a majority. The problem was that the ministry and administration were basically still white. Many of the black members began initiating pressure for the development of regional conferences like in the United States.

In March 1978 then General Conference president Robert H. Pierson and his officers met with the officers of the Northern Europe-West Africa Division to discuss the situation. Out of these proceedings emerged the proposals for greater racial integration of the church in Britain.

The document was generally called the "Pierson Package." With the implementation of these proposals, the demand for a regional conference subsided. Blacks were put into administrative positions and pastors of West Indian background were called to pastor the largest churches.

The Flynn family was one of six families of color sent to England in response to this difficult situation. The other five families were Dr. and Mrs. Silburn Reid, Elder and Mrs.

Everett Howell and family, Elder and Mrs. David Hughes, Elder and Mrs. Cecil Perry and family, and Elder and Mrs. Lewis Preston and family. The Pierson Package worked. The Adventist Church in Britain became alive, prosperous, and started to grow again.

While serving as pastor at the Camp Hill Church, Pastor Flynn conducted a "Christ for the Crises" evangelistic crusade. Evangelist Flynn's short pastorate at Camp Hill resulted in more than sixty new additions to the church. His baptisms for 1979 would total more than 100 souls.

Pastor Flynn tells about an unforgettable experience while working in Britain:

My family and I had scarcely arrived in Birmingham, England, when one of the most challenging experiences of my ministry occurred.

Parts of greater Birmingham were still foreign to me. In fact, just the surrounding areas to my two churches, Camp Hill and Ward End were a little familiar to me. It was on a Friday evening. I had just finished vespers with my family to welcome in the Sabbath and was about to settle down to review my sermon for the Camp Hill church when the telephone rang. I picked it up; it was the mother of Cynthia Woodward. I had just buried Sister Woodward's husband. Her period of grief and mourning had just begun. She was frantic. She was crying and screaming because on top of burying her husband, her only daughter, Cynthia, had just run away with a young man she barely knew. Her plea was that I should find her daughter and bring her home.

Sister Woodward mentioned the name of the little township where this young man had taken Cynthia to his parents' home, and by the way he was not a Seventh-day Adventist. The little township was considered a suburb of Birmingham, but I had never heard of it, nor did I know how to get there.

I had an idea of what direction I should go. To find the address was a different matter. Moreover, I was warned not to take the Motor Ways England Free Way. I would have to enter the Motor Way from what the Brommies call Spaghetti Junction, and if you do not know where you are going one could end up in Scotland, Ireland, Wales or London, not to speak of many other places far from where you wanted to go.

I took the services roads, stopping at every gas station asking for directions. It took me three hours to find the place. I rang the doorbell at exactly 11 p.m. A gentleman came to the door who turned out to be the young man's father. I told him who I was and where I had come from and that I was there to take Cynthia back to her grieving mother.

The gentleman shook his head and said, "She is sleeping."

My response was swift and terse. "Wake her up," I said. I had promised her mother that I was bringing her home, and I meant to do just that.

Cynthia came down the stairs all blurry eyed and sleepy. I told her why I was there. I reasoned, begged, and pleaded with her until 5 o'clock in the morning. Like Judah reasoning with Joseph for Benjamin, my cry was "how can I return to the mother without her daughter?"

At 5 o'clock she broke down in tears and asked, "What do you want me to do?"

"Go get your things and come with me," I said.

She came back with her luggage and the young man. He looked at me and said, "I am coming too."

My response was, "No, no, no, you stay put." I certainly would not be responsible for him if Sister Woodward placed her eyes, let alone her hands on him.

We finally got back to Cynthia's home at 7 o'clock Sabbath morning. I spent an hour reconciling them to each other, and I prayed with them.

After traveling the seven miles to my home, I showered and packed my family into the car

for the fourteen miles to Camp Hill Church. I shut myself in my office and dozed a bit and went out and preached.

Cynthia was a beautiful young lady, and she became very active around the church. We were proud of her. Then one day she came to me to say that she was leaving for London to work and go back to school. I gave her my blessings and she went.

A year and six months went by. One day there was a knock at my office door. Cynthia's mother came in crying. Before she could speak, I said, "It is Cynthia, isn't it?"

She said, "Yes, but this time it is different." Between her sobs she whispered, "Cynthia has terminal cancer. She has but a short time to live." I am sure her tears were not flowing any more copious than mine.

Within a few days I received a letter from Cynthia. She told me that she would be gone in a few weeks. She said, "I know you are going to cry for me, but please don't cry. Just think of all that you did for me. You rescued me. But please promise me you won't forget me, and she sent me a beautiful picture of herself."

Cynthia sleeps in Jesus. Those of us who knew her are sure to meet her soon and very soon.

The Flynn's have two children, Karl Anthony and Donna Fay. Pastor Flynn retired in 2005 to Naples, Florida, but has been kept busy by doing interim pastoral work for the Florida Conference.

Pastor Bruce and Pauline Flynn with their two children while working in Birmingham, England, in 1979.

Pastor Flynn baptizes his son Karl in 1982.

Pastor Flynn and the baptismal candidates at Camp Hill in 1979.

Bruce and Pauline Flynn in 2012

Pastors Flynn and Henry immerse the candidates of Camp Hill.

44

J. Parker and Waustella Laurence

1978–1987 / Zambia, Zimbabwe

Jewerl Parker Laurence attended and graduated from Emmanuel Missionary College and joined the Illinois Conference in 1941 as a ministerial intern. Parker Laurence and Waustella Rickmon were married on November 21, 1943, in Cassopolis, Michigan, by H. W. Kibble Sr.

Before entering the ministry, J. Parker studied toward becoming an electrical engineer. One of the points that was emphasized in those classes was accuracy. A very small error could result in much loss of life and property. He argued that if such great care must be exercised in secular pursuits where only temporal life is involved, then even greater care should be given to the ministry where issues of eternal life and death are involved. He was ordained to the gospel ministry while pastoring in Indiana in 1948. Elder Laurence pastored in the Lake Union and was a teacher in Michigan.

Elder Laurence received additional degrees including a doctorate in education from Wayne State University. The couple left the United States on September 21, 1978, for Zambia, where he served as a science teacher at the Rusangu Secondary School in Monze. After finishing their term of service in Zambia and taking their furlough, they returned to the mission field where he served as a science/mathematics teacher at Solusi College in Bulawayo, Zimbabwe, leaving the States on September 13, 1984.

Waustella worked as a nurse in Michigan, and while in Africa she worked as a part-time nurse and teacher's assistant. J. Parker Laurence retired in 1987, having spent sixteen years as a pastor and thirty-two years as a classroom teacher.

Jewerl Parker and Waustella Laurence celebrated their sixtieth wedding anniversary on November 16, 2003, at a brunch sponsored by the Summit Ridge Church in Harrah, Oklahoma, where they are retired.

*J. Parker Laurence
in 1950*

Jewerl Parker and Waustella Laurence around 2000

45

THEUS AND ELISA YOUNG

1978–1981 / Tanzania

Theus Young was born in Jackson, Mississippi, and came from a large family—five boys and four girls. Theus was next to the youngest. He was brought into the Adventist family by his oldest brother. His mother didn't join the church until years after he did, so Theus struggled to get a Christian education and worked hard as a colporteur to earn the required money to attend Adventist schools.

Theus finally was able to attend Oakwood Academy in Alabama and later Pine Forge Academy, a boarding school in Pennsylvania. In both schools he was active in the temperance oratorical programs, and he demonstrated that healthy living could develop a strong body. He was very active in gymnastics and amazed teachers and students alike with his flexibility and strength in the gym. He completed his undergraduate study at Union College where he obtained his bachelor's degree and where he met his wife, Elisa Papu Siofele.

Elisa and her family would often give concerts and sing songs in their native Samoan language. She was born in Pago Pago, American Samoa, to Pastor Papu and Fa'auliulitoale Tuimanu'a Siofele. She was the third of nine children and oldest daughter. She attended elementary and high school in American Samoa and Suva, Fiji. Elisa's father, Pastor Siolfele Papu was the first Adventist convert in American Samoa. Elisa received a bachelor's degree

in mathematics from Union College and a master's degree in education administration from Loma Linda University.

The intern and his new wife labored in the Central States Conference. On August 22, 1970, he delivered his farewell sermon before leaving his flock in St. Joseph, Missouri, to study at Andrews University. Theus Young, along with eleven other theology students from the Adventist Theological Seminary at Andrews University and their wives, attended a field school of evangelism in Philadelphia, Pennsylvania, during the summer of 1971, assisting with evangelistic meetings conducted by C. D. Brooks.

Theus returned to the Central States to pastor in Kansas, Missouri, and Colorado. He also served as lay activities and community services director of the conference while Elisa served as a teacher and principal. Theus traveled throughout the conference with the new medical van used for screenings. Pastor Young was ordained at the Central States Conference camp meeting in 1974. The Lord blessed the family with four daughters, among them a pair of twins: Tonya, Trina, Teresa, and Elisa.

Elder Young, along with his wife and two children, left Los Angeles on August 30, 1978, to serve as director of the Communication and Sabbath School Department at the Tanzania Union in Musoma, Tanzania.

An experience that Pastor Young is proud

of is the organization of a youth congress for the Tanzania young people. The conference administrators anticipated that approximately 400 youth would attend. On opening night 800 young people assembled, and on Sabbath morning 1,200 crowded into a hall built to seat 600. Their orderly behavior and kind spirit impressed onlookers. The four and a half days of the congress were filled with meetings, workshops, and music from singing groups, choirs, and a brass band. Pastor Young and Dee Hart conducted Sabbath School workshops there.

So impressed was Tanzanian Minister of State for Culture, Youth, and Sports Chediel Mgonja with the behavior of the 1,200 youth gathered for the congress that he called the Tanzanian Union officers and youth leaders to his office in the capital to find out more about the youth and their principles. In his speech at the congress, he referred to Adventist youth as being the "salt" of Tanzania. He called the Seventh-day Adventist Church a "clean" church and exhorted its youth to promote temperance among the young people of the nation.

Later, after the departure of the union youth director, Pastor Young was asked to be the acting youth director in addition to his regular responsibilities of communication and Sabbath School director.

During 1980 Theus Young conducted a six-week evangelistic campaign in the northeast region of Tanzania at Moshi. Young led his four field directors in a practical soul-winning program. A capacity crowd filled the large cinema in town every night of the week. A new church had to be organized in Moshi and in Shinyanga to accommodate the new members, thus making two churches in each city.

Since leaving the mission field, Elder Young has pastored in Florida at the Northside, Mt. Calvary, Elim, and Ephesus churches and served as a departmental director for the Southeastern Conference. During her career Elisa Young served as teacher, principal, and superintendent of education and taught thousands of children, mentored hundreds of teachers, and finally became the superintendent of education for the Southeastern Conference of Seventh-day Adventists located in Mt. Dora, Florida. Unfortunately, she passed away on May 30, 2010, while undergoing treatment for breast cancer.

Theus and Elisa shortly after their marriage

Theus Young, lay activities director of the Central States Conference, just before going to the mission field

The Young's twin girls enjoy a social interlude at the 1990 General Conference Session.

Mrs. Elisa Young as principal and Southeastern Conference superintendent of education

46

EDNA ATKINS THOMAS

1979–1981 / Sierra Leone

Edna Pearlie Atkins was born in Amory, Mississippi, and received her bachelor's degree in home economics education from Hampton Institute (now Hampton University) and a master's degree in home economics education from Ohio State University.

She was not raised an Adventist; however, she became one through her association with some fellow graduate students. The late Dr. Frank Hale who had been the president of Oakwood College was dean of black graduate students at Ohio State University when Edna was a student there in 1974 and 1975. Dr. Hale had made arrangements for several Adventist students from Oakwood College to be in the graduate program at Ohio State. Edna became friends with some of these Adventist students while she was studying there. She was impressed with their spiritual and social values, especially since she was seeking a church after being disillusioned with the traditional Christian church, which she felt showed no conviction to live what the Bible teaches.

Ms. Atkins was reconverted after attending a series of meeting given by Pastor Henry Wright at Hillcrest Church in Columbus, Ohio. She was baptized by Pastor Carl Roger in Springfield, Ohio, and she remembers that Pastor Charles D. Brooks was the guest speaker that special Sabbath.

Being single and a recent graduate, she was really hoping the Lord would lead her to a life partner. One Sabbath at AYS in Springfield, John and Sarah Pitts gave a slide presentation on their work at Masanga in a country called Sierra Leone. She remembers pictures of a big boa constrictor and driver ants. At the time she never thought that any of this would be part of her future.

Her mother passed away in Memphis, Tennessee, which was her hometown, and Edna returned to Memphis and became a founding member of the Breath of Life SDA Church. In 1977 Edna made a commitment to the Lord that she *only* wanted to do with her life what He wanted her to. She had been offered a fellowship to study for her doctorate at Ohio State, but she turned it down after not getting any word from the Lord. She secretly wanted to become the head of the Home Economics Department of a small black college and also to get married.

Her friend Karen (Wells) Williams who led her to the Adventist Church had applied and been offered a missionary posting in Yele, Sierra Leone. Karen decided to refuse the offer but submitted Edna's name without her permission. Edna had been earnestly praying and seeking God's help with the choices she would be making for her life. It took a year of hoping to get a marriage proposal before she just gave up and told the Lord that if the request for mission service was given again she would accept. When it was offered she hesitated and dallied. But a visit from the late Charles Lee Brooks one Wednesday after prayer meeting made her reconsider. He asked if she had prayed about the proposal. She confessed that she hadn't. Elder Brooks told her that she should go home and pray about it again, and Edna said she would.

Edna put some conditions in her prayer. Her first prayer was that the Lord would change the term of mission service from four years to two years. Surprisingly, within the next couple of months the mission committee decided to encourage single people by changing the term to two years! Every other prayer she offered was answered to the tee. The greatest miracle was she got her passport in three days and a leave from her job for two years. Her prayers had all been answered, so there was nothing to prevent her from answering the call to Sierra Leone. She gave up on her last prayer to get married and figured she would never marry and just be a lonely old missionary.

Edna Pearlie Atkins left the States to fulfill her two-year term of service in Sierra Leone in August 1979, and thirty-four years later she is still in Sierra Leone! God even answered her last prayer. She married Valesius Thomas, a young Sierra Leone lawyer who was baptized in 1977 in the town of Waterloo. After she married, she could no longer work because church policy stated that a woman who married a national could not work as an expatriate worker. So Edna Pearlie Atkins Thomas became a mother, lay worker, and teacher in a private American School. Presently, she is self-employed and serves part time as Sabbath School/personal ministries director for the Sierra Leone Mission and is their webmaster.

Edna Atkins became an ambassador of good will even before she left for Sierra Leone. Pastor Victor L. Brooks invited the ambassador to the United States from Sierra Leone to come to the Memphis Church for what Brooks called "International Day."

Congressman Harold Ford Honoréd the ambassador with a reception given at the congressman's home. Governor Lamar Alexander proclaimed April 7, 1979, as "Mohammed M. Turay Day" and gave Ambassador Turay a Certificate of Citizenship, which named the African leader as an honorary citizen of Tennessee. The city mayor and county mayor also proclaimed the day as "Sierra Leone Day."

A Memphis Lincoln dealer provided two Lincoln Continentals for transportation during his visit to Memphis. The ambassador and his entire entourage were moved by the hospitality of that great southern city.

After spending Friday night with Pastor Brooks, the ambassador went to Sabbath School, and then marched in with the ministers and platform guests for the Sabbath worship service. Brooks asked the ambassador, who has a Muslim religious background, to offer prayer. It was clear that he had been exposed to Christianity.

During a planned ceremony, the newly elected first black superintendent of the city school system where Edna Atkins had worked for some time made a touching speech in which he said that the Memphis School System was giving to Sierra Leone a fine teacher. In his acceptance speech, the African ambassador praised the Adventists for their work in his country and for what he called the "cultural exchange" in sending an educator from America to Africa. He felt that it was through such cultural exchange programs that we learned and understood other peoples of the world.

At the reception given by Congressman

Ford, the general managers of all the TV stations in the area were present.

After returning to Washington, D.C., Ambassador Turay invited Brooks, his wife, and Edna Atkins to Washington to join in the celebration of "Republic Day" on April 19. This is to Sierra Leone what Independence Day is to America. Ambassadors from all over the world were there. Adventists were proclaimed as world humanitarians as Pastor Brooks and the newly appointed missionary teacher, Edna Atkins, were introduced. The ambassador later visited the General Conference world headquarters.

On April 7 and 8 the newspapers and radios of Freetown, the capital of Sierra Leone, carried as the lead story the account of the ambassador's visit to Memphis and the fine teacher who was to come to his country. Edna Atkins would be welcomed by the people of Sierra Leone because they already had her picture in their minds and in their hearts.

The ambassador was presented a set of the Conflict of the Ages books. The ambassador later claimed that he had so enjoyed the Sabbath that the next Friday evening and all day Sabbath he could do nothing but rest. He mentioned that he was looking forward to a return visit to Memphis and a Sabbath day of rest with the Adventists there.

Yele Secondary School would later receive a grant of some $200,000 as a result of this special occasion.

There was always a special relationship between African Americans and Sierra Leone. It was Lambert W. Browne and James M. Hyatt, black Americans, who started the Adventist Church in Sierra Leone in the early 1900s. This special relationship would continue to develop between the mission and the government.

That is why His Excellency, The Honorable Siaka Stevens, the president of the Republic of Sierra Leone and the oldest African head of state at the time when he visited America in 1985 requested that his tour include a visit to the Seventh-day Adventist Church during their worship service. At 12:30 p.m. according to his schedule, he along with his entourage arrived at the Longview Heights Seventh-day Adventist Church in Memphis for the worship service.

The program included the singing of the Sierra Leone national anthem and special greetings from Pastors Dana Edmonds, Victor Brooks, Charles E. Dudley, and of course, Edna Atkins.

In his address to the congregation, President Stevens expressed his joy in visiting with Seventh-day Adventists and also expressed his belief in Christianity and revealed that he was a product of the Adventist mission. He expressed good wishes for the members of the church and the work that it was doing in Sierra Leone and around the world. A huge life-size portrait of the president was presented to him at the close of the service.

After he qualified to become a lawyer and returned to Sierra Leone from studies in England, Edna's husband was recently sworn in as a justice of the Supreme Court of Sierra Leone. The Thomas' have two sons, one born in Freetown, Sierra Leone, the other born in Memphis, Tennessee. The elder son is a certified public accountant in Boston. The younger is a pastor who is now on his own missionary journey within the United States. Their younger son has been mentored by Pastor Walton Whaley who also served in Sierra Leone. Pastor Whaley and his wife were a great support to Edna during her early mission service and after her marriage.

The Thomas's have nursed several small Sabbath School branches and helped found

Maranatha SDA Church in Lumley, Sierra Leone. Edna experienced ten years of civil war and was evacuated by the U.S. government in 1997. Edna spent four years back in Memphis before returning to Freetown.

Mrs. Edna Thomas says,

I found that two years of mission service is just a tour. Only a lifetime can equip you to really be used by the Lord to learn enough to become humble enough to be a tool. Short-term tasks maybe can be done in two to four years but one needs to be committed to the Lord's service and the people you are sent to serve. Self has to die. Mission service in NOT glorious … But God is glorious.

I asked the Lord why He sent me to such a difficult field. (By the way I was boarding home matron and home economics teacher at Yele Secondary School. I prayed that God would be glorified through the good that I did and through my fumbles.) The Lord's answer was 1) "This is why it is called a mission field!" and 2) "I needed to bring you here to save you!"

After thirty years my personal testimony is in Lamentations 3:22–24: "It is of the Lord's mercies that we are not consumed, because his compassions fail not. They are new every morning: great is thy faithfulness. The Lord is my portion, saith my soul; therefore will I hope in him."

The Lord has NEVER failed me. I thank Him for the privilege and comfort of knowing that no matter how messed up I may feel or how challenging the circumstances may be there is no joy or comfort than can be compared to being where the Lord wants me to be! Praise Him!

Family reunion in July of 2012

Swearing of Justice Valesius Thomas in March 2013

My son, youth pastor at the Korean Church in Collegedale, Tennessee, and his friend, the son of missionaries to Masanga Leprosy Hospital in Sierra Leone in 2011

47

ART AND HOPE BUSHNELL

1980–1983 / Kenya

The following account was written by Art Bushnell:

My name is Samuel Arthur Bushnell Jr., known as Art Bushnell. My wife who was from Chicago, Illinois, had the beautiful name of Hope (Penn) Bushnell with no middle name.

I was born and raised in Seattle, Washington, the second of thirteen children. The first five of the Bushnell children were raised as Christians, baptized as children in the Presbyterian Church by sprinkling. I graduated from Garfield High School in Seattle and was voted to be the first black Purple and White Day King. This special day was tantamount to voting for the most popular kid in the school as King and Queen for the day.

I gave a speech that day and was applauded with a standing ovation. Some said they were surprised with my ability to speak because I was known as a playboy and a football player, not a student with speaking ability. Even the principal came to me and said that I should think about going into radio or something where I could use my speaking ability. I, of course, brushed it off as fluff. This was a special event held each year for the senior class.

After graduating (1953) at age sixteen, I moved on to Olympic Junior College. This was a time when I got a taste of reality. I had a sponsor who wanted to send me to Oregon State University, but my grades were not good enough. So after a year at OJC in Bremerton, Washington, majoring in football and minoring in foolishness, I got a full scholarship to play football at Idaho State University. Following my stay at ISU, again majoring in football and minoring in foolishness, I left ISU without graduating, but I was invited to come to Canada to play for the Saskatchewan Roughriders professional football team. But I never made it because the Lord stepped in. It was time for some gospel direction.

It was the summer of 1957 when my oldest sister joined an Adventist Church, and I set out to save my sister from this group of fringe so-called Christians. After all, I was a "big-time college student," so I got my party boys together and we met with the Adventist pastor with a list of our questions and objections as to why the Adventists could not be God's true church. The pastor was J. H. Lawrence. He gently shut us down with "thus saith the Lord." I was awestruck. The man knew his Bible so well, and it made so much sense.

After about six weeks, I did a Nicodemus. I called Elder Lawrence and said something strange happened to me and that I was fully convinced that he was right and asked him what I should do next. He asked me to meet him at the church where I told him about my appointment to go to Canada to play football. He told me that was not what God would have me to do. He suggested that I enroll at Walla Walla College and prepare my life for God's team. I told him OK but that I did not want to go alone because I had a girlfriend who lived in Chicago. Hope attended Wright Junior College before becoming an Adventist.

Elder Lawrence asked if she was ready for marriage. I told him that I thought she was. He said that I should go get her, and so we were married on September 7, 1958, in Seattle by Elder Lawrence.

The night we were to leave for Walla Walla College Elder J. H. Lawrence had us come to the church so he could pray for us. As we walked to the front door of the church, there was a knock at the door. It was a white lady in a black neighborhood in a black church. She asked Elder Lawrence if he had any young people who were interested in going to college. There we stood with our mouths wide open wondering if this was for real.

I asked Elder Lawrence afterward if he had ever met this lady or had talked to her before. He said that he had never seen or met her nor had he ever talked to her. He just told me that that is how God works. The lady paid my full college expenses plus she bought my first pair of glasses because now that the Lord was directing my life I had to study books and papers. I needed better eyesight. Surprisingly, I found the reason for my low grades—the answers were in the books, which up to this point in my life I had avoided reading.

I spent two years and two summer schools at Walla Walla and graduated. Then I went on to Andrews University for my master's degree in systematic theology. When I finished Andrews, I had no call to the ministry. Mrs. Jamieson with whom my wife was working in the library asked Hope where we were going to be working. Hope told her that we hadn't received a call yet. Mrs. Jamieson advised us to write to the late Elder Scriven who was the North Pacific Union president at the time and to challenge him. I did.

The following year I received a call to the Washington Conference in the city of Tacoma, Washington. I was given the challenge to raise up a black church there. Within two years we had, with the blessings of the Lord, a church group of fifty or more ready for organization. I stayed there for six years. On Sabbath afternoon, July 10, 1965, I was ordained to the gospel ministry in the Washington Conference. We moved on to Portland, Oregon, for three years, then on to Perris, California, for three years, then on to the Wisconsin Conference as the conference evangelist. Elder Ken Mittleiter was the president. (I had tried to get into a black conference but since I had attended Walla Walla College they would not give me the time of day.)

After three cold years in Wisconsin, I accepted a call back to Washington as conference evangelist, and while there the call came through for the East African Union as conference evangelist. After attending the Institute of World Missions, we left Chicago on July 28, 1980. I was based in Nairobi and worked in both Kenya and Uganda.

I did a lot of traveling. Unfortunately, the union was financially unable to allow my wife to travel most places with me and that was one reason that after three years my wife was ready to come home. We had four children: Scott, Stewart, Faythe, and Melanie. Our two girls went with us, but our boys were having such a good time at Walla Walla College they chose to stay and finish college there. However, while we were in Nairobi, the General Conference allowed our boys to visit us in Kenya.

In one meeting we held in northern Kenya, there was a man who would not come inside our tent. He came every night and sat on the ground outside the tent. I was told that he was a mental case. When I approached him, he got up and bowed to me. I asked him why he did not come inside. He said, "I know what you are teaching. I have been teaching the same thing to my people." I asked him where he had learned the message. He said that he learned it from a book that he was given.

"Who gave you the book," I asked. He said a man dressed in white came by his village one day and gave him this large picture edition of The Great Controversy. He had been teaching his people from that book. He told me the man in white taught him how to read. I asked him how long the man in white stayed with him. He said just a few days.

The next day we visited the man's village and found about forty Sabbathkeepers. Before leaving this area we made sure that the group was organized into a company and equipped with materials to become a church in due time. We made this man who would not come into our meetings and sat outside the tent the official leader of the group. I made a return visit sometime later and the small group had grown considerably.

When we first went there we took five pounds of maize and gave this to each family. This gift was noised around, and the numbers grew in anticipation of getting a bag of maize. We did not disappoint them. Wherever I held meetings, I would go to the city or town fathers and explain to them my work and ask for their help. They would always have in their warehouses United States cornmeal, rice, and beans. So I would avail myself of their supply.

On another occasion again in central Kenya we were conducting meetings and because I had a number of young men working with me I started my meetings at 6 p.m. to 7 p.m. with classes. The young men would reteach the sermon of the night before. I would have lesson outlines done in the native dialect at some nearby typing school. At this time the young lady that was doing our typing seemed interested so I invited her to the meetings. She came and was a faithful attendee.

On the evening that I was to present the Sabbath and the subject of the clean and unclean foods, I took the study outlines to her to be typed in her dialect. The next day when I went to pick up the papers the pastor who was with me said, "You know the people at the typing school are telling your typing lady to stay away from us because we are Adventists and we don't preach the truth. Also that we keep Saturday as the Sabbath."

I let him know that we would just have to let

the Lord take care of the situation. Our lady had been recently baptized into the Full Gospel Church. My series was named "The Gospel Celebration Series." Our typing lady told us later on that she had learned more gospel from us in just three weeks than she had learned all the time she was in the Full Gospel Church. The next day I went to pick up the papers on clean and unclean foods and the Sabbath. I asked her if she had a problem with any of the lessons she had just typed up.

She put her hands on her hips and said, "Yes, I did." I asked her what was the problem. She said, "I never knew there were clean and unclean foods listed in the Bible and God does not want you to eat the unclean foods."

"That's true," I said. "Is that all?"

She said, "Yes."

And I said, "How about the seventh day Sabbath?"

She said, "Oh? Isn't it wonderful that God has a special day for us to worship Him on?"

I replied, "And do you plan to start keeping it?"

"Why of course," she replied. It was a joy to baptize her, and she became a top colporteur.

On another occasion while in Maasai country, we called on as many Maasai villages as we could while giving them sacks of cornmeal (maize) and inviting them to the town meeting hall for Sabbath service. We came upon a village where the village chief lived, and we approached the mud and dung hut and asked the lady of the house could we come in. She told us we could and led us in. She proceeded to call out that visitors were coming in. They responded by making grunting sounds, and the mother immediately turned around and said, "My son does not want you to come into the house."

We turned around and went out. The mother told our translator that when the father is away the sons are in charge and even the mother must obey their requests as it pertains to the house. We offered the mother sacks of maize and asked her to invite the boys to come out for pictures. When they saw the gifts we had given to the mother, they finally came out with spears in hand.

On another occasion while doing evangelism in Uganda, we had some people from the UNICEF office in Kampala attending our meetings. By the grace of God we baptized a young African lady from the office there. She was the product of an African woman and a British soldier. They would come to that area for training in the nearby mountains. While talking to her after baptism, I asked her what she was planning to do with her life, and she expressed her desire to go to America and complete her education. So I inquired of her boss if UNICEF had provision for sending young people to the United States for college. He said that they did, and he would be glad to work on a plan to send her to America.

One day after my return to the United States I got a call. It was Penny from Uganda, and she was in Pasadena, California. My wife and I were in Bakersfield, so we drove down and picked her up, and she stayed with us for a few days. Unfortunately, the school that UNICEF had arranged for was in Kansas. There she had *a less than joyful experience with the Adventist (white) church. She told me they did not act like Christians and the black church was too far away. When she finished school, she returned to Uganda. One day I got a call. She had contracted a brain tumor and had passed away at the young age of twenty-eight.*

The political situation in Uganda was in transition from having just gotten rid of Idi Amin. The country was patrolled by the Tanzanians. There was no salt or sugar and very few fresh vegetables. There was plenty of yellow cornmeal from the United States, which the nationals were hesitant to eat because someone spread the lie that it would take away your manhood. So we had cornmeal mush, cornbread, etc.

I had the richest experiences of my life while in Africa. Except for the long periods away from family, my wife would have stayed a lot longer than she did. But she enjoyed her brief stay. I still have contact with Dr. Wangai in Kenya and have made two trips back to the union and plan to go again.

It was a joy for Arthur and his brother Kenneth, who had arrived ten years earlier to be the youth and communications director, to work in the same union. After returning to the states Elder Bushnell continued to pastor and hold evangelistic meetings in California. In 1990 he held a revival meeting in an old-fashioned red and yellow tent in Anchorage, Alaska. In 2001 he retired.

It's hard to fully retire so after his official retirement he worked in Hawaii for four more years. He also worked in Manilla and other places.

Hope Bushnell doing manual labor in Kisiitown

Mombassa

Village women pose with the distinguished visitor.

The Riff Valley

At this altitude the equator is not that hot.

Somalie brothers wish us farewell.

The Bushnell family in 1972

Preaching on Sabbath through two translators—the first one in Swahili and the second in Masii

Evangelist S. Art Bushnell, ministerial secretary and evangelist, works with his brother Ken L. Bushnell in the East African Union

Evangelist and Mrs. Bushnell share samples from a vegetarian cooking class.

48

SIMON AND SUZANNE HONORÉ

1980–1986 / Rwanda

Simon Mathieu Honoré was born in Haiti. Simon's parents, Disciple Joseph Honoré and Marie-Louise Simeon Honoré, were poor but devout Catholics. They raised their son to have a great respect for the church and the Bible.

Suzanne was born in Martinique. Both Simon and Suzanne trained to be professors.

Simon received his doctorate. Simon Honoré was a colporteur in Canada for many years to help pay for his schooling. Mrs. Honoré had been a principal at the Berea School in Boston. Simon met Suzanne while at Andrews University, and they were married in December of 1967 at Andrews. They had two children: a girl, Katty, and a boy, Karyl. They both were bilingual with French being the language that they used the most. Simon was naturalized as a United States citizen in 1981 and Suzanne in 1983.

Their mission service began in 1980 when they received a call to be teachers at Gitwe College in Rwanda. They left the States in June of that year. Gitwe is a coeducational French-speaking boarding school north of Kigali, the capital. It offered teachers' training and a ministerial course besides the regular high school program. It was located on a 125-acre tract of land.

Dr. Honoré was a professor of physics, chemistry, and math. Mrs. Honoré was the registrar and also taught in the education department. The Honorés were surprised to see that they, as well as all the other missionaries, lived in a very nice big home but the school girls lived in a very small room, six in a room, and several in a bed together. There were no screens on the windows, so mosquitoes could freely come in, and the girls often had malaria. There was also no bathroom inside, so they had to bathe outside and go to the toilet outside. They made it their responsibility to annoy the principal until he provided a larger house for the girls that had screens and better sanitation facilities. They even made a personal donation so that the living condition for the girls was improved.

The principal had to leave the country because his mother was sick. Before he left he assigned Dr. Honoré the job of preparing the union entrance exam that determined which students would be accepted at Gitwe or at any other school in the union. All eighth graders had to take it and pass it if they wanted to continue their education. Simon had to write the exam for French, math, writing, history, science, and several other subjects. At that time there were no copy machines; there were only mimeograph stencils. Simon made enough copies that went to the entire country. But in his innocence he dropped the stencil in the trash, and somebody who was cleaning found the stencil, took it out, and gave it to his friends.

The person did not come to Dr. Honoré or any of the other missionaries with the copy. Just before the exam someone came to Simon and said he saw one of the pastors giving the exam to the kids. That bothered him terribly, but there was little that could be done about it. But what happened next bothered him even more.

When the exams were corrected, those who passed were posted on a list. The eighth grade teacher from one of the schools came to see Dr. Honoré, and she said her daughter was not on the list. "I know my daughter. She couldn't fail, and she has studied hard. You forgot to put her name of the list." The next day she came again. I checked the list again. Her grade was not a passing grade. Her father came and sat under the tree by the school. Dr. Honoré went to his office one day when he was alone to try to get to the bottom of the matter. He searched for her paper again, and when he found her exam, he noticed that it hadn't been graded. Upon grading it, he discovered that she had done very well. She should have received the maximum grade. She had done very well in math and all the other grades, but she had been given a bad grade.

Because of this he called the director of education at the union via radio and told him to come immediately because there was a problem. "What is going on?" Dr. Honoré asked upon arrival.

"I will tell you what is going on. We are Hutus, and if we grade the papers as we should, the Tutsis will have all of the places. She has to fail. You must accept it. She can do nothing about it. You can do nothing about it. Only so many Tutsis can pass. I will let you put her name on the list, but we are going to close the matter. We, Hutus, have to get into school. If you say anything, I will go directly to the president of the country who is from my tribe, and

we will send you home, deport you. Since you saw it, I will let you put the name of the girl on the list. But we are going to close the matter and dig no further into it. Do I make myself clear? This is our time.

The Tutsis must get into school."

Dr. Honoré was shocked. He didn't know who was Hutu and who was Tutsi, and he didn't care, but he had to keep his mouth shut. Simon put her name on the list, and she was admitted to Gitwe and was one of the very best students they ever had. This was just an inkling of the trouble the country would have in the very near future between the two tribes. But Simon was shocked to see it play out in the Adventist Church. They were missionaries and had to obey, but he was deeply troubled over this.

Another problem that occurred in the schools in Rwanda and Burundi was the exam that was given after the completion of high school for entrance into the universities. This exam was always given on the Sabbath. Some of the university courses required class attendance on the Sabbath. Many church leaders had approached the government for them to respect the religious liberties of the Adventists and administer the test on another day for Sabbathkeepers, but this was to no avail. The exams were still given on the Sabbath.

Adventist students had to break the Sabbath and take the exam or go to another country if they wanted to continue their education. Parents wanted their children to succeed and go further than they had, so they looked the other way. Despite the appeals of the Adventist leaders, Adventist students continued to take the exams on the Sabbath. It was a catch-22 situation. Students wanted more education but could not get it unless they broke the Sabbath, and those who broke the Sabbath and took the exam and got more education were promoted in the church to leadership positions because they had more education. The church was losing some of its brightest leaders, and those who stayed with the church knew that they had broken the Sabbath to achieve their education.

In the 1980s the division began planning to build a university in Rwanda that would allow students to further their education without taking the government exam on the Sabbath. Until the time that the university would be completed, the leaders of the Africa-Indian Ocean Division held regular meetings urging the pastors, especially, and the leaders to be faithful to the Sabbath.

The Honorés attended several of these meetings held at the large church at Gitwe College. They were impressed as they saw the interplay of missionary leadership with the African leadership. Preaching and teaching about the Sabbath was conducted all during the week and on Sabbath an altar call was made pleading for faithfulness to the Sabbath even if it meant not taking the exam. The pastors claimed that studying and taking an exam was not really work. We had Sabbath School where we studied and enriched the mind. University study was also enriching the mind and not considered work. In the end, most students continued to take the exam on the Sabbath.

Dr. and Mrs. Honoré are retired now and living in Berrien Springs, Michigan.

The 1980 Mission Institute group held at Andrews University that included the Honorés.

Mrs. Honoré with a promising student

Dr. and Mrs. Honoré (back), Karyl and Katty (front)

Two of the classes at Gitwe College in Rwanda

49

JOHN AND MARY LAVENDER

1980–1984 / Tanzania

John Lavender was born in Greensboro, Alabama, but grew up in Bessemer, Alabama. In 1962 he moved to Cleveland, Ohio. It was in Cleveland that he entered the U.S. Army in 1965 and served for three years. He completed three months of basic training at Fort Knox, Kentucky, and then an additional three months of medic training at Fort Sam in Houston, Texas. He spent the next eighteen months in France (15 months in Orleans, and one month each in Tours, Chattelraux, and Chinon). His last year of service was spent in Mainz, Germany. Receiving an honorable discharge, he returned to the United States in March of 1968.

In 1968 he began his freshman year at Oakwood College in Huntsville, Alabama. John completed his junior year at Cleveland State University. He returned to Oakwood College in 1971 for his senior year, and graduated in 1972 with a bachelor's degree in religion. In that year he was listed in Who's Who in American Colleges and Universities.

After graduation John pastored for one year at the Maranatha SDA church in Cincinnati, Ohio, after which he studied at Andrews University in Berrien Springs, Michigan, where in 1974 he earned a master's degree in Old Testament studies. A summary of Elder Lavender's activities from this point on is as follows:

- 1974–1975 – Pastored churches in Charleston, Huntington, and Beckley, West Virginia. Received invitation from Oakwood College to teach in the Religion and Theology Department.

- 1975–1976 – Completed one year of advance studies in Old Testament at Vanderbilt University.

- 1976–1980 – Served as assistant professor of religion at Oakwood College.

- 1980–1984 – Served as a missionary at Tanzania Adventist College in Arusha, Tanzania. Served alternately as academic dean and registrar. Conducted many evangelistic meetings and speaking engagements in various parts of Tanzania.

- 1984–1995 – Returned from East Africa to Oakwood College to resume position as assistant professor of religion.

- 1989 – Conducted six-week evangelistic crusade in Limbe, Cameroon.

- 1996–2011 – Served as pastor of the Emmanuel Sabbath Assembly in Huntsville, Alabama.

- 2011–Present – Founded Tanzania Missions and Development with a focus on orphanages, medical clinics, education, clean water, agriculture, fisheries, bakeries, and other projects for self-support.

While teaching at Oakwood College, he completed requirements for the associate degree in nursing in 1994. He has since worked as an RN in Huntsville and Birmingham, Alabama, and in Nashville, Tennessee. In 2004 he obtained a master's degree in nursing at Vanderbilt University. He was employed three years as a family nurse practitioner with Quality of Life Health Care in Anniston, Alabama.

Lavender's hobbies and skills include carpentry and building, masonry, gardening, tailoring, reading, writing, art, watercolor and oil painting, photography, word processing, and PowerPoint presentations. Language skills include rudimentary French, Swahili, biblical Hebrew and Greek. Foreign travel includes Canada, France, Germany, England, Spain, Austria, Italy, Greece, the Netherlands, Tanzania, Kenya, Cameroon, and Egypt. He has also traveled to Alaska.

Mary Evelyn Washington began her journey of life on October 14, 1946. Mary was born to godly parents, Jerry and Wanda (Brown) Washington of Margaret, Alabama. Her father was a coal miner and her mother a homemaker. She was the baby of nine other siblings, eight brothers and one sister. At an early age, Mary was baptized at the Beulah Baptist Church in Margaret.

Mary graduated from Reuben Yancy High in 1965 and went on to pursue higher education at Daniel Payne College in Birmingham, Alabama. She later moved to Huntsville, Alabama, to attend Oakwood College where she majored in sociology. It was at Oakwood that Mary accepted the faith of the Seventh-day Adventist Church and was baptized.

It was also at Oakwood that Mary met John Lavender who would later become her husband. Mary and John were united in holy matrimony on August 23, 1970, at the Bethel Seventh-day Adventist Church in Cleveland, Ohio. Their pastor at the time, Elder Isaac Lester, officiated at the ceremony. To their union was born three lovely daughters: Michelle Nicole, Janviere Monique, and Rachel Kiwonna.

Mary served faithfully with her husband in the ministry of the gospel in each of her churches where he pastored. In 1975 Mary and John returned to their alma mater, Oakwood College, where she worked as a teacher at Oakwood's Child Development Center while John taught religion.

In 1980 Mary and John responded to an invitation from the General Conference of Seventh-day Adventists to serve as missionaries. The family spent four years in Usa River near Arusha, Tanzania, in East Africa. Mary served as dean of women, teacher of behavioral sciences, and children's Sabbath School teacher at the Tanzania Adventist Seminary College. She also homeschooled her three daughters. Upon their return to the States in 1984, Mary began working for the Huntsville City School Systems, while John resumed his teaching post at Oakwood College. During this time, Mary acquired her master's degree in elementary education. She enjoyed teaching children and oftentimes went to great lengths to ensure that the children in her classrooms were well-educated.

Some of Mary's hobbies included reading, singing, cooking, traveling. She loved collecting antique clocks and radios, pretty brooches, and little Christmas village houses. Mary was a quiet, gentle spirit and enjoyed spending quality time with her husband, daughters, and granddaughters. Her son-in-law Michael held a special place in heart. She cherished the special times spent with her extended family, especially during the Thanksgiving and Christmas holidays. She was diligent in service to God and in support of her husband in his pastorship of the Emmanuel Sabbath Ministry from 1996 until her very last Sabbath. She was benevolent, a selfless and quiet giver, and would often give to others, seeking no recognition or praise. Her favorite scripture was Psalm 27, which begins, "The Lord is my light and my salvation."

When Mary Lavender passed away on April 5, 2009, John Lavender wrote the following poem:

I Knew You Were the One
A tribute to my wife Mary

I knew you were the one from the day I first saw you
It was winter quarter 1969, across the room in the Oakwood College cafeteria.
At that very moment I knew you were destined to be mine.
I knew you were the one.
I saw you as you entered the dining hall door.
At that moment I knew I had to know you more.
First struck by your petite and pretty form.
Yet beneath the surface I perceived, a woman of character and godly norms.
I knew, I just knew, you were the one.

"Who can find a virtuous woman?" The wise man did ask.
I accepted his challenge, and in you I completed the task.
I knew you were the one

You took me home to meet your father and your mother,
a man and woman of great faith in God.
They liked me, and I liked them. I knew you were the one.
Then I met your seven brothers and one sister, all of them devout Christians, strong in the Lord.
They liked me, and I liked them. I knew you were the one.

We walked down the aisle together and stood before the altar.
There we pledged before God to make the journey through life together.
I knew you were the one.

You labored untiringly to support me in the ministry.
You were faithful in all things pertaining to God and the church.
You were faithful in all things pertaining to the home.
Together we faced many challenges and trials and yet you never complained.
I knew you were the one.

You gave me three beautiful daughters: Michelle, Janviere, and Rachel.
And three beautiful grandchildren: Gabrielle, Aaliyah, and Yeasha.
They have bonded us together in eternal love.
I knew you were the one.

We set out to build a house with no money in our pockets.
I guess I didn't count the cost.
You said, "John, you don't know anything about building a house."
And you were right.
But with your own hands you helped,

encouraged, and supported me.
And together we did it.
I knew you were the one.

We have traveled the world together: Canada,
Alaska, London, Paris, Rome, Greece,
Amsterdam, Germany, Tanzania, Kenya, and
Egypt.
We have been inside the pyramids, rode on
camels' backs, visited the Valley of the
Kings, entered the tomb of King Tut.
We traveled in our new Toyota Camry for
thirty days, just the two of us, across Amer-
ica. We saw the site of the Oklahoma City
bombing,
Looked for alien life forms in Roswell, New
Mexico.
We beheld the splendor and majesty of the
Grand Canyon.
We visited Las Vegas, Loma Linda, San Diego,
drove along the coast of the Pacific Ocean
to Los Angeles. Then northward to visit the
Hearst Castle, Carmel by the Sea, San Fran-
cisco, Portland, Seattle, the Badlands, and on
to the site of the Battle of Little Bighorn.
There we witnessed the ceremony dedicat-
ing a monument to the Indians who died in
that battle. We beheld the grandeur of Mount
Rushmore and toured the Terry Redlin Art
Museum. On to Minneapolis then on to Cleve-
land and finally back home.
We had so much fun together.
I knew you were the one.

As you grew older, your beauty never faded.
You could still thrill me and tickle me.
You could still make my blood flow and my
heart skip a beat.
I knew you were the one.

Your beauty stayed though your health waned.

God gave strength to love and care for you.
As a mother cares for her infant child, you
said so tenderly,
"John, you have taught me how to love."
But it was because you were bone of my bone
and flesh of my flesh.
It was because I knew you were the one.
Caring for you was easy, for I remember the
many times you loved and cared for me when
I was ill. Mary you taught me how to love

Now I am left to complete the journey alone.
I feel so empty without you; the future seems
so dark and drear.
I remember how in your last moments, you
struggled to call my name.
So tenderly and softly you called, "John ...
John ..."
Then with so much affection you laid your
head upon my breast.
My heart melted with love and pain.
I knew you were the one.

Now I commit you into the hands of Him who
is the Resurrection and the Life, into the hand
of Him who first loved you, Him who safe-
guards you in the hollow of His hand.

I always said, "I knew you were the one." And
as I look back on our beautiful thirty-nine
years together, I can now say, "I know you
were the one."

With all my love, John to Mary

Because of Mary's dedication, love, and benevolence shown to the people of Tanzania, Pastor Lavender began developing and building an orphanage and school to be named in her memory. If you would like more information about the organization, search for

Tanzania Missions and Development on the Internet. Their website highlights the organization, which was started in 2010 after Mary passed away.

John and Mary Lavender in 1980

The Lavender family

Mary Lavender in 2009

John Lavender in 2009

J. Lavender with two of the teachers and some of the 771 students at one of the schools in Monduli close to Arusha (the school has only eleven teachers)

J. Lavender (center) with village elders and two female representatives after securing a 100-acre land donation

50
ROLAND AND LILIA MCKENZIE

1980–1991 / Nigeria, Zimbabwe, Kenya

Both Roland Loyd McKenzie and his wife, Lilia Bertina Clarke, were born in Panama.

Roland and Lilia met in high school. Lilia's family was Anglican, but Roland's family was Adventist even though he was not too interested in the church as a teenager. Roland completed his high school education in Panama and came to the United States in 1961. He stayed with his Adventist aunt in California, and out of courtesy to her he went to church on Sabbath.

Elder E. E. Cleveland conducted an evangelistic effort in East Los Angeles in 1962. Little Richard had just joined the church, and he was the singing evangelist for Elder Cleveland.

Roland attended those meetings, and after the meetings were over, Little Richard came to the Miramonte Church where his aunt attended and conducted a two-week revival. Little Richard made an appeal, and Roland took his stand and was baptized.

It had always been his desire to be a professional baseball player or a U.S. marine. He began school at LA City College but was distressed over the social habits of the students there and longed to attend an Adventist school. At this time he was corresponding with Lilia who was still in Panama. Subsequently, she came to the States, took Bible studies, and was baptized into the Adventist Church. It was after that that on November 24, 1962, the couple was married. Soon he was drafted into the army, and they were stationed in Maryland. Lilia worked at the Washington San, and Roland got a chance to see an Adventist College up close, enrolling in nearby Columbia Union College (CUC).

After his discharge from military service, he received a bachelor's degree in history and French from CUC in 1965. In 1971 he completed his master's degree in history at Pepperdine University. He then worked on a doctoral program in history and educational administration at the University of Southern California, completing that degree in 1979. He taught social studies, world history, geography, and America's intercultural heritage at Bret Harte Junior High, a public school in south central Los Angeles.

Dr. Eldon Stratton who had been at CUC while Roland was there saw him at a Saturday night church function and asked him to leave the public school and come to Lynwood Academy where he was the principal. Lynwood Academy was a predominantly white school in a predominantly white neighborhood. After several sleepless nights praying over the decision, they accepted the call, which meant a great reduction in salary. In 1974 he was selected to be the first black principal at Lynwood Academy where he had been a teacher and the vice principal for the previous two years. Then he received a call in 1978 to go to La Sierra University (at that time La Sierra was a part of Loma Linda University). At the end of his second year there, Dr. Grady Smoot of Andrews University invited him to look at the opening for president at a school in Nigeria.

Besides raising their two sons, Roland Jr. and Mark, Mrs. McKenzie worked part time as a nurse's aide. On August 18, 1980, Dr. McKenzie, Lilia, and the two children left Riverside, California, for Africa to accept the position of president of the Adventist Seminary of West Africa (ASWA). The school was initially established as the Adventist College of West Africa (ACWA) in 1959 with seven students. In 1975 it changed its name to ASWA.

In 1983 Dr. McKenzie reported on the work done at ASWA. The seminary had been operating for several years in Nigeria, preparing English-speaking workers for the work in West Africa. The institution faced a number of challenges: financially, in personnel, and with regard to current offerings. However, Dr. McKenzie reported a spirit of optimism. At the time ASWA offered a four-year bachelor's degree in theology. It later became a university on April 20, 1999, and the name was changed to Babcock University. It now has more than 6,000 students.

Babcock has added a postgraduate school, which began in the third quarter of 2010, and a medical school, which took off in January 2012. The Benjamin S. Carson Sr. School of Medicine and Babcock University Teaching Hospital were inaugurated in 2012 during commencement services. It is the Adventist Church's fourth medical school worldwide, and its second English-language medical school. The church operates medical schools in Montemorelos, Mexico; Entre Rios, Argentina; and its flagship school in Loma Linda, California. Babcock trains doctors to be medical missionaries who will go to all parts of the world and administer healthcare from a biblical perspective.

After three years in Nigeria, Dr. McKenzie returned to the States and taught for a quarter at Andrews University. His time there was providential because he was able to meet the educational leaders of Andrews University who would help him transform Solusi into a new kind of institution. In the latter part of 1983, Dr. McKenzie was appointed president of Solusi College. Solusi was a coeducational private university about thirty-two miles from Bulawayo, Zimbabwe. It was initially established in 1894 by a land grant from the famous Cecil Rhoades. Dr. McKenzie applied for a special Sabbath School offering that helped advance the physical plant.

Under his supervision housing for married students and a new administration building were constructed with appropriate space for departmental personnel. He was instrumental in purchasing a 1,200-acre farm. Solusi already had 9,000 acres, but this new land had 2.5 times the water allocation from the government dam (*mananda*). Solusi is located in an area in Zimbabwe with low rainfall.

Under his leadership Solusi became a self-contained institution. With a dairy producing butter, cheese, and milk; orchard producing fruits such as peaches, apples, oranges; a grape orchard that produced enough grapes to bottle the grape juice and sell it on campus as well as in the city; a bakery that produced wholewheat bread and pastries; and a new gardening method that provided fresh vegetables in a drought stricken area, Solusi became well sustained and potentially self-supporting through the continued blessings of the Lord.

The biggest blessing came when Dr. McKenzie was able to affiliate Solusi with Andrews

University so that the degrees they gave actually came from Andrews and was a United States degree. This pleased the African students and the enrollment skyrocketed. One hundred years after it opened, the institution received the authorization from the government of the Republic of Zimbabwe through an act of parliament to operate as a university.

On October 4, 1994, the university opened as the first private institution of higher education in the country. Following the granting of the charter by the government, it was renamed to Solusi University to reflect the institution's expanded roles and academic offerings. The university now follows American grading and business, research, and liberal arts curricular patterns. As of 2006 the university has an enrolment of more than 4,000 students from more than sixteen different countries in and out of Africa. Dr. McKenzie was invited back to Solusi University in 2012 to give the baccalaureate address along with Ted Wilson, world church president, who gave the commencement address.

Seeing the progress and what was happening in Zimbabwe at Solusi, church leaders asked him to go to Kenya to help develop another educational institution. In 1988 Dr. McKenzie was appointed vice chancellor (president) of the University of Eastern Africa in Baraton, Kenya. One of the first things he did was to request an audience with Elder Bekele Heye, the president of the division. They sat down and drew up a three-year plan that would build up the school and enable it to get a charter from the government as a private university.

And that is exactly what happened. At the end of three years, on March 28, 1991, the president of Kenya, Daniel Totoitich Arap Moi, came to the campus and presented the charter to The University of Eastern Africa, Baraton. It became the first private university to be charted by any government or country in English-speaking Africa. In each of the three African institutions where Dr. McKenzie served, he was succeeded by an African. He helped prepare the way for qualified African leaders to take the helm of these institutions.

In 1991 he returned to the United States to serve at Oakwood University as professor and chair of the Department of Education for nine years. From 2000 to 2005 he served as an academy principal in the Florida Conference; he then retired. He now teaches World Civilization at Adventist University of Health Sciences (ADU).

Thanks to Dr. McKenzie's efforts, three struggling school on the continent of Africa became large, productive universities. Praise God for his leadership in educational administration!

At a Mission Institute at Andrews University in 1980: Dr. and Mrs. Honoré (left) and the Mckenzies— Roland Jr., Lilia, and Dr. Roland (right)

51
CHARLES AND PATTIE MILLER

1980–1985 / Kenya

Charles Samuel Miller Jr. was born on July 7, 1938, in Tampa, Florida, the first of two children and the son of Ella Lee and Elder Charles S. Miller Sr. With two God-fearing parents, he was taught and nurtured with Christian principles. Being baptized at an early age, Charles became a child evangelist at age six, accompanied by his sister Naomi, a five-year-old singing evangelist. What a preacher! Little evangelist Charles and his sister provided a ministry that covered most of the southern states. Hundreds of individuals were drawn to the love of a saving Lord and to an awareness of His soon coming by the dynamic duo.

Charles' elementary school years were spent in Florida, Massachusetts, and Pennsylvania, since his father was a minister and his mother a Bible worker. After graduating from Pine Forge Academy in 1956, Charles began his college career at Union College in Lincoln, Nebraska, and later at the U.S. Air Force where he obtained the rank of Airman 1st Class and several awards.

Pattie Rose Reaves was born in Hopewell, Virginia, and attended Prince George High School in Virginia. She moved to Pennsylvania when she was in the tenth grade and later graduated from Chester High in Chester, Pennsylvania. She then went on to graduate from Oakwood College. Charles and Pattie were united in holy matrimony in Chester, Pennsylvania,

in June of 1958. To this union three daughters were born: Shari, Wanda, and Dianne.

Charles completed his bachelor's degree in business administration at Oakwood College in 1972 and his master's degree in accounting at Ohio State University in 1976. He went on to serve as director of the computer center and assistant to institutional research at Oakwood College.

While at Oakwood College a call came that gave him the opportunity to fulfill his lifelong dream of becoming a missionary. With the two youngest girls, they left Huntsville, Alabama, on September 20, 1980, for Africa. They served two terms from 1980 to 1985 at the University College of Eastern Africa in Eldoret, Kenya. Professor Miller served as the business administrator/accountant instructor and developed the first Department of Business at the university. Pattie served as the dean of women.

Both Pattie and Charles had malaria while they were in Africa. Pattie had a strain of malaria that baffled the doctors. When she went to the hospital, they said there was nothing more they could do for her. They believed that she would surely die. Her mother-in-law who was visiting with them felt that they should rush her back to America.

As a last resort her husband took her to a bush doctor that was recommended by some of the students on campus. For a while

Pattie slipped between consciousness and unconsciousness. The medicine man was well acquainted with natural herbs and plants. She stayed with him in a makeshift hut for three days while he administered his herbal concoctions. The family and the campus prayed for her. At the end of the three days she was well again. The good Lord used the medicine man to find the right herbs that healed her body.

Pattie promised the Lord that she would build a church in Africa. Her daughters worked with a very rich attorney whom they called Mr. C. This man had donated $70,000 for the statue of the good Samaritan that was constructed on Oakwood University's campus. Mr. C. was originally from Mississippi, but he became enamored with Africa and built himself a home in Tanzania. He has built a hotel and plans to build four more. After that he has promised to build a suitable church close to the campus of the university.

After returning to the States and serving for three more years in the Business Department of Oakwood College, the U.S. Army Corps of Engineers invited Charles to serve as an accountant in 1988. He was soon recognized as an invaluable employee there and was awarded many honors and recognitions for his service. Unfortunately, Mr. Miller fell victim to a pervasive illness that manifested itself as a tumor on the brain. He was presented at his bedside a certificate of high quality performance and in June of 1995 he received recognition of fifteen years of service to the government of the United States of America. He passed away on July 29, 1995 at age fifty-seven. Pattie continued working at Oakwood as the residence hall director and was greatly loved by the young ladies she counseled and guided.

Pattie later married Harland Landy, a builder/contractor from Bermuda. She spends part of her time in Huntsville, Alabama, and part of her time in Bermuda.

The Millers with some of their local friends: Pattie, Charles, and Shari Lynn (middle).

Charles Miller in his office

Pattie Miller with some village women and children

Charles Miller with some Kenyan friends

The Millers with friends

The Miller's home at the university

Dianne Miller at her Maxwell graduation in Nairobi.

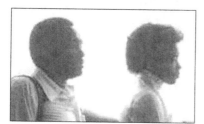

Silhouettes of Charles Miller and his daughter Dianne

The Millers with friends

Pattie and Harland Landy

The Millers with friends

52

ALVIN AND LOIS MOTTLEY

1980–1987 / Tanzania; 1999–2007 / Tobago

Alvin Whitney Mottley was born in Trinidad/Tobago, the fourth child of eight children. He attended schools there, including Caribbean Training College. He worked two or three years in his native country before coming to the United States. He attended Andrews University in 1965 and graduated with a bachelor's degree in biology in 1969.

He found employment with the South Atlantic Conference in North Carolina teaching at Ephesus Junior Academy in Wilmington and before leaving to attend Hinsdale Sanitarium and Hospital where he graduated with a degree in medical technology in August of 1971. His wife, Lois (LaVon Marshall) Mottley, completed her bachelor's degree in nursing at Andrews University in 1972. During the summer of 1966 Alvin was introduced to Lois Marshall, a California native. Alvin and Lois got married in Loma Linda, California, in 1971.

After serving several years as a med tech, Alvin later attended Howard University and completed a degree in dentistry in 1980. Alvin had wanted to join the military at one point to do a tour of duty but later was influenced by Dr. Samuel DeShay and Elder Maurice Battle to be of service to the church and join the Lord's army. At the time he received his call to go to Tanzania, he had just received a scholarship to UCLA. After much prayer he decided, instead, to forego the scholarship and to go to California to attend the Mission Institute that was being held at Loma Linda University.

The family (with two children, Nadine and Nicole) left Maryland in December of 1980 to go to Arusha, Tanzania, where Dr. Mottley would serve as dentist at the Adventist Medical and Dental Clinic.

They discovered, as many missionaries have, that travel is not always a perfect and pleasant experience. They thought they were going to fly directly from New York into the Kilimanjaro airport in Tanzania with a stopover in London. But the airline had cancelled the flights from London, and no one knew that. When they arrived in London they discovered that their direct flight had been cancelled. They waited and waited for their flight to be called. They did not realize it at that time but their luggage had been taken off the plane and was riding around and around on the luggage belt below. It is fortunate that no one took it. Not knowing that their flight was not continuing, they did not think about their luggage at all.

Also, instead of being at Heathrow airport, they were at Gatwick airport. They had to make arrangements to go from Gatwick to Heathrow, and they were able to arrange a Sabena flight to Brussels, Belgium, which was supposed to go on to Arusha, Tanzania. After many hours in the airport, they finally were able to get another flight to Burundi. In Africa at last, but in the wrong country, they were transferred to Dar es Salam and waited there for a long time. Then they got a flight on Air Tanzania to Kilimanjaro.

They still had their winter coats, not realizing that even though it was winter in the States it was summertime in Africa. Because of the mix up in the schedules, nobody was at the airport to meet them. Laden down with coats and baggage, they had to find a pickup truck that could take them and their luggage the rest of the way to the mission station.

Upon arrival no one was around to let them into their house so some Danish missionaries let them spend the night at their house, and the next day they were able to get to the mission station. Here Pastor Theus Young, the Harts, the Thomases, and all the rest of the mission families welcomed them and took them to their house after their tiring travel experience. They were real missionaries now!

Dr. Mottley was able to revive the dental practice that had languished after the departure of Dr. Ted Flaiz. Dr. Mottley's mother, Wilhelmina Mottley, visited them while they were in Africa and enjoyed working with the Tanzanians. She was the one who had inspired Alvin to become involved in outreach ministry. After staying in Tanzania for about two years, she returned to Canada, but in a short time she returned to Tanzania.

She noticed that the Dorcas Society that she had worked with in North America did not exist in Tanzania. She developed a community outreach program similar to the one she had worked with in her church, and it began to expand in Tanzania. This community service style organization called "Love in Action" was greatly appreciated, especially by the women. She made uniforms for the ladies and taught them how to make things that could be sold or given away.

She got ADRA to give them many items that could be used to help the community. She provided many smiles and hugs along with the clothing she distributed to the people. Mrs. Mottley helped with her grandchildren and worked with the community outreach program until the family came home in 1987. She passed away in July of 2013 in Montreal, Canada, at the age of 100.

The Mottleys enjoyed their new African family and enjoyed learning Swahili. They heard a Swahili word that was used often—*muzungu*, which meant "white man." They were amused to hear that the Tanzanians used this word to refer to them. It was sometimes confusing to the Tanzanians to see their dark skin brothers from America whose lifestyle and customs were the same as the white missionaries. By American standards the missionaries had a very simple and conservative lifestyle, but it was so much greater than the Africans that they couldn't help calling their black brother *muzungu*.

They lived in the home that the former missionary dentist had lived in (located on a lovely nine-acre rustic parcel). The Mottleys called it the Garden of Eden because there were an abundance of beautiful flowers. But, as in the Garden of Eden, there were snakes—primarily cobras. They found out that these cobras were often visitors in their house. They had only seen cobras in a zoo, but they found out that often several of these very poisonous crawlers would come and visit them, especially at night.

One day they had their house painted, and the painters were in and out, and the doors were left open more than usual as they brought in their supplies. That night their oldest daughter Nadine got up to go to the bathroom and, half asleep, stepped around a dark object on the floor. She thought the object on the floor was a toy or something. But she noticed on her way back to bed that the dark object she had seen on the floor was moving and realized that it was a large king cobra. Her guardian angel had protected her from stepping on the deadly visitor. In all of Arusha at that time, there were no supplies available to treat snakebites, so the incident could have been fatal.

Another time while they were attending a conference in Nairobi they decided to go to the Masai Mara National Reserve Park in southwestern Kenya. The animals lived naturally there—lions, tigers, elephants, giraffes—on the open plain. There are more than 1.3 million wildebeest there, and often there are predators in hot pursuit of a meal. It's one of the most awesome sights in nature.

It was a beautiful experience for them until it began to rain, an unusually hard tropical downpour. As long as you were in your car and stayed on the road you were pretty safe. They tried to leave the park, but the rain was so hard that they could not see the narrow dirt road and began to wander off the path. All the landmarks that guided them were invisible. They realized that they were lost in the game park, and the sun was setting rapidly. They did not want to spend a night in a place that could be very threatening at night. There were thousands of acres of unknown land in the park, and as they wandered off the road they realized that they were completely lost. They decided to stop and pray and ask God for guidance. When they prayed the downpour abated, and they were able to see the road once more, and God guided them to the gates and out of the park.

About half of Dr. Mottley's patients were nationals, the other half expatriates, including ambassadors, missionaries, Peace Corps workers, and executives of international corporations and their families. The dental practice built a nationwide reputation for high quality service, having added many influential persons to its clientele. Patients were charged on a sliding fee schedule according to their ability to pay. Sometimes this amounted to free dentistry.

Lois Mottley also worked in the dental/medical facility and did book keeping and helped with the nursing program. The medical clinic was downstairs and the dental clinic upstairs, and she acted as the receptionist and office manager for both.

The church leaders discovered that Adventist dental clinics can make more impact in some cases than Adventist hospitals. Large hospitals and institutions are very expensive to staff and operate but small, self-sustaining specialty dental clinics pay for themselves.

Dr. Mottley also provided care to Adventists at camp meetings, and he often traveled to the interior and set up dental services.

Dr. Mottley later obtained his master's degree in public health from Loma Linda, and he and Lois faithfully served in the extension clinic on the beautiful little island of Tobago from 1999 until 2007. Dr. Mottley is currently working in a private dental practice in Georgia.

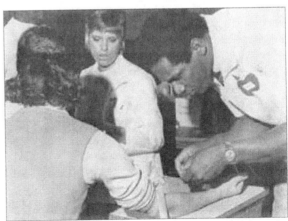

Alvin Mottley, a laboratory technician stateside, prepares to remove a small sample of blood from a participant at a heart screening clinic.

The Mottley family: Lois, Alvin, Nadine, and Nicole

Arriving at Kilimanjaro Airport on December 31, 1980, by way of JFK New York; Heathrow/ Gatwick, London; Brussels, Belgium; Bujumbura, Burundi; and Dar-es-Salaam Tanzania.

Alvin and Lois Mottley with Mission Institute directors at Loma Linda, California, in October-November 1980

Mottley residence at Usa River (pronounced "ooosah river") near Arusha, Tanzania; their residence consisted of three thatched-roof "huts" connected together with concrete bases and hallways

Welcome reception at Tanzania Union Office in 1981: (left) Lois Mottley, office worker, June Moe, office secretary, and Winnie Mottley

53

LARRY AND NATLIE WORD

1980–1982 / Ivory Coast

Larry Doby Word and his wife, the former Natlie Wright, accepted a call to the African-Indian Ocean Division after his graduation from Oakwood College with a degree in business administration. He would serve in Africa as assistant treasurer of the division.

Elder Word tells the story of how he pushed and nurtured the vision of a young man in the Ivory Coast. While working in Abidjan, the Words became acquainted with the Bougui family. The father was an elder in the church and invited the Word family over for Sabbath dinner on several occasions. The Words enjoyed the fellowship and the opportunity to improve their French with a truly French-speaking family.

Their son, Cedric Bougui, admired the treasurer and told him that he would like to go abroad to study. Cedric became acquainted with several of the preachers who passed through the area who were also from Oakwood College (like Elder C. D. Brooks and Elder E. E. Cleveland) and expressed his desire to attend Oakwood. However, there were two problems: Cedric couldn't speak English, and he didn't have any money.

Elder Word explained to young Cedric that all things are possible with God and that if he really believed God would make his dreams come true. They prayed earnestly together and then began to see what avenues would open for the young man.

Elder Word talked to the publishing director, Dale Thomas, and laid the problem before him. Thomas worked out a scholarship plan so that as soon as Cedric graduated from high school he could sell books, and Cedric plunged right in to follow the plan. Cedric canvassed all over Abidjan sowing seeds of truth. After one year of diligent work Cedric had sold enough books to pay for his fare to America and for one year of tuition at Oakwood. He hardly could speak English when he arrived, but with diligent perseverance and good teachers like Alma Blackmon, he got better and better.

Cedric received a bachelor's degree in accounting because he wanted to be like the one who inspired him and then he met a young lady, Victoire, from Martinique who spoke French. She was studying to be a dentist. They both graduated from Oakwood. Cedric then went to Atlanta, and Elder Word drilled and drilled him until he was able to take the difficult CPA exam.

Then Cedric went to Rutgers University where his soon to be wife had just graduated from dental school. He matriculated at Rutgers, finished his master's degree, got married, and the school gave him a full scholarship to work on his doctorate. Victoire became the head dentist at a place in Manhattan.

They now have three sons. A week before he graduated, Cedric received the news that he had succeeded in obtaining his CPA. Victoire and Cedric both got jobs paying them six-figure salaries. Hard work, a vision, and help from his mentor had paid off for the poor boy from the Ivory Coast. In 2012 Cedric and his family returned to Africa to care for his family and to inspire other young people to dream big dreams.

After returning from this mission appointment, Larry Word served as business manager and accountant for the Atlanta-Berean School. During that time he obtained his master's degree in business administration from Mercer University in Atlanta, Georgia. The Words have one daughter, Tomeka. Larry Word was elected assistant treasurer of the South Atlantic Conference on February 21, 1985, and later became the treasurer there in 1988.

In 1997 he was elected treasurer of the Northeastern Conference, and in 1999 he was approved for ordination to the gospel ministry. In 2002 Elder Word moved to Oakwood University as a business teacher and remained there until 2012.

Larry Word is currently working on his doctorate at Walden University.

Larry Word

54
Ronald J. and Equilla Wright

1980–1992 / Liberia, Cameroon, Kenya

Before Pastor Wright became a minister, he was a Vietnam veteran. He was among a rare breed of men who were known as the Airborne Division of the U.S. Army. Simply said, he was trained to parachute out of planes like the c–130 into the thick of battle. His service to his country was more than commendable; it was exceptional.

Ronald Wright is a recipient of the prestigious Purple Heart Medal. The Purple Heart is awarded in the name of the president of the United States to any member of an Armed Forces or any civilian national of the United States who, while serving under competent authority in any capacity with one of the U.S. Armed Services after April 5, 1917, has been wounded or killed or who has died or may hereafter die after being wounded. While clearly an individual decoration, the Purple Heart differs from all other decorations in that an individual is not "recommended" for the decoration; rather he or she is *entitled* to it upon meeting specific criteria. Pastor Wright met the criteria after being wounded in battle in the honorable defense of our country and our way of life.

Pastor Wright is also a recipient of the Distinguished Service Cross. This was awarded to him for extraordinary heroism in connection with military operations involving conflict with an armed hostile force in the Republic of Vietnam while serving with Company B, 2d Battalion, 502d Infantry, 1st Brigade, 101st Airborne Division. Specialist Wright distinguished himself by exceptionally valorous actions on May 18, 1967, while serving as medic of an airborne infantry platoon on a reinforcing mission deep in hostile territory.

While moving to relieve the pressure on a sister platoon that was heavily engaged and pinned down by a numerically superior hostile force, his unit was savagely attacked by enemy soldiers firing automatic weapons. As the intensity of the battle increased, Specialist Wright heard a call for help from a wounded comrade. Completely disregarding his own safety, he began working his way toward the man through a hail of murderous fire. The concussion from an exploding grenade knocked him to the ground and stunned him, but he quickly got up and moved to the wounded soldier. He was seriously wounded while administering aid, but he ignored his injury and moved his comrade to safety. Refusing aid for himself, he again dashed through the withering fire to reach another casualty. Despite his own weakened condition, he carried the man back through a curtain of Viet Cong fire and treated the wounded soldier until he could no longer continue. Specialist Wright's extraordinary heroism and devotion to duty were in keeping with the highest traditions of military service and reflect great credit upon himself, his unit, and the U.S. Army.

After leaving the military, Ronald Wright answered a calling on his life from God. He entered Oakwood University and majored in theology. It was there that he met a lovely young lady by the name of Equilla Green from Oklahoma. They would marry and embark upon their work in the ministry of God as a well-fitted team. Equilla received her bachelor's degree in home economics and business education and later her master's degree in early childhood education. She was very proficient on the piano and vocally. Ronald received his master of divinity degree from Andrews University in 1975 and was called to the South Atlantic Conference where God gifted him in soul winning as pastor-evangelist in Macon and Valdosta, Georgia. On Sabbath afternoon, June 10, 1978, Ronald Jerome Wright was ordained to the gospel ministry at the South Atlantic camp meeting.

His love for God took him from the fields of Vietnam to the mission fields of Africa where he and his family evangelized in God's vineyard for many years. On July 8, 1980, Pastor Wright his wife, and two children, Ron Jr. and Meloni, left New York City for Africa. The Monrovia Seventh-day Adventist Church was filled to capacity on Sabbath, July 12, 1980. It was a day long anticipated by the members since saying farewell to Pastor Cartwright and his family a year earlier. The Wright family arrived in Monrovia on Wednesday, July 9, to assume the responsibility of pastor-evangelist of the Liberia Mission. He and his family were introduced to the Monrovia Church by the president, Pastor Edward Dorsey, and received a very warm welcome.

During a four-week Bible Crusade conducted by Evangelist Wright from April until May 1983, he baptized ninety-nine people in four baptismal services. The praise belonged to God and the victory was His, for the crusade was beset with many problems. The meetings began and continued in the open air for about six days before the tent arrived. On the opening night about 1,500 persons were present. Each night the crowd continued to come, and a separate children's meeting had to be held. Satan tried to disrupt the meetings by having children throw stones at Evangelist Wright from behind the stage. On another night a young man appeared before the pulpit with two rocks in both hands. But God protected Pastor Wright and his family, and souls were baptized. Many of the Tamale Church members prayed all night three times during the campaign.

While people were welcoming in 1984 with partying and dancing, Monrovia Adventist Church members were watching (at 1:35 a.m. New Year's Day) the baptism of the 641st new member as a result of a Revelation Revival Crusade that had begun in October in a town just outside of Monrovia. Ted N. C. Wilson had begun the meetings, which were held in a 40-by-80-foot tent. The tent proved too small for the large crowd of 1,500 people that spilled into the snake-infested grass. At the end of the first three weeks some 321 new members were baptized. It took four pastors, baptizing in shifts, nearly four hours to baptize 225 candidates.

A large brick baptismal pool had been built for the service, but the structure collapsed when its sides were pushed out by the weight of 3,000 gallons of water that had been pumped in from a fire truck. The fire truck was called back to fill a small wooden baptistry that had been built a few days before. Within fifteen minutes the tiny baptistry was filled, but it was a very slow baptism. Pastor Wright coordinated the effort. After Elder Wilson left, Errol Lawrence continued the meetings on the same site. By the time he concluded, another 102 new members had been baptized.

In mid-November the tent was moved to a second location where Pastor Wright and his team began with the topic "The day money will be on the streets of Barnersville and no one will pick it up." A water pressure inadequacy because of limited rain during the rainy season caused power to be switched off often without warning.

On the night when the subject was to have been "The big birthday party," the tent was packed, but there was no electricity. Despite the fact that the advertising referred to a party, candles could not suffice, and the meeting had to be postponed.

When the meeting concluded, there was not enough money to put up the tent in another area, and they moved to a school hall for three more weeks. Six hundred and sixty-six had new significance after the series of meetings because that's how many were baptized in all.

In 1988 Pastor Wright was seriously injured in an automobile accident, but he continued his evangelistic campaign, which resulted in a total of 2,501 persons baptized. He conducted many meetings while in Africa. When he returned to the United States, he pastored in several churches.

At the time of this writing he is the pastor of a church in Augusta, Georgia, and his wife is the principal of Ebenezer Christian Academy. You can find Pastor Wright working with the children at Ebenezer Christian Academy and leading out in devotion or worship. He may also be teaching a physical fitness class to the students. You can find him working hard around the church conducting prayer meetings twice a week, preaching, being active in Sabbath School, business meetings, board meetings, departmental meetings, or giving instruction

and guidance when called upon. He has a burning passion for the work of God and the energy and wisdom to accomplish it.

Ronald Wright with his wife, Equilla, daughter, Melonie, and son, Ronald Jr., when they were serving as missionaries to Liberia. Here they are guests at a camp meeting.

Pastor and Mrs. Wright

55
ROY AND CELIA ADAMS

1981–1986 / Philippines

The following account was written by Roy Adams and provides insight into his and his family's service in the Philippines.

Becoming an overseas missionary was the furthest thing from my mind when I joined the Adventist workforce. When my wife Celia and I left our pastoral assignment in Toronto, Canada, for Andrews University (where I would pursue doctoral studies), I had every intention of returning to the pastorate upon completion. What I didn't know was the dearth of degreed lecturers for our Adventist theological institutions and, accordingly, the amount of pressure that would be brought to bear on me to accept a teaching assignment once I was done.

As it turned out, three teaching calls awaited me upon my completion of a doctorate in systematic theology. I accepted a job at the Seventh-day Adventist Theological Seminary, Far East (now the Adventist International Institute of Advanced Studies, most commonly known by its acronym, AIIAS), near Manila in the Philippines. I arrived in the country in January of 1981 with my wife, Celia, and our two kids, Dwayne (4) and Kimberly (2), to work among some of the most colorful people on the planet.

All the briefings at Missions Institute,

notwithstanding, I had no idea I shouldn't have been dressed in jacket and tie upon arriving in the torrid Filipino capital of Manila. Here I was in the blazing heat and humidity, perspiration bathing my face and neck, lugging a heavy carry-on while holding Kim in my arms. I must have been a sight amid the confusion and the crowd! A van from the seminary picked us up for the fifty-minute trip to the campus.

The church-owned four-bedroom house at the top of the campus where we were placed was practically empty until our furniture and other household things arrived. My family loved the hilltop location that gave us, from our backyard, a view of Laguna de Bay (Laguna Lake) in the distance. There was no air-conditioning, but the hilltop breezes cooled us down. We would often close Sabbath sitting on the back steps looking out over the bay, though it was not the direction of the setting sun.

Our first instinct upon getting to our new home was to call our folks in the United States to inform them of our safe arrival. But we quickly discovered there was no telephone in the house, none on the entire campus, nor any in the immediate surrounding villages. To contact the United States, we had to journey to Manila and have the telephone operator at our North

Philippine Union office put through a call for us. Alternatively, we could use a pay phone in the lobby at one of the major hotels in the city—the Inter-Continental Hotel in Makati (a section of greater Manila) was our favorite choice, offering us the greatest privacy.

The seminary, financed by the division, shared the same campus with Philippine Union College (now the Adventist University of the Philippines), which was financed by the North Philippine Union. And therein lay a long, complicated, and (sometimes) painful story not relevant here. For me, personally, it was an enriching atmosphere.

Not long after we arrived, fellow expat, Sam Robinson, worked out an auto deal for me with one of his friends in Manila for a huge, black Chevrolet, more than a decade old at the time. The price was good. But that first day, as I drove through the campus gate with it, it literally brought the ballgame in the nearby field to a complete stop. In a country where most cars are midsize or smaller, many students had never seen a sight like that, and suddenly I became the object of an entire field of gawkers. In my mind I imagined going around the country and being identified as "the big black American guy in the big black American Chevrolet." Not exactly the image I wanted to create.

Within three days, the vehicle was back outside its owner's house, an outcome made easier by the fact that no money had yet changed hands.

Our second vehicle was a small Ford Escort, which I used to take my family on our first vacation in the Philippines—to the mountain resort of Baguio. Anyone who's ever traveled to that popular destination knows that getting

there involves navigating a long, narrow, winding mountain road with the gradient getting steeper with every meter. Halfway up the mountain, the car began overheating, forcing us to stop more than once on the precipitous incline, and creating some very frightening moments for us.

Eventually, we reached the mountain retreat and had a good time. A few weeks later, however, on a Sunday morning the Escort burned to the ground just about twenty yards from our home, shortly after I'd left the house to run an errand down campus. I'm still so thankful that the incident did not happen during that Baguio trip, or in the middle of Manila traffic, or in any other way that would have put my family or others in danger!

Starting out as an assistant professor of theology (I would become a full professor before leaving), I was operating sometimes just one lesson ahead of my students. It demanded hours and hours of preparation (that first year, especially), developing new lectures in the seven areas of theology I taught—anthropology, soteriology, eschatology, etc. Our students were an international clientele hailing from the Philippines, Indonesia, Singapore, Malaysia, India, Bangladesh, South Korea, Japan, Thailand, Africa, Europe, the Caribbean, and the United States. In addition, the seminary conducted extension schools on location, and I had opportunity to teach classes throughout the region—in Japan, South Korea, Indonesia, and Bangladesh—as well as take seminars and speak at appointments in Singapore, Hong Kong, Taiwan, and elsewhere.

It was stimulating work in a number of ways, providing endless opportunities for interaction and learning—from the Philippines itself (with its colorful traditions and people), from the various cultures present on campus, from the local faculty and staff, and from fellow expatriate colleagues and their families.

Campus life was quiet. We had radios, but no telephones (as mentioned before) and no television. After a few years, a single television set appeared on campus in the home of then seminary president Dr. Werner Vyhmeister. It could pick up, as I recall, two or three local stations. Some Saturday nights saw a lyceum program of some kind, but most times people simply created their own entertainment. My family, with Kim often riding on my shoulder, would often walk down campus, meeting and talking to students and other faculty along the way.

One of the strangest things to happen to me while there came as the General Conference session convened in 1985. The president of the seminary left for the meetings and also to take some furlough time; and the (expat) business manager (together with one or two other expat workers) also left on furlough. So thus it was that yours truly found himself simultaneously holding the offices of theology professor (my main job), chair of the international school board, acting business manager of the seminary, and acting president of the seminary. Imagine that for a moment!

My first morning on the jobs in the seminary found me in some quandary as to which office to occupy first. Eventually, since the business office was the closest as I would enter the complex, I sat there first. Within minutes a woman showed up and requested to see me as the business manager. Her husband was an overseas seminary student, and she'd come to report

that their vehicle had been stolen overnight.

The first thing that came to mind was to advise her to go see the president. Then just as quickly I remembered I was also the president. So after questioning her about the details of her story, we set out in my car to file a report at the nearest police station in the town of Tagaytay, about twenty minutes away.

Out of his office when we arrived, the police chief eventually walked in wearing shorts and flip-flops. Within seconds after we sat down together, he'd put his finger on the single detail we wanted most to avoid: "Was the car registered?" he asked pointedly.

In my questioning of the student's wife, I'd learned that they'd just acquired the vehicle and were currently in the process of registering it. To this day I'm amazed that the casual-looking officer could get so quickly to this central issue. It took a lot of dancing around to avoid a direct answer to that pivotal question. In the end, having no transportation at the station, the chief suggested that I might drive him to Puting Kahoy (the village near the campus, where he suspected the thief came from), so he might conduct an investigation. This I diplomatically declined to do, not wanting my personal vehicle becoming associated with a police investigation. After all, it was the same vehicle I would have to use to drive through that very neighborhood on almost a weekly basis.

How the case eventually was resolved I cannot now remember. But it was certainly a chilling start to my first day in the dual role of business manager-president.

There were other curious stories, many more,

but space does not allow.

Our kids enrolled in the Makiling Adventist School (the international elementary school on campus for the children of expats and foreign graduate and seminary students) and made many friends there. And Celia took time from homemaking to earn a bache-lor's degree in nursing.

We arrived in the Philippines during the time of President Ferdinand Marcos and his colorful (and powerful) wife, Imelda. But before we left, they were both gone, chased out of the country amid the political crisis following the elections of February 1986. It was an exceedingly tense time to live through, with the word "evacuation" surfacing frequently. But it never came to that, and we were able to stay our full term.

That term ended the same year, and the month of October found my family heading back to Canada where I would serve as associate secretary of the Seventh-day Adventist Church in Canada (the Canadian Union) and editor of the Canadian Adventist Messenger.

Apart from the customary farewells, the days before departure were occupied with packing and shipping household stuff, selling some things, and giving away a whole lot to local friends and "helpers" in our home. The specifics of all that have faded in memory now, except this one. When I gave my hammer to the guy whose job it was to repair and fix broken things in homes around the campus—particularly in expat homes—he paused in silence for what felt like thirty seconds; then wistfully he said: "Now I own an American hammer!" It just about blew me away—for here I thought

I was doing just some little, insignificant thing.

My family and I bonded well with the Filipino people, and there remains a deep affection in our hearts for that country and its friendly citizens. Strangers stared at us, to be sure—especially at first. We were different. But throughout our stay the people we met afforded us nothing but honor and respect. Today I feel at home with them wherever they come together in the United States. And whenever the occasion warrants, I wear the Barong Tagalog proudly.

After some two years at the Canadian Union, my family moved to the General Conference, where for the next twenty-two years (until retirement in October 2010), I served as an associate editor of Adventist Review/Adventist World.

Roy Adams was born in Grenada, West Indies, and began his career in the South Caribbean Conference as a teacher in Tobago and as a pastor in Port of Spain, Trinidad, in 1961. After obtaining degrees in theology from Canadian Union College (B.Th.) and Andrews University (M.Div.), Roy spent some seven years in pastoral work in Montreal and Toronto before returning to Andrews University for a doctorate in systematic theology. He was the first candidate to finish a doctoral degree in systematic theology at the Adventist Theological Seminary at Andrews University.

Elder Adams was serving as secretary of the Seventh-day Adventist Church in Canada in 1988 when William Johnsson, then-editor of *Adventist Review*, invited Adams to join the staff of the church's flagship magazine.

In addition to his work writing and editing for *Adventist Review*, and since 2005 for *Adventist World*, Adams has written seven books. In

2008 he authored *The Wonder of Jesus*, a series of Sabbath School Bible studies for the Adult Bible Study Guide.

Adams is often in demand as a camp meeting speaker, and his travels have taken him to nearly every continent on earth. He was twice featured at the Ministry Professional Growth Seminars, cosponsored by *Ministry* magazine and the General Conference Ministerial Association and broadcast live, via satellite, to downlink sites all over the world.

Dr. Adams was the recipient of the Lifetime Achievement Award presented by the Society of Adventist Communicators at its annual convention on October 16, 2010. At that meeting he announced his retirement, capping a career in the Adventist Church that spans nearly fifty years. He has the distinction of being the longest-serving full-time associate editor in the 160-year history of the *Adventist Review*.

Roy (back row, 4th from right) with a wedding party; one of the many weddings he participated in while in the Philippines

Dwayne and Kim with bunnies

Roy with local Filipino faculty friends drinking the real thing.

Celia (left), Kim (next to her), and Dwayne (far right) with guests

Dwayne's graduation at Oakwood University in 1998

Celia and Roy with kids (Dwayne and Kim) on furlough on Vancouver Island, British Columbia (about 1983)

The Adams on furlough on Vancouver Island in 1983.

56
KAREN BURKE-BRIGHT

1981–1984 / Ivory Coast

Karen Ann Burke was born in California and is a former student of La Sierra University.

Her parents are from the Bahamas and from Jamaica. She is a former language teacher who holds a master's degree in French language and civilization from New York University and an advanced certificate in German language from the Intercultural Language School in Vienna, Austria. She is also a graduate of Loma Linda University in California. She served as a missionary in French-speaking West Africa and tells her story below.

Mrs. Burke-Bright has held evangelistic meetings in Rwanda, Central Africa, under the auspices of the Quiet Hour Ministry as well as in Pasadena, Maryland, under the auspices of the Chesapeake Conference. In 2010 she took early retirement from the World Bank to respond to the call of God to pastoral ministry. She is now a graduate seminary student of Andrews University in the pastoral ministries program.

Mrs. Burke-Bright is an experienced preacher, spiritual retreat speaker, workshop facilitator, and university chapel speaker. At her local church, she has served as lay pastor and head elder; she currently serves as an elder and the church administrator.

Karen and her husband Paul live in Silver Spring, Maryland. Her hobbies include reading, writing, singing, and traveling. She tells her own story in the following text.

On January 1, 1981, I arrived in the République de Côte d'Ivoire (the Ivory Coast) to begin service as a regular missionary at the Africa-Indian Ocean Division (AID) of Seventh-day Adventists. I had originally wanted to be a language teacher in Côte d'Ivoire, but the call that came to me was for a bilingual secretary in the division office. It took a while for me to pray about this and accept the call, but I'm glad I did.

This division was the regional administrative office for thirty-three countries in West Africa and in the French-speaking countries of the Indian Ocean. The Ivory Coast is a large country with a population at that time of more than 20 million inhabitants, speaking French as the official language (i.e., the language of business and international relations, but it is considered the second language) with Senoufo and Baoulé as the major languages and thirty additional languages and dialects.

Despite the fact that I had completed background research on Côte d'Ivoire and interviewed students from that country who told me that Abidjan was a modern city and that I did not have to worry about living (that I would have a modern apartment) or shopping (there were modern supermarkets) or finding transportation (I could buy my own car or travel by taxi or bus), etc., I was still a victim to the sociological lessons perpetrated by our American media that Africa is made up of villages full of half-dressed natives living in huts and savannah land full of wild animals.

My surprise was palpable when I arrived in the modern city of Abidjan. It was the capital of the country at the time and very beautiful. The largest hotel that I had ever stayed in anywhere was the Hotel Ivoire, which also boasted the largest pool I'd ever seen. I also had the ultimate surprise—my first time ice skating at a club in the hotel. Cultural life in the city was rich, and the only time I saw wild animals were in the Abidjan zoo.

I had a beautiful, spacious apartment (I was single at the time—families were assigned beautiful homes) and was able to purchase a car later on that year. The supermarkets were lovely, and we even had "The American Store," which sold groceries that we were accustomed to getting at home. In addition to this, we were able to shop at beautiful outdoor markets that offered everything except real estate and automobiles.

During the 1980s the economy of the Côte d'Ivoire was very strong; the CFA franc was robust. International commerce and interests were also very evident. The country still had very close ties to France (its once-time colonialist power), and there was a large French community in the city. I took my first year of German language lessons at the Goethe Institute at the German Embassy and enjoyed some of the social events held at the American Embassy, which was highly respected and very active.

The Ivoirians are a beautiful people who love to dress up and enjoy their lives.

International and local hotels were of high quality, and cultural events brought participants from around the globe to Côte d'Ivoire. For example, Cirque du Soleil, internationally-acclaimed South African and European choirs, troupes, and singers, etc., were the norm. After Sunday morning tennis at one of the hotel courts, I enjoyed meeting friends at the ice cream parlors or one of the many national or international restaurants.

It was a joy to make acquaintances among the local church families and business colleagues. I began my service as a "gopher" (I happily served in whatever area I was needed) as we opened the new division office. On my first day of work I was prepared to receive the incoming families that arrived. Because of my language ability, I was soon moved to the position of a junior accountant, which I enjoyed very much. I was responsible for the installation of all international workers, ensuring that their living arrangements were made, their home-based deposits initiated, and their insurance processed. I also dealt with all travel agents, purchasing tickets for all incoming and outgoing staff, clearing personal effects through customs, and initiating new workers to the city and helping them become settled.

My work entailed some travel, and I served in the accounting department of the Burundi mission for a month and attended quarterly meetings in Accra, Ghana, as part of the treasury team. On my own I had the privilege of traveling to many other countries such as Sénégal, Liberia, Togo, Cotonou, Kenya, Rwanda, Seychelles, Nigeria, Ethiopia, and Djibouti, etc.

We worshipped each Sabbath with the local church family at the Marcory SDA Church. I served as a Sabbath School teacher, and after the first month, I became the interpreter for the divine service to assist the English-speaking division workers (from Ghana, the USA, and Nigeria). After a couple of years, I also attended other churches in Abobo-Gare and a branch Sabbath School in Adjamé.

Because I was the only single person with a car, I generally transported the other single workers (mainly women) to church and to social outings. We socialized quite a bit among ourselves (potlucks, picnics at Grand Bassam beach, canal rides, etc.). Some of the other cities and towns of Côte d'Ivoire that I visited were Daloua, Yamoussoukro, Grand Bassam, Bouaké, Sassandra, San Pédro, and Abengourou.

As a singer/songwriter I had the opportunity to sing at church, our evangelistic meetings, and at a few other events around the city. I appeared a couple of times on Ivoirian television. Some of the music that I wrote in Abidjan included two well-liked numbers:

- *Bless the Family – This song was written during my first month in the country when I was severely missing my family. I shared it with the missionary families, and it became a regularly requested number and served as a spiritual and emotional link to our families.*

- *Mon Ame Béni l'Eternel – This was one of the songs essentially written to share with the French-speaking church members and visitors. I shared it at special events such as camp meeting when we visited the village where the first missionaries set up camp.*

- *Even though I experienced a few negative instances in certain parts of the African continent (car stolen as I waited for a tennis court on a Sunday morning at one of the hotels in Abidjan; sequestered in Accra for almost a month due to a coup d'état and was successfully smuggled out—thank God). I generally do not speak of these events. I try instead to highlight the positive. I will share one incident that took place in Nairobi, Kenya.*

On my way to Burundi on a short assignment I had to remain in Nairobi for about a week in order to secure a visa for Burundi. I lodged in the guest house of Maxwell Adventist Academy, located on Milimani Road, on the property of the headquarters of the Seventh-day Adventist Church for the East-Central African Division. On the Sunday morning before my flight out, I went into the city to purchase a few grocery items. Going down the hill on Milimani Road toward Kenyatta Avenue and the city center, one passes through a section that lies between two parks, one on either side. As I walked, I was delighted to watch the lines of cars filled with beautifully dressed families on their way to church services. Church bells were ringing in the distance, and the scene seemed so bucolic to me.

On my return up the hill with my grocery bag, about two blocks before I arrived at the guest house, someone stealthily snatched my purse from under my arm. I swung around to face two laughing men. A short man, who had the purse, was tossing it back and forth to his taller accomplice.

I dropped my groceries and began to yell at the top of my voice: "Give me my purse, I will give you money. My passport is in there, and you will not get away with this!" I lunged at the younger (and smaller) of the two men, when my purse next landed in his hands. He was so shocked that he stumbled, and I grabbed him. We grappled on the ground for a few moments before he managed to rip my blouse and toss my purse to the bigger man, who then ran across the street into the big park. (Uhuru Park).

I followed as swiftly as possible while yelling at an even higher pitch. "Help, thief! Help, thief!" I had earlier learned a few words in Swahili, but none would come to my rescue at the time. The men were getting away as the distance between us broadened by the minute.

However, at the top of the hill toward which they were running, a growing crowd had gathered and were pointing at us and gesticulating. They had heard my noise and grabbed the thief when he was near enough. I panted up the hill ten minutes later and saw that one of the men had escaped and that the crowd was beating the younger man whom they had caught.

Someone came over to me and handed me my purse asking: "Does this belong to you? Is this what he stole?" I could hardly speak, but managed to squeak out that yes, it was mine. They insisted that I check it to see if anything was missing. After doing this and finding everything in order, I requested that they release the young man, but they insisted that he be punished and continued knocking him about the head.

Suddenly, a large man grabbed my arm and yanked the thief from the crowd and propelled us to his car. I recognized him as one of the men who had earlier taken his family to church, who now happened to be returning by the same way and saw the crowd. He shoved the thief into the back of his car and offered me the front seat. The gentleman took us to the police station where he turned over the thief to the authorities. He refused payment from me and finally left.

The police chief was very upset when I repeatedly refused to press charges. I could hear the young man being slapped around in the next room (possibly his cell). He tried his best to talk me into making sure that the young man was punished, but since I had my purse and was not going to make a later trip back to Nairobi just for the trial of a petty thief, I did not change my mind.

Afterward, it was difficult to follow the same path back toward my guest house for I realized that the situation could repeat itself, but thankfully it didn't. Once back in my room, I thanked the Lord for His protection and care and tossed my torn blouse into the trash. Yes, I felt violated and alone and couldn't wait to take my flight to Burundi the next day.

However, despite my discomfort, my belief in human kindness was greatly strengthened and my love for Nairobi and Kenya had grown immensely.

There is a story in the *Adventist Review* that tells about two families who were involved in a car accident in Abidjan, Ivory Coast, the headquarters for the Africa-Indian Ocean Division office. One worker fractured her pelvis, right femur, and right ankle. Another sustained a fractured pelvis and right femur, and lacerations on her right hand. A third had a fractured pelvis, a broken rib, and minor lacerations. They were all airlifted to their respective countries and left behind disheartened division workers in Abidjan and worried members of their families back home.

Some felt that they would never return to their mission posts, but they all were able to witness while in the hospital, and they shortly returned to work. They were not prepared for the welcome they received when they returned to Abidjan. Waving hands and hearty cheers greeted them as they limped down the stairs. That reunion weekend in September 1983 was very special for the Africa-Indian Ocean Division family.

At the end of the Saturday night vespers program, which was a welcome to the returned workers, Karen Burke sang a song she had written earlier called "Lord, Bless the Family." Karen's composition became the division's unofficial theme song.

Bless The Family

Let's pray for everybody
No matter where we're from
No matter what our story
No matter what we've done
Let's lift our hearts together
Everyone under the sun
And raise a prayer to heaven
To the eternal One
Lord, bless the family

We pray for all the leaders
Of the countries of the world
We strive to keep our freedom
Unfettered and unfurled
We pray for broken people

Who live without a home
For those who are contented
With the lives that they have known

Bridge
We pray for those who know You
And pray for those who don't
We pray for those who follow
And pray for those who won't
As we lift our hearts together
We pray especially
Lord, bless the family

Refrain
Lord, bless the family
It's such a special unity
That brings the world together
Lord, bless the family
It's such a special unity
That makes each one a brother
For the families of earth
Will families in heaven
And the families of heaven
Will be children of the King
As we lift our hearts together
We pray especially
Lord, bless the family

We pray as you have taught us
We pray Thy will be done …
Forgiveness from our debtors
As we forgive each one
We pray that You will keep us
From the evil in the world
Forgive us kindest Father
For every time we fall

Bridge 2
We know You have the power
The glory it is Yours
We praise Your name forever

The King and Lord of lords
As we lift our hearts together
We pray especially
Lord, bless the family
© 1981

Karen Burke with Elder Neal Wilson in Abijan, Ivory Coast

Karen Burke-Bright

57
GEORGE AND PEARL JEAN HUGGINS

1981–1982 / Guatemala; 1983–1984 / Panama; 1992–1998 / Ghana, Liberia

George Edward Huggins is a graduate of Oakwood College. He worked for a long time for the Northeastern Conference as an outstanding literature evangelist and pastor of the Staten Island district in New York. He is married to Pearl Jean Gibbs Huggins, and they have two children, Israel and Winona.

In 1975 he went to Andrews University to study. In 1976 he joined the men's residence hall staff as an assistant dean of men at Andrews University. While at Andrews he finished his ministerial degree (1977) and continued to do colporteur work close to the school. He worked in several Andrews University field schools. In 1977 he worked in Quill Lake, Saskatchewan, Canada, selling books, and his work aroused the interest of a family that joined the church during an evangelistic effort conducted by Pastor Gerry Karst.

In 1980 Elder Huggins became the pastor of the Grand Concourse Church in the Bronx, New York. Under his leadership the church passed the super Ingathering goal for the first time in the history of the Grand Concourse congregation.

On March 5, 1981, Elder Huggins, his wife, and their two children left the States for Guatemala. He was to serve as Bible teacher and principal at the Peten Agricultural School. In 1983 he then moved in Panama.

A few years later Elder Huggins and his wife left New York on February 4, 1992, to serve as ministerial secretary of the West African Union Mission with headquarters in Ghana. In 1995, after his furlough, he returned to Africa to be president of the Liberia Mission. And in 1997 he returned to Liberia as departmental associate director for the Liberia Mission.

Liberia was founded by freed slaves from the United States in 1822. The oldest republic in Africa, it was declared an independent country in 1847. For decades, Liberia was known as one of the most well-to-do countries in the subcontinent due to natural resources that contributed to the economic development of the country.

However, from 1980 to 2003, twenty years of intermittent civil war devastated the infrastructure and impoverished the nation. Despite these hindrances, Liberia is slowly recovering and has of late experienced economic growth.

The Seventh-day Adventist Church in Liberia now has a membership of nearly 25,000, worshipping in 103 churches and companies. In the capital, Monrovia, thirteen organized churches and eight companies meet weekly for services. The Liberia Mission operates six secondary schools. One of them, Konola Academy, is a boarding school with about 350 students. In addition, twenty-one primary schools educate more than 8,000 students.

The church also operates Cooper Memorial

Hospital in Monrovia. Before the political upheaval of the 1980s and 1990s, it was one of the flagship hospitals in the country. In an audience with a Seventh-day Adventist delegation soon after her inauguration in 2006, President Johnson-Sirleaf appealed to the church to upgrade the hospital to the standard of its former days. The hospital was incorporated into the Adventist Health International (AHI) network, and with this new development, improvement in the services and facilities has occurred. The eye clinic connected with the hospital opened in 2004 and provides some of the best ophthalmologic services in the country, including cataract and other surgeries.

Andrews University students who went to assist in the field school in Kelowna, British Columbia: (left to right) Dave Toop, Clarence Baptiste, Gary Birth, Dane Forrester, Ulrich Unruh, Ralph Hollenbeck, Jack Duerken, Irwin Burton, Austin Goodwin, and (far left) George Huggins

Elder and Mrs. George Huggins (center) with son Israel and daughter Winona in 1980

58

ROBERT AND JANICE PRESSLEY

1981–1982 / Nigeria

Robert Pressley shares his thoughts about his short stint of service in Nigeria:

I am Robert Samuel Pressley. My wife's name is Janice. We have four children, and our family is from Charlotte, North Carolina. I was born in Williamston, South Carolina, and graduated from Oakwood College, now Oakwood University, where I received a bachelor's degree in business administration and a minor in religion. I am an ordained local elder.

Prior to moving to Oakwood College, our children were enrolled in church school, but the school only went to the eighth grade. Therefore, we moved to Huntsville, Alabama, so our children could continue their Christian education at Oakwood College. My wife strongly suggested that I complete my education at Oakwood College. Upon graduation, I worked as an accountant in the Allegheny West Conference. After spending two years there, I accepted the position of bookstore manager at Oakwood College.

In the spring of 1980 I received the invitation to serve in the mission field. The call was for me to be the vice president of financial affairs at the Adventist Seminary of West Africa (ASWA) in Nigeria, which was an extension of Andrews University. Two of our children, Adrian and

Gretchen, accompanied my wife and me to the mission field. They were students at ASWA.

My experience in Nigeria could be summed up as wonderfully memorable and challenging. Upon our arrival the nationals and students were very kind and cordial to us. Our children quickly connected with the students, as they were eager to relate with someone their age.

After taking up my responsibilities, I discovered there were many opportunities for growth in the business department. Creating a smoother registration process was one of my first challenges. By God's grace I was able to successfully reorganize the way the students registered for classes. As a result we reduced the registration process to half the time it had previously been.

The college had a bakery, but the money from the sales of the bread, which was being sold as far away as Lagos and other surrounding cities, was going somewhere other than paying for the flour to continue making bread. Some of the employees had not been paid for two months. I went to Lagos and pleaded with the manager of the flour mill to give us a little more time to pay our bill. Initially, the manager showed no mercy; he just wanted his money. But I must say God blessed my persistent and tactful efforts and softened the manager's heart. I was able to offer an acceptable payment schedule, which allowed us to continue to get flour so the bakery could remain operative. Our employees were elated to have their salaries reinstated. To make sure we remained solvent and our invoices were paid in a timely manner, I traveled to the stores that were purchasing our bread and collected the monies. This also gave me an opportunity to personally meet our buyers and witness to them.

While we were in Nigeria, the political situation was stable. There were no government coups, and we moved around the country freely without being harassed.

I enjoyed working with most of the nationals. However, I had problems with some of the Caucasian missionaries from Europe and the United States. They felt they did not have to comply with my authority as vice president of financial affairs. To exemplify, they would go and purchase materials without first coming to the business office and getting approval. As this was not a sound business method, I brought an end to this practice. In their eyes I became their enemy because I would not go along with the mode of operation they were used to before I came. Consequently, they began a conspiracy against my wife and me.

At this point my wife was the accounts analyst for the college. Some of the teachers and other workers did not like the way she was restructuring the business practices. She was organizing the business office in a professional manner that would enhance the day-to-day operation of the office. The conspiracy went so far that my tenure was cut short by two years. I was falsely accused of embezzling $25,000 Naira ($18,000

USD). I demanded an audit by the Treasury Department of the Africa-Indian Ocean Division (AID). The audit, which was conducted by the treasurer of the AID, revealed that the allegation was untrue and that no money was missing.

I must mention that prior to the conclusive findings of the audit I was arrested by the Nigerian police at the behest of the college administration. The ASWA administration went to the immigration authorities and allegedly paid them to have me and my family deported from the country. Most of the people in Nigeria are Muslims, and the immigration authorities were Muslims. They were appalled that as Christians our church leadership was requesting our deportation from the country like common criminals. The authorities' response was, "Since this family has worked for the Seventh-day Adventist Church for a number of years, let them leave this country in a normal and dignified fashion." I was told that the ASWA administration responded by saying, "Get them out of Nigeria as quickly as possible by any means!"

When we were at Andrews University being indoctrinated prior to going overseas, the Adventist Church was trying to find ways and means of witnessing to the Muslims. This dastardly and soulless act was no way to witness to anyone with the hopes of encouraging them to become a Christian.

As I stated earlier, the Nigerian police arrested me for allegedly stealing money. I remained at the police station for about two hours. After my arrest, the ASWA administration had a Kangaroo Court. They tried to convince the police chief to incarcerate me. But the chief *was too wise to be baited into this diabolical scheme. After the meeting, which was attended by the ASWA president, certain teachers, and others, the police chief refused to incarcerate me because he felt it was conspiratorially motivated. This police chief, who didn't even profess to be a Christian, said to me, "I spared you today from what your own people wanted to do to you."*

At one point during this debacle, a high ranking General Conference official called me from Washington, D.C., and told me that "right or wrong, you should return to the U.S. immediately in order to keep the peace." Through divine inspiration, it was clearly revealed to me that this advice was void of any spiritual or ethical substance. It would not have been spiritually responsible or morally ethical for me to have left Nigeria prior to having an audit clear my name and integrity.

During the time of our challenges with the expatriates, the ASWA students said, "If the Pressley family is coerced to leave prematurely, all of the other missionaries will have to leave as well." After my family and I left Nigeria, I learned that the students boycotted their classes and kept the pressure on the administration to vindicate our name. As a result, most of the remaining missionaries were forced to leave Nigeria.

Prominent officials in the hierarchy of the Seventh-day Adventist Church predicted I would never get another job within the denomination because of my refusal to kowtow and truckle to the church officials who heaped gross and outright diabolical injustices on my family and me. However, after arriving in the United States, God had already prepared a place of

service for me. Hallelujah! I was hired by Elder George R. Earle, president of Northeastern Conference (NEC). The position I held was the treasurer of the Publishing Department, and my wife was the manager of the credit union. Several General Conference officials were miffed when they heard this and tried to get Elder Earle to fire us! His response to these officials was, "You tend to your business in Washington, and I will take care of Northeastern Conference's business." My wife and I worked for NEC for almost twenty years. I retired in 2003. We currently reside in Huntsville, Alabama.

The friendships we forged with many of the students and nationals while in Nigeria will forever be cherished. A great number of them now live here in the United States. From time to time we come across them in different cities, shopping malls, groceries stores, at Oakwood University, etc. Even now, when any of our former friends from ASWA visit Huntsville, they are welcomed guests in our home.

Even though our tenure at ASWA was short, it served as a launching pad for the massive expansion that would eventually occur at this great institution. The Adventist Seminary of West Africa has now been renamed Babcock University. There are approximately 7,000 students in attendance, making this one of, if not the largest Adventist university in the world. Being a pioneer private university in Nigeria since 1999, Babcock has continued this legacy of upholding a cutting-edge excellence in education. From her initial four schools, Babcock has added a postgraduate school that took off in the third quarter of 2010 and a medical school that took off in January 2012.

As of 2013 Babcock hosts nine schools and one college: School of Agriculture & Industrial Technology; Babcock Business School; College of Health & Medical Sciences; School of Basic & Applied Science; School of Computing & Engineering Sciences; School of Education and Humanities; School of Law & Security Studies; School of Nursing; School of Public & Allied Health; School of Post Graduate Studies; and The Ben Carson School of Medicine (the denomination's first medical school in Africa).

As I reflect on my service at the Adventist Seminary of West Africa, I am eternally grateful to God for choosing my family and me to serve in this capacity and to make such a lasting impact that will stretch into eternity. I also thank Him for the trying situations I endured there. It crystallizes in my mind the reality that "if God is for me, no one [or any institution] can be against me." And it reassures me that Isaiah 54:17 is true: "No weapon formed against me [or any child of God] will prosper."

Dr. Mensah and Adrian Pressley

Mrs. Mensah and a student that Robin Pressley taught

The marketplace

Janice and Robert Pressley

Downtown Lagos, Nigeria

59

DANIEL AND ELIZABETH DAVIS

1982–1983 / Ivory Coast

Daniel L. Davis was born in Pittsburgh, Pennsylvania. He served in the United States Army Air Force from 1943 to 1946 and saw action in the Pacific. After World War II he was a professional welterweight boxer for a period of time.

His wife, Elizabeth (Betty), led him to the church and to God. Although he was a Christian, when he met Betty, Danny, as he was most often called, knew nothing about the Adventist Church. He learned about the church after he left the military and began attending Friday night services at Elizabeth's house. "He just fell in love with this church and fell in love with God," Betty says. "He was coming to church for a whole year and paying tithe before he was baptized. My husband discovered Daniel 2 and that convinced him of the truth of the Adventist Church."

Davis was a medical student at the University of Pittsburgh when he visited Oakwood College. After that visit he transferred to Oakwood to continue his medical training, but soon he switched to the ministry. He received his bachelor's degree in theology from Oakwood and completed graduate work at the Adventist Theological Seminary. He was ordained to the gospel ministry in 1956.

He began his ministerial career in the Allegheny East Conference (AEC) in 1951 as a pastor-evangelist for some thirteen churches in the states of West Virginia, New Jersey, and Ohio. In 1963 he joined the conference office where he led several ministries for some ten years. Betty was an administrative assistant for AEC. He went on to serve six years as director of youth ministries and health and temperance for the Columbia Union Conference.

From 1982 to 1983 he served the world church as youth ministries director in the former Africa-Indian Ocean Division. According to his wife, when Elder Davis became youth ministries director in the Africa-India Division, he was only the second black American to serve as a division youth director. His tremendous commitment to the Lord and to young people was evident in his life and his work as a missionary.

When he retired in 1994, he continued serving AEC for another seven years as a volunteer trust officer, director of senior citizen housing, and eventually as president of the Fifty-Plus Association. Chillum Oaks, a forty-nine-unit apartment facility for seniors in Hyattsville, Maryland, opened in 1997 on a two-acre lot next to the Metropolitan Church. Davis worked through the maze of paperwork, governmental regulations, and time lines in two years. More than twenty-six county departments and sixteen federal departments reviewed the process, and one high official remarked. "This is the smoothest application that I have seen thus far." The

Chillum Oaks Adventist Apartments program received almost seven million dollars for construction, operation, and subsidy.

Davis' name graces AEC's youth camp—Camp Daniel L. Davis—in Pine Forge, Pennsylvania. He is also credited for innovations in outreach, prison ministries, community services, and Pathfinders.

Pastor Daniel L. Davis, who served the Seventh-day Adventist Church on multiple levels for some sixty years, died on April 3, 2013, at his home in Georgia. He was eighty-eight. Elizabeth, his wife of sixty-five years, still lives in Georgia and is supported by her daughter, Elizabeth Davis-Bell, and her son, Danny, and his wife, Kathy.

Elder Danny Davis, MV director, Allegheny East Conference, with a nine-foot boa constrictor around his neck

Elder Daniel Davis

Change of Command: Danny Davis, Columbia Union youth leader who had just accepted his call to the Africa-Indian Ocean Division, and Norm Middag, General Conference youth department, salute Ron Stretter of Ohio, the newly appointed director of the Columbia Union youth department.

60

Phillip and Naomi Polley

1982–1984 / Marshall Islands; 1996–2007 / Mali

Both Phillip and Naomi were born in Detroit, Michigan. They met at Oakwood College; however, neither of them graduated from Oakwood. Phillip graduated from the University of Texas with a bachelor's degree in psychology and is a graduate student at Regis University, working on a master's degree in nonprofit management. Naomi Jones Polley attended Lake Michigan College and is a certified dental assistant.

They were students at Oakwood when they first were called to serve overseas. After they were married they worked as teachers in Majuro, Marshall Islands, for eighteen months but returned to the States when Naomi became pregnant. They loved their time there, and it was there that the "mission bug" bit them! But earning a living and raising a family kept them busy for several years. Here are their own words about their second term of service.

Our second term of service came years later when we had three children, ages twelve, ten, and three, and homeschooling in Atlanta, Georgia. Phillip was working as a literature evangelist for the Georgia-Cumberland Conference.

It all began with our eldest son Joel's homeschool project. His assignment was to look into short-term mission projects to Native American communities. Eventually he was referred *to Adventist Frontier Missions (AFM) and he sent for an application. AFM sent back the nicest rejection letter, stating that Joel was a bit young (only 11 at the time) to be a missionary, and there were no Native American projects in the works. However, if he wanted to have his parents consider career mission service with AFM, they would send the application. In the meantime, AFM would place us on the mailing list of Adventist Frontiers, their monthly journal of stories written by the AFM missionaries. Thus began six months of prayer and heart searching which eventually led to us submitting the application to be missionaries to Mali, West Africa.*

Following an in-depth application process, we embarked on a year of 'FUN raising.' And boy was it fun! Adventist Frontier Missions is a supporting ministry of the Adventist Church. They work in cooperation with the General Conference and the local administration wherever they have a project to plant an Adventist Church in a location where there is no Adventist presence and often times no Christian presence. Once the church is established, it is turned over to the local conference and the missionaries return home.

Being a supporting ministry, the missionaries are required to raise their support, which is a beautiful system because it builds a team of supporters that become like a large family and safety net beneath you as you serve in some very trying circumstances. With the funds that are raised you have the launching costs, which include plane fares, training costs, other travel expenses, visas, passports, shots, etc. Then you also have monthly costs, which are for your salary, benefits, homeland savings, and administrative expenses. Being a supporting ministry does not provide service credit with the denomination, only with heaven!

We got to travel to different churches and share the vision of missions with so many wonderful people within the Lake Union and around the whole country. We made many friends who now support the work of AFM through their gifts, prayers, and letters. It always amazes us just how many wonderful Adventists there are with such a burden for the unreached! Fundraising truly was a fun way to begin our mission service.

We arrived in Mali, West Africa, in 1996. Our first days were busy and somewhat scary as we encountered sights, sounds, and smells we had never experienced before. Naked little babies ran around with runny noses, sores oozing pus, and covered with dirt from head to toe. Bare-breasted women pounded grain in huge wooden bowls the way I remembered seeing in old black and white movies of Africa from many years ago. Chickens, goats, and sheep were everywhere. Cows roamed the streets like dogs might in the States, looking for something to fill their bellies.

Worst of all, no one spoke our language! Beginning mission service was truly challenging. Excitement builds as you slowly learn to formulate words and phrases in the local tongue. People begin to acknowledge you as a person, not just an amusement. Excitement continues to grow as you find ways to truly help, and people's appreciation floods you. Learning all the aspects of a very different culture keeps the excitement going, especially when someone expresses the very first interest in the gospel you came to share. Yes, being a missionary is truly exciting!

However, God has a sense of humor and maintains balance in the hearts of His missionaries through series of humbling situations. One time we confidently strolled onto the hospital grounds seeking to bring blessings and good cheer to the unfortunate. We greeted the guard, using the few phrases we had mastered. He asked us the purpose of our visit. I boldly stepped forward and said in my best local dialect. 'We are coming to visit the sick people.' But instead of 'sick people' what I actually said was 'lazy people.' Once the laughter died down, we were able to humbly carry on with our task. Being a missionary is, above all other things, a divine privilege. God has allowed us—broken, imperfect, and frail though we be—the opportunity to be His representatives to the unreached people of the world.

Madou was one of those unreached. A karate instructor by trade, he lived life from day to day without purpose. He often expressed disappointment in Islam and rarely practiced his faith. Our meeting happened during my community visiting time. While I talked with his cousin, who was expressing some interest in the Bible, Madou was quite argumentative.

A second and third visit ensued, breaking down barriers and answering the questions in his mind. *Though Madou was initially very resistant, he became an avid student of the scriptures and recently took a stand for Christ in the midst of his Muslim family and village. What a grand and noble task to be a missionary!*

How undeserving we are to be called to such a task. "For whosoever shall call upon the name of the Lord shall be saved. How then shall they call on him in whom they have not believed? And how shall they believe in him of whom they have not heard? And how shall they hear without a preacher? How beautiful are the feet of them that preach the gospel of peace and bring glad tidings of good things!" (Romans 10:13–15).

Maybe you are wondering if being a cross-cultural missionary is for you. Let me warn you, life in the mission field is so fun, so exciting, so challenging, and such a humbling, divine privilege, you may want to devote your whole life to it! And if you do, give Adventist Frontier Missions a call at (800) YES-4-AFM.

Phillip Polley and his family were sponsored by Lake Union Conference members.

Naomi Polley and her canoe

The Polley family in 1999 in Michigan before going to Mali

A Mali man in traditional dress

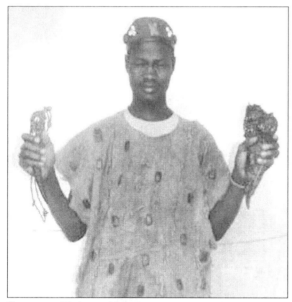

Soma, an idol worshipper

Boli, an idol

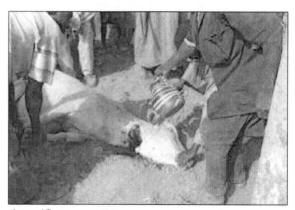

A sacrifice

Phil and Naomi worshipping in their grass church

Worshippers in a mosque

The Polley home in Mali

Most of the women's time is devoted to food preparation and other domestic chores.

Phillip's new friend, Madou, a Muslim karate instructor who took his stand for Jesus.

The Polley family in 2012

61
GOLDSON AND RITA BROWN

1983–1987 / Ethiopa

Goldson Oliver Brown and Rita Maureen (Chen) Brown and two children left Toronto, Canada, on September 5, 1983, to serve as mathematics/chemistry teacher at the Akaki Adventist School in Addis Ababa, Ethiopia. After their furlough they returned for a second term of service on August 31, 1985.

Goldson Brown, a native of Canada, had been a teacher in the eastern province of maritime Canada. He had the privilege of teaching at the Adventist Fredericton School in New Brunswick. Called to mission service in Ethiopia, Mr. and Mrs. Brown responded in the affirmative in 1983. Many prayers were offered by the Canadian membership knowing that they would have to brave loneliness, difficulties, dangers, and the continual adjustment to the surprises of a different culture and a changing political sphere.

Goldson completed his undergraduate studies at McMaster University in 1973 and Rita at the same university in 1976. Goldson followed this degree with a master's degree and doctorate in education from Loma Linda University. He taught in three provinces of Canada before becoming an associate professor of education (curriculum instruction) at Union College in Nebraska in 1990 and later at Southeast Community College and La Sierra University.

Dr. Brown currently resides in California, and his experience includes working in health informatics at Cedars-Sinai Medical Center, where he was lead trainer and curriculum writer. He was also a senior learning consultant at Kaiser Permanente. His administration and consulting work includes operating as CEO of Griltech Associates and working as dean of student services at SCC. He has also worked as a director of corrections education and director of student records.

Dr. Goldson Brown

62

RONALD AND DOROTHY FORDE

1983–1999 / Zaire, Zimbabwe

Ron E. Forde was born on the island of Barbados in the early 1950s along with his brother and two sisters. He is the oldest of four children, born into a Seventh-day Adventist family. In 1965 the family moved from Barbados to Montreal, Canada, where a new chapter in his life began.

Ronald completed high school there in 1969, followed by a one-year stint at Sir George Williams University, where he discovered that electrical engineering was not to his liking.

Following this effort, he trained on the job and worked as a respiratory technologist for about two years and then decided to return to school. This time it was to pursue a degree in medical laboratory technology.

He enrolled at Dawson College in Montreal and completed the course, becoming a registered medical laboratory technician in 1974. With degree in hand it was time to leave home, so off to Toronto he moved where he worked at York-Finch hospital for two years.

In 1975 Ron Forde married the former Dorothy Sinclair, his childhood sweetheart. She joined him in Toronto as they began their life together. As they were enjoying the early routines of married life, a recruiting team (Pastors Harold Lee and Wintley Phipps) from Oakwood College came to town, and before

they knew it, they found themselves in Alabama. Dorothy graduated in 1978 as a registered nurse, and Ron in 1979 with a bachelor's degree in biology and an invitation to join the incoming class of dental students at Loma Linda University (LLU) in 1980.

Upon graduation from LLU in 1982, Dr. and Mrs. Forde along with their two small children accepted a call from the General Conference of Seventh-day Adventists to go to Zaire and open a new dental practice in the city of Lubumbashi.

It was a challenging practice for a new graduate. Working with his patients who spoke French, being out of contact with friends and family back in North America, and hoping to avoid tropical illnesses were among the realities of daily life. It was also an opportunity to meet the local population and learn the culture while serving the large expatriate community, including many from the American consulate nearby where Dorothy also worked as a nurse.

After six years there, a call came to move to Bulawayo, Zimbabwe, to join a growing Seventh-day Adventist dental clinic there. The call was accepted, and the family of five (an additional child had been added) made the move. They lived and worked there for ten years (1989 to 1999).

Dr. Forde's expanding dental skills began during the early years in Africa. In dental school, he recalls, he had relied principally on handouts and notes to learn the basics of dentistry. Isolated from other professionals, he found textbooks to be what he called his "security blanket." During three-week mission furloughs, he observed oral surgery and other procedures at Loma Linda University School of Dentistry (LLUSD) that would never occur in his mission area unless he performed them.

His teaching skills were honed by necessity. There being no trained office staff in the area, Dr. Forde recruited and trained his office staff. Along with the indigenous population, he treated patients who worked for the Peace Corps, USAID, and World Vision. It was an opportunity to provide his dental associates an education in oral health and care. Under Dr. Forde's tutelage, there were others who were trained to provide basic dental care in more remote settings. Later, facing a difficult case, the bush "dentist" would call Dr. Forde, who would talk him through the procedure. Licensure was no problem for the new "dentist" practicing in a country with no dental school.

Returning to his dental alma mater in 1999, Dr. Forde became director of service learning, bringing insights from his years in Africa. He oversaw senior dental students as they rotated through community clinics, becoming perhaps the only faculty member with the privilege of working one on one with every graduate. He also oriented students for overseas mission service and outfitted their trips, packing dental units and supplies at the warehouse, then checking them after the trips for any needed maintenance. He also accompanied students on some of these trips.

Embarking on the Advanced Education in Prosthodontics at LLUSD in 2006, Dr. Forde completed the course in 2010 and presented his research, "Changes in the Retentive Force of Locator Attachments at Selected Angulations," in 2011. He then accepted an assignment as prosthodontics faculty for the International Dentist Program and main clinics. Following this position he came under the tutelage of then Restorative Dentistry chair Dr. Douglass Roberts whose pending retirement prompted a grooming of Dr. Forde for the position, exposing Dr. Forde to administrative meetings, regional education meetings, and emphasizing the necessity of expanding the educator's view from a day-to-day focus to incorporate long-term planning and anticipating curricular changes and additions that would better prepare the graduating dentist to meet the needs of patients in today's world.

In November of 2012 Dr. Forde assumed the chair of the Department of Restorative Dentistry at Loma Linda University.[84]

Dr. Ron Forde

84. Excerpted from Nicole R. Cheatham, "Black Alumni of LLU & LSU names alumnus of the year," TODAY news for Thursday, March 23, 2006.

63
GLENN AND WINNIE HOWELL

1983–1985 / Ghana

Glenn Douglass Howell was born in Oklahoma City and graduated from Oakwood College in 1953 with a bachelor's degree in theology. He served as a colporteur in the Missouri and Southern California Conferences. He then served as a ministerial intern in the Central California Conference for two years after which he went into a private business for several years. He later pastored and served as the youth director for the Southwest Region Conference.

Mrs. Howell is the former Winnie Mae Jackson. The Howells have five children: Jenice, Renée, Glenn, Judy, and Michelle. After pastoring several churches, Elder Howell was ordained to the gospel ministry at the annual convocation in Lynnwood on September 19, 1970. At the time he was the MV Department associate secretary.

On January 17, 1983, Elder and Mrs. Howell and one child left New York City for Africa. Elder Howell was to serve as youth/temperance and SAWS director (Seventh-day Adventist World Service, the predecessor of ADRA) for the West African Union headquartered in Accra, Ghana, West Africa.

In late January and early February 1983, the country of Ghana faced a crisis. The Nigerian government ordered nearly 1,000,000 Ghanaian immigrants to leave Nigeria for their homeland of Ghana by February 1.

The forced repatriation turned into a chaotic exodus that left many of the Ghanaians sick and hungry. To help combat the problem, an official of the Ghanaian government phoned Glenn Howell, who had just arrived as the youth director of the West African Union Mission and asked whether the Adventist Church could provide some badly needed medicines and medical supplies. Elder Howell forwarded the request to the SAWS office at the General Conference.

An organization called the Inner City Broadcasting Corporation (ICBC) had been raising money to help but was not quite sure what to do with it or where to send it. After investigating a number of relief agencies suggested by the United States government, they concluded that the Adventists had the best program. The Lord in His providence had prepared the church to meet the emergency.

For eight days Elder Howell marshaled a small army of Pathfinders smartly dressed in their uniforms who distributed high protein biscuits to an estimated 200,000 hungry people.

Thirty tons of the highly nutritional dry biscuits had been sent to Ghana by the Northern European Division several months earlier and seemed to be waiting there for this crisis.

The mutual desire of SAWS and the ICBC to provide relief dovetailed into a cooperative effort including the Upjohn Corporation and

Inter-Church Medical Assistance as well.

Lufthansa Airlines charged a preferential rate for the air cargo and Pan-American Airways gave a free ticket to a representative.

A Ghanaian television crew covered the event and a taped report was broadcast over the ICBC radio stations. Elder Ted Wilson and Elder Bediako and other officials supervised the unloading and clearance of the medical supplies from the airport and the supplies were distributed by the Adventists over a period of time.

Pastor Glenn Howell (tall man on left) and Pathfinders passing out high protein biscuits to hungry Ghanaian returnees.

Glenn Howell in native costume

Glenn Howell in casual dress

64

ALCEGA AND VERONICA JEANNITON

1983–1987 / Zaire; 1988–1996 / Cameroon; 1997–1999 / Equatorial Guinea

Alcega believed one hundred percent in the publishing work. He began his career in the Northeastern Conference and set delivery and sales records. He worked in this conference as assistant and director of publishing from 1975 until 1983.

When he received a call to serve as publishing director in the Zaire Union, he and his wife, Veronica Davis Jeanniton, moved to Lubumbashi from Providence, Rhode Island, with their three children on September 5, 1983.

As Zaire Union publishing director, he set a goal to have more than 1,000 literature evangelists working in Zaire by the end of 1985. He also set up a goal to organize a colporteur club in every church. His literature evangelists made major contributions to the spread of the third angel's message not only through the sale of literature but also through personal involvement in conducting evangelistic campaigns, opening new branch Sabbath Schools, and inviting interested individuals to weekly church services. They became faithful frontline troops for bringing the gospel message to unbelievers and for baptisms. The Jeannitons remained in Zaire until 1987.

In 1988 they moved to Yaoundé, Cameroon where he again served as publishing director. It was the publishing work that brought a very illustrious leader into the Adventist Church in Cameroon.

For a long time Jean-Marie Tchoualeu had not been happy. He felt that something was missing from his life. He grew up in a Catholic Church but had lost faith in the God of Christianity, and later he declared himself a deist. He stopped going to church altogether except for special social occasions like weddings.

He had a lot of respect for the Catholic Church and was convinced it was the church of Saint Peter, Saint Paul, and Saint John. He thought the Catholic Church was the church the historical Jesus left on this earth. He did not feel that Jesus was the Son of God but felt He was the wisest man the world had ever known.

Jean-Marie later received his bachelor's degree in law and became a judge. While he was searching for answers, one of his friends introduced him to books on parapsychology, occultism, and spiritism, and he was immediately captivated with this strange new way of thinking. But after six months he saw that this was not the answer to his questions.

One day an old colporteur came to his office with some books, and one of them had a title that captured his attention: *Who Will Dominate the World?* by Pierre Lanares. The white front cover of the book carried pictures of the White House, the Kremlin, and the Vatican. He actually did not feel it was a religious book, but when he started reading it, he found out that it was. The book dealt with the prophecies of Daniel and Revelation and the statue of Daniel 2. It was 1986 and he was thirty-six years old. For the first time in his life, he realized that the God of heaven had spoken to humanity through the Bible, and he decided to study the Bible.

He went to his library and took the old Bible that had been given to him on his wedding day by the officiating priest off the shelf. He removed the dust, which had accumulated on the book because of disuse. He had never once read it. Now he determined to read it all the way through, starting with the very first page.

It was difficult reading Leviticus and Numbers, but the old colporteur would drop in from time to time to study with him. He was very patient, and he felt he was a Jehovah's Witness.

One day the colporteur sold him a copy of a book titled *God's Answers to Man's Questions,* and this book really did answer most of the questions that he had been seeking all his life. By now Jean-Marie Tchoualeu had become a judge and a very important individual in Cameroon. He bought the entire conflict series of Ellen G. White and decided to give his life to God.

He had never heard of Seventh-day Adventists before, but his search finally led him to this church, and he was baptized on March 28, 1987. After his conversion he was so happy he began to wonder what he could do for God to thank God for how He had changed his life. It was at this point that Pastor Jeanniton suggested: "You became acquainted with the message through publishing, so it is your responsibility to be a part-time colporteur for the Lord."

Judge Tchoualeu didn't see how he could do that in his position. He went to Pastor Jeanniton and told him that the Lord had impressed him to be a colporteur, but he was not going to go from door to door selling books. He decided to put the books on his desk. While people were talking with him in his office, the visitors would glance over the pages of the books, and suddenly they would say, "You have very nice books. Where can we get them?" The judge would answer, "Right here, they are for sale." He became one of the best colporteurs in Yaoundé.

He was extremely proud of his job as a judge. He had great influence in his country. However, the Lord clearly showed him that he had to work full time for Him for the rest of his life. He sold his car, television, VCR, and some luxurious furniture he had bought in Italy a year before in order to have money to go to school. Finally he gave up his career as a judge and began to study at the Adventist Seminary of West Africa in Nigeria and Andrews University where he obtained his master's degree in pastoral ministry.

In September 1990 he received a call to work as an evangelist with the union and was greatly blessed. In 1995 he was elected union secretary; and five years later, on November 1, 2000, the former judge was elected union president. When he decided to leave his job as judge to go into the ministry, his wife, a staunch Roman Catholic, opposed him. So did his parents, his relatives, and his friends. His wife nearly divorced him, but he received more and more acceptance from them over time. He later baptized his wife, his sons, and one of his magistrate colleagues.

He gave the magistrate one of Mrs. White's books, and after he read it, he was converted and was baptized. The magistrate is doing a wonderful work for the Lord while remaining an outstanding court president. His wife is doing a wonderful job as shepherdess and evangelist and has developed a gift of prayer and prayer ministry. Once delivered by literature evangelists like Pastor Jeanniton, the books of the church silently did their work. Praise God![85]

Alcega Jeanniton, then the assistant publishing director of the Northeastern Conference, in 1978 with a group of believers who met regularly in Providence, Rhode Island. This interest was first started by literature evangelists, and the number kept on growing.

Jean-Marie Tchoualeu, former judge in Cameroon who is now president of the Central African Union Mission in Yaounde, Cameroon

Pastor Tchoualeu baptized his two youngest sons, Rodrique (right) and Arnold.

A very happy Mrs. Tchoualeu who nearly divorced her husband for becoming an Adventist being baptized by her husband, Pastor Tchoualeu.

Pastor and Mrs. Tchoualeu fellowship with an Adventist judge, (left), Mr. Fotso Jean.

85. Jean-Marie Tchoualeu. "God Found Me on the Bench," *Adventist Review*, February 13, 2003.

65

ERROL AND PAMELA LAWRENCE

1983–1990 / Liberia

Errol Lawrence was born in Cornwall Barracks, Portland, Jamaica. He started his education on the lap of his mother, Doris, and then under the tutelage of Mrs. Nell Marshalleck at Cornwall Barracks Basic School. He later attended Moore Town Elementary School under the tutelage of Principal Colin L. G. Harris. His high school education began at Portland High School, Port Antonio, Jamaica, with Headmaster Samuel Campbell, but he completed his high school education at Battersea County School in London, England.

Errol received his bachelor's degree in theology from Newbold College, England, in 1975, and his Master of Divinity in 1992 and Doctor of Ministry in 1995 from Andrews University in Michigan. He is an ordained minister in the Seventh-day Adventist Church.

After graduating from Newbold College, he served as a pastor/evangelist in London, England from 1975 to 1983. The first "big tent" evangelistic campaign to be held in South London, England, for nearly forty years opened under the direction of two young ministers, Errol Lawrence (pastor of Brixton and Battersea) and Lester Elliott (pastor of Balham and Peckham and the main evangelist for the series). They had spent time praying and planning for a year. Then with the assistance of eager, committed members they distributed 30,000 handbills and advertised in newspapers and on buses.

The tent, which could seat 1,000, was pitched on Clapham Common, one of London's "green lungs." The series was titled "Better Living" and consisted of more than just preaching. A health-education series of films and lectures was presented, which included a Five-Day Plan to Stop Smoking conducted by Dr. Keith Hertogs and South England Conference Health and Temperance Director Lionel Acton-Hubbard, in an adjoining tent. On the final Sabbath eighteen persons were baptized, with 1,300 people crowding together to witness the service. Thirty more people were prepared for a later baptism.

In September 1983 Pastor Errol and Pam Lawrence and their two daughters, Abigail and Michaela, arrived in Monrovia, Liberia, from Croydon, England. Pastor Lawrence served as the district pastor for the churches in Monrovia and as communication, stewardship, temperance, health, and family life director for the Liberia Mission.

Pastor Lawrence recounts these incidents:

The first day we arrived in Liberia there was no one to meet us at the airport. We had written to the mission secretary to give the date of our arrival. We had sent telex messages. We had attempted phone calls without success. So when we arrived at Roberts International Airport, there was no one to meet us.

As we negotiated our way through the busy customs area, a young man named Andrew approached us and volunteered his assistance. With a watchful eye and close by his side, I followed every move he made with our passports and other travel documents.

After everything was cleared through customs and immigration, he asked us who was picking us up to take us to the mission office, which was thirty-five miles away. Since there was no one in sight, we tried to make a phone call. The phone kept ringing and ringing, but no one answered. At that time we did not realize that the phone service had been disconnected because the bills had not been paid.

Andrew saw our desperation and asked me if I had another number I could call. It was then I remembered that a couple of months before Borge Schantz, the director of the Missions Institute we attended in Newbold College, had introduced us to Ron Oliver, an Englishman who had a business in Monrovia, Liberia, and who had given me a business card. He had told us to look him up when we got to Liberia. I was delighted that in my desperation when I called his number he answered. I told him about my plight and asked him for directions that I could give to the taxi driver, but he was not familiar with the location of the mission office. However, as God had designed it, his assistant, Louise Gibson, was an Adventist. So he put her on the line, and she gave me the directions.

That incident produced lifelong friendships. God has used those two people to bless our lives in many and various ways to this very day.

Another surprise that awaited us was that when we got to the house that had been so nicely decorated and prepared for our family, we found the living room carpet under two inches of water. The rainy season was just ending. Water had backed up on the flat roof above the porch. Finding a small crack in the structure the water leaked in and flooded the place. When the gutters were unblocked, the water cascaded off the roof like a mini Niagara Falls. We had to wait several weeks for the walls to dry out before they could be repainted. But God saw us through.

Apart from experiencing attempted coups, my most harrowing experience was a near-death experience with malaria. I will always be grateful for the support of my wife and the prayers of the saints during those troubled two weeks in bed. I will always remember the fervent prayer of one of our outstanding elders, Mother Diggs. In her prayer she said, "Lord, we beg You, please heal your man servant because You have a great work for him to do, and You did not bring him here for us to send him back home in a body bag."

One of his first official tasks upon arrival in Liberia was to participate in the preparatory organization for a major evangelistic campaign organized by outgoing union/mission evangelist, Pastor Ronald J. Wright and conducted in Monrovia by Elder Ted N. C. Wilson

In addition, he was the follow-up speaker after Elder Wilson's departure. The whole series was coordinated by Pastor R. J. Wright, West African Union evangelist and ministerial secretary. Night after night thousands came to hear about the way to a better life. As a result of this campaign, 666 souls were baptized and four new church groups were established.

In the Liberia Mission eight pastors served approximately 6,000 baptized members. There were insufficient finances to employ an office secretary or to pay an outstanding phone bill of $900, the non-payment of which led to the cutting off of the telephones.

The mission office was in great need of a duplicating machine and was endeavoring to raise $500 to buy a secondhand one. They were also seeking funds to complete two buildings at the lovely youth camp that had begun in 1975.

Pastor Lawrence got special recognition for services to the World Health Organization and the HIV/AIDS program, The Christian Health Association of Liberia, and the Cancer Society in Liberia (1985–1990). Special recognition was also given for conducting Breathe Free Stop Smoking Programs in Liberia from the Liberia Cancer Society (1985–1990).

Pastor and Mrs. Lawrence's two daughters, Abigail and Michaela, attended the British School in Monrovia. Pastor Lawrence learned how to do plumbing out of necessity. He also learned how to do carpentry and painting and typing. Twins, Anthony and Antonia, were added to their family while they were missionaries.

When they returned from Liberia, Pastor Lawrence went to Andrews University with his family of six. At Andrews University the whole family was involved in some from of educational pursuit, from kindergarten to the doctoral level. After completing his Doctor of Ministry degree, Errol and his family were called to Canada where he served as senior pastor at Apple Creek Seventh-day Adventist Church in Markham, Toronto (1995–1998). Dr. Lawrence then joined the staff of Canadian University College in 1998 and taught subjects such as homiletics, pastoral ministry, pastoral practicum, pastoral counseling, worship,

church history, and theology. He was chair of the Religious Studies Department from 1999–2005. He has taken students and others on mission trips to Kenya, Zimbabwe, Togo, Jamaica, Nicaragua, and the Philippines.

In January 2006 Dr. Lawrence was called to take up the position as ministerial director of the Ontario Conference of the Seventh-day Adventist Church, as well as evangelism and church growth coordinator. He served in this position from 2006 to 2013

When asked to give his motto in life, Errol Lawrence replied: "It is not enough to dream about what you want to do; you must begin to do something about what you have spent so long dreaming about."

Dr. Errol Lawrence has written and published various articles and papers, and in 2012 he published a poetry book, *JUXTAPOETRY: Lessons from Life*. He is soon to publish another book titled *Life Lessons from Liberia and Other Places*.

When asked who inspires him, he replied: "Dr. Martin Luther King Jr. has always been one of my heroes. I am inspired by the work that NASA does. And Dr. Oswald E. Gordon, whom I worked with in Africa, has been a great mentor because he sees everything as possible."

Besides providing him with a deeper commitment to God and service to humanity, the mission field provided Errol Lawrence with the fulfillment of his life motto and provided him with a great mentor.

Since January 2014, Dr. Errol Lawrence has been serving as the lead pastor of the first black church in Canada, Toronto West (former Shaw Street, former Harvey St.) Seventh-day Adventist Church in Etobicoke, Toronto, which celebrated fifty years in 2013.

Remember, says Lawrence, "If you cannot cross the ocean and the heathen lands explore, you can find many heathens nearer. Some are just outside your door."

While she was in Liberia, Pam Lawrence worked for a while as administrative assistant to the mission president, O. E. Gordon, as well as communications secretary for the mission, for a year. She also worked as a teacher's assistant at the British Independent Preparatory School (BIPS) and tutored non-English speaking parents and children as a part of her missionary contribution. She is trained in secretarial science but has worked as a nursing assistant as well as accounting clerk and office manager.

According to her, "missionaries" must have the greater good of the people they minister to at heart. It should never be an "us" and "them" situation. It should always be "us" because we are in it together.

She remembers teaching deacons or deaconesses to make Communion bread after an experience at one church where the Communion bread was so hard you could hear people trying to crunch the pieces and anxiously waiting for the wine to be blessed to help with the swallowing.

As well as doing all the other things she did, she managed a family of four children, including twins born in Liberia, and kept her busy husband in line.

She loved the people of Liberia and was blessed by their lovingkindness in spite of their poverty. Pam says that mission service opened her eyes to some very interesting and intriguing aspects of church life.

As of 2014, their daughter Abigail is a French teacher in Edmonton, Alberta. Their married daughter, Michaela Lawrence-Jeffery, works as campus chaplain at the University of Tennessee in Knoxville where she lives with her husband, Justin. Their son Anthony is pursuing his physical therapy course and his twin sister,

Antonia, is seeking to fulfill her dream in international relations. Pam and Errol are enjoying ministry at Toronto West Seventh-day Adventist Church.

Pastors R. J. Wright and Errol Lawrence baptizing a candidate in the Revelation Revival Crusade in Liberia.

Liberian boys with a wasp nest

Pastor Lawrence and the director of the Christian Health Association of Liberia who is holding a sign indicating that "The Best Man for the Job is a Woman"

Pastor Lawrence at the office of Mrs. Sandolo Belleh, then minister of health; the gentleman beside her was her assistant

Errol and Pam Lawrence making a presentation to Liberian officials at the time of the visit of the International Commission for the Prevention of Alcoholism and Drug Dependency (ICPA) officials from the States.

Pastor Errol Lawrence

66

RANDOLPH AND DEBRAH STAFFORD

1983–1988 / Kenya, Zimbabwe

Randolph Poten Stafford was born in Hamlet, North Carolina, and had two brothers and one sister. Randy, as he was called, was always taller than the other kids. Some thought he would become a football or basketball player.

Debrah Wright came from Germantown, Ohio, and was born into a very musical family. Everybody in her family knew how to sing and perform. While a student at Oakwood College, Randy worked as a Bible instructor with Charles D. Brooks in Cincinnati in 1968.

Randy attended Oakwood and majored in religion. He later went on to receive a bachelor's degree in behavior science from the University of Southern Mississippi.

Pastor Stafford entered the gospel ministry in 1969 for the South Central Conference. From 1969 to 1973 he pastored several churches in the South, including Meridian, Laurel, Soso, and Hattiesburg, Mississippi. He was pastor of twelve churches in Mississippi.

In 1973 Stafford was called to be the youth director for the Southwest Region Conference in Dallas, Texas. He served also as public relations director during this time. From Dallas, Stafford accepted a call to the Lake Region Conference to pastor the Capitol City Church in Indianapolis, Indiana. Perhaps the greatest challenge in his ministry up to that point was when he entered the pulpit of the large City Temple Church of Detroit, Michigan. At that time the church had a membership of more than 1,500 members.

In September of 1979, Pastor Stafford accepted a call to pastor Lynwood Boulevard Temple in Kansas City, Missouri. The church had a large membership and operated its own preschool program with extended care.

It was while he was pastoring in Kansas City that he received a call from the General Conference to go to Africa. He took Africa by storm by holding amazingly large evangelistic meetings. Below is an account of his first meeting.

The impact of the six-foot, seven-inch, 275-pound black evangelist was felt five days before his crusade's opening night on April 10. Several television spot announcements advertised the crusade, and all of Bulawayo knew that something big was about to happen. Crusade officials estimated that nearly 4,000 people came the first night, but the city hall, the largest meeting place in Bulawayo, had a regular seating capacity of only 1,600. Immediately the officials decided to have two meetings per night to accommodate the crowds. Thereafter, the attendance averaged 3,000 per night throughout the three weeks of the crusade. Over the weekends, when the hall was not available, the meetings were held in an amphitheater in the nearby city park.

Many no doubt came at first to see the big black man from America preaching in his long white, gray, or maroon robes. But the Holy Spirit wooed them back, night after night, to hear Pastor Stafford pure, simple gospel message. It was solid Bible doctrines full of the love of Jesus. The people came to the meetings hungry and went away fed.

At first the manager of the city hall was hostile toward Adventists. But as he listened to the message and saw the steady attendance of so many people night after night he kept saying, "This thing is serious; this thing is serious."

When Pastor Stafford made a call asking people to accept Jesus as their Savior, be baptized, and become members of the Adventist Church, the response was overwhelming. The crusade organizers were faced with new challenges—how and where to baptize hundreds of people; how to get the names and addresses of all the candidates; how to determine which of the Bulawayo churches they should join; and how the church boards could meet and examine the candidates for their churches.

The first baptism was scheduled for Sabbath evening, April 23, 1983, in the swimming pool at Bulawayo Adventist Secondary School. Observers surrounded the pool, five to ten people deep. Adequate preparation had not been made to facilitate such a crowd of observers and such a large number of candidates. A hastily set up floodlight partially illuminated the otherwise dark pool, but no one foresaw the need for a public address system soon enough to set one up. The candidates had to force their way from the dressing rooms through the crowd to the shallow end of the pool, and at first there was some confusion as to which was the shallow end!

Eventually ten pastors took their places in the pool. Pastor Stafford, seated precariously on the end of the diving board, called out, "In the name of the Father, the Son, and the Holy Ghost," and the pastors began baptizing the 545 candidates. Three nights later another 300 people were baptized. And on the final Sabbath of the crusade, another 505 people followed their example, bringing the total to 1,350 baptisms.

The crusade had been Pastor Stafford's first encounter with the people of Africa, but it clearly was not to be his last.[86]

The Zambezi Union later invited Stafford to Harare, capital of Zimbabwe, to be the evangelist there. They secured the city's sports arena for the series. Some 836 people were baptized. During that year some 2,000 persons were baptized into the church by Evangelist Stafford.

But God's greatest blessings came in Kisii, Kenya. More than 3,100 people were baptized in his first baptism there in April of 1985. The Kenya National News Service reported the campaign's first baptismal service, giving it major television and radio coverage that evening. Liquor and cigarette sales dropped, and town officials noticed a remarkable difference in the attitude of local residents. It is reported that in subsequent baptisms in Kisii the total baptisms amounted to more than 4,000. When they organized a church there, the first day it became the largest church in the conference, and this church has been responsible for birthing and mothering twenty-two churches in Kenya.

The family lived in Nairobi for two years and in Zimbabwe for three years. When they returned to the States, Randy Stafford began a self-supporting ministry and conducted evangelistic meetings all over the world. A four-week evangelistic campaign in 1991 in Jamaica ended with nearly 300 baptisms.

---

86. Excerpted from "Bible preaching in Bulawayo results in 1,350 baptisms," Janice Erntson, *Adventist Review*, October 6, 1983, pp. 14, 15.

There is a Kenyan Adventist Church in Arlington, Texas. There are people there that Stafford baptized who have moved to America. Stafford recently preached there when he was invited to be the guest speaker for a weekend. They have given Stafford a Kisi name "Kundi," which means father of the Kisi. This was the place where he baptized the most people.

In August of 2012 Elder Stafford retired and now lives in Tennessee. He serves as a business consultant and spends his spare time fishing. Debrah worked in the juvenile justice system for the state of Tennessee, and in her retirement has just defended her thesis for her doctoral dissertation.

Elder and Mrs. Randolph Stafford and son, Randy, standing with J. R. Wagner (left), conference president, who introduced them to their new church and the members of the Capitol Avenue Church in Indianapolis, Indiana, in 1975.

Pastor and Evangelist Randy Stafford

More than 5,000 attended the Sabbath service at the Bulawayo amphitheater. As a result of this three-week campaign by Randolph Stafford in 1983, 1,350 people were baptized.

Evangelist Stafford talks to the children.

Debrah Stafford (one of the Wrights from Ohio) delivers a message in song.

Pastor Stafford preaches in his robe.

Pastor Stafford teaching with a translator.

Debrah Stafford receives her doctoral degree.

67

Disciple and Ninon Amertil

1984–1986 / Zaire; 2013–Present / Ghana

Ninon Philogene grew up in Brooklyn, New York, with her parents where she attended Sarah J. Hale High School. After her graduation she attended Atlantic Union College and completed a bachelor's degree in personal ministry and modern language. There she married Disciple Amertil who also graduated in 1980. The couple went to Andrews University where Ninon graduated with a degree in nursing in 1984 and 1993.

Their first mission assignment was to Songa Hospital in Zaire (Congo) in 1984 where Ninon served as head of the nursing department. Songa was an isolated hospital and one of the oldest mission stations in Africa. Mission work among the Baluba people was established in 1921 on a 500-acre plot, and medical work began there in 1927. The station is about 400 miles northwest of Lubumbashi, the second largest city in the Congo. Their three children accompanied them there.

On their return both worked at Atlantic Union College, Disciple as college dean of men and assistant chaplain and Ninon in the Nursing Department. While at Atlantic Union College, she completed her doctoral degree from the University of Massachusetts, which she added to her RN and NP degrees. Also while at Atlantic Union College, Professor Amertil initiated the International Health Mission, which had as its purpose to provide culturally sensitive health care to underserved groups of people in overseas locations.

The second international trip was to the Dominican Republic from May 28 through June 12, 2000. The clinical sites for this trip were in nine areas of Santo Domingo and San Cristobal. More than 200 patients were seen each day and received medications free of charge. An evangelistic campaign was also conducted during the trip. Many came forward to acknowledge their acceptance of the teachings of Christ and others to renew their commitment to Him. More than 3,000 patients were seen in the clinics. Dr. Amertil was the driving force behind this project, and Pastor Amertil served as the transportation coordinator, translator, and college recruiter.

In 2013 the General Conference called Dr. Amertil to Ghana to help develop the Valley View University's Nursing Department. She plans to put in place a strategic plan for the department during her five-year mission commitment to Ghana. Besides her official role as the head of the Nursing Department, her greatest undertaking and passion is helping children and teenagers to invest their energy and talents to church activities and businesses and present Jesus to them as a forever helpful friend. Pastor Amertil is teaching theology at Valley View.

The Nursing Department at Valley View has several projects, including opening a nursing bookstore in the fall semester of 2014. The university does not have a bookstore yet. Students depend mostly on faculty notes and are encouraged to find other resources at the university library. Having a nursing bookstore will facilitate their learning as well as enhance accountability and ownership for their schooling.

Dr. Ninon and Pastor Disciple Amertil

68
BYRON AND ALFREDIA CONNER

1984–1987 / Ethiopia

Byron E. Conner wrote the following pages, which are included in a book titled *The Face of Hunger: Reflections on a Famine in Ethiopia* that he hopes to have published in the near future.

Intractable insomnia led my family and me to a life-changing and unforgettable chapter in our lives. My wife, my two children, and I were living in Visalia, California, during my two-year stint as a physician with the U.S. Public Health Service in nearby Earlimart, California. The term of service was nearly at an end, and I was pondering what to do next as far as future employment was concerned. My insomnia became even worse while I considered where we should go and what to do. During one of the many nights when sleep fled from me, I found myself sitting in front of the television surfing the channels.

Suddenly pictures on the screen had my undivided and rapt attention. It was an informational and fundraising presentation by the aid organization World Vision. It revealed that there was a famine in Ethiopia. Ethiopia, I thought, just where is that? I learned it was a large portion of the "horn of Africa" in the northeastern region of the continent. I was to learn more than I had ever known before.

The rains had failed, and the drought produced food shortfalls in Ethiopia. Eight million people were at risk of being subjected to a devastating famine. The country was being run by a Marxist, and it seemed to me an incompetent and brutal government. I have to admit I was somewhat callous at first in considering this news. As terrible as it seemed, what was happening had some political overtones in my view. I did not see that the victims were the powerless and innocent.

Night after night with my family asleep, I sat and watched the same scenes replayed over and over. There before my eyes were wasted, emaciated children with their faces covered with flies and looking miserable beyond belief. The mothers of those children looked hopeless as they tried to breast feed their skeletal children. I became obsessed with watching those pictures. It was not a morbid fascination but a growing feeling that someone should do something about this. Gradually, I started to feel that that "someone" should be me. I was nearing the end of my term of service on my job at the time, so I thought, Perhaps I can go to Ethiopia to help out somehow.

Most importantly, I came to believe that it was God's will that I go about doing something to help. In other words I had a mission to perform. I did not know how to do it, but I had to do whatever I could. There were, however, other concerns. First of all, I had a wife and two children: my daughter, Kellie, was ten years old, and my son, Kevin, was five years of age. If I went to Ethiopia, they would have to go with me. How was I going to support them if I became a missionary? Secondly, I had a plan to take a fellowship to become a specialist in taking care of cancer patients in the field of hematology/oncology. If I went to Africa as I was thinking, I would have to give up on the idea of entering the specialty I was considering.

I also did an introspective look back on my life. I thought about everything that had happened to lead me to that point in my life. I relived many experiences, and it seemed to me that overall, God had had a master plan for my life and I believed also a plan for the future.

I was born in Denver, Colorado. I was the oldest of eleven children of a large African American family. I thought of the major milestones in my life. I joined the Seventh-day Adventist Church at the age of nine. I learned in the church the value of education and the notion that the education you received empowered you to serve. I attended a Seventh-day Adventist college in Lincoln, Nebraska—Union College—from 1966 to 1968 and 1970 to 1972. I had been a premed student for a time, but an undisciplined one.

I served in the U.S. Army from 1968 to 1970, including a tour in Vietnam. I returned to Union College from 1970 to 1972, majoring in sociology and then theology. I returned to Denver, Colorado, and met my wife, Alfredia, in our church parking lot! She was from San Bernardino, California. We moved to my wife's hometown and got married in 1973. We discussed my finishing up a degree in theology and my becoming a church pastor. However, one month after our marriage, I had a rather dramatic and sudden change of plans. I had a strong impression that the Lord was leading me to go into medicine.

I attended Loma Linda University School of Medicine from 1976 to 1979. Our two children were born in the medical center where I trained. I was blessed in that I graduated in the upper third of my class. I subsequently did an arduous and hectic three-year residency in internal medicine in Denver at Saint Joseph Hospital from 1979 to 1982. After my training, we moved to Visalia, California, to do two years of duty with the U.S. Public Health Service to pay back the scholarship that had helped pay for my medical school expenses. I worked in a clinic that gave primary medical care to mostly farm workers in the San Joaquin Valley, many of them natives of Mexico, Central America, and the Philippines. In retrospect, this was good preparation for being in the mission field as I learned the need to respect other cultures, and I learned the need to communicate despite language barriers.

I repeatedly replayed in my mind my life's history. I also thought about the powerful compulsion I was feeling to go to Ethiopia. I discussed things with my wife. She was supportive in my desire to go, and my desire became her desire! However, I still had misgivings. My children were so young. We were going to travel so far away. Would my family and I be safe? What would happen after our stay in Ethiopia?

Meanwhile, the news reports from Ethiopia revealed an immense human tragedy like none that I had ever heard of before. I thought again about eight million people being at risk for starvation. In addition, millions lived in abject poverty and in inhuman conditions. I was in a position to help. If I was going to go help, it would have to be now. It seemed that the needs of the people I was going to serve were more important than all other considerations. I felt compelled to act. The future was uncertain, but I prayed that I was making the right decision.

I contacted the headquarters of the Seventh-day Adventist Church in Maryland and told them that essentially we were at their service. We wanted to go help out however we could in the crisis in Ethiopia. They hadn't called me; I was calling them to offer my time and my efforts. After some discussion, I learned what the church expected of me. It was to be six years of service as a missionary, with a mid-term three-month furlough. My job title was to be the health and temperance director of the Ethiopian Union Mission. My job description was to be in charge of eight clinics and a rural hospital. I was also being asked to help set up something called a "Better Living Center" in the capital city, Addis Ababa, and to conduct Five Day Plans to Quit Smoking seminars. I was a little uneasy with the fact that my brief job description did not really mention anything about famine relief. I just thought this was an oversight or an out-of-date job description that did not fully describe what I would be doing. It was June of 1984.

Prior to beginning our mission service, we went to Andrew University in Berrien Springs, Michigan, for a one-month orientation. This time of orientation was referred to as "Mission Institute." We then had one month to visit our families in Denver and California before leaving for Ethiopia in September 1984.

I had some second thoughts. I was concerned that I was going to put my family in danger. After all, there was famine and warfare going on in Ethiopia. The country was very poor, and I was concerned about the type of house we would live in, what we would eat, what type of medical care would be available, and what unknown threats and dangers awaited us. We prayed about the move, and we were convinced we were doing the right thing. Our help was in fact needed in Ethiopia. There was hunger in the country, along with disease and a shortage of physicians. It looked like I was going to have to defer and perhaps give up my desire to be a specialist in hematology/oncology at home in America.

During our training at Andrews, we were exhorted to go to serve and to serve with dedication in whatever place we were to end up. It was a well-structured program and well intentioned. The most important things I learned was to "scratch where it itches" in the country we were to serve. I also learned to expect the unexpected. In retrospect, however, it seems that the course did not prepare us adequately for what we were to actually experience in Ethiopia. We had to learn to be resilient and resourceful in the mission field. We had to pray for endurance and tell ourselves that what we were going through would not last forever. On the other hand, our mission service gave us a new passion for service despite whatever situation we found ourselves in. We were never the same after the years we spent in Ethiopia.

There is considerable time for personal reflection on a long trip to your final destination. Following farewells to our families, we found ourselves on a tiring trip to Ethiopia. We flew via Lufthansa Airlines from Los Angles, California, to Frankfurt, Germany, for the first leg of our journey. It was a non-stop ten-hour ride. I thought frequently during the trip about what we would find after arriving at our destination. I wondered if I had made the right decision.

We landed in Frankfurt and had a twenty-four-hour layover. However, our jet lag did not permit us to do any sightseeing, and we spent the bulk of the time before the next leg of our journey sleeping. The next phase of our journey was from Frankfurt to Jeddah, Saudi Arabia. We did not deplane and were on the ground just a short time. Then we were set to land in Addis Ababa, Ethiopia.

The name Addis Ababa means "new flower." We arrived after nightfall on a Thursday evening in August 1984. As the door to the aircraft opened and we descended the mobile staircase, we were greeted by the pungent odor of a new land and a new part of the world. It seemed surreal that we were now on the other side of the world. We were greeted by a fellow American missionary, Irwin Dulan, and I was grateful for his warm and enthusiastic greeting. I was a little taken aback that the officials of the mission who were Ethiopians were not present to greet us.

We traveled by car from Bole International Airport to our place of residence on a fenced church compound referred to as kabana. On the compound with us were a small church, a school, and a printing house that published church literature. Pastor Irwin Dulan gave us a running commentary and orientation to the city. We drove along the streets of a modern

looking city as near as we could tell. We drove past many office buildings, hotels, and foreign embassies. Our compound was behind Menelek II Hospital, which was operated by the Ethiopian Ministry of Health. We were to find ourselves in a comfortable modern house with many of the comforts of home, and we were grateful for this.

Addis Ababa was actually a city I came to love. It was a big sprawling city of over one million in 1984. It is a high-altitude capital with an elevation of more than 7,500 feet as I was informed, even higher than my native Denver. The high altitude allowed us to escape the risk of malaria. The climate was awesome with an average high in the 70s. We had arrived during the end of the rainy season, but I loved the daily brief rainfall. The city was a mixture of modern buildings and mud houses, which were the residences of the urban poor, and there were plenty of poor people.

I was grateful that we lived in a comfortable home that exceeded my expectations. I would have to do some traveling, so I was grateful that at least my wife and children would be in a comfortable place. We even were able to shop and eat our usual vegetarian diet that we had consumed at home. There was a good variety of food and plenty of it, which seemed surprising in a country in the grip of a devastating famine.

The following morning Pastor Dulan took us to the Ethiopian Union Mission office, which was near the center of town. It was quite striking to see the juxtaposition of the old and new. There were small herds of goats, cattle, and sheep in the streets, and drivers had to weave their way around them. Near the center of town were soldiers standing on the streets holding AK47s. Needless to say this was an intimidating sight, but they were actually non-threatening.

The compound for the Ethiopian Union Mission included a large church, and an office building. I was introduced to the workers on the compound and the union officials who seemed cordial enough. I had my own separate office. There was in the office building a large committee room where I was to spend too many hours in my view sitting in committee meetings. This setup was not what I had envisioned when I thought of coming to Ethiopia to serve victims of the famine. I was to be an administrator, not my concept of being a missionary.

I was able to spend some time walking the streets of Addis Ababa around the mission compound. It gave me more of a perspective to add to what I could see driving around. There were modern hotels and restaurants near the compound that served western-style food. There were also beggars on the streets of Addis Ababa, and they readily approached foreigners. They could quickly tell I was not a native despite the fact that the hue of my skin was like theirs. They held out their hands and made what sounded like a hissing noise. I saw some beggars who were maimed and had been the victims of polio as I surmised. These individuals actually crawled on the ground dragging their withered legs and their hands inside a pair of shoes.

Near the church compound was the Black Lion Hospital, which was a huge teaching hospital for the country's medical school. There were offices for the United Nations and the World Health Organization. Scattered around the center of town were signs that said "Long Live Marxism-Leninism" and others that said "COPWE's Mission Shall be Fulfilled!" COPWE was a committee that was working to organize the Worker's Party of Ethiopia, which was meant essentially to be a one party Marxist government. There were a number of embassies near the center of town, which made for a fascinating urban arrangement.

The Marxist government seemed oppressive. The soldiers in the streets and the obvious censorship of books and newspapers affected even foreigners. There were significant travel restrictions and one had to obtain permission to travel outside Addis Ababa unless it was a relatively short trip. We even had a worker tasked with going to a government office to get travel documents for us expatriates to visit different parts of the country. I had to travel to visit the medical facilities we had in the country, but I learned that I did not dare travel to a place without travel documents as required.

I felt sympathetic with the Ethiopians as they did in fact live in a repressive regime. We had arrived ten years after a Marxist coup had overthrown Emperor Haile Selassie. The country was ruled be an Ethiopian despot Mengistu Haile Mariam. This ruler reigned with brutality. He had a political system that kept close surveillance it seemed over everyone. The people who lived in Addis Ababa were part of kebeles, which were also in the rural area, or a so-called urban dwellers association that included about 2,000 people. The head of this kebele could be a small dictator himself, and I learned of situations where the kebele head had jailed people. We expatriates learned to live and function in the political atmosphere as it existed then.

The day we arrived at our new residence in Addis Ababa, my five-year-old son was really impressed that we were now in Africa. He kept saying repeatedly: "I can't believe we are in Africa!" My son and daughter adapted rapidly to our new country. Their only complaint came from my daughter who thought the locals stared at us too much when we were out and about around town. It was obvious to me that the locals knew we were not Ethiopians, and perhaps they stared at us to figure out where we were from. My son quickly picked up Amharic, which was along with English an official language. There were actually about eighty languages in the country. My wife and I had not had formal language studies as we had thought we would have, and we were far less proficient in learning Amharic. As it turned out, many people spoke English, and in fact the instruction in schools across the country was often in English.

We arrived on a Thursday evening, and I received a surprise on Friday evening when someone came to our house, greeted us cordially, and then informed me that I would be preaching the sermon on Saturday morning in the small Seventh-day Adventist Church on the compound. I then spent a good part of the night preparing for this. I spoke the next day on the subject "Where Is Your True Home?" The thrust of my sermon was that we are all just passing through this world, and our true home is in heaven. This was a good initiation for me as I was to preach many sermons there, including in the largest Seventh-day Adventist Church in Addis Ababa. When I preached a translator translated into Amharic. I learned that this meant my message had to be relatively brief.

In our home we entertained many of the visitors who came to Addis Ababa from abroad and had business at the Ethiopian Union Mission. My wife became quite proficient at preparing awesome meals for our guests. Also, we had an Ethiopian helper, a young lady who assisted my wife in preparing food and house cleaning. We learned how to cook Ethiopian dishes that consisted of injera, the local equivalent of bread that was flat with a spongy texture and was eaten with wat. This wat was various vegetable stews, and for people who ate meat there was a wat made with meat such as chicken. The wat was seasoned with a hot reddish spice called beriberi. I developed a real taste for Ethiopian food as long as it is vegetarian. I still love it too this day.

There was a large expatriate community in Addis Ababa. Given the many NGOs (non-governmental organizations with a humanitarian focus), churches, international health agencies, and foreign embassies, there was a true international group. We got to know people from every part of the globe. There were a number of missionaries both within and outside of the church who we spent considerable time with. Some of us are still friends and keep in touch to this day.

From time to time representatives of the various NGOs assembled to meet with the Ethiopian Relief and Rehabilitation Committee. We received briefings about the needs of the country in terms of famine relief from the person in charge of the government entity at that time: Comrade Dawit. There were also unofficial channels of communication that were surprisingly accurate but not approved by the government. All of us expatriates were aware of proper precautions and protocols to live and work in *an authoritarian regime and be there to help the millions at risk. At times we disagreed with the government's policies and practices, but we did not openly contest things.*

From time to time my wife and I and our children visited the American Embassy in Addis Ababa. In fact, my wife worked there briefly as a teacher. We attended a briefing there at the embassy, and we heard a report from an American economist. She told us that Ethiopia was the poorest country in the world at that time. It did not seem so apparent living in Addis Ababa as the government tried as much as possible to create as rosy a picture as possible. However, those of us who traveled to the countryside knew better.

Our children were blessed to be able to attend a school for expatriate children called Bingham Academy. The teachers were from the United States, and my son had a teacher from Australia. The students were from America, Europe, Asia, South America, and other African countries. The importance of our children's education was one reason why we did not stay in Ethiopia as long as we should have as the school only went to the eighth grade.

We witnessed an unbelievable celebration one night on September 10. The skies over Addis Ababa were filled with fireworks. The display of pyrotechnics was to celebrate the tenth year of the revolution that overthrew Emperor Haile Selassie. It seemed almost obscene to see such a display for the poorest country in the world in the grip of famine, disease, and internal warfare. It made me more determined to try to understand the reasons for the famine of 1984 and to just reinforce and focus my passion for being in Ethiopia.

Mothers and children in the feeding center in Makele.

Dr. Conner with a mother and her child

Food grain for those in need

Adventist Relief and Development Agency (ADRA) trucks

A tent hospital

Traveling to a remote village

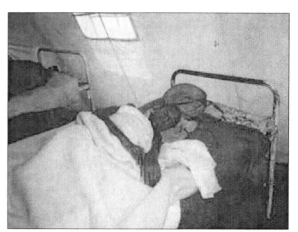

Inside a tent hospital

69
CARL AND LAVETTA DENT

1984–1987 / Kenya

Carl Ashley Dent was born in May of 1914 in St. Simon Island, Georgia, to Ernest and Josephine Dent. His mother, the former Josephine Green, was born in Green Landing, Mississippi. With the death of her mother, their family moved to Natchez, Mississippi. At age twenty she attended school on the Morning Star and became a Seventh-day Adventist. Years later her father joined the church.

Elder Halladay, superintendent of education for the Southern Missionary Society, urged her to attend Oakwood Training School, where she took the nurses training course. It was in 1908 at Oakwood where she met her future husband, Ernest Alton Dent, who was also taking the nursing course. After graduating from Oakwood in 1910, they were married.

Ernest Alton Dent was born in St. Simon Island, Georgia. His father, Samuel G. Dent, was a Baptist minister who later became a Seventh-day Adventist. Later, he contracted tuberculosis and went to the Oakwood Sanitarium. Soon afterwards he died.

Ernest Dent had a love for knowledge. He attended Atlanta Baptist College and completed his nurses training at Oakwood. He dreamed of becoming a doctor, but he never reached his goal because he, like his father, died of tuberculosis while still a young man.

After his death, his wife, Josephine Dent, took their three children—Ernest Jr. (at the age of eighteen he died of tuberculosis also), Thelma, and Carl—and moved to Redlands, California, in search of a warmer climate and better opportunities.

In 1917 Redlands was a sunny, picturesque town filled with orange groves. It had a population of 15,000. The Dents numbered among the four or five black families in the town. They attended the only Adventist Church in the town and were actively involved.

Life was filled with hard work, challenges, and fun. Josephine Dent worked as a domestic to provide for the family. At an early age she instilled within her children a sense of pride and commitment to excellence that made a lasting impression upon their lives.

Mrs. Dent constantly reminded her children that they were "first class people from good stock." They didn't really understand the meaning of those words because they were the poorest kids on the block. Their playmates had fathers, bikes, and toys. They had none of these things. They lived on the wrong side of the tracks. Yet, their mother's words left an indelible impression upon their young minds that made them strive for mastery.

Thrift, industry, and detailed attention to their duties were some of the values instilled in them by their mother. As a young boy Carl sold newspapers every Sunday to earn money for the family. By the time he reached junior high school he was practically self-supporting.

He bought a bike and delivered milk rain or shine. Many times he came in soaking wet, but the milk was delivered. By working he was able to buy his clothes, school supplies, and meals at the school cafeteria for his sister and himself. This lightened his mother's load.

Carl also worked as a caddy for his mother's employer and soon became a caddy in demand because of his strict attention to detail and his diligence.

As a student young Carl possessed great intellectual ability. He was always an honor student. While in high school he became a life member of the California Scholarship Federation.

During his early teens he began to seriously consider his life's vocation. One teacher encouraged him to enter engineering because of his love for mathematics. After giving it serious thought and taking into consideration his religious beliefs, he decided to become a doctor.

He chose to enter medicine for two reasons: he could control his employment and not encounter Sabbath problems; and secondly, he lived near Loma Linda and on Sabbaths he would often listen to the doctors talk about their missionary experiences. After listening to their stories, he knew he wanted to be a missionary doctor.

The summer of Carl's junior and senior years in high school, he pruned orange trees eight hours a day, five days a week to earn money for college. Upon enrolling at Pacific Union College in Angwin, California, in 1931 and until he graduated, Carl worked in the school cafeteria. He did all sorts of jobs in the kitchen—mopping the floors, cleaning tables, carrying linens to the laundry, washing kettles, and occasionally helping cook.

During his freshman year Carl worked 40 to 50 hours a week. His hard work paid off. At the end of his freshman year, his bill was paid in full. His work in no way affected his studies. He took eighteen hours each school term and still maintained a high academic standing. He was gifted with a photogenic mind. Carl could listen to his professor's lectures and on a test write verbatim what had been said. His intellectual prowess became the campus talk, and soon he became recognized as a scholar on campus.

The summer after his freshman year he spent at Bluff Lake, California, as a cook boy. He helped prepare meals and wash clothes. Carl chopped weeds, swept floors, and cleaned house. He lived in a tent and remembers "it being quite an exciting summer." On Sabbath he would hitchhike to San Bernardino and remain there until the sun set.

In 1932 the Depression was in full swing and affecting the life of every American. Carl's sophomore year was accentuated with work, work, and more work. He still maintained his job in the kitchen, but his wages were decreased from $.25 to $.22 an hour. Yet the expenses were the same. He took sixteen hours each term and maintained his high scholastic average.

During the summer after his sophomore year, Carl worked in an auto paint shop owned by Dennis Black who later became a minister. By the end of the summer he had earned $150, which enabled him to pay off his school bill and buy some clothes.

In his junior year Carl encountered a financial problem that changed the focus of his life and taught him about God's providence. During this year he had to study less and work more. He was taking a three-year pre-medicine course, but had to drop back and take a two-year course. The business office took notice of his school bill and gave him less than a week's notice to pay his bill or leave school.

After receiving the notice, he put in a long distance call to his mother and explained his predicament. Mrs. Dent immediately enlisted the aid of her employer. He sent a telegram asking the school if they would let Carl graduate if he sent fifty dollars. During that same weekend Carl went down to Oakland, California, to see Mr. Ridgeway, who sent a note stating he would send fifty dollars toward Carl's bill. Carl spent much time praying and crying out to God to help him out of this crisis.

The last of the money arrived in a letter addressed to Carl from the General Conference. Carl was quite surprised because he couldn't figure out who knew him there. When he opened the letter, he found a check for $10. A wealthy Chinese had read a story he wrote in the *Youth's Instructor* about the hardships he faced in school. The man was so impressed that he sent him a check for 100 Chinese dollars. When this total was converted to American currency, the sum came to $10. Carl knew beyond a shadow of a doubt that God had heard and answered his prayers. When Monday came Carl had enough money to pay his school bill and complete his education. He also had the assurance that God is able to do more than he could ask or think. Carl completed his pre-medicine course and set his sights on medical school.

With bated breath Carl waited for acceptance into Loma Linda Medical School. To his surprise, he was one of the first students to be accepted in his class. He was excited by the prospects of realizing his dream but silenced by the thought that he didn't have any money.

Carl immediately went to work as a call boy at Loma Linda Sanitarium. He ran errands, delivered messages, and did whatever his supervisor instructed him to do. He worked for two months during the summer and earned enough to pay off his college debt.

With great fear and anticipation the day came to enter medical school, but he didn't have any money. Once again he prayed to the Lord and asked Him to open up the doors of heaven and pour out a blessing.

School was scheduled to begin Sunday morning. On Saturday night he went to ask for the assistance of a wealthy couple, Mr. and Mrs. James Finley. At about 8:00 p.m. that evening he met with them and told them of his desire to become a doctor. He told them of his acceptance into medical school and his lack of finances. He asked if they could help him or if they knew of someone who could.

After Carl presented his case, he produced his report card with all As. Mrs. Finley exclaimed, "Such nice grades!" She told him to return the next morning. Sunday morning at the appointed time Carl came to the Finley's home. After a brief conversation, Mrs. Finley wrote him a check for $350.

What an answer to prayer! He immediately went to Loma Linda and registered as a medical student. Then he went to the student loan office and borrowed $175. The money Mrs. Finley gave him, along with the student loan and his wages from working in the hospital lasted throughout his sophomore year.

At the end of his second year in medical school, he had a debt of $100. He borrowed from every friend and relative he knew. The man that employed him to deliver milk gave him $100, and he gathered $35 from friends and relatives. He hitchhiked back to school and registered for the session. The regular school session was about to begin and he needed $500.

Once again he found himself penniless, and as in times past he got on his knees and prayed for a miracle. School was to begin Monday morning. Already it was Sunday, yet there he was without a cent. When his friend heard of his dire financial needs, it was suggested he apply for a job in the paint factory.

Monday morning he talked to the owner of the factory. When he found out that he was a medical student, the owner suggested that Carl get a job in the hospital rather than the factory. He thanked the man for the advice and left, discouraged and heartbroken.

One of the clerks in the registrar's office suggested he go see the chaplain. Carl went to Dr. Worth and asked him to point him to someone who could help. He replied, "I don't know a soul. Half a dozen students are faced with the same problem. But don't be discouraged. The Lord isn't dead yet. Let's get down on our knees and pray." Carl got up and thanked him with tears in his eyes. He remembers, "It was pretty hard to keep from crying because I was sure I was out of school."

He hitchhiked to Redlands and went to see Mrs. Wagner, a black Seventh-day Adventist who had always taken a special interest in him. She had always wanted to help him in school, but she had lost all her money in the Depression. Carl went back to see her and explained his situation to her. He borrowed her car and went to several wealthy people to see if they could help him, but even the wealthy were affected by the Depression.

He then remembered that as a boy he had delivered papers to a Mrs. Shirk, a wealthy woman whom Mrs. Wagner worked for. With fear and trembling, he knocked on her door. The maid answered, and Carl asked to see Mrs. Shirk.

"Is she expecting you?" she asked.

"No, she's not expecting me, but I would like to see her."

The maid invited him in and led him to the library. Mrs. Shirk, a portly woman, greeted Carl. He immediately began to introduce himself.

"I'm Carl Dent. I've just finished two years of medical training at Loma Linda Medical School. It is time for me to start my third year, but I don't have any money. I was wondering if possibly you could help me through medical school."

She looked at him and asked, "What kind of student are you?"

"A fairly good one," he responded.

"Who do you know that could give you a reference?"

"I know Mrs. Wagner who works for you. Mr. Clement, my high school principal, and the dean of the medical school at Loma Linda." Mrs. Shirk immediately sat down and began to call these people. She received a glowing report.

"My, those were some tremendous recommendations you received from them. I'll help you out." She loaned him $550. Once again God had performed another miracle for Carl! He immediately caught the bus back to school. The next day he was back in school with the rest of his class. During the next two years he faced financial difficulties, but he knew he could depend upon the Lord to make a way for him.

In 1938, after four years of intense study and financial problems, Carl Dent graduated from Loma Linda Medical School. A dream realized! Carl married Lavetta Lucas of Phoenix, Arizona, in 1938. Lavetta had been a nursing student at Loma Linda. Lavetta had been a victim of polio in 1934. While she was confined to a nursing home to recover from this sickness, she became acquainted with her Adventist roommate and was led by the Spirit of God to become a member of the Adventist Church.

Her new friend recommended that she attend Loma Linda where she met Carl.[87]

Carl tells his story about his mission service.

My lifelong dream to work as a missionary was realized three years ago when the GC Mission Board asked me to serve as a missionary to Nairobi, Kenya. My wife, Lavetta and I accepted the call. We attended the month long Mission Institute at Andrew University. Our group consisted of eight couples——two doctors, two dentists, two evangelists, a computer expert, and an ADRA (Adventist Development and Relief Agency International) couple. Six were assigned to Africa, two to the Far East.

The instruction I received at the Institute was most valuable. We were educated by our instructors, and inspired by returning missionaries, to give our best. I think the most impressive part of the Institute was the ability of the faculty to wield a group of strangers into a family unit so strong that within 30 days our ties were as close as those of relatives.

After completing the Institute, we were on our way as full-fledged missionaries. We boarded the plane for Kenya. First, we stopped in Amsterdam. We made a quick inspection of Dutch shops (wooden shoe making factory, cheese factory, etc.) took a short nap in the Tulip Hotel, boarded another overnight flight, and finally arrived in Nairobi.

We were met at the airport by a friend and colleague, Elder Ted Cantrell, then the treasurer of the East African Union Mission. We

were received with a warm welcome, and a delicious meal. During the first three days of our stay, the missionaries took turns inviting us to their homes for meals. We were given the necessities to start housekeeping (even food in the pantry and refrigerator).

We were pleasantly surprised at our accommodations; the house was spacious with four bedrooms and two baths. It was situated on 1 1/2 acres of land, landscaped with roses, bird of paradise and a large variety of tropical flowers. Everything was fine, with the exception of lizards walking on the bedroom walls and an occasional monkey sneaking in the house through an open window.

The day after our arrival was the Sabbath. The church designed for 350 members, held 800 with an estimated 100 or more seated on the outside, listening to the services over a loudspeaker. There are two services held: one at 8 a.m. and the other at 11 a.m., both of which were well attended. The Sabbath School program was conducted by our hostess Mrs. Frankie Cantrell.

When the classes were divided for study, who should be one of the teachers but my old friend and medical colleague, Dr. S.B.M. Kesseka. We had worked side by side at Riverside Hospital, now he was living in Nairobi because of the civil war in Uganda. Dr. Kisseka is now Prime Minister in Uganda. My wife and I sampled Sabbath School classes and finally joined a class taught by one of the City High Court Judges. His class was one of the most stimulating I've attended; being comprised of doctors, educators, Ph.D.'s, lawyers, businessmen and thinkers. This class also attracted most of the other missionaries that were not assigned to teach.

87. Stephanie D. Johnson, "Dr. C. A. Dent: A Citadel of Commitment and Dedication," *North American Regional Voice*, November 1980, pp. 2–4.

"This is mission service," I thought, "I like it."

Church service was prompt and well organized. The choirs sang familiar songs with a slightly different accent and an occasional variation in the melody and timing.

Everything proceeded fine until the minister began to preach. I asked what language is he speaking? I was informed it was English, Kenyan English. Soon I became accustomed to the accent and discovered the pastor was delivering powerful, well prepared sermons. One Sabbath I was asked to preach, I can imagine my American English sounded alien to them.

Shortly, after catching up on my sleep, I was taken to the S.D.A. clinic, located on the same ground as the church and Maxwell Academy. It is housed in a three story building with dental offices and Better Living Lecture Hall on the first floor; medical offices and laboratory on the 2nd floor; and three apartments on the third floor for medical and dental professionals.

I had brought several instruments from the States, but, to my delight, the medical offices were fully equipped. All I had to do was start working.

Dr. Ross Jose, an Australian physician, was filling the S.O.S. call at the Center, due to the return of Dr. B. Nelson to the U.S. Ross was being assisted part-time by Dr. John Amwega, Medical Secretary for the Division. Practice was slow at first, but that was good. I had to learn new medicines that were in use there.

Surprisingly, most of my patients were missionaries from various denominations, most of whom where Americans. I began to call myself "missionary to the missionaries." They assured me that my work was an important work for God—keeping them on the job.

My real mission experience had to be obtained vicariously through them. Many were working in real hardship areas in Northern Kenya, Somalia, Ethiopia and Sudan. They talked of the massive starvation in these areas, and their attempts to get food distributed to the people.

They faced constant danger. They recounted experiences of lying on the floor while insurgents and government troops riddled their house with bullets. I enjoyed their mission stories and listened with rapt attention.

Finally, I had a genuine experience of my own. On Sabbath afternoon, I was called back to the clinic for an emergency case. From all appearances the patient didn't seem ill. He calmly explained that he had been bitten by a hippopotamus and that he had to catch a plane to the U.S. that night.

If you have ever seen a hippopotamus you know that his mouth is so big that he could bite you in half. On the outskirts of Nairobi, there is a game park where animals live without human interference. A fence around three sides of the park prevents the animals from coming into town but allows free migration out of the park into the plains of the Mara and Serengiti.

This tourist was walking along the trail beside the river when he rounded a bend and came face to face with a baby hippopotamus. He turned to back off only to meet face to face with the mother coming to rescue her child. The river was on the left, so he tried to dive through the bush on his right as mother hippopotamus opened her mouth. She took a bite out of his rear knocking him down. Of course, thinking his end had come, he turned over and as mother lowered her head for a second bite he remembered someone had told him that animals were sensitive in the nose. In his remaining split second of life, he kicked the hippopotamus on her menacing snout. Instead of a second bite, she gave a snort, turned and went to rescue her baby.

My patient examined himself. He could still get up, his trousers were ripped and bloody, but he was able to drive his car, and he rushed to the clinic. I, in turn, examined the man; he had a three inch scratch on his bottom. I painted it with antiseptic, gave him a tetanus booster, and wished him a pleasant flight to the U.S.

Not all people are as fortunate as my patient. One day, a tall, very erect, soldierly appearing Briton brought his wife to the clinic for malaria treatment. I noticed that his voice was very hoarse. He had a large scar running from his chin to the right collarbone, and he walked with a limp. To satisfy my curiosity, he confided that he was and had been a "white hunter" for many years; conducting hunting safaris.

On one of his expeditions, he faced a charging rhinoceros. With calm assurance he stood his ground and, just as he was about to fire, he shifted his foot where there was a hole in the ground. The shot was misfired. The rhinoceros attacked him and began gnawing on his thigh, neck and ribs. The expedition members

shot the rhinoceros. Unconscious, his friends carried him to the nearest first aid station, radioed air medical rescue, and within a few hours he was being transfused and surgically repaired. Four days later, he awakened to find out that he was still alive. Within six months he was back at his chosen profession and there he remains.

During summer vacation, Lavetta and I, along with the Newborns and the Harts went camping in Masai, Mara, an extension of the Serengete Safari Park in Kenya. During the early morning hours, Dee Hart was awakened by something moving outside of the tent. It was a lion! The only thing separating the king of the jungle from his midnight snack was a plastic wall. The lion ripped a couple of jagged holes, thrust in a claw, snatched a basket from beside Dee and scattered its contents in the surrounding bush. The rest of the group now awake, signaled to Todd Hart, sleeping in the car to blow the horn, turn on the lights and start the motor. The lion abruptly disappeared, not from fear but from annoyance. Like Daniel, Dee can say, "My God has shut the lion's mouths."

My medical work was rather routine after 40 years of surgery in the United States. I treated simple injuries, hepatitis, diarrhea, malaria, simple injuries, migraines, infections, and minor surgical procedures.

Since many specialties are present in Nairobi, specialty board qualifications are required of those using major hospital facilities such as theatre and coronary care. Not having a surgical degree, my hospital cases were limited to diagnostic work and treatment of medical cases.

Language adjustment in Kenya wasn't too difficult because English is the official language and Swahili is widely spoken. Swahili is a relatively easy language to learn. Since I never used it regularly, I didn't become fluent. However, I was able to speak a few words, "open your mouth," "breathe," "turn over," "take off your clothes," "does this hurt?" and other expressions. My Swahili was sufficient for a complete examination, but detailed histories had to be done through a translator.

My working staff was dedicated and well trained. Sellina Onimba, the secretary-receptionist was a 4'10" Tanzanian who spoke Swahili and British English. "Kidogo," my nickname for her, translated in Swahili means little, was a perfectionist. She would write out my dictation in long hand, make me correct it, then submit her perfect copy for my signature. Nahoshon Kiamba, laboratory technician, did all the lab work for 3 doctors. He is an industrious, hardworking, Christian man. Kiamba is the father of five, who on a monthly salary of $450 managed to put a down payment on a house and pay $1250 cash for a used car.

Mrs. Damaris Mainda, the wife of a banker, is the accountant and business manager for the clinic. For 14 years she has worked faithfully with the Health and Welfare Association not out of necessity but rather out of love for God. Mrs. Mainda pays all the bills, keeps up the physical plant, watches the budget, supervises the maintenance crew and manages personnel.

My medical colleagues, Drs. Zofia and Jonazz Lypo, a husband and wife team, joined me in August 1985. Jonazz is an internist and his wife, Zofia is a gynecologist. The Lypo's are a dedicated missionary team having previously served in Nigeria for seven years. They are an asset to the clinic; their arrival has professionally and financially strengthened the clinic. Dr. Zofia Lypo has been granted a place on the gynecological and surgical staff of the Nairobi and Aga Khan Hospitals. Dr. Jonazz Lypo's practice is growing steadily.

During my stay in Kenya, I came in contact with the rich, the poor, the powerful and the influential. Shortly after beginning my work an American gentleman was brought to the clinic suffering with influenza. After treating him, one of his friends asked if I were acquainted with the Living Bible. "Of course," I answered. He then revealed that my patient was Dr. Ken Taylor, translator of the Living Bible. Dr. Taylor, a very warm, Christian man, spoke of the 18 years he devoted to prayerful study of the Greek and Hebrew text trying to find the real meaning of the text. Dr. Taylor remembered with enthusiasm the satisfaction he received when his work was accepted. Before his final visit, he gave my wife and me an autographed copy of the Living Bible.

During my mission service, I discovered the respect that one multicorporation has for our church. Every year we would examine the executive staff of the Kenya Canners, a subsidiary of Del Monte. These executives who traveled around the world confided that wherever their business takes them they always look for an Adventist clinic or hospital.

One patient that stands out in my mind was a fragile Kenyan woman who came into my office with her hand swollen nearly twice *the normal size. She explained, it all started as a small cut on her little finger. After one week of home care, the finger grew worse. Upon closer examination I discovered she was diabetic and her condition was quite serious. I administered penicillin, drained the abscessed pocket. Soaking along with oral antibiotics reduced the swelling and pain but the little finger was turning black. I regrettably had to amputate her finger. I gave her the best medical care and with overwhelming gratitude, this "shilling less" woman, left the clinic overjoyed.*

During a routine checkup one of my patients, a friendly man, confided in me that he had just been appointed the Kenyan Ambassador to China. During the course of our conversation, Mr. Jelian Habib invited my wife and me to stop in Peking on our return to the States. Was he just being gracious or did he really mean that we should be his guest at the embassy? The offer was too good to be true.

Before making our final travel plans I checked with the Kenyan Office of Foreign Affairs and was told the offer was genuine. I was also informed that Mr. Habib would be returning to Kenya for surgery on the advice of an SDA physician in Hong Kong. As soon as Mr. Habib arrived from Peking he came in for consultation. It was my privilege to assist with his surgery and visit him during his convalescence. Before returning to China, he invited Lavetta and me to attend the inspection of the new 60,000 seat stadium built and donated by China to Kenya.

We accepted his invitation, arrived at the appointed time and received a special welcome from the Chinese Ambassador, the

Somalian Ambassador, the Greek Ambassador, the Kenyan Permanent Secretary for Foreign Affairs (both the Secretary and his wife were my patients), and members of the Kenyan and Chinese Foreign Offices.

The facilities were elegant. Our host, the Chinese Embassy entourage, was especially kind. They had been informed of our proposed trip to Kenya. Following the tour the Chinese Embassy hosted a dinner. The specially prepared vegetarian dishes for us were delicious.

We did make our planned trip to Peking. We were treated royally. I don't know why God gave me favor with these men, but I do hope I'll not fail to accomplish His purpose.

At a recent East African Union Session, following my report, one of the ministers asked the question, "How many souls have you baptized?" Of course, I answered, none, our function is to be an entering wedge softening hearts and allaying prejudice so the gospel might do its work when presented.

One prime example of my role as a sower is the relationship I have developed with a Sikh attorney. We have had some deep discussions about Christianity. Who knows what God will do?

The gospel is spreading throughout Africa like an epidemic. The church in Kenya doesn't need to conduct an evangelistic crusade; they have only to indoctrinate the people knocking on the church's door. The baptismal class conducted by Mutoku Mutinga, Ph.D., has outgrown its small room in the church, filled the available space in the Better Living Center Auditorium and continues to grow. When the Bible students have finished their studies they always bring one or more relatives to take their place.

Finding seating for a newly baptized member poses a problem. There are no seats left, no aisles left vacant. Soon the converts will have to meet house to house like the early Christian church. A 4,000 seat church will be filled to the capacity before it can be completed.

Kenya has one of the fastest growing Christian populations in Africa. Religious freedom is guaranteed to every Kenyan. Public school facilities are made available for Christians to give Bible instructions to students willing to attend classes during their free time.

President Daniel Arap Moi recognizes the importance of religion. He attends a different church every week. Recently, he established an official five-day work week. He specifically mentioned that one of his primary reasons was to make sure that Adventist could worship freely without having to jeopardize their livelihood.

It was rewarding having the privilege to spread the gospel in Africa.[88]

Dr. Dent would return to Africa several more times as a short term volunteer both in Kenya and Nigeria. He died on February 1, 1995, at age eighty in Nashville, Tennessee.

Carl Dent as a young man

Lavetta Dent as a young woman

Dr. C. A. Dent

---

88. Carl Dent, "Reflections on a Mission Experience," *North American Regional Voice*, August and September 1987, pp. 12, 13.

Dr. Dent as a pilot

The Dent home while they were in Kenya

The Dents in their later years

70

OSWALD AND THELMA GORDON

1984–1990 / Liberia

Oswald and Thelma Albertha Gordon are from Panama. He worked in Guyana for two years and in Jamaica for ten years. Elder Gordon was ordained to the gospel ministry in 1954 while working as the district superintendent of the British West Indies Union Mission. In 1964 they were teachers at the West Indies College in Jamaica. Mrs. Gordon was also a legal secretary. They had two sons, Vernon and Maurice, and two daughters, Sheila and Norma.

He pastored in the Lake Region, Northeaster at Hanson Place and then in California. In 1984 while pastoring at the Los Angeles Tamarind Avenue Church he was called to Liberia to work in the Education Department and was soon made the president of the Liberia Mission. The Liberia Mission had thirty-four churches and a membership of 4,769 at the time and was headquartered in Monrovia.

While in Liberia a civil war broke out, and for a while the missionaries were in danger.

Pastor Gordon had to see to the safety of all the missionaries at the Liberia Mission. For a while the General Conference felt that all the families should be evacuated. The minutes of the General Conference Committee for May 3, 1990, indicate that he called Elder C. D. Watson and affirmed that all of the missionaries serving in Liberia were safe and for the present time, at least, could remain at their posts of duty in Liberia.

Together with an expatriate from the country of Ghana named Andrews Ewoo, Pastor Gordon conducted a Harvest 90 evangelistic campaign in a town about fifty miles north of Monrovia. At the close of the series, about 100 converts were baptized.

Mrs. Gordon was responsible for many people joining the church because of her kindness. She was in charge of the Voice of Prophecy Bible lessons. Magnus Kallon, a former Muslim in Monrovia, Liberia, joined the Adventist Church because of her and later became a literature evangelist.

Magnus became friends with Dwight Barnest, a Christian who worked with him at the Universal Insurance Company. Both came from the neighboring West African country of Sierra Leone. When Magnus shared his problems with Dwight, he became intrigued by the way Dwight prayed. This aroused his interest in Christianity.

One day Magnus visited the Adventist headquarters in Monrovia to inquire about the church's beliefs. With Mrs. Gordon's help, he was soon enjoying the Voice of Prophecy Bible lessons and sharing them with Dwight. After attending a Revelation Seminar at Monrovia's Better Living Church, they were both baptized.

The local publishing director recognized the potential of these young men and invited them to sell gospel literature to prepare people for eternal life rather than selling insurance policies for this present world. Both men resigned from their jobs and enrolled in Liberia's new Literature Ministry Seminary to prepare to become literature evangelists.

Pastor Gordon received his doctorate from Andrews University in 1991. When he returned from Liberia, he moved to Florida, where he became an assistant to the president of the Southeastern Conference. It was his responsibility to oversee churches without pastors until a pastor was selected for the church. He relocated the Mount Olive church in Apopka that had been in a drug-infected community for more than fifty years. Under his leadership they found new land, sold the old church, raised money, and built a lovely new church seating close to 500 members.

Thelma Gordon died in April of 2010, and Pastor Gordon married Edris Dailey, a nurse.

Tom Neslund, director of the International Commission for the Prevention of Alcohol, standing with Oswald Gordon, president of the Liberia Mission.

The Gordons as professors at West Indies College: Oswald Gordon (left) standing, and Thelma Gordon (left) seated

Pastor Errol Lawrence (left), Dr. DeWitt Williams, and Elder Oswald Gordon discuss the program of emperance with a Liberian health official.

Thelma Gordon with two friends

71
BOYD AND WANDA GIBSON

1986–1992 / Kenya

Boyd E. Gibson grew up in a musical family in Pottstown, Pennsylvania. His brother Stephen is an accomplished pianist. Boyd directed choirs and played strings. He began his musical skills on the violin with Evan Hallman at Reading Junior Academy and later switched to viola during his freshman year at Columbia Union College, now Washington Adventist University, with Robert Walters. He was drafted into the U.S. Army during that summer.

After serving his time in the army, Boyd entered Howard University where he earned his undergraduate degree. Boyd began his professional musical career at Pine Forge Academy as music teacher, choir director, and chair of the Music Department between 1980 and 1982.

During his second year at Pine Forge Academy, he married the former Wanda Marie Lester. In 1982 he returned to graduate school at Howard University where he earned a master's degree in music in 1986.

After his graduation Boyd and Wanda accepted a call to the University of Eastern Africa in Kenya, East Africa. Boyd served as director of choral activities, and Wanda worked as a nurse in the school clinic and later developed a child daycare for married students' children. The daycare became so successful that the Home Economics Department made the daycare part of their curriculum.

During his time in Kenya, the university became well known throughout the country for its outstanding musical ensembles. The choir also became the favorite choir of the president of Kenya, the Honorable Daniel Arap Moi, and would be called to sing at the State House on various occasions. The Chorale and University Chamber Singers sang on a weekly basis for every worship service during the school year and performed annual Christmas and spring concerts. The chorale also presented two major Christmas concerts at All Saints Cathedral in Nairobi.

Even with the wonderful musical success, Boyd considers the lifetime relationships that were forged to be the most rewarding aspect of his time abroad. The choir also became a Sabbath School class and would study the lesson together on a weekly basis. There were more than eighty baptisms from the choirs that took place during Boyd's time spent at UEAB. In addition to developing a wonderful choral tradition at the university, Boyd also developed a music minor program that was eventually developed into a music major.

After his return to the United States, he completed additional graduate studies in musicology and composition at Duke University. Boyd now serves as the director of the strings program at the Durham School of the Arts and the music director of the Church of the Holy

Family in Chapel Hill, North Carolina.

As a composer he has been blessed to have his compositions performed by the Duke University String School, the Ciompi String Quartet, the resident string quartet of Duke University, the Durham School of the Arts String Orchestra, the adult choir of The Church of the Holy Family, and his brother, pianist, Stephen Gibson. He has also been the featured composer at the Raleigh/Durham Chapter of the American Guild of Organist. Boyd had another premiere of his Spiritual Celebrations for Mixed Chorus and String Orchestra with the Shaw University Chorale in Raleigh, North Carolina, in May of 2010. His "Gates of Hell" composition, based on the sculpture of Rodin, was performed by the Durham School of the Arts Dance Company and String Orchestra at the North Carolina Museum in June of 2011.

His family includes his beautiful wife, Wanda, and three lovely daughters, Eugenia Marie, Deborah Eileen, and Faith Lee Ann.

Boyd Gibson conducting an orchestra

Boyd Gibson tuning his violin

Boyd Gibson leading an orchestra

Mr. and Mrs. Gibson and their three lovely daughters

72
CHAUNCEY AND BERNADINE CONNER

1987–1991 / Cameroon

Chauncey Lloyd Conner was born and raised in Brooklyn, New York, and his interest in dentistry came from early childhood dental issues that he and his family encountered. He obtained his bachelor's degree in chemistry with a minor in mathematics from Howard University. Dr. Conner also obtained his doctorate of dental surgery (DDS) degree from Howard University.

After obtaining his DDS, he volunteered for Special Services to serve as a relief dentist at the Health Centre in Blantyre, Malawi. This short episode created a desire to serve full time as a missionary in Yaounde, Cameroon, as the dental director for three years.

Later Dr. Conner served as the director of the Brooklyn Plaza Dental Center, which serviced a large diverse population. As the owner and co-founder of Conner Dental Associates, he has the opportunity to practice dentistry using the latest technology—very different from his primitive conditions in the mission field.

Dr. Conner is now affiliated with various professional organizations such as the American Orthodontic Society, Implant Seminars, American Dental Association, and the Academy of Laser Dentistry. He believes in supporting the community, and to this extent his practice partners with local schools and also does community outreach activities. His future goals include lecturing and helping other young doctors become proficient in private practice. In his spare time, Dr. Conner enjoys exercise, sports, travel, chess, photography, and spending quality time with his family.

Chauncey Conner, DDS

73
MISHAEL AND RUTH MUZE

1987–1991 / Zimbabwe; 1991–2001 / Kenya

Dr. Mishael Muze and his wife, Ruth, currently reside in North Carolina. He tells his own story very nicely in *Dialogue*. I will let him tell his own story.

The road has been long; the journey has been rough; the struggles have been many. Yet through it all, I have seen God bid me come higher, holding on to His unmistakable guiding hand.

I grew up looking to the snow-capped peaks of Kilimanjaro. From our Tanzanian village of Suji, the mountain seemed insurmountable, reaching to the skies. Born in an Adventist home, privileged to be raised by Christian standards, I have more than the mountains on which to focus my life. Early in my childhood, my parents taught me that nothing in life mattered as much as faith in God and reliance upon His Word.

I wanted to be a teacher, like my father. My mother, a gifted homemaker, knew exactly how to motivate her children. But our village had nothing more than a primary school. So as a teenager I was sent to a teacher-training school 1000 kilometers away. By 18, I was a primary school teacher. My father was not satisfied. He urged me to study further. I left home for the nearest Adventist school, Bugema

Missionary College, in Uganda. The cost was high, the environment new and strange, but Adventist education was worth pursuing, and it made all the difference in my life.

After completing my education there, I returned to my village to teach science and mathematics. When my students achieved the number two position in state government examinations, I knew I could make it as a teacher. Even as I breathed the fresh air of success as a teacher, I could feel the rumblings of strange winds from another direction. The winds of freedom were blowing across the African continent. Tanzania was no exception. Political leaders were conscious of the need for trained national leadership. The Tanganyikan National Union sponsored me to study abroad, and I chose Emmanuel Missionary College, later to become Andrews University, in Berrien Springs Michigan.

Armed with a bachelor's degree in mathematics, I was ready to return in 1964 to serve a free Tanzania. But the government offered to extend the sponsorship for a graduate program in education, and I joined the California State University at Fresno. Two blessings awaited me there: I got my Master's degree and I met Siphiwe, soon to be my wife.

I returned to Tanzania in 1966, married and began my government educational career. For the next 20 years, I worked for the state, using the opportunity to be a witness for my faith and to influence peers and policies for the good of Adventism.

My first test of loyalty came in my first appointment as a teacher at a public (government) secondary school. I told my headmaster about my faith as a Seventh-day Adventist and requested Sabbath privileges. The headmaster had no power to grant such requests, and he sought advice from the Ministry of Education. The assistant director of the ministry gave permission so long as the syllabus was covered by holding classes on other days. I rejoiced. But my joy was premature, as the director of education insisted that no such special privilege was possible. "If one is granted Saturday off," he argued, "another may ask for Friday, also on the bases of religion." I explained my position to the director. Getting nowhere, I told him I would have to resign my position rather than disobey God. To my amazement, the matter was dropped. I learned a valuable lesson: The God who commands also enables.

After several years of teaching, I was appointed headmaster (principal) of a Lutheran Secondary School at Mwenge. Wherever we served, my wife and I made our working a means for witnesses as well, usually by starting a branch Sabbath School. We did this at Mwenge, targeting our witness to the town of Singida. Eventually a church was organized there.

As the head of the school, I had an opportunity to experiment with an educational philosophy that had been incubating in me over the years. Under the inviting title, "Education for Self-reliance," I aimed to transform Mwenge into a model institution where staff and students would not only implement the routine curriculum but also adopt self-reliance as a goal for the institution and its community. The experiment succeeded so well that the then-president of Tanzania, Julius Nyerere, visited the school and commended its accomplishments. Regional and national media covered the school's activities as well.

Not long after this, I received a presidential appointment to be the district director for development. This job had prestige, power, and a good salary, and one should think twice before turning down a presidential appointment. But I loved the classroom, and reluctantly declined the offer. Unexpectedly, my action created a backlash, misunderstanding that I harbored negative attitudes toward the government. The result? I received a government reprimand and a demotion.

However, I had learned early in life that "all things work together for good to them that love God, to them who are the called according to his purpose" (Romas 8:28). A few years later after my demotion, I transferred to the University of Dar es Salaam as a lecturer, an opening that eventually led to the completion of doctoral studies.

In 1978 came another presidential appointment, this time to be chief education officer. The job involved supervision of more than 80,000 teachers and heading a number of departments, with 10 directors answerable to me. I did not expect this appointment, for I thought I was under disfavor for declining the previous presidential appointment. But God has a way to change things when we follow his directions. I accepted the new offer and served in that national responsibility for seven years.

The new office provided me with opportunities to improve the quality of elementary education in the country. Upon my recommendation, the government adopted a five day week for primary schools, an action that delighted Seventh-day Adventist teachers and students. I traveled widely to many countries in Africa, Europe, and Asia. Wherever I visited, my profession became an avenue to let the light of Christ shine. Sabbath and my Adventist lifestyle became conversation starters with colleagues from many countries.

While attending the General Conference session in 1985 at New Orleans, I had a chance meeting with Roland McKenzie, then principal of Solusi College in Zimbabwe. Just a joke, perhaps, but I remember telling him that should he need a teacher at Solusi, he did not need to look too far. Dr. McKenzie must have taken me seriously. Or perhaps God did. Soon I received a call to join the Solusi faculty. In 1987 I became part of that great historic institution. After serving for a few years as professor of education and mathematics, I was appointed the first black African Adventist principal of the college.

My agenda for Solusi became clear: it should become a University. Upgrading of facilities, negotiations with authorities, prayer and hard work of a dedicated faculty and students led to Solusi's gaining a University charter from the Zimbabwe government in 1994.

However, three years before that, I moved to Kenya to be the vice Chancellor of the University of Eastern Africa, near the town of

Baraton. Within months, tragedy struck. The companion of my life for 25 years, Siphiwe, was suddenly called to rest.

A statement from Ellen White brought me much courage and comfort: "In future life the mysteries that here have annoyed and disappointed us will be made plain. We shall see that our seemingly unasnswered prayers and disappointed hopes have been among our greatest blessings" (The Ministry of Healing, p. 474).

Our disappointments turn to become God's appointments. That is the lesson I have learned in my long journey of faith, work, and witness. In 1993 the Lord led me to meet Ruth Sihlangu, former head of the nursing sciences department at the University of Zimbabwe. My remarriage has not only helped in my emotional recovery, but together Ruth and I have clasped God's hand to continue the journey that He has set before us.[89]

---

89. Mishael S. Muze, "The Journey Must Go On!" *Dialogue* 7:2, 1995, pp. 32, 33.

From a hill near the East African Union office one gets a clear view of the Nairobi skyline. University of Eastern Africa, Baraton, Kenya president Dr. M. S. Muze (right) stands with some of the union leaders: (left to right) Phillip Ombuyi (secretary), Peter Bwana (education director), and Samuel Misiani (communication director).

Dr. Mishael Muze and wife, Ruth

74

LESTER AND PRISCILLA PARKINSON

1987–1997 / Zimbabwe, Kenya

Pastor Lester Parkinson holds a masters of divinity, masters certificate in project management, and a bachelor of arts in English and theology, church leadership, and administration management strategies. He possesses great interpersonal and people skills and is sensitive to cultural and gender diversity issues.

While pastor of the Ypsilanti and Ann Arbor, Michigan, churches he baptized his former teacher, Dr. Urius George, who was now employed by the University of Michigan in Ann Arbor as a professor of biometrics and as an environmentalist.

It was during his early school years that he met this teacher who made a profound influence upon him as a child in his native country of Guyana, South America. Years went by before Pastor Parkinson met him again while visiting a member's home. He invited his former teacher to take Bible studies. It did not take many Bible studies before Dr. George was ready to accept the teachings of the Adventist Church. Pastor Parkinson later baptized him in the Ypsilanti Church.

Dr. George was asked about his feelings in having his former student as his pastor. He said, "It is a feeling of admiration. I would like to think that I inspired Lester, or was an example that he respected. Pastor Parkinson's achievements are commendable. I feel real good about having him as my pastor."

Nineteen eighty-five was a very interesting year for the Parkinsons. Pastor Parkinson was attending the General Conference session in New Orleans. His wife remained at home expecting a baby. Priscilla's doctor finally gave her permission to fly to New Orleans to join her husband. She was assured that the birth would not take place until she was safely back home.

However, toward the end of the General Conference session, there were indications of an early arrival. The Parkinson's were hastily rushed to Tulane University Medical Center in a borrowed car. Little Ryan Charles Lester Parkinson weighed in at six pounds and four ounces and was born far from his father's home in South America, far from his mother's home in Zimbabwe, Africa, and far from their adopted home in Ann Arbor, Michigan. However, he was welcomed into this world by many friends and well-wishers. Ryan was blessed and dedicated to the Lord before hundreds of people at the Lake Region's fortieth anniversary weekend where his father was ordained to the gospel ministry.

Elder Parkinson, his wife, and two children left Illinois on July 29, 1987, to serve as the Sabbath School/lay activities/temperance director for the Zambezi Union Mission in Bulawayo, Zimbabwe. Shortly after arriving in Zimbabwe, he conducted two evangelistic crusades in two different towns, which resulted in approximately 500 baptisms.

On December 16, 1989, a brand-new church was dedicated in Gwanda, Zimbabwe. Church dedications are not uncommon or unusual in themselves, but this church opening was different. The 300-seat church was built in just sixteen and a half days by thirty-seven youth volunteers from Britain. The group included twenty-eight men who worked just as hard as the nine women!

The Zimbabwe Youth Project was the brainchild of Lester Parkinson and Hymers Wilson, youth ministries director of South England conference, and others. Early in 1988 planning began to raise funds for the project. Throughout North and South England young people energetically raised funds through a variety of sponsorship schemes: sponsored walks, runs, hymn singing sessions, and parachute jumps to name a few. In one instance young people from an area known for racial troubles and serious tensions between police and youth washed the local police squad cars to raise funds for the project.

British youth volunteers of diverse ethnic backgrounds all responded to the invitation to give one month of their time to help build the church. Some even gave up their jobs in order to make the trip. Only a handful were professional builders. There was one time when it looked like the team was falling behind schedule with the building, but, like angels from heaven, a group of about fifty church members arrived from Bulawayo to give a well-needed boost.

This brand-new "miracle" church now stands as a testimony that heaven continues to work in concert with human frailty to alleviate suffering and shortages.

Zimbabwe, formerly Rhodesia, became independent in April of 1980 following fourteen years of bitter guerrilla warfare by nationals against the white colonial rulers. The country now has a parliamentary form of government headed by a prime minister. Surrounded by Zambia on the north, Mozambique on the east, South Africa on the south, and Botswana on the west, Zimbabwe is completely landlocked, a significant factor in regards to the country's political and economic security.

Harare, the capital, is Zimbabwe's largest city, followed by Bulawayo. The official language is English with the population also speaking one or the other of two main indigenous languages: Shona and Sindebele. The literacy rate is very high, approximately 70 percent. The Zambezi Union, established in 1919, embraces the entire country.

After a needed furlough, the Parkinson's returned to Africa, this time to serve as chaplain and pastor of the University of Eastern Africa in Baraton, Kenya, in August of 1993.

On his arrival the baptistry at the church was kept busy. The first baptism involved twelve university students from Pastor Parkinson's Sabbath School class, which had about 350 students studying Bible doctrines. Another subsequent baptism saw five more university students joining the church. Pastor Parkinson used mostly evangelistic sermons that concluded with an appeal to respond. During the first quarter of 1993, 145 young people were baptized, the fruits of the secondary school outreach program conducted by the university church in area schools. In addition to these young people, twenty-nine more were baptized as a result of meetings conducted by the university church in a town about twelve miles away.

Pastor Parkinson also conducted a seminar on love, courtship, and marriage for about 120 students. He was also available for counseling with students. The combined effort of evangelistic sermons ending with calls, Sabbath School programs, seminars, and counseling helped the church to add 196 new members during the first five months of the year.

Lester A. Parkinson, then pastor of the Ypsilanti and Ann Arbor, Michigan, churches, baptizes his former teacher, Dr. Urius George.

The waters in the baptistry at the University of Eastern Africa were "troubled" by frequent baptisms of Pastor Parkinson's students.

University Pastor L. A. Parkinson (center front) rejoices with newly baptized students.

75

JAMES AND SARAH WASHINGTON

1987–1992 / Kenya

James Washington graduated from Oakwood College with a bachelor's degree in theology and a minor in business administration. He received his master's degree from Andrews University Theological Seminary and did additional study through the Ohio State University School of Commerce and Administration.

Pastor Washington and his wife, nee Sarah E. Costen (the older of a set of twins) of New Haven, Connecticut, were blessed with three daughters, Costena, Sarah, and Nancy.

James Washington began his ministry as a student colporteur intern in his hometown of Coatesville, Pennsylvania. He was ordained to the gospel ministry in 1960 while he was pastoring the Danville and Roanoke, Virginia, churches. His evangelistic crusade in Martinsville, Virginia, resulted in the organization of a new church there. He was then transferred to the Ephesus Church in Columbus, Ohio. Early in 1964 the church inaugurated a mortgage liquidation drive, and on April 3, 1965, the church was dedicated free of debt.

He later pastored the Shiloh congregation of Cincinnati, Ohio, and from there he was invited by the executive committee to become the new secretary-treasurer of the Allegheny West Conference.

Pastor Washington was serving as the African American affairs director in Sacramento, California, when he received a call to become the treasurer of the East African Union, which is headquartered in Nairobi, Kenya. They attended an Institute of World Missions at Andrews University, which ran for about six weeks while their passports were getting ready. When the institute was over, it was still not settled as to exactly where they were going to serve.

There was a strong nationalistic spirit where they were going and a national leader from Uganda was placed in the spot that he was to fill. While they were working this out, the Washingtons returned home to California. It was more than a year after attending the Institute of World Missions before the call was finally arranged. Secretary M. T. Battle had taken their passports to work on securing their visa, but he wasn't quite sure where they were to go. The Washingtons thought about visiting Africa on their own to get some prior knowledge of the continent, but now they didn't have their passports, so they were not able to get a visa. The Uganda Field had now become organized into the Uganda Conference, and the national leader was called to be the treasurer in Uganda, leaving the spot in Kenya open for Elder Washington.

Finally, with the call worked out, the General Conference was able to get their visas, and Elder Washington left to be the treasurer of the East Africa Union. At that time, although the membership was large, the East Africa Union was not financially self-sufficient. Elder Washington and the leaders there set up goals to meet this challenge and become financially independent. Before he returned to America, the union was nearly financially independent.

Their youngest daughter was about to attend an Adventist school in Spain, and the two older girls were already in college, so the children did not go with them. Before they left Africa, all three of the girls had an opportunity to visit their parents in Nairobi. In 2006 fifteen years after they had returned home, the Washingtons were called back to be the main feature of a camp meeting in the Kenyan Lake Field. The two youngest girls, who were nurses, along with their children, also gave lectures at the camp meeting.

Pastor James Washington

Elder and Mrs. J. A. Washington and their three daughters

76

LEONARD AND ORA NEWTON

1989–1995 / Madagascar, Cameroon

Leonard Gillyard Newton was born in Shreveport, Louisiana, on July 30, 1929. Newton's family moved to Los Angeles where the young man first encountered the Adventist Church. He was baptized at age seventeen after attending tent meetings and Bible studies.

Leonard attended Oakwood Academy his senior year of high school and afterwards earned a theology degree from Oakwood College. His first assignment after graduating from Oakwood was to work alongside E. E. Cleveland in a tent effort in Gulfport, Mississippi.

Ora Lee Davis was born in Calera, Alabama, but moved to Chattanooga, Tennessee, when she was very small. She was not an Adventist at the time. When she was about eighteen years old Elder D. B. Reid conducted evangelistic meetings in Chattanooga, and Ora attended every night. She was the only one in her family that was baptized as a result of that meeting, but later her mother was baptized in Wilmington, Delaware, by Elder C. D. Brooks. Leonard and Ora met at Oakwood and were married in 1952. Elder Newton was ordained to the gospel ministry in 1955.

Elder Newton's pastoral ministry spanned forty-seven years and eight states that included locations in the South Central Conference—Gulfport, Meridian, Hattiesburg, Soso, Mississippi; Tuscaloosa, Alabama; and Nashville, Tennessee; Southwest Region

Conference—Oklahoma City, Oklahoma; Dallas-Fort Worth, Texas; and Baton Rouge, Louisiana; Allegheny East Conference—Newport News, Virginia; and Northeastern Conference—Boston, Massachusetts. He served as the Northeastern Conference Stewardship Department director from 1976 to 1985 and later as the fifth president of the Northeastern Conference from 1985 to 1988.

His strong commitment to Christian education was demonstrated by the founding of two schools, Grace Temple Seventh-day Adventist School in Fort Worth, Texas, and Calvary Seventh-day Adventist School in Newport News, Virginia. His five children—Leonard G. Newton Jr., Gayle Newton-Taylor, Leonora D. Coopwood, Valeria F. Newton, and Lionel D. Newton—birthed in him a desire for good Christian education facilities.

In anticipation of someday serving in a French-speaking country, he studied French at Harvard University Extension School and later at Saleve Adventist Seminary in France. Ora had taken French in high school and at Oakwood and was also prepared to deal with the foreign language. It was during the time that he was serving as president of the Northeastern Conference that Newton was called to the mission field, which he and his wife readily embraced. Serving in the mission field had been a lifelong desire for the family. Sister Newton says her only regret as she looks back on her mission experience was that they didn't go sooner. They immediately left the Northeastern Conference to go to Tananarive, Madagascar where Elder Newton served as ministerial secretary of the Indian Ocean Union Mission and Sister Newton taught English in one of the schools. The kids were grown, so none of them went with their parents.

In 1992 Elder Newton went to Yaounde, Cameroon, to serve as president of the Central African Union Mission. They remained there until his retirement from denominational service in 1995. The Newtons retired to Anniston, Alabama, where they unofficially worked with the Mount Olive congregation in whatever capacity they were needed.

Elder Newton died in Anniston on June 14, 2009, at age seventy-nine, six weeks short of his eightieth birthday. Ora now resides in Georgia with one of her daughters.

Mrs. Ora Newton

President of the Central African Union Mission, the late Elder Leonard Newton (far right) and wife (center) with the Gibbons' family and a local leader

Elder Leonard Newton

77
ELLIOTT C. AND SONIA MARIE OSBORNE

1989–1991 / Kenya

Elliott C. Osborne and his wife, Sonia Marie Duroncelet, were both born in California and raised as Seventh-day Adventists. Both became educators with a desire to serve God in the mission field. Here is their story as written by Elliott:

I was born and brought up from the cradle in the city of Oakland, California. My parents raised me within the confines of the Adventist Church. I was baptized under B. R. Spears in 1961 during a tent meeting in East Oakland. This became the Elmhurst Church. I was eleven years old at the time.

My status today is emeritus having retired in regular standing as an ordained minister with thirty-two years of active service and employment with the church. I live in Pittsburg, California. I am still married to Sonia, now celebrating thirty-eight years of marriage. We have five children and three grandchildren as of 2014.

My educational background includes degrees in counseling, psychology, theology, education, and sociology, ranging from associate degrees to a doctoral degree.

I was a local church pastor in Fontana, California, before receiving my call to mission

service. I had worked for the SECC (Southeastern California Conference) office for twelve and a half years. My wife was a public elementary school teacher who had previously been employed in the Adventist school system.

I was called to pastor the university church and teach theology at the University of Eastern Africa. As chaplain I had the responsibility for two churches on campus, the larger one English speaking and the other Kiswahili. I also inherited fourteen Sabbath school classes that met off campus. I organized the lessons and teaching teams for the Sabbath school classes, and I preached both services for the campus churches. My wife also received a call to teach at Baraton School on the university campus.

As a professor it was my responsibility to teach three courses. The most challenging was World Religions since I had Muslim students in my class. I had to be very exact and sure of what I taught. I only had one complaint in two years. An Islamic female student had to write a paper on the pros and cons of Islam, and she protested because there were no cons to Islam in her reasoning. Fortunately, we both survived the assignment.

My whole family spent those two years with me in Kenya at the University of Eastern Africa,

Baraton. Meshach, the eldest and only male child, was thirteen. Keziah was eleven, and the twins, Fawn and Acacia, were nine, followed by Berniece, age seven.

Our experiences were positive, negative, political, and dangerous. I will speak to only one experience to illustrate each aspect of our stay. However, I want to state up front I would not exchange my two years for anything on earth. The positive far outweighed the negative and the benefits are reaping rewards still after these many years.

I begin with the positive. Before we actually left the States, my children received some teasing. Huts, savages, living in trees, and other very ignorant comments came from underexposed American children. Thus, when we arrived and found black Africans to be more than capable students, with strong family ties and loyalty to God and tribe, we were pleased. Tarzan was the only one living and swinging in trees and that was a movie.

Our children went to school with Africans as well as children from other parts of the world whose parents were part of the university faculty. They made friends that have stuck for life. My son was in his African roommate's wedding many years later. The computer keeps them all connected, and I have had the privilege of seeing my ex-students rise to high responsibilities in the EAD and EAU. Some are now professors in universities around the globe.

We learned how different African tribes vary in custom and tradition. The Luo is not a Kisii and the Massai are far apart from the Kikuyu in dress, speech, and manner. We left great

debtors. We learned so much more than we ever taught. This is one of the positive realities that came our way.

One negative story I share at this point is not to discourage but to enlighten. We humans have besetting sins that the spirit must dispel. Our family was greeted by the harsh reality that there are some men and women in mission service who do not cherish the people they signed up to serve. We saw missionaries treat black Africans in their own country like they were sub-human. We heard college professionals call grown men "boy" and never allow 'workers' to come to their front doors or socially mix with Africans. I was told that "these 'people' are brutish and childlike," as if this was a nineteenth century racial bigot speaking.

I witnessed children of whites from other countries whose parents were missionaries demand menial tasks from adult males as if they were personal servants, never using the word please or thank you. This was very difficult to watch. We had come to teach, serve, and learn, not to rule, control, and undermine the African population. These are not the kind of encounters authors are anxious to write about, but I witnessed it.

Politics of the day were very strained. President Bush Sr. attacked Iraq while we were in Kenya, which made our stay very stressful. The Kenyan government was not favorable to the U.S. aggression on a small nation. We were put on alert by our own embassy. We were prepared to leave the country at a moment's notice.

Also, the nation of Kenya was experiencing political strain. It was a single party state when we arrived, and there was a push for a multi-party system. A Luo decided to challenge his government and run for president. He was not officially recognized. There was only one name on the ballot for president. Essentially you are in the office for life as long as there is only one party, and the president is the head of the party, unopposed. Robert was told not to come to a certain town close to the university or his life would be at risk. He went anyway, and as he left, he died in a head-on collision. The atmosphere was hostile, and we felt the tension daily.

The dangerous nature of our service was not just perceived. The closed knit nature of tribe and family translates controversy into a personal response often filled with emotion. I traveled to my great-grandfather's homeland of Ethiopia. This had many fearful aspects to it, but I will not speak of those. While I was away, the students on campus protested our administration. The authorities on campus called it a riot. No stones were thrown and no fights were fought, which doesn't equate to much of a riot in my mind.

My wife and children were still on campus at the time even though I was out of the country. Several of my students came to our house seeking advice. My wife is a peacemaker at heart. She did not want violence to break out, so she escorted a few of my students to the president's home so they could speak face to face.

The response to the riot in the minds of our leaders was to call the Kenyan police. They came on our Adventist campus with automatic weapons and batons to encounter unarmed students on a religious campus. They shut the school down and told the students they had to leave immediately. Kenya is not America. These students were boarding students. Many were from other East African countries. Turning our students out on the street was especially cruel. So they marched off the campus down the muddy road on foot.

When I returned to campus, the place was ghostly quiet. I had no clue what had happened in my absence. My wife tried to explain the events. Soon after my arrival, I was part of a meeting to discuss what our next move would be as a university. Our president wanted to exact a heavy toll on the students, and especially my students. He began putting together a plan of attack. He and his academic dean actually began to assemble a retroactive diary of events pointing to the ringleaders. I protested this outrage. I was then dismissed from the meeting.

I was on the Administration Council, so I had a rightful place at the "hearings" that took place when the students returned. I took the stance of defense lawyer, not prosecutor. I was able to spare several of my students because I would not allow the retro diary to be used as evidence against the students. I was attacked and accused by my leaders of being responsible for the "riot" event though I was not on campus. When these proceedings were over, I was terminated. I appealed to the General Conference president. He came and heard my case. He did not see where I had done any wrong, and the fact that I was not in the country when the "riot" occurred seemed conclusive. But he told me to my face someone was going to have to take the fall for this fiasco, and I was the new kid on the block. So he upheld the wrongful termination and sacrificed my family for the sake of peace and harmony.

We finished our second year and were then sent back to the States. We had no jobs and no help seeking employment. We were on our own and totally dependent on our Lord. If a man ever finds himself alone, the best arms to fall into belong to Jesus. We never suffered. A man I did not know recommended me for a teaching position I had not applied for, and I was hired before my last paycheck was spent from mission service.

We returned in 1991, and I worked for the church until December 2010 when I retired. I am currently a tenured faculty member for City College of San Francisco. I teach classes and am an academic counselor. My wife is in the final year of her contract with Alameda County Office of Education, teaching in the Juvenile Justice System. She will retire in June 2015.

The five Osborne children: Meshach, Keziah, Fawn, Berniece, and Acacia

Four of our children are married, and they all have Adventist spouses. My wife and I are members of our local Pittsburg, California, church and are proud members of the California returned missionary families.

I would be remiss without mentioning the harvest the Lord gave us in our two years of service. We baptized 300 precious souls for the kingdom. We have a godchild named Mary Osborne born of Kenyan parents. Mary is my wife's nickname. We have lifelong friends with cherished memories that can never be removed. But the greatest blessing in this life was to have nothing—no job, no home, no prospects, no hope, five children, a wife—and one promise, "I will be with you always."

Sonia Marie and her fifth and eighth grade students

Our mission experience took away every security we had on earth except our Lord, and we found that He is enough for today, tomorrow, and forever more. Had we not taken the call, my family might never have known the firsthand intimacy and charity of God. I have a thousand stories but only one testimony—the Lord is faithful!

The Baraon overseas elementary school choir

The Osborne girls with their Ethiopian friends, the Dakas

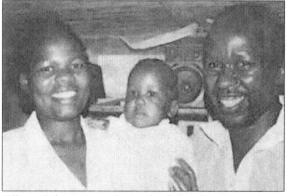

Elliott Osborne's students, the future Drs. Amenias—both would go to the United States and complete their doctorates

Thirteen-year-old Meshach riding a motorcycle

River baptism. (one of 44 that day)

Elliott and Sonia Marie with a theology student and wife on campus

The Osbornes with students at the University of Eastern Africa.

78

PAUL AND PATRICIA BRYANT

1990–1995 / Ghana, Sierra Leone

Paul A. Bryant was born in Richmond, Virginia, and attended Virginia Union University where he earned a bachelor's degree in elementary education. He later attended Andrews University and earned a bachelor's degree in religion and a master's degree in religious education. He also is a graduate of Bethany Theological Seminary and has a doctor of ministry degree from there. He was ordained an Adventist minister.

Paul married Patricia Royleen Perry and served as principal of the Ephesus church school in Richmond, Virginia, for a while.

While Paul was attending Andrews University, the Bryant family received the call to go to the mission field where Pastor Bryant would serve as a departmental director and mission evangelist in Liberia. When missionaries leave home, they are not sure what they will face in the new territory. Sometimes there are great dangers. Sometimes there are debilitating diseases.

Sometimes there are unforeseen circumstances. They go in faith knowing that God has promised to protect them.

The Bryants were originally scheduled to go to Liberia. They later found out that there was a great conflict and political unrest in Liberia. This unrest spilled over into Sierra Leone, which had a coup d'état. The division leaders decided that the family should instead go to Ghana. For a while their lives were very unstable. Then the division had to withdraw them from that country. Next, they were sent to Abidjan, Ivory Coast, and then back to the States. They enrolled their son, Christopher, at Maxwell Academy in Nairobi, Kenya. Finally conditions settled down, and they were able to return to a more peaceful Sierra Leone.

While in Freetown, Sierra Leone, they were privileged to work with the local members to rebuild the church that had burned down there. Also, they were privileged to work in a small community called Lumbly close to the beach. One day Pastor Bryant was driving through the area, and the Holy Spirit impressed him that this would be a wonderful place to have an evangelistic meeting and establish a church. However, he could not find any place like an auditorium or hall where he could have a meeting. There was only a nightclub there. He went in to speak with the owner, and she said they could have an evangelistic meeting there, but they had to be finished by 10:00 p.m. each night.

His team went in each evening and removed all of the tables and the things from the dance floor and put in chairs. For three weeks they conducted their meetings like that, taking down the tables, rearranging the seats, and then putting everything back again by 10:00 p.m. During those hours the Holy Spirit replaced the alcoholic spirits with God's spirit. God blessed his efforts with twelve souls, which became the nucleus of a beautiful church that has been built in Lumbly.

Elder Bryant is now serving as a district pastor in Salisbury and Cambridge, Maryland.

Pastor Paul Bryant officiating at a baptism in Northern Ghana (1990).

Pastor and Mrs. Patricia Bryant stand with some nationals in Northern Ghana (1990).

79

CLYDE AND BARBARA CASSIMY

1990–1996 / Kenya

The Cassimys left Oakland, California, at the end of May 1990 for mission service in Kenya, Africa. Clyde was pastoring in the Northern California Conference at the Elmhurst SDA Church at the time. On June 1 they arrived at the University of Eastern Africa where Pastor Clyde Peter Cassimy served as professor of theology while his wife, Barbara (Elaine Brown), functioned as an administrative assistant in the Business Office.

They finished their six-year term and returned to the States on July 30, 1996, settling near Loma Linda where Pastor Cassimy now serves at the Behavioral Medicine Center of the Loma Linda University Hospital as a spirituality-focused psychotherapist (chaplain) and in the School of Religion as an assistant professor. Barbara functions as the senior administrative assistant in the School of Allied Health Care Professionals.

We were born in the Caribbean—Barbara in Jamaica and I in Trinidad and Tobago. I attended Atlantic Union College and Andrews University and finished a doctor of ministry degree at Vanderbilt University in the department of pastoral psychology and pastoral counseling.

Kenya was relatively peaceful while we were there. The country was under the leadership of

President Daniel Arap Moi, who favored our university. We were the first private university in Kenya, or in Africa, to be chartered by a national government. It occurred in 1991.

The six years we spent in Kenya were probably the best six years of our lives. We made many lifelong friends and still correspond and visit with the Binas family from Tanzania.

I did week of prayers and spoke at camp meetings in several countries including, of course, Kenya, Tanzania, Zimbabwe, Uganda ,and South Africa. My first and most memorable camp meeting took place in Kampala, Uganda.

Uganda was still quite tense after the overthrow of the government by Yoweri Museveni. There were male and female soldiers everywhere toting guns, and our vehicle was stopped and searched at least six times as we traveled from Busia to Kampala. I preached to thousands of Ugandans on that occasion, in the open air, with the gun-toting military affecting a very threatening presence. The vice president at that time, who became the prime minister soon thereafter, was a physician by the name of Kiseka. He lived in exile in Kenya for a number of years and assisted Museveni in their successful coup. Kiseka was a devout

Seventh-day Adventist. He and his wife were positioned prominently in the audience as I preached twice daily. I later learned that while a medical student in the 1950s Kiseka was baptized by E. E. Cleveland in Kampala.

Dr. Cassimy and his wife Barbara with their ministerial students

Pastor Cassimy officiating at a baptism at the university

Officiating at a wedding

Dr. Cassimy with his class outdoors studying

At a tent service

80
RAY AND JOAN RICKETTS

1990–1997 / Kenya

Ray Ricketts' ministry has taken him around the world. Born in Belize, Central America, he attended college at Northern Caribbean University, the former West Indies College in Mandeville, Jamaica, began his ministry in the West Jamaica Conference, went to graduate school at Andrews University in Michigan, then was called to the Southern California Conference where he pastored for ten years.

Ricketts later received a call from the Eastern Africa Division to serve as Adventist Chaplaincy Ministries Director/ University Chaplain for the East African Union in Nairobi, Kenya. He left the United States on August 19, 1990, with Joan Elizabeth Collins Ricketts and their two children. He served with distinction for seven years, primarily in Kenya, ministering to Adventist young people attending secular university campuses throughout the republic. In his dual role he also gave leadership to and mentored other chaplains in the conferences and missions within the East African Union. Joan served as a medication procurement officer for the East African Union Rural Health Ministries and later worked for ADRA Kenya as a liaison officer for ASAID, WHO, and other NGOs, writing proposals for grants to enhance the health and well-being of Kenyans in rural areas.

Chaplain Ricketts spoke of his ministry on secular campuses as an exciting and challenging experience. According to Ricketts there are countless thousands of Seventh-day Adventist students on secular college and university campuses worldwide. With this in mind, the Adventist Church has the responsibility and the mandate of developing and sustaining a credible program/ministry to meet the spiritual needs of this ever growing constituency of intellectuals and scholars.

So then, Seventh-day Adventist chaplains ministering on secular campuses are among a new breed, born of necessity and called upon to serve in a highly specialized ministry. For this reason, these chaplains should have certain basic qualifications and understand the nature of their work in order to be effective in their ministry. Ricketts feels that campuses are like people. They each have their own personality and peculiarities; therefore, the campus chaplain is faced with the challenge of developing "programs" to best meet the unique needs of his/her particular campus and ultimately making the gospel culturally relevant to the country, region, and campus.

As a campus chaplain it was his desire to see young people experiencing the joy of salvation. He wanted them not only to fall in love with Jesus but to remain connected with the Lord for the rest of their lives. He often said, "Students must be offered something real, something that was transformative and of enduring value; sometime that will keep then for now as well as for eternity ... spiritual 'gimmicks' don't work."

While in Kenya Pastor Ricketts was often invited to minister to large groups of young people and to preach at camp meetings in Tanzania, Uganda, Botswana, Zambia, Zimbabwe, South Africa, and even India. His ministry was fruitful, and hundreds received the Lord as their personal Savior and were baptized under the unction of the Holy Spirit. After returning from Kenya, he was called to be the campus chaplain at Atlantic Union College in Massachusetts; currently he serves as a health care chaplain in Orlando, Florida.

Ray Ricketts with Elder James Washington (fourth from right)

Ray Ricketts casual at Atlantic Union College

Ray Ricketts with other campus leaders

Ray Ricketts addressing students on the campus

Some university students with the Ricketts family, including sons Ricky and Andrew

Chaplains Ricketts and Nymwanda in the pool at a student baptism

Joan Ricketts singing a favorite on the campus

81
Danforth and Vera Francis

1991–2010 / Madagascar

Barbadian born, Robinson Danforth Francis was the tenth child of eleven children born to the late Dorcas and Urbane Francis of Fitts Village, St. James. He is a third generation Adventist and has been active in all areas of church work from an early age. He was a youth who was not afraid to challenge the leadership to do better when he thought there was a better way.

Robinson taught school for six years before he began the ministerial course at Caribbean Union College, graduating in 1979 with his bachelor's degree in theology. He served as a departmental director of the Surinam Mission and pastor of the Bethel church.

Two months after graduation, he married his soul mate, the former Vera Samuel of Antigua, who became a great asset to his ministry in the various places they've worked. Both Pastor Francis and his wife are the tenth child of their parents and were considered the "tithe" of their parents increase. Their call to the mission field, which spanned a total of nearly twenty-nine years, was providential.

In April 1983 Pastor Francis was ordained to the gospel ministry, one month after becoming a father. The same year he was elected a departmental director for Personal Ministries and Stewardship. He continued working in Suriname during the turbulent years of the revolution until 1985 when he answered the call from the East Caribbean Conference to work as a pastor in Georgetown and later the Richland Park districts in St. Vincent. While in St Vincent, Pastor Francis completed his master's degree in religion at Andrews University and became the proud father of a baby girl. After three fruitful years, he was called to Barbados to pastor six churches in the north of the island.

Pastor Francis' passion for the work led to greater responsibilities, and in 1991 he was again elected to the Church Ministries Department with special responsibilities for youth; also to the Health and Communication Departments in the East Caribbean Conference. Seven months later he received and accepted a mission service call from the General Conference to the Indian Ocean Union located in Madagascar. He served as church ministries director with responsibilities for youth and stewardship along with communication. As communication director he was instrumental in starting a television program that is still vibrant today. This union included Mauritius, Madagascar (the fourth largest island in the world), Comoros, Seychelles, Mayotte, and Reunion. Most of these islands are French speaking. He also served as president of the Mauritius Conference.

There were approximately 34,000 Adventists in Madagascar (the union headquarters) at the time of his service; 70 percent were under thirty years of age. There was a continuing struggle for economic survival due in part to the country's seventeen-year experiment with Marxist social-ism (1975–1992).

The 100 percent wage factor for their pastors and other workers was 250,000 Madagascar francs (about US$74.32). A senior worker at the 160 percent level earned about US$119 per month. Most of the workers were unable to afford their own home, car, or motorcycle. However, food was relatively inexpensive.

His leadership qualities soon became obvious to the administration of the Indian Ocean Union, and he was asked to go to the beautiful Seychelles Islands to be the president of the mission. With the help of God, he was able to mobilize the laity in several evangelistic thrusts, utilizing the different methods learned in the Caribbean to double the membership of the mission in three years.

The neighboring Mauritius Conference, seeing what was happening in the Seychelles Mission, was motivated to elect Pastor Francis as president at their next session in November 1999. Once again, his evangelistic skills, which were new to the area, brought hundreds into the church, swelling the membership and planting new churches.

He was only two years in Mauritius when the then Africa-Indian Ocean Division (AID) invited him to Liberia to be the president of the West African Union. His tenure there was shortened by the escalating civil conflict during the last days of the Charles Taylor regime. On his second evacuation from Liberia, he and his family took refuge in Sierra Leone, and it was from there they were called to the division headquarters to serve as a field secretary with special responsibilities for strategic planning and stewardship. Later in 2005 at the General Conference Session in St. Louis, he was elected field secretary with responsibilities for strategic planning, the ministerial association, and global mission coordinator.

Pastor Francis was an invaluable asset to the WAD President, Pastor Luka Daniel, under whom he served six of the eight years he spent at the division. Pastor Francis always credits his success to the mantra, a quotation taken from E. G White: "There is no limit to the usefulness of the one who, putting self aside, makes room for the working of the Holy Spirit upon his heart, and lives a life wholly consecrated to God."

The poolside of the Riviera Seventh-day Adventist Church in Abidjan, Côte d'Ivoire, was the setting of an exciting baptism of eleven new converts. The event could have passed as any other, for it was not the first baptism held at the church, which began years ago as a small group meeting in the chapel of the West-Central Africa Division (WAD), then known as the Africa-Indian Ocean Division. But these baptismal candidates were unique. They were the fruits from the first-ever Adventist-held evangelistic campaign on the campus of the University of Cocody in Abidjan, once a hotbed of social unrest during the country's five-year civil conflict that displaced hundreds of thousands of people.

The decision of the Riviera Church's Women's and Personal Ministries Departments to target the campus as their mission field for the year 2007 had finally materialized. The campaign began with a week of prayer. WAD Ministerial Director R. Danforth Francis was the speaker. For three weeks, June 1 to 23, he spoke passionately of his message titled "Steps to Better Life." Yet the ground remained tough and unyielding. Other social and sporting events on campus competed for attention. Some nights music from outside the gymnasium in which the meetings were being held resonated and bounced off the walls. Other nights, it was the chill and rain that dampened spirits.

"Ideally, the gymnasium [in which the meetings were being held] could seat 1,000 persons," Francis said, "but we had an average of only 35 guests each time."

He added, "If I were in a position to do it all over again, we would have a longer time for contact with the people before launching the campaign. The community didn't know us well enough, so we did not attract more people to come to the meetings. Because my responsibilities at the office had been increased to include Adventist Mission, I will be promoting more sowing so we can reap more from where we have sown."

But the church members persisted—and that persistence paid off. Finally, eleven people indicated their desire to be baptized. Among those was one man whose story stood out. Though bound to a wheelchair, he radiated the joy and confidence that comes from an intimate relationship with Christ.

"When I am depressed, I sing and my spirit is lifted up," said Ivorian-born Jacquelin Brou Kouaku, the tenth among twelve siblings, who jokingly refers to himself as a living tithe for God. His search for the truth took him through several challenging experiences.

Today, Kouaku is a composer of numerous songs awaiting production. During the 2006 Radio/Television Ivoirienne (RTI) musical contest, he emerged among the finalists, touching a chord in the hearts of his listeners. This singular event became a turning point in his life, an acceptance of what God could use him to accomplish. In spite of this new turn, Kouaku describes his journey for truth and success as long and tortuous, but he remains stoic: "I know music does not immediately translate into wealth in Africa," Kouaku said, "but if it's God's will for me, He will provide the means."

Indeed, Kouaku's life had not been easy. Inadequate funds and his father's initial reluctance to let him out of his presence delayed his early education. But during a visit to one of the mission hospitals in Divo, a town in Côte d'Ivoire, West Africa, a missionary doctor encouraged his father to send him to school, and he relented. On Kouaku's first day of school, he recalled that his father had to carry him on his back because Kouaku could not use his legs. The missionaries later provided him with a wheelchair, easing the problem of transportation.

Kouaku's high intelligence earned him a promotion in elementary school. He skipped second grade and advanced to third grade. But then a lingering ailment forced him to remain out of school for five years. By the time he reached the final year of high school, a bout of typhoid fever robbed him of the joy of successfully completing his final exams. That was in 2002. The next year his mother died. His father had predeceased her in 2000. The combined tragedy of the loss of his parents and his inability to take his school exams drove him to the edge of despair, and he contemplated suicide. Still, God's grace kept him going. He spent 2004 trying to survive by cultivating and selling tomatoes. Then his older sister died in 2005, leaving him broken with grief.

Kouaku's determination to overcome his pain and discouragement compelled him to continue composing songs and maintaining a small shop his sister had left behind. Then he learned about the musical contest, and this experience opened other doors. Not only did Kouaku receive invitations to sing for special occasions, he also had the privilege of signing up for musical training at RTI.

The church where he previously worshipped provided for his upkeep. Although he shared a room with another student on the university campus, the church met his other basic needs.

Thus it was a struggle to make the decision for baptism following the evangelistic meeting on the campus where he lived. He faced a dilemma.

Kouaku did not want to let his previous church down; the issue of his financial support was also at stake. Still, he felt he had encountered the truth and needed to take a stand for what he believed. He felt conflicted until the last day of the meetings, but then he made up his mind to totally commit his life to Christ.

"I realized that my former church might cut off my stipend [because of] my new decision, and I realized I might face tough times," Kouaku said. "But I would rather lose my stipend and privileges than lose my faith in Christ. After all, He is the real Provider."

"This is a testimony of the power of the gospel," Francis says. "Kouaku's stand was very encouraging indeed."

So on that bright, sunny day, Kouaku, like ten others, sealed that faith in baptism.

The challenges and struggles are just as real today for Kouaku as they were in the past, but the assurance of God's promises strengthens his faith. He acknowledges that beyond the glitz and frills the world offers lives a God who loves and cares for him. Indeed, He who has given the gift of music and the promise of eternal life had also given Kouaku hope amid pain.[89]

At the last East Caribbean Conference Session held from August 14–17, 2013, Pastor R. Danforth Francis was elected president of the conference for the quadrennium 2013–2017. At the time of his election, Pastor Francis was serving as the personal ministries and Sabbath School director for the Caribbean Union Conference of Seventh-day Adventists, with headquarters in Trinidad.

Madagascar Union Church Ministries Director Danforth Francis, his wife, Verna, and their children with a crowd of Sabbath keeprs

Composer and Ivorian-born Jacquelin Brou Kouaku sitting by the baptismal pool after his baptism

Pastor Francis and his wife at a General Conference session dressed in their stylish African garb.

---

89. Information from Josephine Akarue, a freelance journalist based in Abidjan, Côte d'Ivoire.

82
WILLIAM AND RUTH HUGHES

1991–1996 / Tanzania

William Edward Hughes, a graduate of Oakwood College (class of 1978) worked in Southern California Conference and was ordained to the gospel ministry during the Southern California Conference's black convocation held at Lynwood Academy during the summer of 1985. Pastor Hughes was serving as pastor of the Miramonte Boulevard church in Los Angeles at the time of his ordination.

While serving in the United States Navy, he met his wife-to-be at the Philadelphian SDA Church in Long Beach, California. Soon after his release from military service, William and Ruth became husband and wife in November of 1970. To this union were added their son, Paul Jermaine and their daughter, Kelwy Marie. They are presently the proud and blessed grandparents of four beautiful grandchildren; Ariana, Aliyah and Josiah Hughes and Kaizsha El-Haj.

While serving as Senior Pastor of the University SDA Church in Los Angeles, California, he and Ruth were called to serve the East African Division at the Tanzania Adventist Seminary and College, located in Usa River, Tanzania. Ruth served as the on-campus Shepherdess Director, elementary school teacher and tutor for expatriate children. Pastor Hughes served as the Vice-President of Student Affairs as well as an instructor in evangelism, religion and theology. Pastor Hughes also served as the Director of Affiliation and was instrumental in helping to move the college theology program from a certificate program to a Bachelor Degree program through affiliation with Griggs University.

Life on campus and in the classroom provided many wonderful opportunities for building friendship and witness. One such opportunity came to me (William) during my first Communion Service on campus. During the foot washing service I noticed a quite shy villager standing alone, not being served. I approached him and offered to wash his feet. He accepted and with everything prepared, I knelt down before him. He placed his feet in the pan and to my surprise the water began to turn black. I must admit, there was an initial recoil in my heart but then it came to me that this is the way it was in the time of Christ—what an opportunity! And so, I dug in and washed those feet until they were squeaky clean. My brother was overwhelmed that a foreigner would not only serve him but serve him like this. Thus our brotherhood and friendship in Christ was affirmed.

One of our joys while serving in Tanzania was the joy of baptism. I was privileged to baptize under some very interesting situations. One such situation is pictured here:

This is African genius! This pool was filled by ladies carrying water jugs from a not so nearby stream in order to baptize about 20 precious souls. Below is pictured another baptism that took place on campus. It was the baptism of a young Somali student who converted from Islam to Christianity. Gathered around the pool are faculty, staff, and a mixture of Christian and Muslim students.

This baptism provided us with an awesome experience and education in Somali/Islamic culture. Ruth and I had met with Ismail's family, we enjoyed dinner at her home and were developing a good relationship with her mother and siblings. We also were encouraging her to share with them her decision to be baptized. Ismail was very reluctant to do this, but, because she was a young adult a decision was made to honor her request for baptism.

As it turned out, some of the Muslim students who witnessed her baptism, decided to inform her family of what had taken place. The family was outraged! That's with an emphasis on 'raged'.

The family communicated with her that her brothers were coming to take her from the campus and under the threat of beating and death, force her to recant. And not only this, but they had vowed to do harm to the person who had baptized her. Imagine my surprise!

The administration informed the police but the police had no one that they could send to the campus, especially when it was unclear as to when this was to take place. One evening, word reached the president of the college that the brothers were indeed on their way. It was determined that it would not be safe for Ismail to stay in the dormitory that evening. So the decision was made that she should stay with us. And so, there gathered in our little duplex, the president of the collage, some fellow students, friends and our daughter who was visiting from Maxwell Academy in Nairobi, Kenya.

This gathering is pictured above. We prayed, and prayed and talked and prayed. The brothers came and at one point we could actually hear them outside our door. But a strange thing happened that night. We later found out that even though the brothers were told where their sister was, they left the campus because they could not find the duplex. Some say it was the blackness of the African night, for no moon shown that night and at that time no star twinkled from the sky. But for me, I now know what it feels like to be hidden in the shadow of the Almighty God.

In consultation with the president of the East African Division, it was agreed that Ismail should be given safe haven outside of Tanzania. Therefore, arrangements were made to relocate her to another African institution of higher learning. And so, on the night pictured below we said our farewell.

An additional part of our activity involved the joy of giving bible studies. On one occasion I visited a public elementary school not far from our campus. After building some relationships with the principal and teachers, I was able to interest three of the teachers in bible studies. We were permitted to study at the school. After we studied the lessons on the Sabbath, two of the teachers dropped out. With the one remaining teacher, we agreed to continue studies at his home. His home was a good hike from the college and among the most humble that I had the privilege to visit. The walls were made of woven wooden sticks and boards covered with a cow dung mixture that was whitewashed. The roof was tin and had some problems with leaks and severe structural lean.

His wife joined us in bible study and always looked forward to our meetings. Eventually, they shared with me their plan to build a new home for their growing family and showed me how much they had accomplished in making bricks and laying the foundation and the challenges they faced that made for slow progress. They asked for nothing but prayer. While teaching my Sabbath School class one Sabbath morning, the discussion centered on spiritual gifts and talents and their use within the church and for outreach. There I shared the circumstance of Kitiomari and how it would be awesome if a group of believers, with various gifts, could get together and make bricks and help to finish building his house. As it turned out, one of the members of my class had brick making experience. Another member had construction experience and another could frame a roof. As we discovered the gifts that we had present among ourselves the consensus evolved that we could do this and this we did!

The bible studies were completed, the house was completed and the Kitiomari family was baptized. He shortly thereafter joined the college as a ministerial student to become a pastor to his Meru tribe.

There was a time in Tanzania that when a person was admitted to the hospital, a family member had to stay in the hospital with them to cook for them and nurse them back to health. This happened to little Sinasali. One day she had a terrible fall that resulted in a broken and infected leg. I met this little bundle of joy through her older brothers and sister.

In my teaching evangelism, students were encouraged to go into the hillsides and villages and establish friendships, meet the needs of people and learn that this created opportunities for witness and bible studies.

On one of these excursions, one of my students found a dire situation and asked me to please visit with him to see what we could do. He led me to a home in the bush that was in extreme disrepair and where three elementary aged children were living alone and who were trying to care for themselves. One of the boys was covered with open sores and had a distended belly. His brother's tummy was just as distended and all three were showing signs of malnutrition. These were Sinasali's siblings whose mother had to abandon them while she stayed in the hospital to care for Sinasali. We were able to locate the mother at the hospital and offer our help. She agreed and we first took the boys and their sister to the Adventist Clinic in Arusha. It was determined that the boys had a severe case of hook worms and bacterial skin infection.

It was also determined that the cause of this condition was more likely due to the fact that there was no Cho (toilet facility) on the property and the children were defecating around the property and thereby picking up hookworms. Through some generous donations from the U.S., we were able to build a Cho on the property, hire a sitter/cook, purchase some food staples, and repair some of the house. After the boys' physical situation improved we were able to arrange for them to visit their mom and sister in the hospital as pictured below.

The Hughes' returned to the States in 1996 and continued to pastor in the Lake Region Conference of Seventh-day Adventist. He retired in August, 2012 while pastor of the Ecorse and Living Water district. He and his wife Ruth now live in the state of Washington and are thrilled to know that their works in Momma Africa do follow them.

The Hughes family at Maxwell Academy in Nairobi, Kenya

A handmade baptism pool in the bush

The baptism of Ismail

President Muganda (far left) and friends gather with Ismail at the Hughes home to avoid her brothers

Pastor Hughes, Ismail, and Sister Hughes on the night of Ismail's departure

Ruth with Kitiomari and his family beside their new home the Sabbath School class helped to build.

Ruth Hughes and Ruth Tuvako with Bible study interests

Pastor and Mrs. Hughes often facilitated interaction with TASC students and international students visiting Tanzania hosted by Pete and Charlotte O'Neal.

Little Sinasali and her mother receive a hospital visit from her family and friends.

Pastor Hughes sponsored annual climbs of Mount Kilimanjaro for students and expatriates.

Pastor Hughes, his son Paul, and guides on the summit of Mount Kilimanjaro

83

MAX AND ELIANE PIERRE

1991–1999 / Gabon, Cameroon

Max Jose Pierre was born and raised in Haiti, a third generation Adventist. His grandmother, Inelie Mercier, was a pioneer Bible worker and his parents, Duvillard and Germaine Pierre, were missionaries in their native land.

As a teenager Max distinguished himself by his devotion to Bible study and interest in missionary activity. In 1967 he came to the United States and settled in New York City. He worked as a layman, pioneering the publishing work among the Franco Haitian people. In 1968 he returned to Haiti and married the former Eliane Joseph. Their combined ministry was instrumental to the formation of the Morija, Bethanie, and the Bethel French church.

In 1972 he assisted in the planning of a three-day workshop that was to prepare workers for a full summer of public meetings. Elder E. E. Cleveland was the principal lecturer on evangelism at the workshop. On the spot demonstrations enabled the literature evangelists to see what might help them do their job more effectively.

In 1974 the Lord blessed the student literature evangelism program that took place during the summer in the New York metropolitan area. As a district director, Max Pierre helped make the program a success. The combined efforts of college, academy, and elementary students resulted in the sale of more than 50,000 truth filled journals.

The students' task was hard, but every day they worked it seemed easier. The students were able to earn scholarships, return to school, and continue their education.

In 1981 he attended Andrews University to pursue a degree in religion. His wife also matriculated, seeking a degree in diet and nutrition. He graduated in 1984 and began study on a master's degree. He was ordained to the gospel ministry on July 4, 1987, at the Victory Lake camp meeting.

The Pierre family left New York on October 5, 1991, so that Elder Pierre could serve as mission president in the small French-speaking country of Gabon. At that time he was the only Adventist worker there. Gabon was basically a Muslim country, and the work had started there some three years earlier. However, with help from literature evangelists from the Adventist Seminary of West Africa, a local radio ministry, and public evangelism, Adventist membership rose from 205 in 1990 to 1,500 in 1995.

On the outskirts of Libreville, the capital of Gabon, the political leader of the local township organized an independent Christian church, an unusual move in a land where most political figures were not Christian. The congregation grew so rapidly, however, that it soon outgrew the building, and members began constructing a large building on the same premises.

At the same time the congregation was

earnestly studying the Bible and evaluating its beliefs. From this study, members learned of a seventh-day Sabbath and began to wonder if anyone else in the country observed it.

Providentially, members learned about the Seventh-day Adventist congregation in Libreville and sent a number of members to investigate it. This led to an invitation for Pastor Pierre to visit the nondenominational church and to present the Adventist message.

When members learned that Adventists beliefs are based on Scripture alone, almost the entire congregation was baptized, and the new church building became a Seventh-day Adventist Church.

There were fifteen congregations in 1995. Elder Pierre formulated plans to establish forty new churches, and leaders succeeded in purchasing land for seventeen of those churches. A member in America from the Upper Columbia Conference donated $1 million to put roofs on the many open-air churches in Africa. African churches were invited to submit requests for assistance in which they agreed to erect the buildings, with the exception of the metal roofs.

Materials for most elements of construction are readily available and within a congregation's financial capability; however, metal roofing material is virtually impossible for the average congregation to afford.

The initial $1 million fund provided 704 roofs on buildings of varying sizes at an average cost of $1,400 per roof. The program provided not only a place of worship but also became an evangelistic center. The average congregation applying for a new roof had about 40 members but would build a facility to seat 400 to 500 members. Typically, that new building would be filled to overflowing within a couple of years and then work would begin to establish satellite churches. From just a few members, hundreds

and hundreds of members joined the church as a result of this activity. Max Pierre assisted in the building of forty churches in Gabon.

Pastor and Mrs. Pierre have two children: Josue and Mirelande.

Some of the Atlantic Union and local conference officers and literature evangelists: (left to right) Leonard Harris, Vernon Cartright, Silas McClanb, Paul Bernet, Robert Smith, Max Pierre, and Matthew Dennis

Pastor and Mrs. Max Pierre and children

A large attendance at a tent crusade

Evangelist Max Pierre at the tent crusade

84
RUBY LEE JONES

1991–1992 / Zimbabwe

Ruby Lee Jones was born in the little village of Durand, Michigan, where her father worked in the hoop mills, the fourth child in what was to become a family of nine children. She tells the story of her life of service:

My eldest brother tells me there were very few African Americans living in the white community of Durand. I was so accustomed to playing with little white children that I was afraid of black folks.

My first recollection, as I look back on my childhood, was standing in a huge field with a little black and white dog. I can only conjecture that I was in Arkansas where my mother took her younger children to visit relatives. I must have been about two years old. The next scene that comes before me is the house on Grant Street after Daddy moved our family to Flint, Michigan, to work in the booming General Motors automobile industry. I faintly remember beginning first grade at the Dewey Elementary Public School.

Shortly after that time, Elder A. E. Webb, a Seventh-day Adventist evangelist, came to town and our family accepted the Advent message. Our family's decision caused many changes. I sometimes wonder what my life would have been like if this divine change had

not happened. Our worship changed, our diet changed, and our education was changed to an elementary "church" school. My remembrances before joining the Adventist Church are rather sketchy, but two things stand out— chewing on a greasy pig's foot and Sunday mornings, with three or four of us strolling down the street to Antioch Baptist Church for Sunday school. Only the children in our family attended this service.

The new religion, along with the Depression and Daddy's refusal to work on the Sabbath, resulted in the loss of his job and our home. I have always had a very soft place in my heart for Sister Aslena Friend, the devout Adventist sister, and her husband, Felix, who took our large family into their small home. Brother Friend was a short, Indian looking man, the son of a slave—he must have been in his late seventies or early eighties. He was the world's best storyteller, and he kept all of us children entertained for hours on end. My stay in the Friend home was a happy one.

One Wednesday night I attended prayer meeting with Daddy (I can't remember why I was the only one with him that night) and the speaker was Elder Frank L. Peterson! It was unheard of for such a dignitary to visit our little church, and especially in the middle of the week! As a young girl, even in my most fanciful imagination, I never dreamed that one day I would become his secretary at the General Conference, the world headquarters of the Seventh-day Adventist Church, but God had a mission and blessings in store for this little girl and her family from Flint, Michigan.

Daddy was determined to move to the country so as to make a better life for his large family. The first move was to a rental house on Frances Road in Mt. Morris. I was a teenager when we moved to the country the second time, this time to five acres of land he purchased at 7335 Vassar Road and to a house Daddy built himself. It was nothing to look at in the beginning stages, but gradually it became livable——HOME.

After high school graduation, I worked in the AC Spark Plug factory, a job that lasted about a week because I would not work on God's Sabbath. By working about three months in the Buick factory, I was able to save all of my wages for college. My sister worked in a clothing store, so I was able to purchase some lovely clothes. With the ones Mama made, I had a more than adequate wardrobe. Excited, I boarded the train to Alabama. I remember riding back and forth to Oakwood in Huntsville, Alabama, on the train. When we got to Cincinnati, Ohio, we had to get on the Jim Crow coach. Returning home we were able to breathe free again in Cincinnati and ride in a decent coach. This was my first overt discrimination experience in the South. (I was quite familiar with the covert brand practiced in Michigan.) I found it quite humorous as I made a deliberate practice of drinking out of "white" water fountains.

My days at Oakwood were very pleasant. A whole new world opened up to me. I was enrolled in a class with five others as we went through the two-year associate program of secretarial training. Mr. Charles Galley, my favorite teacher, during the latter part of the first year, felt that I should have some actual experience in doing office work. He sent me to the very precise Dr. O. B. Edwards, of all people, for dictation. The letter was short, but I missed one word. I inserted a word that I thought made sense, but Dr. Edwards pointed it out to me, and I had to redo the letter. He probably knew the letter verbatim and gave it to each new raw recruit, but his training experience was good for me. The second year I worked in the office of the business manager of the college. My work there was very enjoyable. The boss was strict, but he instilled in the students the desire to excel.

After graduating with an associate's degree from Oakwood's secretarial course, the next twelve years flew by quickly. The Lord provided exciting and fulfilling labor throughout His field: secretarial positions in the business office of Oakwood College, in the Nashville treasury department of the South Central Conference, and in the Book and Bible House of the Northeastern Conference of Seventh-day Adventists in New York City.

I was enjoying the excitement of my five years in New York City when a surprising contact came one day from the General Conference of Seventh-day Adventists. I was invited to serve as secretary for Elder F. L. Peterson.

While in the nation's capital, my sister Vera and my sister Esther and her husband, Edward Mattox, were also transferred to the *area. For the first time in years I had family nearby. Along with the excitement of working at the world headquarters of the Seventh-day Adventist Church, another dimension was added to my lifestyle—that of travel. In 1962 when missionaries Pastor Leland and Lottie (my sister) Mitchell were scheduled to return to the states on furlough, I decided to journey to Africa and spend time there, then tour Europe with them. (Until that time, my California trips were the highlight of my travels.) In April 1962 I boarded a large Pan American plane bound for the continent of Africa!*

This was the beginning of many personal world travel experiences to places such as Italy, Mexico, Germany, Russia, England, many countries of Africa, and my own North America (to name a few). In addition, of the many trips I have been able to take in connection with my position at the General Conference, the one to Vienna, Austria, was especially memorable.

In 1986, after forty years of denominational service, I retired from the General Conference. The Lord blessed me with many expressions of appreciation. My retirement reception was as large as those usually given for the "important brethren." One of the men stated, "This is the end of an era!"

I moved to the homestead at 7335 Vassar Road in Michigan and had fun remodeling my new home! I had attended college classes toward the completion of a bachelor's degree while in Washington and was looking forward to the completion of that program. I enrolled in the University of Michigan (Flint) and began classes, but a telephone call put that plan on hold for a year. In July of 1990 I received a call from the General Conference headquarters

asking me if I would go to Zimbabwe, Africa, as a volunteer worker to aid in the organization of their union office. I consulted the Lord, and the Tribunal of Six (five sisters and one brother).

Most felt that it was a good idea to re-enter the Lord's work at this point. Correspondence with Pastor P. R. Ndhlova, the president of the Zambesi Union, invited me to work with him for two years. I asked the Lord to help me blend in with the culture because there were three groups: the Native Africans, the coloreds, and the whites. The president wanted an older woman with no ties to any of these groups. I was on the road again!

After the all the red tape was completed and all the tests taken, I left for Bulawayo, Zimbabwe, on March 1, 1991. From New York I flew to Brussels, Belgium, to Zaire, to Johannesburg, South Africa, and then to Bulawayo. At first the General Conference travel agency arranged for me to spend a weekend in Johannesburg, but my advisor, Pastor Maurice Battle of the General Conference secretariat, changed my travel schedule. He informed the travel agency that I should not enter South Africa, as it might be a hindrance later to my visiting other African countries. South Africa should not be on my passport!

My plane flew into Bulawayo on a bright and sunshiny day in early March. Never have I seen such blue sky and white clouds. Upon disembarking from the airplane, I saw a very dignified couple waving to me. I immediately knew that this was Pastor Ndhlovu, and Daisy, his wife. The next time they saw me, I was being supported by someone because I could not walk. In those few short minutes, I had slipped and fallen, and "could not get up!"

The next day the Ndhlovus took me to the doctor, and it was discovered that I had fractured my knee. Pastor was kind enough to give me until the latter part of the week to recuperate before beginning work.

Zimbabwe is a beautiful landlocked country (about the size of the state of California) in southeast Africa surrounded by Zambia on the north, South Africa on the south, Mozambique on the east, and Botswana on the west. The stately bauba tree is found throughout Zimbabwe and other parts of Africa. The mighty Zambezi River, which is over 1,670 miles long, suddenly tumbles 300 feet into a gorge called Victoria Falls, an awesome world renowned display of nature, renamed by European David Livingston in his explorations in honor of Queen Victoria. Kariba Dam was built in the late 1950s to provide hydroelectric power for Zimbabwe and its neighbors. It is the second largest manmade dam in the world.

When the dam was completed and the water rose higher and higher, a tremendous effort was made to save the animals that had lived on the flooded land. In a rescue effort called "Operation Noah," people worldwide sent funds to save the animals that had lived on the flooded land. Over 50,000 people were also relocated. The Great Zimbabwe Ruins, the Vumba Mountains, and Hwange National Park are all a part of the beautiful Zimbabwe country.

The Zambesi Union Mission of Seventh-day Adventists has its headquarters in the city of Bulawayo, the second largest city in Zimbabwe. The downtown streets in Bulawayo are wide and beautiful with flowering trees and shrubbery. The streets in most Zimbabwean cities are named for the Freedom Fighters who helped to gain independence in 1980. The union's territory covers the entire country of Zimbabwe. The president, for whom I worked, was R. P. Ndhlovu; the executive secretary, P. R. Machamire; and the treasurer, K. J. Seligmann. As of February 1992 the membership of the union was 166,617 with 395 churches.

The union buildings were formerly a girl's boarding school, but it was built around the time of the country's independence, and the existing administration could never get enough students to enroll; therefore, the union brethren were blessed to acquire the property at a very reasonable price. On the grounds you will find the Better Living Center that houses a thriving dental practice and a training center for literature evangelists. The Bulawayo Adventist Secondary School (BASS), with an enrollment of 500 plus students, is also on the property.

The workday began each morning at 8:00 a.m. with a fifteen-minute worship. The president believed in starting worship right on time. You could hear his strong voice starting the hymn if there was only one person present. We sang a song, offered prayer, and the message was presented. We formed a prayer circle, and a worker from one of the conferences would be highlighted for prayer that day. At the close, any worker who had just returned to the office would give a report of the meetings or the work God had done. Most of the workers held tent efforts, and God mightily blessed their endeavors. Even witch doctors were converted. A number were changed when they heard the gospel message, and they gathered their equipment in a central place and torched it all.

President Ndhlovu's day, as with most presidents, was filled with meetings, visitors, workers, and laymen who needed his ear. At the Ingathering season, Pastor Ndhlovu would schedule a week from the office to participate in raising thousands of dollars for the advancement of God's cause in the union. There were many wealthy farmers of Chiping, and they looked forward to his coming every year to collect the money. Upon his return to the office, he corresponded with the donors to let them know he was interested in their spiritual welfare as well as their financial aid.

Under the direction of the Zambezi Union, Solusi College was established in 1894 and is approximately thirty miles from Bulawayo. It is affiliated with Andrews University in Michigan and offers bachelor's and master's degree programs. However, the sad thing is that many students wish to attend, but funds are not available to them. On October 8, 1991, there was a groundbreaking ceremony for the Solusi Adventist Vocational School on the grounds of Solusi College. A great deal of money was provided by ADRA Germany. A wide range of academic and vocational skills will be taught, including agricultural training, building, woodworking, fashion and fabrics, food and nutrition.

There are a number of clinics in the Zambezi Union, and the Health Services Department is attempting to elevate them to a higher standard. The staffing has been greatly improved, and Honda gasoline lighting has been installed in some of the clinics. Base holes (deep wells) have been drilled at twelve clinics to insure sufficient water; however, at the Montgomery Farm training program, a shortage of water remains a serious problem. At Montgomery

Farm, just outside Bulawayo, the union operates an experimental farm. Young men and women from the interior are brought there and taught to raise vegetables and fruit. After the period of instruction at the farm, they return home to put their knowledge into practice in their communities. Each week a load of vegetables such as celery, broccoli, greens, beets, onions, etc., was brought to the union office to sell. The produce was beautiful!

The Fordes and their three children became my close friends. Ron was one of the dentists, and Dorothy, his wife, taught at the church school. They went home to Canada on furlough in August, and this left me without a way to get to church. But when the Lord closes one door, He opens another!

About two blocks from my home was the Hillside Teachers' Training College, and I was told that the Adventist students held services there in a small chapel on the campus. I started attending and enjoyed it so much that when the Fordes returned from furlough, I remained at my little church. The stewardship director of the union and his family lived in my neighborhood, and they also attended church there. The students seemed to enjoy our company. Just before graduation, I invited the whole church to dinner. I started cooking early in the week because there were about fifteen young men and five young ladies. The students gave us a musical program, and the whole afternoon was just delightful!

In October the union administration loaned me the use of a car, a Peugeot, and never was anyone so happy! I think they felt it would be quite undignified for me to be pedaling around town on a bicycle. In Zimbabwe, the steering wheel is on the right side, and we drive on the left-hand side of the road. One day I had just turned the corner slowly and found myself looking into the horrified face of a gentleman—we were on the same side of the road! It very quickly occurred to me that I was not in America, and I straightway switched to the left-hand side of the road. I decided then and there to always keep my mind on my driving because that was a very good way to cause one's expiration!

In addition to the familiar daily duties of an administrative assistant/executive secretary (organizing, scheduling, dictation, keyboarding, editing, publishing, communicating, etc.). which had been my routine over the past forty years in the States, it was rewarding to travel out into the union to view and enjoy the field side of God's work in Zimbabwe, Africa.

The Zambezi Conference camp meeting is always held at our Anderson School near Gweru, Zimbabwe. Anderson is one of six academies under the auspices of the union. My first trip after arriving in Zimbabwe was camp meeting attendance.

I was given a grand welcome at the eleven o'clock worship hour by Conference President Robert Hall. He mentioned that I had come all the way from America to be with them. A young couple from New York, Brother and Sister James, blended their talents in song, and the guest speaker's sermon was powerfully delivered. I was happy to see my American friends, Pastor and Mrs. Louis Preston, stewardship director of the Eastern African Division in Harare, the capital of Zimbabwe. It was also a joy to meet new friends and converse about our respective homelands.

One Sabbath, Pastor Msimanga, union church ministries director, took a group of us to visit a church he had pastored in the Quanda. Pastor and his wife, Bussie, had a very busy day. We left very early because he wanted to visit some of the members before Sabbath School. Upon arriving he was informed that the husband of one of the members had died, and the wife requested that he conduct the eulogy. After the funeral service, we hastened straightway for a baptism far out in the bush. Several districts had gathered (some pastors have as many as eighteen districts), and Pastor Msimanga was the guest speaker. We sang and prayed and had a joyous time in the Lord. En route home to Bulawayo we stopped at the home of one of the young ladies who had come with us. She had already informed me that her mother did not speak English but was a very friendly person. As we entered her home I was reminded that God blesses His children in many ways. Evidently her friendly family was quite blessed financially, because the beautiful sprawling residence was not a village, it was a one family compound.

One of my most memorable trips was the one to Binga in a very destitute part of the country. This was what is called "out in the bush." Paula Leen, an independent ADRA worker, supplied clothing and food to the needy. She also held classes, teaching the women to sew, cook nutritious food, and make their own soap and body lotion. Many African ladies are very adept when it comes to crafts. They do very exquisite needlework and make beautiful baskets of all sizes. Paula teaches them the business end of this talent, how to manage their money after the goods are sold.

When I heard she was taking the three-day trip to Binga, I truly desired to go. My boss,

Pastor Ndhlovu, consented. He told me he wanted me to enjoy myself while in Africa and have many varied experiences. So we set out for Binga in Paula's large van. The back was filled with clothes. She has three regular helpers, and we met Pastor Lunga, director of the Binga district, en route. He had left a message at the police station as to his whereabouts. (The established system of communication was to leave a message at the police station: the first thing a person would do upon arriving in town would be to go to the police station to see if there were any messages.) Before we picked up Pastor Lunga, however, the van broke down, fortunately near St. Luke's Hospital in Lupane. The Lord must have had some purpose in mind for this circumstance.

While the van was being repaired, we had a chance to visit patients in the hospital. We went to the ward where there were three premature babies. I took a picture of two of them. The third child was in a more secluded place and later died while we were there. The hospital, operated by doctors from Poland and Germany, has other workers from Great Britain and America, including a black lady from Ohio. When patients come to the hospital, their relatives come also with food and bedding and stay with the sick the entire time. Paula was able to supply some with clothes. One young lady who had fallen into the fire had horrible burns on her body. She had apparently just been left there. Her sister had been with her, but it seemed made no effort to rescue her. Someone else eventually did. I was told later that people do not want to touch such a person as they feel the same thing will happen to them.

When we arrived in Binga with Pastor Lunga

to deliver clothes, we first had to pay our respects to the chief of the village and his large family. Polygamy is acceptable in Zimbabwe. The chief was very gracious in welcoming us to his village, and clothes were left there. I took a photo of him seated with his headman standing beside him. We continued on to the place where the majority of the people were and passed out more clothing. Paula had the people organized by groups—women, men, then younger women and men, girls and boys.

At one point things started to get a bit unruly, and Paula got in the van and slowly started moving away. I looked around and saw the van moving and realized that I was the only one of our party of six left! Never have you seen anyone move so rapidly. I took a running leap and jumped into the van. Paula later said she always backs in when she delivers clothes, and if conditions warrant it, she starts the motor, and this is a signal that she plans to depart. The only problem was that everybody knew the signal except me! The remainder of the clothes was distributed to those on the roadway en route home.

From December 1 through 21, 1991, Dr. Calvin B. Rock, vice president of the General Conference, and his team conducted a crusade in Bulawayo, Zimbabwe, at the open-air amphitheater. The slogan for the crusade was "21 Meetings in 21 Nights." Dr. Rock introduced so many interesting features. On "twin night" fifty sets of twins were present along with the crusade's singing twins, the Jones Sisters from Charlotte, North Carolina. On one night he honored the oldest couple, the youngest couple, and the couple with the most children. Pastor Thompson Kay conducted a signing class on learning to communicate with the hearing impaired, and certificates were given at the end of the crusade. The average nightly attendance was 4,500!

In the end a total of 592 precious souls were baptized. I had always wondered how so many were baptized. There were fifteen ministers in the pool, each with a candidate and fifteen waiting on the side of the pool; therefore the baptismal service was quickly and efficiently conducted. A local businessman offered to pay the salaries of five to eight Bible workers to assure that the members were well grounded in the newfound faith. Modern miracles still occur. The campaign was in the height of the rainy season, and not a single meeting was cancelled because of rain. After the crusade was over, it rained for the next three days. This was an awesome experience for me!

When I realized that my year of service in Africa (1991–1992) was coming to an end, I was determined that I would see some of the country before I departed. It was always my desire to see South Africa. Now the time had come! I traveled to South Africa, visiting Johannesburg, Durban, and Cape Town (at my expense).

Upon returning to Bulawayo, Zimbabwe, I left that same evening to view the beauty of Victoria Falls, which was my magnificent, breathtaking "farewell gift" from the Zambezi Union in Zimbabwe. The beauties of God's creation, the awesome splendor of Victoria Falls, recall the words of religious writer, Ellen G. White:

"This world is not all sorrow and misery. 'God is love,' is written upon every opening bud, upon the petals of every flower, and upon every spire of grass. Though the curse of sin has caused the earth to bring forth thorns and thistles, there are flowers upon the thistles and the thorns are hidden…. All things in nature testify to the tender, fatherly care of our God and to His desire to make His children happy" (Patriarchs and Prophets, pp. 599, 600).

The year flew by rapidly, and before I knew it, it was time for me to depart. Over and over I thank the Lord for the privilege afforded me in assisting His work there in Africa. Pastor Ndhlovu told me at one point that when I came his work "just clicked and fell into place." Whatever I did and whatever the impact was, I give all the glory and honor to God!

Upon returning to the States, I was surprised to learn from the officer at headquarters in charge of Adventist volunteers that I was the first black to go as a volunteer worker. I thank God for the many experiences I have had in His service. "All things work together for good" is the testimony of the little girl from the small church in Michigan whose life has been guided by God.

Ruby Lee Jones was a "trailblazer" and had this awesome experience at age seventy after she had retired. Besides traveling, Ruby loved photography, walking, crocheting, reading, and gardening. Ruby went on to complete a bachelor's degree in history at the University of Michigan-Flint on August 17, 1994. God blessed Ruby with a long, useful, and fulfilling life! Born on June 6, 1924, she passed away on April 16, 2009.

Oakwood Chamber of Commerce Officers (1946): (left to right) Vivian Gardner, Pauline Jones, Charlye Mae Porter, Ruby Jones

Ruby Jones in later life (picture on her passport).

85
GOSNEL AND DOREEN YORKE

1991–1997 / Kenya

Gosnel Lenox Yorke is originally from St. Kitts, and his wife from Jamaica. Gosnell is a naturalized citizen of both Canada and South Africa. In 1989 he was ordained to the gospel ministry in the Quebec Conference, Canada. Doreen has worked as a child life specialist at Montreal's Children Hospital and other places.

The Yorkes are the parents of three Canadian-born and university-graduated working adults—two girls and one boy. Oumari arrived on August 29, 1984, becoming the younger brother of Crystal Claire Yorke. Kanyika Yorke joined the family as the youngest sibling.

Dr. Yorke is fluent in English, French, Spanish, and Portuguese, a working knowledge of Kiswahili (East Africa), more than a "nodding acquaintance" with various South African languages, a reading knowledge of German, and both Hellenistic Greek and classical Hebrew. He taught at Canadian University College for four years (1981–1985) as well as at Atlantic Union College for two (1989–1991).

He earned a bachelor's degree in theology (University of the Southern Caribbean, Trinidad in 1976); a master's degree in biblical and cognate languages (Andrews University, Michigan, 1977); and a master's of sacred theology in biblical studies and a doctorate in biblical studies with an emphasis in New Testament studies (McGill University, Canada, 1979 and 1987 respectively). In addition, he successfully completed a post-doctoral program in African languages and linguistics at the University of South Africa (Unisa) in 1999.

In 1991 he and his family left the United States to serve as a teacher at the University of Eastern Africa in Eldoret, Kenya. In 1994 he became the chair of the Department of Religion. One of his goals has been to get the true meaning of the Bible to as many people as possible.

After working at the university, he spent several years as a translation consultant with the United Bible Societies. Yorke supervised the translation of the Bible into indigenous African languages in the Portuguese-speaking countries of Africa.

In 1990 the University Press of America published his doctoral dissertation as a book, and Professor Yorke began a five-week teaching and preaching tour of southern Africa, presenting lectures on "The Book of Hebrews," "Bible Manuscripts," and "Contemporary Issues in Christian Theology" from his book *A Re-examination of the Apostle Paul's Concept of the Church as the Body of Christ*. Weekend and evening speaking appointments took Yorke all over South Africa.

He went on to serve as an adjunct professor in the College of Human Sciences, Department of New Testament, at the University of South Africa (Unisa). He also did some lecturing at the postgraduate level for Andrews University in Nigeria and Zimbabwe and served, in 1992, as a visiting professor in the Department of Religious Studies, Classics and Philosophy at the University of Zimbabwe.

For ten years (1996–2006) Professor Yorke was recommended by the General Conference to serve the United Bible Societies as a translation consultant. He was based in South Africa at the time and was responsible for mentoring African translators and monitoring the translation of the Bible from its original languages of Hebrew, Aramaic, and Greek into various indigenous African languages in the Lusophone (Portuguese-speaking) countries of Angola, Guinea-Bissau, and Mozambique, plus the Anglophone (English-speaking) countries of Botswana and Zimbabwe. He also worked briefly in the Spanish-speaking country of Equatorial Guinea in West Africa and in French-speaking Africa, mainly Cameroon and Ivory Coast.

While working as a professor of theology at the Mandeville-based Northern Caribbean University, Yorke worked to translate the Bible into a Jamaican patois. When criticized for becoming involved in this project, he said that we must also remember that Jesus used his mother tongue, Aramaic, and Jamaican patois is as eligible as any other to be a vehicle for the Word of God. He added that a number of countries in that region, including Haiti, Dominica, St. Lucia, Suriname, and the Dutch Antilles, had already translated some or all of the Bible into their local creoles.

More recently he also facilitated access for biblical studies students to the most sophisticated Bible translation software program available. The program helps students gain a keener appreciation of the cultural, exegetical, theological, and other intricacies involved in the translation of the Bible into the various African languages.

Dr. Gosnell Yorke

Clyde and Barbara Cassimy (left) stand with Roy Adams and Gosnell and Doreen Yorke (right) at the University of Eastern Africa in Kenya.

86

SYDNEY AND KATHERINA GIBBONS

1992–1998 / Cameroon; 2000–2001 / Jamaica

Sydney C. Gibbons holds master of divinity and the doctor of ministry degrees from Andrews University. He is currently the executive secretary of the Bermuda Conference of Seventh-day Adventists. Also, he is pastor of the Southampton Seventh-day Adventist Church, founder/director of the Bermuda Conference School of Evangelism, and director of human relations and intercultural ministries for the Bermuda Conference. He was employed as a consultant and executive officer of the Commission for Unity and Racial Equality for the government of Bermuda for five years.

Mrs. Katherina Gibbons holds a bachelor of arts degree in history from Atlantic Union College and a master of science degree in community counseling from Andrews University. She is a social worker for the government of Bermuda. The Gibbons' served as missionaries in Central Africa (1992–1998) and in Jamaica (2000–2001).

For the Gibbons family, arriving in West and then Central Africa can only be described as walking right into a *National Geographic* magazine. Their work was set in the backdrop of majestic mountains, enormous rain forests, miles of white sandy beaches, and the varied abundance of fresh fruit and vegetables. Added to this were the people. From the Bulu preaching elder, to the drum beating mother and the swaying singing children, all lent to the rich culture that was to be their home for six years. Of course, all was not joy and beauty. There were the strange and the bizarre: river bathing and monkeys and rats sold for eating. But an answer to the call of mission service made a world of difference for the family, which included Sydney, Katherina, Meliseanna, and Gianluca. Mystere joined them along the journey.

The post that landed them in Africa was Sydney's position as director of the Department of Church Ministries for the Central African Union Mission (CAUM). The assignment began in January 1992 with language studies in Lomé, Togo.

This Bermudian family did not know then that accepting a call from the General Conference of Seventh-day Adventists to serve in the Africa-Indian Ocean Division would redefine how they would view the world and life. This effect was most impressionable on their children; Meliseanna, age three, and Gianluca, age one. It was through the childhood friendship of Meliseanna and Mystere that the Gibbons' sensed God's leading to make Mystere a part of the family through adoption. So in December 1999 Meliseana and Gianluca welcomed a new sister to the family. Today, Mystere lives with her husband, Patrick Monteiro, in California. She is completing a master of science degree in communication science disorders and audiology at Loma Linda University. Meliseanna is a medical student at St. George's University in

Grenada, and Gianluca is a senior at La Sierra University pursuing a double major in music technology and marketing.

The Gibbons recalled many experiences of culture shock. When they arrived in Togo, West Africa, to study French in 1992, their accommodation greeted them with spiders, ants, and twenty-two flying cockroaches, which was somewhat terrifying. Then there was the political instability when tanks patrolled the streets and random acts of violence took place in the neighborhoods. While in Yaoundé, Cameroon, the Gibbons resided in a political opposition stronghold. As a political attack on these individuals, the government would turn off the water and electricity for three to four days, sometimes up to two weeks.

The most significant shock for the Gibbons was being called "white people." They identified with their black heritage and relished the idea of returning to their roots in Africa. But a rude awakening occurred when children and adults in Togo and Cameroon, from the street market to the church, referred to them as *les blancs* (French for "white people"). It took them many months to learn that the phrase *les blancs* was not about color. It was about culture. The reference was neither racist nor derogatory. It was a neutral expression of a fact that those who came from the West thought from a European cultural context and thus were considered white. The Gibbons realized that understanding differences in culture is vital to effectiveness and personal satisfaction for missionaries living in a cross-cultural context.

Another culture shock for them was in the area of health. They were exposed to extreme poverty and diseases that were long gone from western living. As a mother, Katherina, always prided herself in cleanliness. How was she going to keep her young children from sickness and disease? She remembers holding on to her daughter's arms so tightly when walking in the streets that she would leave fingernail marks in her arms. Managing culture shock was further put to the test when Gianluca was overcome with five days of vomiting and diarrhea when they first arrived in Togo. When Katherina picked him up from his little bed, his body went limp and his eyes rolled to the back of his head. Neither Katherina nor Sydney could speak French yet, the language spoken in Togo. Receiving medical care in a community where AIDS and STDs were rampant added fear to the unknown. Would their son be safe being treated in the local health facilities? They traveled to a clinic where he was diagnosed with malaria along with severe dehydration. Intravenous fluids were administered amidst his screams—all his parents could do was helplessly watch. They prayed and prayed and stayed with him that night. Thankfully he recovered, but their minds screamed for some normalcy.

As time went on these little annoyances became a way of life for the family. They became accustomed to the machine guns held by the soldiers that lined the street and the members of their congregation who had to run for their lives due to either political or religious threats. And then there was always the shadow of voodoo worship with its reality becoming more evident when members needed reassurance through prayers and intercessions that God was more powerful than the devil.

One of Sydney's highlights was receiving news that his private French tutor, a Togolese national, had requested baptism. Sydney remembers when the tutor asked him to give him a Bible study in French. The tutor knew that if Sydney became passionate about the subject he would forget about the fear of speaking French. He was right. But he too became a learner. He gave Sydney permission to choose the topic, and the first study was on salvation. The second study was on the Christian Sabbath. Sydney learned French, and the tutor found Christ through the Adventist message of hope and wholeness. Unfortunately, the joy of learning about a tutor's conversion turned to sorrow when Sydney heard the sad news after two years of residing in Cameroon that his beloved tutor had died in a road accident. Death is an ever-present reality in mission service.

Another account of unexpected death came when a close missionary friend of the family who learned French with them in Togo later died by a gun shot as a victim of mistaken identity on the border of Benin. Mission service was like living on the edge of time, survival of the fittest. However, the family knew that God would be their ever-present help in time of trouble.

In June 1992, on the first Sabbath they arrived in Yaoundé, Cameroon, Sydney was introduced to a joint assembly of 400 believers who met in a tent. The late Elder Leonard Newton who was the president of the union assigned him to preach there that Sabbath. Under the guidance of the Holy Spirit, Sydney decided to preach in French, to the surprise and fear of the president. The strong affirmations from the congregation, despite grammatical errors and unrefined accent, dissipated the fears of the president and relieved Sydney's anxiety. Sydney's willingness to speak the language of the people opened the door of their hearts to him. Also, Katherina sang on that Sabbath, and they both were welcomed and respected from the start. They bonded with the people. The love was mutual and sustained over the years they served there.

While in Yaoundé Sydney was responsible for the departments of Sabbath School, Personal Ministries, Youth Ministries, Community Services, and Family Ministries. It wasn't long before the list grew. His union roles also included interim director for ADRA, and director of ministerial and global mission. However, the honeymoon in Yaoundé was short-lived. A greater need for his service was identified by the executive committee of the union, and he became president of the West Cameroon Mission from January 1993 to June 1998. This was one of four mission territories of the union in Cameroon.

Pastor Gibbons was asked to bridge the gap, primarily, between two language groups of people and to provide neutrality of leadership to advance the work of the West Mission. The mission served five of the ten provinces of the country. The provinces were divided by the two official languages of Cameroon—French and English—eight spoke French and two spoke English. Both English-speaking provinces, along with three French-speaking provinces, were in the West Mission.

Cameroon is a cosmopolitan country of about 250 ethnic African groups and languages with a population under 13 million in 1992, and 21.7 million in 2012. About 53 percent of the citizens in 1992 were loyal to ethnic religions; some 37 percent were Christians; about 10 percent were Muslim. Diversity of people groups and languages decorate the landscape of Cameroonian citizens. The two official languages of the country permitted people to communicate across the diverse spectrum of local dialects. Unfortunately, the official languages became a point of tension for the nation. Loyalties were divided, to a significant degree, between the French-speaking, francophone, and English-speaking, anglophone, peoples of Cameroon. The tension between the groups displayed itself in the political, socio-economic, cultural, and religious life of Cameroonians.

The Seventh-day Adventist Church was not free from the effects of historical factors that contributed to conflict between persons considered francophone and those considered anglophone.

The West Mission was directed from its headquarters in Bali, Doula, the economic capital of the country. Pastor Gibbons traveled extensively throughout his mission territory of 124,041 km² over the first two months of service for orientation to the field. According to the 1987 census report of Cameroon, the population of that mission territory was 5,141,812; the total population of Cameroon in 1987 was 10,493,655.

After reflecting, Pastor Gibbons concluded that breakdown in communication was the cause of much distrust and division in the field. The great distance between subregions and the mission headquarters further alienated interest groups from each other. Decisions at the headquarters did not always reflect equal access to privilege and opportunity across all people groups within the mission. He recommended decentralization of the mission by establishing four regional boards accountable to the mission executive committee. His recommendation was accepted. The new arrangement provided autonomy for respective regions, both English and French. Decentralization improved communication and advanced the mission. The membership doubled from about 3,500 to about 7,000 during Pastor Gibbons' presidency.

Pastor Gibbons won the respect of mission employees and members by empowering the regions to direct regional affairs. Whenever he traveled in the field, he would live in the homes of the people, eat their food, sleep in their beds, and mingle with all who assembled to receive him. This endeared him to the masses, aided his effectiveness in leading people who were willing to follow him and who wanted him and his family to remain in Cameroon when their term of service had ended. When the Gibbons' left Cameroon, the mission had fifteen pastors who served 100 churches and companies, a clinic, two elementary schools, and one high school.

Mission service is known to demand much from missionaries. In addition to being the mission president, Sydney was the pastor of two districts, each having a principle church and a growing company. Also, he was visiting professor in the Department of Theology at Nanga Eboko in Cameroon, He taught a range of college courses in French and some in English.

One highlight was teaching a course in public evangelism. The students, about fifty plus, were divided into three groups. Each group had to plan and conduct an evangelistic crusade. The crusades were conducted simultaneously and concluded in a joint baptism. Three weeks later, students and converts celebrated victory in Jesus as 113 souls were baptized.

Pastor Gibbons was happy to secure scholarships to sponsor the training of pastors to raise the quality of professional, pastoral care and leadership in the West Mission. A progressive Cameroonian pastor was sponsored from funds raised by Sydney in Bermuda. He returned as pastor in the field with a bachelor of theology degree before Sydney left Cameroon. He later served in different administrative posts within the CAUM. Currently he is pursuing higher learner in Nigeria to better advance the work of Adventist missions in Africa.

Life in Cameroon was slow paced, and often salaries were delayed, thus limiting funds to purchase life's necessities for the Gibbons. Yet they were able to take care of many needs of others. Katherina accounts how she, along with another church member, was able to save the life of two children because of her previous nursing experience. She recounts how she was able to detect a physical defect and report her concerns to the family. The sick child was eventually flown to Paris for needed open-heart surgery. Another child was so malnourished, without proper medical attention he was going to die. Katherina and the church member were able to garner the services of a pediatrician who provided services for free until the child recovered.

On December 15, 1996, Sydney was awarded a title of merit by the village chief of Bandenkop in the West Province of Cameroon. He was recognized for services rendered by the mission in the areas of education and health. He was given the official name, Sah Ghomsi, which appears on the certificate and means *Messenger of God*. Katherina left Cameroon with lifelong friends and a journal of memories that will become the content of her book on mission service. She will be remembered in Cameroon for her extensive, spirited singing in church services, and in particular, accompanying Sydney as singing evangelist for crusades they conducted. Katherina and Sydney also remember a major blessing to the mission in the last year of their service in Cameroon. They sold several hundred pairs of shoes and collected one million francs, $3,000.00US dollars. These funds provided academic scholarships, purchased camping equipment for the Pathfinders, and afforded opportunity for many youth to attend a youth congress.

After Cameroon, the family re-entered mission service at Northern Caribbean University (NCU, 2000–2001) in Mandeville, Jamaica. Sydney served as an associate professor in the Department of Religion and Theology, teaching Bible doctrines, church leadership and administration, church history, and Revelation. The wide spectrum of courses taught in Jamaica was another evidence of great expectations from Inter-division employees. Katherina's position was resident counselor for the university. The

short stay at NCU was productive and satisfying. The longer stay in Cameroon left more indelible impressions for missions by virtue of the length of time invested in service.

The Gibbons children made a positive impact on others in Cameroon, even though they were young. Gianluca formed multiple friendships and was known for his prayers of faith.

Meliseanna defied the norm in Cameroon and was rewarded for her faith in God. She attended a private French school in Cameroon, Dominique Savio, which required weekly class attendance on Sabbath. She never attended classes on the Sabbath, and God blessed her with top grades, helping her to end the school year at the top of her class. Mystere returned to Cameroon with her father in 2003 and conducted a crusade through a Global Evangelism program. As a result, thirteen people were baptized.

The Gibbons wished to expose Mystere to a different culture, so they requested the permission of her parents to take her to Bermuda on a visit. While visiting, the Bermuda Institute of Seventh-day Adventists offered her free schooling for one year to further expand her cross-cultural learning. They soon found it difficult to take Mystere with them when they traveled overseas due to immigration restrictions. Her maternal parents had welcomed the Gibbons family as their extended family. They were happy for the Gibbons willingness to help sponsor Mystere's education.

When Mystere's parents learned about the difficulty of travel, since Pastor and Mrs. Gibbons needed legal permission from them every time they traveled, they consented for the Gibbons to adopt Mystere. They provided the documents required by the government of Bermuda to support the process. It would not have been possible for the Gibbons to adopt Mystere in

Cameroon. If they had intended to adopt her when they first took her from Cameroon, their request for travel would have been denied. God orchestrated the adoption of Mystere, and the Gibbons were happy to follow His lead.

Mystere became an integral part of the Gibbons family, their country, and their world. All the while she maintained contact with her maternal family. Her father was the secretary of the West Mission when Pastor Gibbons was the president. They worked well together. Her maternal father died in recent years, but Mystere had the joy of reuniting with him, her mother, and her family in 2003 when Pastor Gibbons returned to Cameroon with her to preach in Global Evangelism.

Mystere is now happily married to a Cape Verdean whom she met at Atlantic Union College. They also discovered that they had connections from Cameroon. Her mother-in-law is a Cameroonian. Her father-in-law is from Cape Verde, but he had studied with Mystere's father in Cameroon. He is also a pastor, leading a district of Cape Verdean churches in the Southern New England Conference in Atlantic Union. God orchestrated their marriage too.

Mystere was the last child born to her parents. They named her Mystere because of the mysterious circumstances of her unexpected birth. The mystery has continued to follow her. The Gibbons two daughters, Meliseanna and Mystere, made history in Bermuda. They both, among other successful applicants, received the highest government educational scholarship offered for successful applicants leaving Bermuda to begin college. It was the first time that two siblings received the same scholarship in the same year. Just another mystery! The Gibbons call it another miracle of divine intervention!

The Gibbons family left Cameroon speaking French. They left mission service with the knowledge that they had been blessed, their children forever changed, and the sense that God had given them an experience of a lifetime. John records in his book, "There are so many things that Jesus did. If they were all written down, each of them, one by one, I can't imagine a world big enough to hold such a library of books" (John 21:25, *The Message*). Also, the Gibbons' could write forever of the many wonderful and awesome experiences of their journey in mission service.

Gianluca (left) and Meliseanna (right) with the babies of the Gibbons' house assistant in Bali, Douala

Dr. Gibbons with local pastors baptizing after a crusade

Pathfinders at federation, Bali, Douala, receive gifts from a fund-raising project led by Katherina Gibbons

Meliseanna, Gianluca, and Mystere (middle) enjoying a festive occasion

Katherina Gibbons, ministering in song, at a subregional year-end event

The Gibbons in the village of Bandenkop holding the certificate of honor given to Dr. Gibbons for mission services rendered to the community

Dr. Gibbons and his wife (front row) with pastors and administrators of the West Cameroon Mission

Dr. Gibbons preaching the Word of God

Dr. Gibbons and a local pastor of the West Mission baptizing a new believer

Prison officials in Kumba receive clothing for inmates, donated by the West Mission

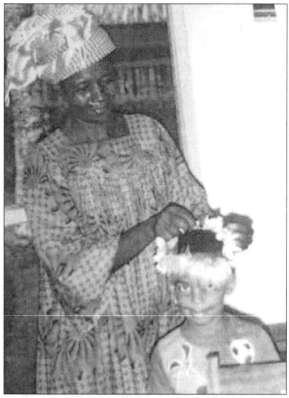

The maternal mother of Mystere, the Gibbons' adopted daughter, places traditional local flowers on Gianluca's head to celebrate his birthday

Dr. Gibbons shows his knowledge of soccer with some of his mission pastors supporting him in the background

Dr. Gibbons receives a certificate and gift of honor from the village chief of Bandenkop for services rendered in the village

The Gibbons celebrate the marriage of Mystere and Patrick, June 2012, in California: (left to right) Gianluca, Meliseanna, Patrick, Mystere, Katherina, and Sydney

87
Howard and Lois Bullard

1993–1995 / Mexico

We don't often think of Mexico as the mission field since it is so close to our home base, but service there requires a passport, travel, an unfamiliar culture and language, and time away from home, family, and friends. Sometimes countries and universities need special skills that cannot be found in their own borders, so they make calls for specially trained individuals.

In his early days Howard Israel Bullard Jr. was involved in gangs, drugs, and stealing on the streets of Los Angeles. He left the street life when he encountered Christ as revealed in the Seventh-day Adventist message. Since that time he has spearheaded a variety of ministries for the disenfranchised. He married Lois Ellison, and they had five children: Adrena, Victoria, Sherri, Paul, and Joel.

At one time Howard Bullard was the assistant art director for the Review and Herald Publishing Association and the designer for the magazines *Life and Health* and *Message.*

Howard is a very creative person with a head full of ideas. These ideas coupled with his training made him an artist in demand.

He spent five and a half years at art schools studying commercial art: first at the Art Center College of Design in Los Angeles, then at the Los Angeles Trade Technical College, and finally at the San Francisco Academy of Art. Additionally, he received degrees at Oakwood University and Howard University. He worked as a commercial artist for more than twenty years: as a layout artist and designer for design studios, as art director/designer for the Oakland Post, as graphic designer for an ABC television station in San Francisco, and as art director for United Way in San Francisco, and for an advertising agency in San Jose, California.

In the mid-1980s Bullard was called to Oakwood University to be an instructor of communication and commercial art and graphic design with an emphasis on layout and design and be the director of *Graphixx.* In addition to teaching communication art and graphic design, television commercials, and advertising art, he, with the Office of College Relations, produced the *Oakwood Magazine,* which won national and international recognition.

Prior to joining the Oakwood college staff, he was senior graphic designer and art director at the prestigious B'nai B'rith Foundation in Washington, D.C. When he left Oakwood University he operated his own studio: the Howard Bullard Graphic Design Studio in Adelphi, Maryland, where he emphasized design of brochures, logos, newsletters, and magazines.

In 1993, while living in Maryland and operating his own graphic design studio, Howard Bullard responded to an unusual call from Mexico. The University of Montemorelos wanted him to be a professor of visual communications with the purpose of developing their first four-year degree program in graphic designing and computer technology. They wanted the program to be first class, one that would prepare the students for a career in graphic design, art direction, and desktop publishing, and one that the Mexican government would approve for accreditation.

After a few years of building the program, the Mexican government heartily approved and accepted the program for accreditation. The missionary project Howard Bullard started at Montemorelos University is one of the most successful in their school history and is growing yearly. "The University of Montemorelos now has some of the most outstanding visual communications students in the world. It is my desire that one day Oakwood University will have such a program," said Bullard.

Howard Bullard

Howard Bullard at his drawing board

88

GERTRUDE JORDAN

1993–2002 / Kenya

Gertrude Jordan grew up in a small town in Pennsylvania. She says there were more trees than people there. Her father had gone to a trade school for three years, and her mother had taken a college prep class in high school but was never able to get to college. They were determined that their children would go to college, and they worked several jobs to put their four children through school. Gertrude graduated from Andrews University in 1965, and then went to Youngstown, Ohio, to teach. Then she moved to Chicago where she decided to pursue further education.

While she was getting her master's degree, her professor said, "Why don't you get a doctorate?" She got a fellowship and paid all her back bills as well as her doctoral studies. When she finished that degree, she went to Michigan State and then to Baltimore as a counselor.

While in Baltimore she met Dr. Muze who invited her to go to Kenya to teach. Gertrude Elizabeth Jordan of Ellicott City, Maryland, left the States on September 26, 1993, to serve as psychology instructor at the University of Eastern Africa in Baraton, Kenya.

While in Kenya, she taught classes in home economics, education, and general psychology/ sociology. Every quarter it seems that she had every student at the school. The textbook was too advanced, so during the years she was there, she made her own textbook. The school was just starting the master's program, and she had to develop course outlines.

Art education was a delight for her. She would give the students pictures and ask them questions in a formal test. Each student had a different picture. They had to tell everything about the picture: the color, the period it was produced in, etc. She had seen an art textbook in Maryland that she really liked, but she didn't buy it. She thought about it and later regretted very much that she hadn't purchased copies for her students. Surprisingly, while visiting Zimbabwe some years later, she saw the very same book and bought every one of them for her students.

Below is a portrayal of her life, written by Dr. Jordan herself, which will add some details to her life and mission experience.

What can I say that could possibly interest you? Here I am, seventy years old and living in Michigan, where it is currently raining and snowing at the same time.

Well, I was born in July 1943 to a mixed black family in a small town in Pennsylvania. I grew up, hardworking, picking blueberries in the summer (age seven to twelve), and cleaning smoked-filled rooms with spittoons and dirty floors as a teenager, because my older sister wanted to go to college.

Andrews University was a life-changing experience: 1) After three years I was still afraid to go into the dining room alone and sit down because I didn't know the people at the table. 2) My roommate was a Nigerian who was "engaged" at age fifteen to her boyfriend, but she was a pure "rose," marrying him after both of them had completed their doctor of medicine studies. 3) My one time cheating experience in which I wrote the answers on my fingernails. A fellow student observed me and passed the information around before telling me he had seen me cheating. I never cheated in college again. 4) Canvassing with Ruthie in Detroit and with students from the Lake Region Conference of Seventh-day Adventists in Chicago and Toronto, Canada, was hard work. 5) The words "I waited until you were twenty-one [before raping you] so your father wouldn't intervene [and stop you from marrying me]" haunted me for years. I carried those words with me and felt that God couldn't forgive me for stepping outside of His hedge of protection into outer darkness.

At one time I contemplated suicide. I had married outside of God's guidelines and lived a lifetime—thirty years—working for God's redemptive grace. But, it was free! Oh, to believe in the Bible promises—Matthew 7:7; Mark 11:24; John 11:41.

By age 50 I had completed several teaching contracts and a doctorate with an emphasis on character development, all the while shying away from several marriage proposals. At this same time I had two alternatives before me, an attractive position of supervising/teaching/monitoring teachers/students in character development for the school system in Baltimore, Maryland, or being a missionary teacher

at the University of Eastern Africa in Kenya, East Africa. "Take Kenya," my Arab-American dentist uttered into my ear as he cleaned my teeth. "Take Kenya."

And so I did. An old college friend, an international student when I knew him at Andrews University, called my older sister, asking, "Where is Gertrude? What is she doing?" He interviewed me and prompted me on what to write. The result? I became a missionary, an overseas worker—something I had intermittently thought/wanted/dreamed about but had stopped. Now I was a single, divorced mother with all of the "baggage" that a divorce carried in the late 1960s, and beyond.

I remember in Kenya the inquisitive conversation I had over dinner with Koleth K. in Nairobi asking why I had taken the UEAB contract. I remember the first purple flowering tree I saw in Nairobi, the pine tree forest I traveled through when I traveled from Nairobi to Baraton, dinner with the Mwangi's, my meeting the first class, and the diarrhea from eating too much cheese. I remember my first apartment (three stories up), my first suite mate, Ms. Lemon, the vacation trip to Dar es Salaam, and the purchase of art/culture books in that city that I had first seen in Baltimore (and didn't buy them). I remember that I would be teaching every student art history that came through the doors of UEAB.

I remember the challenge of staying ahead of the students in developing curriculum, and test and lecture materials that were relevant, interesting, and new. I remember the copying I had to do and the glorious interactions I had with students.

For instance, with Emma A. "Who knows if you have come into the kingdom for such a time as this?" For instance, with Theresa K., a student who had "daughter privileges" but did not take advantage of them. For instance, with Ms. Obegi and Samuel Obara in Test and Measurement class who taught me more then I taught them. For instance, Kate Namirembe and the marathon week we had with her while working on her master's thesis; with Gladys who "had to change her major" because she couldn't stand up to the sexual harassments of a teacher. I remember two young men, both of who wanted a college education but lacked the funds to make it a reality. I remember the cultural exchanges, some delightful (i.e. giving of gifts to say "job well done"), others dangerous ("if we have a slaughter/killing … would you stand between … and?").

I remember the comradeship between teacher and students (i.e. Friday night potlucks at my house). I remember the interactions, the nuances, etc., between administrators, supervisors, teachers, campus workers, and students. I remember two brothers who both died of AIDS and a student publicly announcing the information. I remember the young woman buried in her wedding dress. I remember one of three brothers whose life was saved when his two brothers insisted that they go on to Nairobi where they were able to get the necessary medical help. I remember assisting in two mass marriages we had on campus for several workers who, having cultural tribal weddings wanted a Christian wedding with all the trimmings (i.e. the wedding dresses, western styled suits, cake, preacher, flowers, etc.).

I remember the tension/confrontation between people, i.e., the sweetness of Emily Dube, a teacher on campus, the attitude of one person who did not like either divorced or single woman as teachers on campus. Steven K., a good worker who "never let through the campus gates persons of questionable character and intent," perhaps "saved my life" when I hired him first as my gardener, later as my indoor worker. Through it all I remember that God's grace is there for all who love Him, working together for good.

Gertrude Jordan

Gertrude Jordan with Lydia Andrews at the opening of the Ellen G. White Research Center at the University of Eastern Africa

89

DELBERT AND CURDELL PEARMAN

1997–2008 / Sri Lanka, Lebanon, Ethiopia

Delbert's taste of foreign mission service began in November 1983. He had just graduated from Oakwood College that June with a major in religion and a minor in business administration. Unmarried and still without any prospects, and unsure what he wanted to do in life, he accepted an invitation from the Adventist Volunteer Service Corp to serve as accountant for the Tuberculosis and Leprosy Research Center (TALRES) in Southeast Africa for one year. It was there, 7,330 miles from home, that he found his life calling.

While in rural, southern Malawi, he quickly bonded with the nationals. In addition to his work, he started a youth choir, led out in Pathfinders, held evangelistic meetings, played soccer for the Ngabu Village team, and courted the girls. Being a foreigner, yet like them, was something they had never experienced before, so he became the center of attention. Noticing the increase in interests his presence brought to the church, the leaders requested that he go home, get married, and return as a regular missionary. It was good counsel since the life span for women in the country at the time was only forty-four years of age.

At home again Delbert began sharing his recent mission experiences at area churches. During one such presentation one Sabbath afternoon, he stuttered, mid-sentence. He saw a girl in the audience with the prettiest face he had ever seen. On their first date, she watched him play basketball at a church social, and then they took a quiet walk through the city streets together.

They began to see each other more frequently. She always baked his favorite peanut butter cookies and brought them to prayer meeting each Tuesday evening. Those pastries never saw the light of day.

The young lady was Marilyn Curdell Ebbin. Everybody called her Curdell. She had attended the Bermuda Institute, then Berkeley Secretarial School and had graduated from Columbia Union College with a bachelor's degree.

They grew closer together until he got the nerve to ask if she would like to be a missionary wife someday. She thought it would be exciting. Even though the flower girl stumbled over her dress walking up to the altar, it was a blissful wedding. Soon after the honeymoon, Delbert reminded Curdell of the need to get back to Africa. She responded, "Not so fast, buddy!" It wasn't until twelve years later that he got back into mission service, and it was not to Africa!

During those first twelve years of marriage, beginning June 1986, Delbert served as accountant, under treasurer, treasurer, and then secretary/treasurer for the Bermuda Conference of Seventh-day Adventists. Within that time they acquired a lovely home overlooking the Atlantic Ocean, and a beautiful daughter, Cierra, was added to the family.

Elder Ted Jones initiated a call for them to serve as treasurer for the Sri Lanka Union of Churches. Curdell missed home sorely. It was even further away than Malawi. Six-year-old Cierra tried to console her mother, and eventually Curdell adjusted and got involved in Sabbath School, women's ministries, and children's ministries. She conducted workshops to train the leaders and personally led many of the children to baptism.

Today, Sri Lanka is her favorite place on earth. Delbert was kept busy as there were several schools, including a junior college, a forty-bed primary care hospital, an ADRA operation, a publishing house, an Adventist World Radio studio, and forty churches to care for. Also, he had to train his assistants so they could support him in his work. Curdell and Cierra enjoyed accompanying Delbert in his preaching assignments all over the island nation. They served the church in Sri Lanka from August 1997 until January 2001.

Following Sri Lanka they accepted a call to serve as secretary/treasurer for the East Mediterranean Field, which was comprised of the countries of Jordan, Lebanon, and Syria. It was a life-changing experience to work in the place where Abraham, Lot, Moses, and Ruth called home. A whole lot has not changed over the millennia, and to live in the same neighborhood where Jezebel grew up as a little girl brought many of the Bible stories their parents had read to them as children alive. "It is amazing what can grow in the desert. It is the best food we have ever tasted, even to this day, better than IHOP," Delbert exclaimed. They lived in the mountains overlooking the city of Beirut and the Mediterranean Sea. A beautiful sight to behold! Curdell took advantage of this time to continue her university studies. They served the church in these Middle Eastern countries from January 2001 until January 2005.

The greatest responsibility came in their service with the Ethiopian Union. Finally back in Africa, as union treasurer, Delbert's responsibilities were to give financial oversight to more than 1,000 churches, thirty-six schools with a combined enrollment of 18,000 students including a senior college, an Adventist World Radio studio that produced daily programs in three languages, an eighty-bed primary care hospital and sixteen clinics, and a publishing house. The baptized membership was about 136,000 with average baptisms of one thousand per month.

"Our greatest achievement was to adopt Lidette, a stunningly attractive Ethiopian orphan girl who had lost both of her parents. Having her with us now for ten years, I can't imagine how we could have been a family without her."

The country of Djibouti also came under the jurisdiction of the Ethiopian Union. There the church operated a healthcare center composed of an eye clinic, dental clinic, medical clinic, and an English language school. Even though the country was 98 percent Muslim, the Adventist clinic made a good impression among the people. Once again, Curdell put her gifts to work, leading out and training Sabbath School leaders and working among the women and children. Their service in Ethiopia and Djibouti spanned from January 2005 until September 2008.

Pastor Alex Bryant, president of the Central States Conference, kept calling for Delbert to come and serve as his treasurer in Kansas City, Missouri. By this time, Cierra was about ready to go into her third year of high school. From age six she had lived overseas, and now at age seventeen, it was time to introduce her to the Western culture where she would probably spend her adult life. So they accepted the call and put Cierra in an Adventist boarding academy in Georgia and kept Lidette with them. Even though they soon missed foreign mission service, it was a good move. Within a couple of months at their new posting, Alex apologized for calling Delbert away from Ethiopia because he was leaving to accept a call as executive secretary of the North American Division. Little did Delbert know at the time that about a year and a half later, they would be called to the General Conference also as planning director for the Office of Adventist Mission. Curdell would take a position as administrative assistant in ADRA International and later in the General Conference Treasury, working in the same building together.

Working in Adventist Mission puts Delbert back in touch with the people and places they have served during their foreign mission service. He is able to speak passionately about the needs on the frontlines to the leadership in Silver Spring because he has "been there and done that."

Cierra went on to marry Jamal, a pre-med student at Andrews University, and together they have added a grandson to the family clan. Lidette is completing her senior year at Spencerville Academy.

Delbert adds, "God has given us a full life of service for Him, and that cute face that stopped me in my tracks hasn't lost its charm in our twenty-eight years of marriage." Even though they are now working at the highest levels of the church organization, they often ask themselves, "Why did we leave foreign mission service?"

Delbert Pearman, then treasurer of the Bermuda Conference, receiving the Jewell W. Peek Award for Excellence from Robert L. Sweezey, executive director of Risk Management Services.

Delbert and Curdell Pearman

90
NEWTON AND LYDIA ANDREWS

1998–2004 / Kenya; 2006–2009 / Ghana

Newton and Lydia are natives of the beautiful twin islands of Trinidad and Tobago located in the sunny Caribbean. Newton graduated from Caribbean Union College (now the University of Southern Caribbean) in 1962 with an associate's degree in theology, which was the highest degree offered at that time. He was immediately appointed as a ministerial intern by the South Caribbean Conference and was assigned to the San Fernando district to work with Senior Pastor Henry Gabriel.

Lydia graduated from Southern Academy in San Fernando in 1960 and was accepted to study nursing at San Fernando General Hospital. This was a three-year diploma program. Lydia was very involved in church activities, and Newton watched with keenness her devotion and spirituality.

One day while they were both engaged in harvest ingathering Newton decided to look no further for a life companion. The rest is history.

Shortly after their marriage in June 1965 Newton was accepted to Atlantic Union College to complete a bachelor's degree in theology. Lydia remained in Trinidad to complete the final year of her nursing program. However, God had another plan. She soon realized that final year lectures were to be held on Sabbath, and together with five other classmates they decided not to attend. They petitioned everyone, including the Conference president who was unable to intervene on their behalf. They were told that since other Adventist students before them had attended lectures on Sabbath there was nothing to be done. Eventually Lydia left to join Newton in South Lancaster, Massachusetts. After Newton's graduation from AUC and with their first baby on the way, they packed their few earthly belongings in a Ford and moved to Washington, D.C. to join other family members. Over the years three children were born to the couple, and in time all started attending Adventist schools in Takoma Park, Maryland.

Both Newton and Lydia attended Howard University. Newton enrolled in the master of divinity program but graduated with a master's degree in social work. Since Lydia was not able to complete her nurses training in Trinidad, she requested to have her credits transferred. Her request was denied, so she had to start all over again. Juggling work, studying, and caring for a home and two young children kept her busy, but she persevered and graduated with a bachelor's degree in nursing in 1973. During the children's early years Lydia and Newton were both very active in Pathfinders and became founding members of the Metropolitan SDA Church in Hyattsville, Maryland.

After repeated invitations from Lydia's uncle, Dr. Emmanuel Saunders, now retired chair of the History Department, Lydia and the children, along with another family, the

Applewhites whom the Andrews had brought to the church, relocated to Huntsville, Alabama, in August 1983 to enable their children to attend Oakwood Academy. Moving south was quite a challenge for the children, but it was important for them to experience their "own" in high profile positions.

Newton commuted for two years while waiting to sell their home in Maryland. He eventually joined the family and was employed with the State of Alabama. When Lydia announced to her coworkers at Howard University Hospital of her decision to move south, they tried to discourage her. One nurse said, "Huntsville, where is that?"

Lydia began working the night shift at Huntsville Hospital, and in 1984 was offered a part-time clinical instructor position at Oakwood College in their Department of Nursing. At the same time Naomi Bullard, who had recently returned to the United States after thirteen years of mission service in Rwanda, joined the staff. They quickly bonded and became teaching buddies. Naomi worked until 1996 when she received a call to the University of Eastern Africa in Kenya to head the Department of Nursing. By this time Lydia had earned a master's degree and was working full time. Later Lydia completed another master's degree in midwifery at the University of Alabama, Birmingham. Because laws in midwifery are different in each state, Lydia could not practice in Alabama. After ten years at Oakwood College as an assistant professor, she accepted a three-year contract at the Gardenview Women's Rural Clinic, Manchester Memorial Hospital, in Kentucky as a full-time midwife.

While in Kentucky Lydia was invited by Naomi Bullard to join the faculty at the University of Eastern Africa since there was a need for a midwifery instructor. Nursing students were also trained to perform deliveries when they graduated. Neither Lydia nor Newton had been to Africa. In fact, they had never given it a thought. About ten years earlier Newton had developed an interest in a call to a chaplaincy position in Trinidad, but since Lydia was not ready academically the call had not materialized. This time a formal call for a six-year contract came from Elder Maurice Battle at the General Conference. They prayed and discussed the idea with their children and family as they asked for God's guidance with such a serious decision.

Just then the hospital administrator announced that they needed to downsize the clinic and wanted to start with the women's section. Lydia agreed to be released from her contract with severance pay. At the same time Newton was offered early retirement with the State of Alabama to which he also agreed. Now they were both free to accept the call to Africa. God was working out everything. Their daughter was married, one son was doing a residency in internal medicine in Ohio, and their last son had just completed his first semester of medical school at Loma Linda University. How could they refuse such an opportunity to serve? They had no excuse but to say, "Here am I, Lord, send me."

After completing all the necessary paperwork, Lydia and Newton needed to obtain financial and medical clearance. All went well, but they wanted to keep their home. The General Conference committee agreed since their newly married daughter who was employed at Oakwood College consented to live in it and care for it. They also attended Mission Institute at Loma Linda University to prepare them for transition to another culture. Next began the arduous task of packing. Family and friends provided assistance to pack household items and put them on the truck. They wanted to make sure their shipment reached the General Conference warehouse before they left the country, so Newton agreed to drive the U-Haul truck from Alabama to Maryland, a sixteen-hour trip. When they arrived, tired and exhausted, at 1:00 a.m., Marvin Robinson met them at the warehouse. After securing the truck, he took them to a hotel where they rested for a few hours before leaving for the airport on their way to Kenya.

Their first layover was in Amsterdam where they boarded a Kenya Airways jet for Nairobi, Kenya. After two days of travel, they arrived in Nairobi and had to board a smaller aircraft to Kisumu, which was one hour away. They were met at the airport by Naomi Bullard and Dr. Maradufu, dean of the School of Science and Technology. Finally, after traveling one hour by road, they arrived on the beautiful, green, exquisitely landscaped campus and were taken to their one-floor brick furnished home. All the faculty lived on campus. The house had three bedrooms, a large living room with a fireplace, a dining room, and a kitchen equipped with a five-burner gas range and oven, as well as a large double door refrigerator. There was a full bath with hot and cold water and a washing machine. Expatriates were expected to hire house help, gardeners, and babysitters from the local community. So as soon as they arrived, many came for hire. One young helper that they hired, a long-distance runner, eventually received a scholarship to the United States where she completed her nursing degree thanks to assistance from the Andrews. She still keeps in contact with them.

The Andrews were surprised to experience such mild weather in spite of the fact that the equator passes through Kenya. They crossed that imaginary line many times on their way to Nairobi. Due to the high elevation, the climate

is very cool, especially in the rainy season. In fact, their shipment included floor and ceiling fans because they anticipated a hot, humid African climate. Instead the fans were brought back to the United States in unopened boxes and the fireplace was constantly in use, especially in the rainy season.

They experienced great anxiety upon their arrival because they were unable to communicate with family, letting them know they had arrived safely to Africa. It took one week before such news reached family and friends. A switchboard system that was used by the university only functioned during business hours and was closed on weekends. If there was an emergency, someone was sent to the operator's home to ask her to come to the office. Sometimes when she was off campus you just had to wait until she returned. The cafeteria was supplied with vegetables from the farm, milk from the dairy, eggs, and bread from the bakery. This provided work for many students, which helped them with their tuition.

At that time the university functioned under the quarter system, and Lydia had to jump right into teaching second quarter after being on campus just two weeks. There was little time to be completely oriented. They did receive an abbreviated orientation for new faculty conducted by the deputy vice chancellor for academic affairs, Dr. James Mbyirukira, who is presently dean and chair of the Education Department at Oakwood University. The president of the University used the title of vice chancellor because by law in Kenya no one can use the title of president. That title is reserved only for the president of the country.

Nursing was one of the largest departments on campus and was housed in a separate building that included classrooms, faculty offices, and a skills lab. Total enrollment of the university fluctuated around 3,000 students, 70 percent of whom were non-Adventists. However, all students were required to attend all religious services. At registration every student received a Sabbath School quarterly and was assigned to a Sabbath School class. What an opportunity for evangelism!

The university had a unique hospitality department. While waiting for their shipment, all new workers were assigned to the homes of different faculty members for each meal. This was exciting because they were able to become acquainted with the families and enjoy dishes from different cultures. There were workers from different countries in Africa as well as the Philippines and the United States. Students were also from different East African countries. It was during their first year in Kenya that the Andrews experienced the terrorist bomb attack on the American Embassy in Nairobi, which killed and wounded many citizens. During that attack their youngest son, who was in medical school at Loma Linda, was in Malawi for his SIMS (Students in Missionary Service) rotation. He decided to visit his parents in Kenya and had to take an alternate route to the airport because some of the roads were barricaded by police. It was a horrifying experience for everyone.

Because of their love for students, the Andrews agreed to become AY sponsors. This gave them the opportunity to assist in planning off-campus retreats, which took them to beautiful sites all over Kenya. They planned two retreats to Mombasa, which is on the coast of Kenya on the Indian Ocean. There they witnessed the most beautiful sunrise and sunset. One retreat was in conjunction with the East Africa Division Youth Congress in Rwanda. All these trips were done by rail or road. In Rwanda they visited the skull museum, the Adventist Church in Mugenero where hundreds were slaughtered when they ran there for refuge, and other sites that held replicas of the 1994 genocide.

Their home was always open to on and off campus students and community people. Some came for financial assistance, some for a meal or food items. Some came to hold student association or AY meetings, birthday parties or a potluck. Whatever the reason, all were made to feel welcome, and none left with their needs unmet. One student, an electronic technology major who received financial assistance in exchange for typing assignments for Lydia, won the green card lottery to the United States after his graduation. He and his wife needed an address in the States and someone to receive them on arrival. The Andrews provided the necessary documentation required by the U.S. embassy in Kenya, and when the couple arrived, they stayed in the Andrews' home until they were able to launch out on their own. At present they have completed further studies, bought a home, started their family, and the husband is presently on the staff of the media department at the Oakwood University Church.

Elder Andrews taught classes in the Counseling and Religion Departments and later became the director of the Ellen G. White Center, which was established while they worked at UEAB. One of his classes, Christian Ethics, was a requirement for all students, and almost 150 students registered for the class each quarter. This was quite a daunting task because most of the examination questions were in the form of essays. Lydia taught almost every nursing course, became acting chair of the Nursing Department and director of the Maternal and Child Campus Clinic. Lydia obtained her Kenyan midwifery license and had several opportunities to practice her skills both on campus and in the community. One night a man came to their home to report that his wife was in labor. Lydia got her flash-light and bag, which was always packed, and fol-lowed the man on foot to his house in the village a short distance away. When they arrived, sure enough the wife was having labor pains and too far along to make it to the Catholic Mission Hos-pital. Lydia continued to monitor the mother and delivered a healthy baby boy right there in the home. Many times the Andrews were called to transport workers or students to the clinic, hospital, or other locations. The road from cam-pus to the nearest town was about twelve miles and not paved, so in the rainy season vehicles were frequently stuck. This meant spending long hours navigating the roadway due to the heavy red mud. In the dry season they had to contend with the red dust that blew everywhere.

Shortly after their arrival in Kenya a Cau-casian couple came as volunteers from Phila-delphia. This Lutheran couple came during the spring semester of each year, and they eventu-ally spent five consecutive years at UEAB. The wife, Helen, taught in the Nursing Department, and her husband Ron taught calculus and math-ematics. This couple went with the Andrews on safaris and enjoyed many potluck dinners together. Both families also took a class in Swa-hili in order to effectively communicate with the Kenyan community. Various ethnic groups speak local dialects, but the two official lan-guages spoken in the country are English and Swahili. English is widely used in commerce, education, and government.

While in Kenya the Andrews visited other African countries, namely Tanzania, Uganda, the magnificent Victoria Falls in Zambia, South Africa, and Ethiopia.

The following experience is one that Lydia will never forget. One morning as she was about to leave home for the office she heard a knock on the door. At first she thought it was a lay midwife from the village in need of gloves or other supplies or bringing gifts such as a large pumpkin on her head, pineapples, avocados, eggs, a chicken, or *mursik* (milk with pieces of charcoal used as a preservative). When Lydia opened the door, she was greeted by a nurs-ing student who lived off campus. The student looked troubled, so Lydia asked her what was wrong. The student informed Lydia that she had mixed up a poisonous concoction, waited for her roommate to leave, and was about to drink it to commit suicide when a voice said, "Go see Mrs. Andrews." She explained that her mother, who was funding her education, had just been diag-nosed with HIV/AIDS. She felt that there was no hope for her to complete her education, plus she could not live to face the shame and stigma of the disease. Lydia prayer with the student and promised to find a way to assist her. Sometime later Lydia related the situation to Helen, who turned around and placed the student's name on the list of young people whom Helen's Lutheran church members were sponsoring. In the end, the student completed her nursing degree and was able to afford medication for her mother and support her other siblings.

The Andrews spent six wonderful years at the University of Eastern Africa, Baraton. It was a very exciting and rewarding experience. They returned every two years on furlough to visit with family and friends. They established many long-standing relationships and touched many lives during their sojourn in Kenya. They returned home in April 2004. They give all praise and glory to God for preserving their lives as they ministered overseas.

After returning to the United States, Lydia accepted part-time nursing positions at the Uni-versity of Alabama, Huntsville, and Oakwood University. Just before Thanksgiving, Novem-ber 2005, Lydia received a telephone call from

Elder Bediako, General Conference secretary. He explained that he had seen her name on the list of returning missionaries and asked if she would consider going to Valley View University in Ghana to establish a bachelor's degree in nursing program. The request sounded challenging yet exciting. With prayer and much discussion with the family, Newton and Lydia decided to accept another missionary post.

When Lydia called to give her response, Elder Bediako informed her that the union president, Dr. Lami, and the president of the university, Dr. Laryea, would be attending the Ministerial Evangelism Program at Oakwood University Church and she should find time to meet with them for further details. Since they lived close to the church, Lydia agreed to attend the program. Neither Lydia nor the two men knew each other. However, as God would have it that night Lydia arrived just in time to see the men being introduced to the congregation. They met after the meeting and discussed the urgency of the situation. Lydia was invited to Valley View all expenses paid to meet with a team of consultants to plan for the project.

Lydia arrived at Valley View in January 2006 along with Dr. Gina Brown, Mrs. Minnie McNeil, and members of the administration. They spent two weeks meeting with the Ghana Education Board and the Nurses and Midwives Council. They received the criteria for starting a new program and began to prepare the required documents, including the nursing curriculum.

They also needed to discuss erecting a building to house the program. Several meetings were held with the librarian, Mrs. Vida Mensah, and the registrar, Mr. Okyere-Darko. The vice president for academics, Dr. Swansi, and his staff were very supportive and allowed them access to their computers and duplicating machine.

The Columbia Union Conference, under Dr. Harold Lee, provided part of the funding for the erection of the three-story building to house the nursing program. Other requirements included a skills lab, which was equipped by Loma Linda University and Johnson and Johnson, and a separate nursing library. Books for the library were donated by Oakwood University's Department of Nursing and Loma Linda University. Other funding for the building and laboratory supplies was received thanks to the generosity of Dr. Andrew Clerk, a dentist and native Ghanaian living in California.

Lydia returned to the States and began making plans to move to Ghana. They would be spending another five years overseas. This time God again made it possible for them to keep their home. Their daughter was again available to move in with her young son, since her military husband was being sent on a single assignment to Korea and could not take his family. Lydia and Newton arrived in Accra, Ghana, in November 2006 and traveled one hour by road to the campus, which is located along a main highway. Lydia immediately started classes at the Nursing Council to obtain her license to practice in Ghana. Two months of clinical rotation was done at Ridge Hospital followed by a written examination. Unlike Kenya the climate in Ghana is hot and humid. The Andrews occupied a large four-bedroom house with two baths and all modern appliances—refrigerator, microwave, washer, gas range, hot and cold water. There was a ceiling fan in each room and in the master bedroom was an air-conditioning unit. Almost everyone in Ghana owns a cell phone. Laptops are also common, even among students.

The building was finally completed, nursing faculty were hired, and a date was announced for the nursing council to make their site visit to see whether all criteria and specifications were met before granting permission to begin the program. All went well and advertising for the program began in late June 2007. Also in June two other nurses came from the States to assist in preparing the final documents. They were Afriye Johnson who was born in Ghana to missionary parents and Kathleen Farrell. Students were interviewed in July and August, and the first class of nursing students began the bachelor's degree in nursing program in September 2007.

There are many challenges when starting a new program, but a nursing program presents additional challenges such as finding clinical sites in various hospitals, arranging transportation for students to clinical sites, partnering with faculty and hospital staff from other institutions, and finding adjunct faculty to teach nursing courses as well as science courses required for nursing students. Lydia also prepared the syllabus for each nursing course in the curriculum, including the science courses. Valley View University did not offer any science courses. Lydia was appointed head of the Department of Nursing.

Newton was given a local appointment in the Counseling Department. His position was probably misunderstood because he frequently received requests from students and/or parents for financial assistance. On one occasion a student requested funds for medication. About one week later he came to their home to thank Newton, and the couple offered him a meal. The student obviously felt comfortable in their company and decided to share his story. His native country was Rwanda, which he had left because of the genocide. He had been nine years old when the rebels came to his home. He hid in the attic, and when they left he came down to find all the other members of his family lying dead in the house. He began wandering in the streets until a kind lady took him to a refugee camp. He was later taken to South Africa where he completed high school. Somehow an Uncle found him and sent him to a Muslim school in Ghana. While in Ghana he was browsing on the Internet and found Valley View University. He visited and liked what he saw. He transferred to the university, but when his uncle found out, he stopped all support. He was later baptized.

In Kenya Lydia and Newton were allowed to return home on furlough every two years. By the time they went to Ghana the policy had changed to an annual leave. During those times the Andrews were frequently asked to speak in various churches at which time they made appeals for needy students as well as recruiting faculty. On one occasion they presented the case of the student from Rwanda and received enough funds for him to complete his computer program. At present he is employed at the Rwandan embassy in Nigeria.

During their physical examination before leaving the United States, Newton was told by his physician that he needed a checkup every six months. As a nurse Lydia became very concerned, and they made arrangements accordingly. However, in African culture health is not a priority. There is no such thing as yearly physicals. If someone is not bleeding or in pain there is no need to visit a doctor. As a result many people just die suddenly, which is sometimes attributed to witchcraft. Therefore, Newton sought permission from the administration to visit his doctor in the States twice a year. These visits were scheduled during the summer and Christmas when the school was on break. During the summer they took their paid annual leave, and for the Christmas visit they paid their own expenses. However, the administration felt that they were traveling too much, and the Andrews began to feel very uncomfortable about the situation. Finally, in the interest of

Newton's health and the stress Lydia was experiencing, after three years they decided to request permanent return.

Along with the nursing program responsibilities, Lydia was required to attend various administrative committee meetings, travel, mentor new faculty, and prepare for accreditation. She spent long hours at the office, which affected her health and she contracted malaria. Many students came to assist her in their home during this time. Their home was always open and inviting to anyone in need. One semester they allowed two male students to live in their home because they were unable to pay dormitory expenses. They also provided housework for female students who needed funds for books or off-campus rent. One such student who was being sponsored by the Andrews was advised to change her major to international studies. She did so and graduated in 2012 and now works with ADRA in her country of Burkina Faso. Ghana is surrounded by French countries, and students who attend Valley View come from many West African French-speaking countries.

In July 2009 Valley View University and the Department of Nursing hosted a group of medical professionals who came from New York to present a nursing conference. The leader of the team was Mrs. Kathleen Farrell. There were more than 300 attendees from all ten regions in Ghana. Many officials from the Ministry of Health and the SDA Health Ministries were in attendance. The majority of attendees were nurses who received continuing education credits toward the renewal of their nursing license. A similar conference was held in 2012. The group also held two conferences in Nigeria at Babcock University.

After their request for permanent return was granted, the Andrews sold most of their household items, including their vehicle, and returned to the States in September 2009. In November 2011 Lydia returned to Ghana with a team of ten ladies, including the registrar from Oakwood University, Mrs. Henrietta Lathon, to attend the graduation of the first class of nursing students. There were fifteen nursing students, eleven females and four males, among over 600 graduates. Lydia was the speaker for the dedication ceremony. Oakwood University also presented each student with an Oakwood bag and a medallion, as well as giving the president of Valley View a quilt with the story of Oakwood on it. Oakwood's Nursing Department donated the lamps for the candlelighting ceremony. Mrs. Ruth Swan, sister of Mrs. Minnie McNeil who visited Valley View some years ago, collected funds from her Sabbath School class in Florida to provide stethoscopes for each one of the nursing students. It was a very beautiful occasion that will be forever remembered.

The Andrews feel blessed to have given service in the motherland, and they continue to encourage young people to use their talents to glorify God. They enjoy spending time with their four grandsons, three of whom live in Huntsville. Lydia continues to go on yearly mission trips with the Office of Spiritual Life at Oakwood University. In 2012 they went to Malawi and 2013 to Madagascar. She also serves in the Nursing Department at Oakwood University whenever she is called upon as an adjunct professor or as a clinical instructor. Recently she was appointed as interim chairperson.

They have no regrets about their time spent in mission service and look forward to many wonderful years of retirement. To God be the glory!

Throughout her life Lydia Andrews experienced a series of "firsts." She was the first among her twelve siblings to migrate to the United States. She graduated in the first class of the bachelor of nursing degree program at Howard University in 1973. She graduated in the first class of the midwifery certificate program at Georgetown University. She was the first black student to graduate with a master's degree in midwifery from the University of Alabama, Birmingham. She joined the faculty at the University of Eastern Africa, Baraton, which was the first to start a bachelor of nursing degree program in Kenya. And she started the first bachelor of nursing degree program at Valley View University, Ghana, and became its first director of nursing. God used Lydia to accomplish great things for Him during her career.

Pastor Newton and Lydia Andrews in their academic attire at a Valley View University graduation ceremony, Ghana

Arrival of Lydia and Newton Andrews at Baraton— they were met at the airport by Naomi Bullard and Dr. Maradufu, dean of health sciences.

Team who came to accreditate Valley View University in Ghana: Lisa Beardsley and Dr. Johnson in center

A group of Muslim students who attended Valley View University

Lydia with a group of nursing students who were attending an international conference in Accra during a nurses and midwife conference

Lydia at the home of Mrs. Lagat, one of the teachers, trying to milk a cow—this was her first and last attempt at this feat.

Mrs. Minnie McNeil presenting one of her nursing students with a stethoscope donated by her sister, Ruth Swan, from Florida. Mrs. McNeil was one of the participants who helped in the training of the first graduating class.

A well-trained automatic milk carrying donkey on the campus of UEAB resting in front of the nursing building. The donkey gets the milk daily from the farm and delivers it without anyone guiding him. When they load his cart at the farm, he goes directly to the cafeteria with the milk and then returns to the farm for the second load.

Traditional birth attendants from a nearby village talking with the nursing students on campus at Baraton in an effort to upgrade their skills.

Attending a Ghanaian funeral of one of the conference workers. The men dress in a solid piece of cloth wrapped in a special way for the funeral. They don't wear shoes with this attire. They may also wear this garb for special occasions.

The first class of nursing graduates at Valley View University

A group of students and members during a health fair and temperance parade listening to the mayor and city officials.

91

MAXWELL AND DESIREE BLAKENEY

1998–2005 / Zimbabwe

The Blakeney's inter-division service began when they accepted the call for Maxwell to serve as associate director of the General Conference Auditing Service (GCAS) in the Eastern Africa Division with headquarters in Harare, Zimbabwe.

Maxwell began working for the church in July 1967 after graduating with an associate of arts degree in accounting from Caribbean Union College. He worked as the accountant at Davis Memorial Hospital in his native Guyana until 1970 when he was transferred to the Guyana Mission where he served briefly as manager of the book center and accountant of the mission. He and Desiree, a registered nurse, were married in March 1971, and he was appointed youth director of the Guyana Conference in 1972. In 1973 he was ordained to the gospel ministry.

Maxwell served briefly as the business manager of Davis Memorial Hospital in 1975 and 1976 before they left for West Indies College in Jamaica where he completed a bachelor's degree in business and Desiree worked on the staff of the Mandeville hospital. After Maxwell's graduation they proceeded to Andrews University where he completed a master's degree in business administration. They returned to Guyana in January 1980 where they both worked at Davis Memorial Hospital, he as administrator and she as staff nurse.

Service outside of Guyana began in 1983 when Maxwell accepted the call to serve as vice president for finance at Caribbean Union College. In July 1986 Maxwell was appointed as a staff auditor of GCAS and stationed in St. Croix in the U.S. Virgin Islands. From there he worked on audits in the Caribbean Islands and Mexico, while she served as secretary of the SDA Academy in St. Croix until 1998 when they moved to Zimbabwe in response to another GCAS appointment.

After their marriage in 1971 they were blessed with three children: Melissa, Deann, and Maxwell. Melissa had completed college by the time they transferred to Africa. Deann was in her second year at college, and Paul graduated from high school in the same year and began his freshman year of college. None of the children lived with them in Africa but all visited during their period of service there.

The Eastern Africa Division comprised the countries of Ethiopia, Kenya, Uganda, Tanzania, Zambia, Zimbabwe, Malawi, and Botswana in 1998, and Maxwell's assignment was to supervise a group of ten staff auditors performing audits of church organizations in those countries. All of the auditors were male, and none was a certified accountant. Later the assignment was enlarged to include the staff in the Africa-Indian Ocean Division and countries from Liberia to Angola in West Africa, as well as those in Central Africa along with Madagascar and other islands in the

Indian Ocean. The staff was increased to twenty-two men and now included one chartered accountant from Ghana. The two divisions were merged in 2004. During this period Desiree worked in an Orthodontic Clinic in Zimbabwe for two years before transferring to the division office as a departmental administrative assistant.

The primary concern of Maxwell's supervision was to implement the GCAS aim of improving the professional quality of its audits internationally by training and recruiting staff capable of becoming certified accountants. The Blakeneys returned to the United States after their work in Africa, but Maxwell continued to supervise the auditors from the General Conference headquarters in Silver Spring, Maryland. By the end of 2008 the staff in Africa included ten staff members who were certified accountants and several others who were in the process of completing their certification. There were also four women on the staff, two of whom were among those who were certified accountants. Three of the staff certifications were country specific in Africa, and the others were from international bodies, including seven with Association of Chartered Certified Accountants (ACCA) certification. A member of the staff with whom he began in 1998, and who completed ACCA certification while in service, was appointed area director for the divisions in Africa in 2010.

In addition to their assigned duties, Maxwell and Desiree actively participated in the process of leadership from the division office. She was a regular presenter in the division office and at local congregations, primarily speaking about the inclusion of women in leadership of the church. He employed his pastoral skills as a speaker in evangelistic meetings in Zimbabwe, also at union and conference sessions, committee meetings, camp meetings, weeks-of-prayer, and seminars in many of the countries of the

divisions in which they served. They developed many relationships with local African church members and leaders as well as with other missionaries in Africa from the Philippines, India, Europe, and the United States.

(Left to right) Leonidas and Anita Ayivi-Togbassa, Philippe and Christine Agbovor, Furaha and Fifi Mpozembizi, Maxwell and Desiree Blakeney. Leonidas completed ACCA certification in service and is now a regional manager of GCAS in Africa. Philippe completed ACCA certification in service and served as GCAS area director for ECD. Furaha completed ACCA certification in service and is now director of the Southern Africa-Indian Ocean Division of GCAS.

Francisca Anti was recruited in Ghana as a university graduate with an accounting degree. She was single then. She is now a mother of two and works as a staff auditor for GCAS out of the London office of the Trans European area of GCAS.

Delilah Mutai (née Migwa) and family—Delilah was recruited immediately after graduation from UEAB. She was Migwa then. She married and is raising a family with her husband. She is now ACCA certified, having studied in service. GCAS accommodated Delilah during her pregnancies and the infancy of her children so that she could continue working.

Maxwell and Desiree Blakeney with Danforth and Verna Francis of Barbados and Antigua, respectively, in front of the East Africa Union office while attending Mission Institute in Kenya

Tahina Ramandimbiarison (and husband) was recruited in Madagascar and is currently working toward ACCA certification.

The fourth woman recruited was called from the staff of EAD. Her name is Joy Mokotedi (née Mliswa). She is now a mother of one, internationally certified, and a regional manager for GCAS in Africa.

92
CARL AND DEBORAH MACKENZIE

1999–2000 / Kenya

Carl Liscott MacKenzie was born in New York although his mother was from Bermuda. He did his undergraduate work at the University of California, Riverside, and lived there for two years. He later attended Howard University Dental School where he met Deborah who would soon become his wife. They set up a dental practice in Maryland but sold it when they received a call to go to the mission field. He and his wife, Deborah, who was also a dentist served in the Adventist Health Services clinic in Nairobi, Kenya. They left for Kenya in 1999 and took their two children with them. One child attended Maxwell Academy, and the other son attended a private Christian school.

The dental clinic was in the city of Kenya on the conference grounds. They often arranged to go to nearby villages and set up a free dental clinic for those who were unable to come to the city. Dr. MacKenzie also visited many churches on the weekends, preaching and bringing encouragement to the members. He also visited the University of Eastern Africa and preached there and in some of the surrounding churches. The MacKenzies lived fairly close to the clinic.

The family was devastated by the bombing of the U.S. embassy that took place while they were there. One of Deborah's closest friends was killed in the bombing, and she became very depressed after that. She found it necessary to return to the States several times to recharge her spirits. When her good friend, the treasurer of the conference, and his family returned to the States, she felt she needed to return also. So after a short stay of two years, the MacKenzies returned to the States. Dr. MacKenzie feels that those two years in Kenya were the best and most productive years of his life.

Carl is very active in their church in Bermuda and serves on the board of the conference.

Their children are grown now, and their daughter is following in their footsteps and attending Howard University dental school. They now practice dentistry in Bermuda.

93

KENNETH AND BELYNDA MULZAC

2000–2005 / Philippines

Kenneth D. Mulzac earned a bachelor's degree in theology and psychology from Columbia Union College in Maryland in 1985. In 1988 he earned a master of divinity degree, and in 1995 he earned a doctor of philosophy degree, both from Andrews University.

He served as associate professor of Christian Ministry at the Seventh-day Adventist Theological Seminary at Andrews University in Berrien Springs, Michigan, and pastored the Highland Seventh-day Adventist Church in Benton Harbor, Michigan.

Before joining the seminary faculty in 2006, Mulzac served as associate professor at the Adventist International Institute of Advanced Studies (AIIAS) in the Philippines from 2000 to 2005 and Oakwood University in Alabama from 1995 to 2000.

It was a shock to the students and faculty alike when he died on July 23, 2008, at Lakeland Hospital in St. Joseph, Michigan, following a long illness. He was forty-five.

"Ken Mulzac came to Andrews University to teach preaching, but sadly, he barely had a chance to share his many gifts with our seminary students. We will greatly miss Ken and all he had to offer the students, staff, and faculty at Andrews University," said Niels-Erik Andreasen, president of Andrews University.

During his career Mulzac published a number of scholarly books and articles on Old Testament prophets and other biblical themes. He also authored several articles in the Eerdmans Dictionary of the Bible, which was published in 2000. Mulzac was a well-known speaker and preacher and was often invited to speak at international conferences, congresses, and churches.

Students appreciated him for his passionate teaching and personal care. The Pilipino community where the Mulzacs worked for five years were shocked to hear this news and issued the following statement, which appeared in the July 2008 edition of *AIIAS Highlights*:

"Those of the AIIAS community who either worked or studied with Dr. Kenneth Mulzac in the time that he served here from 2000 – 2005 were deeply saddened to receive the news this last Thursday of his untimely passing on July 23. It was while Dr. Mulzac was here as a Seminary professor that he was diagnosed with bone cancer in his leg.

"He, with his family, took permanent return to the US, where Dr. Mulzac was appointed to Andrews University Seventh-day Adventist Theological Seminary in Berrien Springs, Michigan, as an associate professor of Christian Ministry. He also pastored the Highland Seventh-day Adventist Church in Benton Harbor, nearby. While receiving specialist treatment, secondary tumors were discovered in a lung, and despite a valiant struggle on his part, our beloved colleague has passed away. Ken is remembered for his exuberant, warm, generous nature, inspirational preaching and teaching, and scholarly work. He will be greatly missed. Our sympathy and prayers are extended to his wife Belynda, who taught in the AIIAS English Center, while also accomplishing an MPH degree from AIIAS, and a Doctorate of Public Health from AUP; and his two daughters Breanda and Karla, whom he showed great affection for."

Belynda Mulzac

Ken Mulzac

94
FRED AND BIRDIE WILLIAMS

2001–2008 / Hong Kong

Fred A. Williams was born in Butler County, Pennsylvania, and grew up in the city of Pittsburgh where the family of three siblings, along with his mother and father, attended the Ethnan Temple Seventh-day Adventist Church. During his high school years at a public high school, Fred was an outstanding basketball player. In 1958 when the state championship game was scheduled to play on Friday night, he refused to play and was ridiculed by students and staff. After graduating from Westinghouse High School that same year, he matriculated to Oakwood College in Huntsville, Alabama.

At Oakwood Fred majored in religion with a history minor. It was there that he met Birdie Wright from Chicago, Illinois. Birdie was a new Adventist. In 1957 Birdie, along with an older sister and grandmother, was baptized into the Seventh-day Adventist Church during a tent meeting conducted by Elder E. E. Cleveland in Chicago. In 1959 Birdie became a student at Oakwood College where she majored in elementary education.

Having completed their studies in Huntsville in 1963, Fred and Birdie returned to Chicago where Birdie obtained a job in the public school system as an elementary school teacher. Fred worked as a youth pastor under the guidance of Elder Samuel D. Meyers, pastor of Shiloh SDA Church. In December of 1963, Fred and Birdie were united in marriage by their former college professor Elder C. T. Richards. Following their marriage, the Lake Region Conference sponsored them to attend Andrews University in Berrien Springs, Michigan.

After completing his studies at the seminary and the birth of their first child in 1965, Fred was assigned as an associate youth pastor at the Burns Avenue SDA Church in Detroit, under the tutelage of Elder Franklin S. Hill. While in Detroit, Fred also had the responsibility of working with a fledgling church, the Essex Company, which was the offspring of Burns Avenue's outreach endeavor. Fred pastored in several other areas of the conference, and with his talented and supportive wife, he was successful in his pastoral leadership.

It was the summer of 1971 during the annual Lake Region camp meeting that Fred was ordained to the gospel ministry under the guidance of Elder C. E. Bradford, president. That same summer during a conference constituency meeting, Fred was invited to serve as the conference youth director and communications director. Birdie left her teaching profession and came to work in the conference as her husband's. Under their leadership, the youth work blossomed around the conference: the Pathfinder program grew; Youth Federations were more frequent; and youth leadership training programs took place on a regular basis. Relevant articles on the work and growth of the conference were submitted to the union paper, the *Lake Union Herald*. During their leadership, more basketball teams were formed among the churches, and the Christian Fellowship League was organized, which is still in operation. This program was a way for the Missionary Volunteer Societies to share their faith in the community.

After seven years of serving in the Lake Region Conference, Fred was invited to serve as the associate youth director, with emphasis on leading the Pathfinder organization, for Northern California, in Pleasant Hill, California. After prayer and consultation with President Jesse Wagner, Fred and Birdie and their three children accepted the call and moved to Concord, California. Birdie began teaching at Golden Gate Academy (GGA) in Oakland.

The conference area coordinators for the Pathfinder work were well-organized. The hundreds of volunteers working with the young people strengthened the Pathfinder clubs and made them an integral arm of the many churches. Camporees, fairs, bicycle marathons, and church school promotions of junior-age activities contributed greatly to a healthy organization for the church's young people. Training seminars contributed to the Northern California Conference having the largest number of Pathfinders in the North American Division.

In 1985 Fred began to think of other areas of ministry. At the suggestion of a friend, he looked into chaplaincy. After completing the required Clinical Pastoral Education (CPE) training, he was assigned to the Veterans Hospital and Merrithew Community Hospital for training in patient care. In 1987 Fred accepted a call to the Eastern Oregon Psychiatric Hospital in Pendleton, Oregon. Birdie, now principal of GGA, and their children chose to stay in Oakland. After two years state funding became an issue in the operating of the facility, and

the chaplaincy position along with others was cut. At the same time a job announcement was posted for a Protestant chaplain at the Oregon State Penitentiary located in Salem. Fred applied for the position and was hired. With this job change, Birdie decided to leave her position, and the family moved to Oregon. Fred began his duties as prison chaplain, and Birdie obtained a teaching position with the Oregon Conference at Portland Adventist Academy.

In 1997 Fred received a call from Richard Bland, founder and president of United Prison Ministries, expressing the need for a chaplain to direct spiritual programs for a new prison. He explained that a Bakersfield, California, Adventist contractor had built a prison in Adelanto, California, with the intent of offering prison inmates the choice of learning a healthful lifestyle we know as the WEIMAR diet. It was a vegan diet that would contrast the regular state menu. Inmates would have the option to enroll in the special program or to follow the regular prison program. This was a totally new concept of prison management for the state of California, and Fred was eager to accept the challenge. Fred and family moved to Southern California. However, the prison was not able to sustain this special program, and after two years, the prison program came to an end in January 2001.

Unemployed for the first time in his career, Fred served as a volunteer chaplain for St. Mary's Medical Center in Apple Valley, California. A few months later he received a call from Elder Ted Jones, General Conference field secretary responsible for the work in the Northern Asia Pacific Division, saying a search was underway for a lead chaplain for two Adventist hospitals in Hong Kong. Feeling that this was a fulfillment of a long-held dream of serving the church as a missionary, and after prayer and consultation with their family, they felt that this indeed was a call in answer to their prayers for a place of service. On February 14, 2002, they arrived in Hong Kong.

Hong Kong Adventist Hospital and Heart Center was an international hospital actually composed of two hospitals. The first hospital opened in 1964 in Tsuen Wan, a satellite town of Hong Kong. Tsuen Wan Hospital was mainly a hospital for Chinese patients. On May 4, 1971, the second hospital, Hong Kong Adventist Hospital, was opened on Hong Kong Island. It is a circular shaped, eight-story steel and concrete building. Many modern additions had been added to both buildings. Both hospitals are respected and have a very distinguished clientele. Hong Kong Adventist Hospital caters to Americans, diplomats, businessmen, and government officials. The Williams family lived and worked at the Hong Kong Adventist Hospital.

Pastor Williams served as chaplain at both hospitals. His main responsibility was to build the spiritual atmosphere and train a core of Chinese chaplains. Jesus said, "I was sick, and you visited Me." Chaplain Williams visited many of the patients in the hospital and provided devotional services for the staff. He successfully brought the 3ABN channel via satellite to the hospital rooms for additional spiritual help.

Chaplain Fred took up his duties of supervising the Chinese chaplains working in the hospitals, and under the guidance of hospital administrator and CEO, Dr. Y. C. Wong, he worked with the staff to develop programs to enhance the spiritual climate of the hospitals. One of the innovative services developed was an annual Thanksgiving service. In conjunction with the holiday celebrated in the United States, the chaplain's office planned a service of music and the spoken word, featuring messages of thankfulness by various staff persons.

Part of the work of the chaplain is to be on call in times of trauma and grief. When the area was hit by a tsunami, the chaplains were available and worked with local Adventist Community Service agencies and ADRA International to bring relief to the many grief stricken citizens. They were later joined by Loma Linda University's trauma response team. This represented the best of Adventist Chaplaincy Ministry and the Adventist Church in going where the people were and following Christ's method of ministry.

Yearly the gospel seed was planted in millions of hearts and untold goodwill was generated toward the church. All of this is done at very low cost to the church since the chaplains' salaries were being paid for by the hospital.

Clinically trained full-time chaplains are on call twenty-four hours a day, seven days a week to offer spiritual and emotional support to patients, family members, and staff at critical moments of their lives. This service extends to patients' family members and staff regardless of their religious background. When the patient is anxious, angry, lonely, or depressed, such emotions can negatively affect his or her physical health. The chaplain sees that each patients' spiritual and emotional needs have been met.

Ministry to the Chinese was very difficult. The Chinese pastors were not used to sharing their faith and doing evangelistic work. They were not particularly interested in bringing new people into the church. One program that Chaplain Williams began was to work with mothers who delivered babies. When an expectant mother came into the hospital and was from the territory of a particular church, the chaplains contacted the pastor who would encourage that mother and her family to visit their church.

A special gift Bible and other well baby literature was given to new mothers. One young mother had never heard of a Bible or read one. However, during her stay at the hospital, she completely read through the New Testament. She was fascinated to learn the story of Jesus.

Birdie was employed in the outpatient department of Hong Kong Hospital. Language was not a problem because the majority of Chinese in Hong Kong speak English.

During the six years of their stay in Hong Kong, Chaplain Fred, along with his hospital duties, assisted in the hospital church as well as worked with the Filipino Adventist overseas workers. After their years of service in the North Pacific Asia Division, the Fred and Birdie returned to the States in May 2008 and retired near Oakwood University. Chaplain Fred's favorite Bible text is a verse that he said guided their spiritual journey throughout their years of ministry: "In all thy ways acknowledge Him, and He will direct thy path" (Proverbs 3:6).

Fred and Birdie Williams

95
TIMOTHY AND BEVERLY MCDONALD

2003–2007 / Kenya

R. Timothy McDonald was born and reared in Pittsburgh, Pennsylvania, the oldest of four children born to Ralph and Harriett McDonald. When he was a teenager, the family joined the Seventh-day Adventist Church as the result of an evangelistic campaign.

Tim graduated from Oakwood College in 1963 with a bachelor's degree in elementary education; from Atlanta University with a master's degree in education and supervision; and from the University of Miami with a doctorate in higher education administration.

Tim met Beverly Clark, who was originally from Dayton, Ohio, and was swept off of his feet. They were married in October 1964. They have four adult children: Lawana, Monica, Lanita, Patrick, and eight grandchildren.

Dr. McDonald has served at all levels of education within the Adventist Church and at secular institutions as well. He currently serves as provost and senior vice president at Oakwood University. Previously he worked at Oakwood as director of the Adult and Continuing Education Program (LEAP). Other administrative posts included vice president for information technology and vice president of advancement and development at Oakwood University; director of development at Morehouse School of Medicine; director of development at Baltimore County Community College; and director of program development, research, and evaluation

of Ohio State University.

Earlier, he served as director of education for the Columbia Union Conference and vice president for academic affairs at Barber Scotia College. He has also worked as a teacher and principal in several places, including Greater Atlanta Adventist Academy, DuPont Park School in Washington, D.C., and the Larchwood School in Philadelphia, Pennsylvania.

The McDonalds were called to Africa in 2003. Dr. McDonald accepted the position of vice chancellor of the University of Eastern Africa, Baraton (UEAB), which is the equivalent of being the president of the university. Mrs. McDonald served as dean of the School of Education, taught a class in quilting, and was the editor of the university bulletin/catalog.

Alice was a Kenyan young woman who developed a relationship with Beverly McDonald. Alice was one of the young ladies who swept the floors in several of the buildings on the campus. Beverly kept a close eye on this young woman, for she perceived that Alice was a very smart young person and should be attending school rather than sweeping the floors of the school. Although Alice was a Christian, she kept company with and was very intimate with Paul, a Christian young man who lived nearby. Paul and Alice were not married, but they had a child together.

Beverly mentored and instructed these two

young people for a long time and let them know that they needed to be married or they would be living in sin. She pointed out what the Bible says about marriage and what the church taught. The McDonalds established a very good relationship with the couple, and over time Alice and Paul came to see that they would be better off if they blended their lives in a permanent bond. They agreed to get married. The news spread across the campus along with the reasons they were getting married.

The appointed Sunday when the pastor of the church arrived to marry Alice and Paul, there were twenty-four other couples who wanted to get married. Instead of marrying just one couple, the pastor performed a ceremony for a total of twenty-five couples who formerly had been living together who now had decided to change their way of life and commit to the Lord and each other in marriage! The whole community was blessed by the decision of one couple to do the right thing.

Dr. McDonald was the vice chancellor at the university when it celebrated its twenty-fifth anniversary. UEAB came into existence in 1980 when the school in Lebanon closed down because of war and was moved to Kenya. Then President Daniel arap Moi gave a plot of land to the Adventist Church, which was quite controversial. Many Kenyans felt that it was not proper to give land to a church organization, but President Moi held the Adventist Church in high esteem and insisted on the donation.

UEAB is now accredited and legally chartered by the government of Kenya as well as the board of regents of the General Conference. Its rural campus, five hours by car from Nairobi, is an appealing campus graced by stately trees and modern buildings. UEAB provides advanced degrees to Kenyans and also serves the entire Eastern Africa region. Students come from many places and the faculty and teaching staff is equally diverse. This cosmopolitan church resembles the multi ethnicity of the Adventist Church. Approximately 50 percent of the student body are non-Adventist, thus providing the school with great evangelism potential.

Dr. McDonald invited all the former vice chancellors to be present, including Dr. Roland McKenzie and Dr. Matuko Mutinga, as well as former students and alumni. Dr. McDonald went to Daniel arap Moi's private mansion and invited him to be present at the occasion. He had retired from office three years earlier and was no longer the president of the country but was still very popular and well known. His respect for the Adventist Church was so great that he agreed to come and be a speaker for this special occasion. A new science building, medical center, humanities building, and dormitory had just been completed. Special funds came from USAID to build a new training center.

The highlight of the service was seeing Daniel arap Moi fly onto the campus in his private plane surrounded by a retinue of officials and security people. Thousands of Kenyans from miles around came to see him and celebrate the twenty-fifth anniversary with their friends the Adventists. Moi was treated royally by the university and presented with all kinds of gifts and mementoes. By now the school had grown to about 2,000 students and about 200 faculty and staff and was probably one of the best-known institutions of learning in the entire country.

Dr. McDonald impersonating Lawrence of Arabia on vacation in Egypt

Dr. McDonald surrounded by a group of visitors to the University of Eastern Africa, Baraton

Dr. and Mrs. McDonald enjoying the beauty and mystery of the pyramids during their Egyptian vacation

Dr. McDonald on safari with Peter, his loyal driver, and a fascinating Masai warrior giving a tribal blessing

Mrs. Beverly McDonald enjoying an afternoon visit to the traditional home of Alice, one of her students, and Paul and their children

Dr. McDonald dressed up as a royal African prince about to "address his subjects".

Dr. McDonald with former Kenyan President Daniel arap Moi touring the campus during the silver anniversary celebration

ALPHABETICAL LISTING OF AFRICAN AMERICAN MISSIONARIES

There were many African Americans sent out from the Inter-American Division and Europe who also served as missionaries. This list includes only those with permanent residence in the North American Division (NAD) or citizens of NAD countries (United States, Canada, Bermuda).

I have not made Bermuda a mission field. It was a mission when Alvin Goulbourne was a missionary there in 1957, but in 1959 Bermuda was officially organized and became a part of the Atlantic Union, thus a part of the NAD. Except for Alvin Goulbourne, I did not include anyone who worked in Bermuda, Hawaii, or Alaska.

In some instances, I was not sure if missionaries were sent out under the Inter-American Division (IAD) or the NAD. Some lived and worked in both places. If they retired, and since retirement, are not living in the NAD but are living in the IAD, I did *NOT* include them.

There were many who volunteered for special service and volunteer service for a short period, and there were many student missionaries; however, these are not included here. Included here are those who served for more than a year outside of the North American Division.

Last names are in bold. Single women who served before they were married will show their maiden name in bold followed by their married name in regular type (i.e. Ruth Faye **Smith** Davis). Many missionaries have doctorates in various fields. In these two lists, I only used the term "Dr." to designate medical personnel.

Those with an asterisk (*) in front of the name were included in the first book and are not detailed in this second book. Their names are on the list so that we can get a complete picture of those who served as missionaries. Those who served before 1920 will be detailed again in book two since I have more information on them.

*Benjamin W. and Celia **Abney**	South Africa	1931–1938
Roy and Celia **Adams**	Philippines	1981–1986
Dolly **Alexander**-Johnson	Zambia, Rwanda, Ethiopia	1965–1967, 1970–1972, 1975–1979
Disciple and Ninon **Amertil**	Zaire, Ghana	1984–1986, 2013–
Newton and Lydia **Andrews**	Kenya, Ghana	1998–2004, 2006–2009

Robert T. and Cordelia **Andrews**	Jamaica	1969–1978
*Lloyd G. and Etta **Antonio**	Ghana	1979–1984
Edna Pearlie **Atkins** Thomas	Sierra Leone	1979–1981
*G. Nathaniel and Etta **Banks**	Liberia	1945–1952
*Maurice T. and Esther **Battle**	Liberia, Sierra Leone,	
	Ghana, England, Lebanon	1956–1979
Dr. George and Lois **Benson**	Libya, Ethiopia	1967–1970
Dr. David and Dr. Lottie **Blake**	Panama, Haiti	1913–1917
Maxwell and Desiree **Blakeney**	Zimbabwe	1998–2005
*Mabel **Branch** Webb	Malawi	1902–1908
*Thomas and Henrietta **Branch**	Malawi	1902–1908
Elysee D. and Alice **Brantley**	Jamaica	1969–1972
Goldson and Rita **Brown**	Ethiopia	1983–1987
*Benjamin and Janice **Browne**	Ethiopia	2001–2005
Lambert Wellington **Browne**	Sierra Leone	1906–1908
Paul and Patricia **Bryant**	Ghana, Sierra Leone	1990–1995
Howard and Lois **Bullard**	Mexico	1993–1995
Naomi **Bullard**	Rwanda	1967–1982
Karen A. **Burke** Bright	Ivory Coast	1981–1984
William and Cynthia **Burns**	Rwanda, Ivory Coast, Ethiopia	1971–1974,
		1985–1988
Art and Hope **Bushnell**	Kenya	1980–1983
*Ken and Elizabeth **Bushnell**	Kenya, Uganda	1977–1987
Theodore and Frankie **Cantrell**	Liberia, Ghana, Nigeria	1955–1968
*Ray and Carol **Cantu**	Kenya	1987–1994
*Robert H. and Rose **Carter**	Uganda	1971–1972
*Harry and Beverly **Cartwright**	Sierra Leone, Kenya,	1974–1979
	Gambia, Zambia, Zimbabwe	1981–1986
Clyde and Barbara **Cassimy**	Kenya	1990–1996
J. Michelet and Elmire **Cherenfant**	Ivory Coast, Togo, Cameroon	1972–1986
Dr. Chauncey and Bernardine **Conner**	Cameroon	1987–1991
Dr. Byron and Alfredia **Conner**	Ethiopia	1984–1987
Donald L. and Carrie **Crowder**	Jamaica	1978–1982
Loretta **Daniels** Wassie	Ethiopia	1962–1966
Lucius and Naomi **Daniels**	Liberia	1957–1964
Daniel L. and Elizabeth **Davis**	Ivory Coast	1982–1983
Dr. Carl and Lavetta **Dent**	Kenya	1984–1987
*Dr. Samuel and Bernice **DeShay**	Nigeria, Sierra Leone	1961–1973
*Pierre and Jocelyn **Deshommes**	Ethiopia, Cameroon	1982–1986,
		1994–1998
*Edward and Dorothy **Dorsey**	Liberia	1979–1981

Irwin and Laura **Dulan**	Ethiopia	1977–1985
*James and Geraldine **Edgecombe**	Trinidad	1967–1970
Bruce and Pauline **Flynn**	England	1978–1984
Dr. Ronald and Dorothy **Forde**	Zaire, Zimbabwe	1983–1999
R. Danforth and Vera **Francis**	Madagascar	1991–2010
Sydney and Katherina **Gibbons**	Cameroon, Jamaica	1992-1998
		2000-2001
Boyd and Wanda **Gibson**	Kenya	1986–1992
*Philip E. and Violet **Giddings**	Ivory Coast, Liberia	1945–1954
		1964–1979
*Samuel and Elita **Gooden**	Nigeria	1963–1967
Claudienne **Gordon**	Nigeria	1958–1960
Oswald and Thelma **Gordon**	Liberia	1984–1990
*Alvin and Lucy **Goulbourne**	Bermuda	1959–1965
		1977–1986
Gretel **Graham** Ashley	Uganda	1957–1958
*Ruby Dolores **Graves**	Nigeria, Sierra Leone	1966–1970
Alfonzo and Estella **Greene**	Jamaica	1974–1977
*Eula **Gunther** Evans	Ghana	1964–1967
*James and Carol **Hammond**	Ghana, Sierra Leone	1961–1974
*Victor and Candice **Harewood**	Dubai	2002–
Helene **Harris**	Zambia	1976–1981
*Dunbar and Lorraine **Henri**	Liberia, Kenya, Ghana	1945–1973
Simon and Suzanne **Honore**	Rwanda	1980–1986
Glen and Winnie **Howell**	Ghana	1983–1985
Lucille **Hubert**	Guyana	1977–1978
George and Pearl Jean **Huggins**	Guatemala, Panama,	1981–1984
	Ghana, Liberia	1992–1998
*David and Jane **Hughes**	Liberia, Nigeria, England	1953–1967,
		1979–1982
William and Ruth **Hughes**	Tanzania	1991–1996
*Dr. James and Marian **Hyatt**	Ghana, Sierra Leone, Nigeria	1903–1907
Morris and Shirley **Iheanacho**	Nigeria	1975–1979
Caddie **Jackson** Howell	Nigeria	1961–1963
*Samuel and Sarah **Jackson**	Jamaica, Lebanon, Kenya	1973–1985
*Anita S. (Moreland) **James**	Palau, Koror	1992–1997
Alcega and Veronica **Jeanniton**	Zaire, Cameroon, Equatorial Guinea	1983–1999
Roland and Marie Solange **Joachim**	Ivory Coast, Burkina Faso, Sengal	1973–1996
	Cameroon, Ghana	
*Johnny and Ida **Johnson**	Liberia, Ghana, Nigeria	1957–1985
*Carol Ann **Jones**	Ethiopia	1962–1966

Ruby Lee **Jones**	Zimbabwe	1991–1992
*Theodore and Esther **Jones**	Indonesia, Uganda	1968–1971
		1974–1975
Gertrude **Jordan**	Kenya	1993–2002
*Dennis and Dorothy **Keith**	Sierra Leone, Korea	1967–1975
*Anna **Knight**	India	1901–1907
J. Parker and Waustella **Laurence**	Zambia, Zimbabwe	1978–1987
John and Mary **Lavender**	Tanzania	1980–1984
Errol and Pamela **Lawrence**	Liberia	1983–1990
*Harold and Barbara **Lee**	Trinidad	1968–1975
Celeste **Lewis**	Nigeria, Liberia	1960–1964
*Ronald and Marilyn **Lindsay**	Zimbabwe	1985–1990
Dr. Carl and Dr. Deborah **MacKenzie**	Kenya	1999–2000
Gloria **Mackson** Hemphill	Tanzania	1958–1961
*Jason and Carolyn **McCracken**	Brazil, South Africa	1975–1976
		1979–1986
Timothy and Beverly **McDonald**	Kenya	2003–2007
Monica **McKenzie**	Zaire	1977–1981
Roland L. and Lilia **McKenzie**	Nigeria, Zimbabwe, Kenya	1980–1991
Charles and Pattie **Miller**	Kenya	1980–1985
*Leland and Lottie **Mitchell**-Harris	Liberia	1959–1963
*Hannah **More** (not an African American)		
Dr. Alvin and Lois **Mottley**	Tanzania, Tobago	1980–1987,
		1999–2007
Ken and Belynda **Mulzac**	Philippines	2000–2005
Mishael and Ruth **Muze**	Zimbabwe, Kenya	1987–2001
Milton and Ivy **Nebblett**	Guyana	1963–1966
Craig and Janis **Newborn**	Kenya, Iran, Lebanon	1975–1989
Leonard and Ora **Newton**	Madagascar, Cameroon	1989–1995
Elliott C. and Sonia Marie **Osborne**	Kenya	1989–1991
Lester A. and Priscilla **Parkinson**	Zimbabwe, Kenya	1987–1997
*James E. **Patterson**	Jamaica, Barbados, Panama, Haiti	1892–1896
	Columbia	1910
*Robert and Barbara **Patterson**	Burundi	1980–1984
Delbert and Curdell **Pearman**	Sri Lanka, Lebanon, Ethiopia	1997–2008
Max and Eliane **Pierre**	Gabon, Cameroon	1991–1999
*John C. and Sarah **Pitts**	Sierra Leone	1971–1977
Phillip and Naomi **Polley**	Marshall Islands, Mali	1982–1984
		1996–2007
*Jerome and Yvonne **Pondexter**	Zaire	1981–1988
Robert S. and Janice **Pressley**	Nigeria	1981–1982

*Louis R. Jr and Janice **Preston**	England, Zimbabwe	1979–1991
*Lois **Raymond**	Sierra Leone	1966–1978
*Ruth **Rhone**	Rwanda	1976–1986
Dr. Earl and Ann **Richards**	Kenya	1973–1985
W. Ray and Joan **Ricketts**	Kenya	1990–1995
William R. and Hortense **Robinson**	Uganda	1957–1959
John and Dora E. **Rodgers**	Puerto Rico, Costa Rica	1967–1975, 1980–1991
Henry T. **Saulter**	Bahamas	1928–1929
Donald B. and Dorothy **Simons**	Sierra Leone	1947–1950
Richard W. and Ruth **Simons**	Liberia, Nigeria	1952–1960
*Ruth Faye **Smith** Davis	Ghana	1954–1957
Randolph and Debrah **Stafford**	Kenya, Zimbabwe	1983–1988
Douglas T. and Helena **Tate**	Liberia	1955–1957
*Clarence and Carol Baron **Thomas**	Brazil, Haiti	1971–1983
Lindsay and Dr. Evelyan **Thomas**	Ivory Coast	1964–1966
*Carmelita **Troy**	England, Cyprus, Lebanon	1989–1996
*Owen A. Jr. and Ann **Troy**	Sierra Leone, Ghana, Trinidad	1964–1966, 1972–1977
Herman and Phillipa **Vanderburg**	Liberia	1967–1969
James A. and Sarah **Washington**	Kenya	1987–1992
*Walton S. and Leola **Whaley**	Sierra Leone, Ghana, Ivory Coast	1968–1998
*DeWitt and Margaret **Williams**	Zaire, Burundi	1967–1972, 1979–1982
Fred and Birdie **Williams**	Hong Kong	2001–2008
Larry D. and Natalie **Word**	Ivory Coast	1980–1982
Ronald J. and Equilla **Wright**	Liberia, Kenya, Cameroon	1980–1990
Gosnell and Doreen **Yorke**	Kenya	1991–1997
Theus and Elisa **Young**	Tanzania	1978–1981

Chronological Listing of African American Missionaries

(* indicates that their biography appeared in vol. 1)

1.	*James E. **Patterson**	Jamaica, Barbados, Panama, Haiti	1892–1896
		Columbia	1910
2.	*Anna **Knight**	India	1901–1907
3.	*Mabel **Branch** Webb	Malawi	1902–1908
4.	*Thomas and Henrietta **Branch**	Malawi	1902–1908
5.	* Dr.James and Marian **Hyatt**	Ghana, Sierra Leone, Nigeria	1903–1907
6.	Lambert Wellington **Browne**	Sierra Leone	1906–1908
7.	Dr. David and Dr. Lottie **Blake**	Panama, Haiti	1913–1917
8.	Henry T. **Saulter**	Bahamas	1928–1929
9.	*Benjamin W. and Celia **Abney**	South Africa	1931–1938
10.	*Nathaniel G. and Etta **Banks**	Liberia	1945–1952
11.	*Philip E. and Violet **Giddings**	Ivory Coast, Liberia	1945–1954, 1964–1979
12.	* Dunbar and Lorraine **Henri**	Liberia, Kenya, Ghana	1945–1973
13.	Donald B. and Dorothy **Simons**	Sierra Leone	1947–1950
14.	Richard W. and Ruth **Simons**	Liberia, Nigeria	1952–1960
15.	*David and Jane **Hughes**	Liberia, Nigeria, England	1953–1967; 1979–1982
16.	*Ruth Faye **Smith** Davis	Ghana	1954–1957
17.	Theodore and Frankie **Cantrell**	Liberia, Ghana, Nigeria	1955–1968
18.	Douglas T. and Helena **Tate**	Liberia	1955–1957
19.	*Maurice T. and Esther **Battle**	Liberia, Sierra Leone, Ghana, England, Lebanon	1956–1979
20.	Lucius and Naomi **Daniels**	Liberia	1957–1964
21.	Gretel **Graham** Ashley	Uganda	1957–1958
22.	*Johnny and Ida **Johnson**	Liberia, Ghana, and Nigeria	1957–1985
23.	William R. and Hortense **Robinson**	Uganda	1957–1959
24.	Claudienne **Gordon**	Nigeria	1958–1960
25.	Gloria **Mackson** Hemphill	Tanzania	1958–1961
26.	*Alvin and Lucy **Goulbourne**	Bermuda	1959–1965,

			1977–1986
27.	*Leland and Lottie **Mitchell**-Harris	Liberia	1959–1963
28.	Celeste **Lewis**	Nigeria, Liberia	1960–1964
29.	*Dr. Samuel and Bernice **DeShay**	Nigeria, Sierra Leone	1961–1973
30.	*James and Carol **Hammond**	Ghana, Sierra Leone	1961–1974
31.	Caddie **Jackson** Howell	Nigeria	1961–1963
32.	Loretta **Daniels** Wassie	Ethiopia	1962–1966
33.	*Carol Ann **Jones**	Ethiopia	1962–1966
34.	*Samuel and Elita **Gooden**	Nigeria	1963–1967
35.	Milton and Ivy **Nebblett**	Guyana	1963–1966
36.	*Eula **Gunther** Evans	Ghana	1964–1967
37.	Lindsay and Dr. Evelyan **Thomas**	Ivory Coast	1964–1966
38.	*Owen A. Jr. and Ann **Troy**	Sierra Leone, Ghana, Trinidad	1964–1966, 1972–1977
39.	Dolly **Alexander**-Johnson	Zambia, Rwanda, Ethiopia	1965–1967, 1970–1972, 1975–1979
40.	*Ruby Dolores **Graves**	Nigeria, Sierra Leone	1966–1970
41.	*Lois **Raymond**	Sierra Leone	1966–1978
42.	Dr. George and Lois **Benson**	Libya, Ethiopia	1967–1970
43.	Naomi **Bullard**	Rwanda	1967–1982
44.	*James and Geraldine **Edgecombe**	Trinidad	1967–1970
45.	*Dennis and Dorothy **Keith**	Sierra Leone, Korea	1967–1975
46.	John and Dora E. **Rodgers**	Puerto Rico, Costa Rica	1967–1979, 1980–1991
47.	Herman and Phillipa **Vanderburg**	Liberia	1967–1969
48.	*DeWitt and Margaret **Williams**	Zaire, Burundi	1967–1972, 1979–1982
49.	*Theodore and Esther **Jones**	Indonesia, Uganda	1968–1971, 1974–1975
50.	*Harold and Barbara **Lee**	Trinidad	1968–1975
51.	*Walton S. and Leola **Whaley**	Sierra Leone, Ghana, Ivory Coast	1968–1998
52.	Robert T. and Cordelia **Andrews**	Jamaica	1969–1978
53.	Elysee D. and Alice **Brantley**	Jamaica	1969–1972
54.	William and Cynthia **Burns**	Rwanda, Ivory Coast, Ethiopia	1971–1974, 1985–1988
55.	*Robert H. and Rose **Carter**	Uganda	1971–1972
56.	*John C. and Sarah **Pitts**	Sierra Leone	1971–1977
57.	*Clarence and Carol Baron **Thomas**	Brazil, Haiti	1971–1983
58.	J. Michelet and Elmire **Cherenfant**	Ivory Coast, Togo, Cameroon	1972–1986

59.	*Samuel and Sarah **Jackson**	Jamaica. Lebanon. Kenya	1973–1985
60.	Roland and Solange **Joachim**	Ivory Coast. Burkina Faso Senegal. Cameroon. Ghana	1973–1996
61.	Dr. Earl and Ann **Richards**	Kenya	1973–1985
62.	*Harry and Beverly **Cartwright**	Sierra Leone, Kenya, Gambia, Zambia. Zimbabwe	1974–1979 1981–1986
63.	Alfonzo and Estella **Greene**	Jamaica	1974–1977
64.	Morris and Shirley **Iheanacho**	Nigeria	1975–1979
65.	*Jason and Carolyn **McCracken**	Brazil, South Africa	1975–1976, 1979–1986
66.	Craig and Janis **Newborn**	Kenya, Iran. Lebanon	1975–1989
67.	Helene **Harris**	Zambia	1976–1981
68.	*Ruth **Rhone**	Rwanda	1976–1986
69.	*Ken and Elizabeth **Bushnell**	Kenya, Uganda	1977–1987
70.	Irwin and Laura **Dulan**	Ethiopia	1977–1985
71.	Lucille **Hubert**	Guyana	1977–1978
72.	Monica **McKenzie**	Zaire	1977–1981
73.	Donald L. and Carrie **Crowder**	Jamaica	1978–1982
74.	Bruce and Pauline **Flynn**	England	1978–1984
75.	J. Parker and Waustella **Laurence**	Zambia, Zimbabwe	1978–1987
76.	Theus and Elisa **Young**	Tanzania	1978–1981
77.	*Edward and Dorothy **Dorsey**	Liberia	1979–1981
78.	*Lloyd G. and Etta **Antonio**	Ghana	1979–1984
79.	*Louis R. Jr and Janice A. **Preston**	England. Zimbabwe	1979–1991
80.	Edna Pearlie **Atkins** Thomas	Sierra Leone	1979–1981
81.	Art and Hope **Bushnell**	Kenya	1980–1983
82.	Simon and Suzanne **Honore**	Rwanda	1980–1986
83.	John and Mary **Lavender**	Tanzania	1980–1984
84.	Roland L. and Lilia **McKenzie**	Nigeria. Zimbabwe, Kenya	1980–1991
85.	Charles and Pattie **Miller**	Kenya	1980–1985
86.	Dr. Alvin and Lois **Mottley**	Tanzania, Tobago	1980–1987, 1999–2007
87.	*Robert and Barbara **Patterson**	Burundi	1980–1984
88.	Larry D. and Natlie **Word**	Ivory Coast	1980–1982
89.	Ronald J. and Equilla **Wright**	Liberia. Kenya. Cameroon	1980–1990
90.	Roy and Celia **Adams**	Philippines	1981–1986
91.	Karen A. **Burke** Bright	Ivory Coast	1981–1984
92.	George and Pearl Jean **Huggins**	Guatemala, Panama, Ghana, Liberia	1981–1984, 1992–1998
93.	*Jerome and Yvonne **Pondexter**	Zaire	1981–1988
94.	Robert and Janice **Pressley**	Nigeria	1981–1982

95.	Daniel L and Elizabeth **Davis**	Ivory Coast	1982–1983
96.	*Pierre and Jocelyn **Deshommes**	Ethiopia, Cameroon	1982–1986, 1994–1998
97.	Phillip and Naomi **Polley**	Marshall Islands, Mali	1982–1984, 1996–2007
98.	Goldson and Rita **Brown**	Ethiopia	1983–1987
99.	Dr. Ronald and Dorothy **Forde**	Zaire, Zimbabwe	1983–1999
100.	Glen and Winnie **Howell**	Ghana	1983–1985
101.	Alcega and Veronica **Jeanniton**	Zaire, Cameroon, Equatorial Guinea	1983–1999
102.	Errol and Pamela **Lawrence**	Liberia	1983–1990
103.	Randolph and Debrah **Stafford**	Kenya, Zimbabwe	1983–1988
104.	Disciple and Ninon **Amertil**	Zaire, Ghana	1984–1986, 2013–
105.	Dr. Byron and Alfredia **Conner**	Ethiopia	1984–1987
106.	Dr. Carl and Lavetta **Dent**	Kenya	1984–1987
107.	Oswald and Thelma **Gordon**	Liberia	1984–1990
108.	*Ronald and Marilyn **Lindsey**	Zimbabwe	1985–1990
109.	Boyd and Wanda **Gibson**	Kenya	1986–1992
110.	*Ray and Carol **Cantu**	Kenya	1987–1994
111.	Dr. Chauncey and Bernardine **Conner**	Cameroon	1987–1991
112.	Mishael and Ruth **Muze**	Zimbabwe, Kenya	1987–2001
113.	Lester A. and Priscilla **Parkinson**	Zimbabwe, Kenya	1987–1997
114.	James A and Sarah **Washington**	Kenya	1987–1992
115.	Leonard and Ora **Newton**	Madagascar, Cameroon	1989–1995
116.	*Carmelita **Troy**	England, Cyprus, Lebanon	1989–1996
117.	Elliott C. and Sonia Marie **Osborne**	Kenya	1989–1991
118.	Paul and Patricia **Bryant**	Ghana, Sierra Leone	1990–1995
119.	Clyde and Barbara **Cassimy**	Kenya	1990–1996
120.	W. Ray and Joan **Ricketts**	Kenya	1990–1995
121.	R. Danforth and Vera **Francis**	Madagascar	1991–2010
122.	William and Ruth **Hughes**	Tanzania	1991–1996
123.	Max and Eliane **Pierre**	Gabon, Cameroon	1991–1999
124.	Ruby Lee **Jones**	Zimbabwe	1991–1992
125.	Gosnell and Doreen **Yorke**	Kenya	1991–1997
126.	Sydney and Katherina **Gibbons**	Cameroon, Jamaica	1992–1998, 2000–2001
127.	*Anita S. (Moreland) **James**	Palau, Koror	1992–1997
128.	Howard and Lois **Bullard**	Mexico	1993–1995
129.	Gertrude **Jordan**	Kenya	1993–2002
130.	Delbert and Curdell **Pearman**	Sri Lanka, Lebanon, Ethiopia	1997–2008

131.	Newton and Lydia **Andrews**	Kenya, Ghana	1998–2004, 2006–2009
132.	Maxwell and Desiree **Blakeney**	Zimbabwe	1998–2005
133.	Dr. Carl and Dr. Deborah **MacKenzie**	Kenya	1999–2000
134.	Ken and Belynda **Mulzac**	Philippines	2000–2005
135.	*Benjamin and Janice **Browne**	Ethiopia	2001–2005
136.	Fred and Birdie **Williams**	Hong Kong	2001–2008
137.	*Victor and Candice **Harewood**	Dubai	2002–
138.	Timothy and Beverly **McDonald**	Kenya	2003–2007

We invite you to view the complete
selection of titles we publish at:

www.TEACHServices.com

Scan with your mobile
device to go directly
to our website.

Please write or email us your praises, reactions, or
thoughts about this or any other book we publish at:

P.O. Box 954
Ringgold, GA 30736

info@TEACHServices.com

TEACH Services, Inc., titles may be purchased in bulk for
educational, business, fund-raising, or sales promotional use.
For information, please e-mail:

BulkSales@TEACHServices.com

Finally, if you are interested in seeing
your own book in print, please contact us at

publishing@TEACHServices.com

We would be happy to review your manuscript for free.